Western Power in Asia

Its Slow Rise and Swift Fall,
1415–1999

Western Power in Asia

Its Slow Rise and Swift Fall, 1415–1999

Arthur Cotterell

WILEY

John Wiley & Sons (Asia) Pte. Ltd.

Other Wiley Editorial Offices

John Wiley & Sons, 111 River Street, Hoboken, NJ 07030, USA
John Wiley & Sons, The Atrium, Southern Gate, Chichester, West Sussex, P019 8SQ,
    United Kingdom
John Wiley & Sons (Canada) Ltd., 5353 Dundas Street West, Suite 400, Toronto,
    Ontario, M9B 6HB, Canada
John Wiley & Sons Australia Ltd, 42 McDougall Street, Milton, Queensland 4064,
    Australia
Wiley-VCH, Boschstrasse 12, D-69469 Weinheim, Germany

Library of Congress Cataloging-in-Publication Data

ISBN 978-0-470-82489-4

Typeset in 11/14pt ITC Gallard by Macmillian.
Printed in Singapore by Saik Wah Press Pte Ltd.

10 9 8 7 6 5 4 3 2 1

In piam memoriam
Professoris Johannis Crookii
Magistri carissimi discipulisque benevolentis

Contents

Contents

Preface

The idea for *Western Power in Asia* arose from discovering an old account of a courtesy visit paid by an Austria-Hungarian warship to the Paris of the East, French Saigon. This late nineteenth-century event evoked a world that has completely vanished. Although Ho Chi Minh City still has its Catholic cathedral and opera house, and in its squares and avenues the look of a French provincial town, there is little else to recall more than a century of colonial rule. Neither Austria nor Hungary now possesses a coastline, let alone a navy capable of sailing in Asian waters. So altered is the face of present-day Asia that the length of Western dominion there is easily forgotten, from the arrival of the Portuguese at the close of the fifteenth century to the liberation of their last colony at the close of the twentieth. And overlooked, too, is the extent to which all Asian peoples were drawn into the colonial scheme of things. The Chinese and the Japanese played their very different parts in the rise and fall of Western power. This book endeavours to chart the whole course of European and American imperialism in Asia during the colonial era, from the perspective of both the rulers and the ruled.

In publishing this book I must acknowledge the invaluable contributions made by several people. First of all, my wife Yong Yap, through the translation of documents from both European and Asian languages; second, Graham Guest, an old friend whose amazingly extensive archive of pre-1900 illustrations, Imperial Images, furnished most of the fascinating material in the early chapters; third, my stalwart designer Ray Dunning, for the excellent maps as well as the work he has done once again on the illustrations; and last but not least, my publisher Nick Wallwork, a world history enthusiast. Without his timely support, *Western Power in Asia* would never have appeared in its present form.

Introduction

At the height of the Boxer rebellion, as an international relief force closed on Beijing, the great Qing minister Li Hongzhang pointed out how continued resistance was worse than useless until conditions changed in China. Having witnessed at first hand the military advantage enjoyed by a modernised Japan, he was under no illusion about the need for Asian states to match the technology of the Western colonial powers. The British, the Russians, the French, the Germans and even the Japanese had easily extracted concessions and territory from a tottering Chinese empire, because an unwillingness to embrace the modern world was the root cause of its weakness. There was nothing Li Hongzhang could do to stop Empress Ci Xi endorsing in 1900 the anti-Western sentiments of the Boxers, although he knew that their assault on the Legation Quarter would lead to Beijing's second foreign occupation. His own efforts to introduce up-to-date methods in industry and the armed forces had met with a degree of success; but Li Hongzhang's struggle to reconcile the adoption of foreign ways with traditional values—"Western learning for practical purposes" as opposed to "Chinese learning for fundamentals"—indicates the problem he encountered in strengthening China. This worldly man was still appalled by the looting of Beijing on its fall. Forty years earlier, Lord Elgin had authorised the plundering of the Summer Palace as a punishment for the deaths of captives: in 1900, there was an unauthorised free-for-all. Afterwards, Li Hongzhang suggested that the eighth commandment should be amended to: "Thou shalt not steal, but thou mayst loot."

The vulnerability of China throughout the period of modernisation in Asia profoundly influenced the outlook of the Chinese people. They were acutely aware of the abyss into which their country sank as the imperial system declined, and the republic that followed its disintegration proved no match for either warlord politics or Japanese imperialism. It is something of a paradox, therefore, that Japan's attempt to subdue China led to the downfall of Western power in Asia. No one could foresee in July 1937 how a skirmish between Chinese and Japanese soldiers at the Marco Polo bridge, southwest of Beijing, would start Japan along a path leading not only to the surprise attack on Pearl Harbor and the capture of Singapore, but also to unconditional surrender after the United States dropped atomic bombs on Hiroshima and Nagasaki. Few could have guessed that the nationalist aspirations stimulated by the short-lived but spectacular Japanese advance were to be beyond the capability of the returning colonial powers. Britain alone was spared the agony of a bloody retreat from empire because the Labour government of the day regarded decolonisation as an absolute necessity. The granting of independence to India, Pakistan and Burma in 1947 spelt the end of Western power in Asia. London had tacitly acknowledged how conditions there had changed in the half century since Li Hongzhang deplored the looting of Beijing. The resurgence of Asia remains the most significant historical event of our time.

Western Power in Asia narrates the recent liquidation of the colonial empires belonging to Europe and the United States, as well as their gradual accumulation of territory from the sixteenth century onwards. Quite remarkable is the fact that the last colony to gain its independence in Asia was founded by the very first colonial power, Portugal. The expulsion of the Indonesians in 1999 from East Timor represented a delayed liberation since Jakarta had taken advantage of the overthrow of a dictatorship in Lisbon to annex this Portuguese possession shortly after the colony's own declaration of independence in 1975. Because of its abundant sandalwood forests, the Portuguese had established a trading post there in 1642.

Chapter 1 surveys Iberian expansion overseas after a brief comparison of Chinese and Portuguese maritime exploration. The decision of the Ming dynasty to turn away from the sea left a power vacuum in the Indian Ocean into which Vasco da Gama unwittingly sailed. Had the Portuguese explorer rounded the Cape of Good Hope 70 years earlier, he would have found his own vessels of 300 tonnes sailing alongside a Chinese fleet with ships of 1,500 tonnes. Da Gama arrived instead at Calicut in 1498 quite unaware of China's naval reconnaissance of the Arabian, African and Indian coasts. Delighted to set foot safely on land, he and his men gave thanks inside a Hindu temple in the mistaken belief that it was a Christian shrine. While the legendary mission of St. Thomas in India probably explains the error, it was really the absence of any sign of Moslem worship that clinched the matter. Despite this first embassy to an Indian king going off without too much misunderstanding, the Portuguese soon tired of such diplomatic exchanges and looked for a permanent trading post of their own. This foothold they secured in the Moslem settlement of Goa, which was taken by force in 1510. The colony functioned as the headquarters of the Estado da India, the name given to the Portuguese empire in Asia. While Portugal's maritime expansion was overshadowed by Spanish exploits in the New World, the speed with which the Portuguese travelled eastwards was staggering, their ships reaching China in 1517. The first Europeans to visit Japan were three Portuguese traders who made the voyage from Guangzhou on a Chinese junk. Within a few years of their arrival in 1542, Portugal dominated Japan's international commerce.

From the outset, the Estado da India was determined to control the spice trade, the most lucrative of all European markets. By planting fortresses at strategic locations and conducting regular sweeps of the seas, the Portuguese were able to add customs duties to the profits derived from their own trading activities. Only in disunited Sri Lanka did they manage to hold a sizable territory; elsewhere, their tiny population discouraged any challenge to organised Asian states. The total number of Portuguese men in Asia at the height of the Estado da India's power never topped 10,000. But it was the ripple effect of European conflicts that brought this privileged position to a close: the temporary union of Spain and Portugal between 1580 and 1640 meant that the Estado da India came under assault from Spain's enemies, most notably the Dutch.

The arrival of European competitors in Asia is the subject of Chapter 2. After the ratification of the Treaty of Münster in 1647–48, by which Spain recognised Holland's independence, the Dutch replaced the Portuguese. Except for Britain at the start of the nineteenth century, no power ever approached the reach of early Dutch trading ventures. Once the Vereenigde Oost-Indische Compagnie, or the United East-Indian Company, persuaded merchants in Amsterdam of the value of cooperation, a concerted effort was made to monopolise the import of spices to Europe. But setting up a fortified settlement on the island of Java was to have unexpected consequences for Holland, because the steady extension of its influence throughout the Indonesian archipelago laid the foundation of a land-based colonial empire. The advent of the English and the French converted commercial rivalry into outright warfare, especially in India, where the decline of Mughal power provided ample scope for the acquisition of territory. And the discovery that properly trained Indian recruits could perform as well on the battlefield as European soldiers increased the possibilities of colonialism overnight. Here was an almost inexhaustible reservoir of military manpower. As Field Marshal Slim noted in his memoirs, victory over the Imperial Japanese Army in Burma had been achieved by "an army that was largely Asian".[1] Other colonial peoples under his command in 1945 hailed from as far away as Africa. By this date some 200,000 West Africans had volunteered to fight for "King Georgi", Biyi Bandele reminds us in his novel *Burma Boy*.

The English East India Company eventually won the contest for India. The Treaty of Paris between the United Kingdom and the United States, along with related treaties ending wars with France, Spain and Holland, left Britain in 1783 as the major European power in Asia. If anything, the loss of the North American colonies redirected British imperial interests eastwards, where India received most attention. Yet China was soon seen as an adjunct of growing dominion in the subcontinent through the expanding trade of the English East India Company. Lord Macartney's mission to Emperor Qian Long in 1793 was intended to place Anglo-Chinese commerce on a regular footing. What London failed to understand was China's indifference to international trade and the anxiety of the Qing dynasty about the adverse effect foreign influences might have on its Chinese subjects. That this mission was not a success can be explained perhaps in the darker side of the English East India Company's trading activities. So that it could acquire sufficient silver to sustain an unfavourable balance of payments involved in the China trade, caused largely by massive purchases of tea, it had deliberately stimulated the production of opium in India. Except for a single year, 1782, when its own ships sold the drug in Guangzhou because of an acute shortage of bullion, the English East India Company was careful to leave opium distribution to private merchants. This policy did not fool Beijing and in 1839 a special commissioner was sent to southern China with orders to stamp out the whole business.

Chapter 3 begins with the Opium Wars fought between China and Britain, which led to the cession of the island of Hong Kong as a sovereign base and the lease of a large stretch of land opposite, on the mainland itself. That the Second Opium War concluded with the fall of Beijing reveals how vulnerable the Chinese empire had become: fewer than 20,000 British, Indian and French soldiers were needed to force its surrender in 1860. But in India, Britain was seriously challenged by the Indian Mutiny, an uprising in the north of the subcontinent, which delayed the attack on China for almost one year. Even though the British scraped through this unexpected crisis, things could never be the same again. After the last Mughal emperor was dethroned, attitudes hardened among the Indians and their colonial masters, and the utter dominance of British authority in the subcontinent left no escape route other than the pursuit of outright independence. Its architect, Mohandas Karamchand Gandhi, was born in 1869, seven years after the last of the Great Mughals died in exile at Rangoon. Not to be outdone by the British, the French pushed their way into mainland Southeast Asia, the last remaining colonial prize. Even the Americans were drawn into an imperial role through the annexation of the Philippines after a brief war with Spain. The Filipinos were baffled that "the Land of the Free" felt no sympathy for their desire for immediate freedom. Although it suited President William McKinley to portray the American colony of the Philippines as an incidental result of American intervention in the Spanish Caribbean, the truth is that he had already decided to advance the United States' position in the Pacific by the acquisition of key islands. In his mind, the chief threat to American interests was Japan, whose rapid modernisation had introduced a new imperial player on the Asian stage. Prescient though this judgement proved to be on 7 December 1941, when Japanese aircraft caught most of the US Pacific Fleet at anchor in Pearl Harbor, Japan drew European blood first in its defeat of Russia in 1905.

The mediation of the United States brought the Russo-Japanese War to a close. By the Treaty of Portsmouth, Russia allowed Japan to occupy the Liaodong peninsula, assume railway rights in Manchuria, take over the southern half of the island of Sakhalin, and act as protector of Korea. Chapter 4 traces the Asian challenge that Japan's rise as an imperial power represented for the Western colonial empires. It shows how different the Japanese experience of economic as well as constitutional change was to that of Europe. Even though the emperor, his court and leading reformers all dressed in Western-style clothes, the constitution they announced by imperial decree in 1889 was unnegotiable and an "immutable fundamental law". Influenced by Germany rather than Britain or France, the new system of government was in effect an oligarchy of shared power between civilian politicians and military leaders, which in the 1920s and 1930s tilted in favour of the latter. Revolution in China and unrest in the colonies of the Western powers seemed to create an ideal moment for an increasingly militarised Japan to strike out on its own. The result was the Pacific dimension of the Second World War, a catastrophe for imperialism throughout Asia. Everywhere Japan's opponents were taken by surprise. Western confidence and prestige plummeted with defeats as widespread as Hong Kong, the Philippines, Malaya, Singapore, Burma and Indonesia.

As Tsuji Masonobu, staff officer responsible for operations under Yamashita Tomoyuki during the Malayan campaign, commented well after the Japanese surrender:

> In military operations we conquered splendidly, but in the war we were severely defeated. But, as if by magic, India, Pakistan, Ceylon, Burma, the Dutch East Indies, and the Philippine islands one after the other gained independence overnight. The reduction of Singapore was the hinge of fate for the peoples of Asia.[2]

Britain never really recovered from the surrender of the supposedly impregnable "fortress" of Singapore. Its fall heralded the end of the colonial era in Asia.

In Chapter 5, the rise and fall of the Greater East Asia Co-Prosperity Sphere provides the narrative focus. By using this name for its newly conquered empire, Japan hoped to enthuse the Asian peoples it had liberated from Western rule. They were encouraged to believe that a modernisation programme akin to Japan's would be a reward for active participation in the Greater East Asia Co-Prosperity Sphere. No concessions were made to nationalist demands for independence until it became obvious that the tide of war had turned against the

Japanese. As a Burmese nationalist remarked: "If the British sucked our blood, the Japanese ground our bones!" Because the Indonesians had such a pronounced hatred for Dutch rule, they tolerated the Japanese occupation for two years without complaint. Yet their anti-Western outlook was not proof against Japan's inability to administer conquered territories with restraint. Forced labour, rice requisitions and the Japanese military police had undermined Indonesian acquiescence by 1945. In March that year, Tokyo virtually acknowledged that its authority was at an end by asking Sukarno and Mohammad Hatta, the leading nationalists, to devise a formula for political cooperation based on the so-called five principles of nationalism, internationalism, representative government, social justice and Islam. They were even allowed to draft a constitution for an independent republic, which was to incorporate under a strong presidency not only the territories of the Dutch East Indies but those belonging to Britain in Malaya and Borneo too. Because the Indonesian leaders did not want independence as a gift from the Japanese, on 17 August 1945, two days after the surrender of Japan, Sukarno proclaimed the Republic of Indonesia.

The abysmal failure of the Dutch to reassert themselves in Indonesia was a signal that the days of Western power were numbered. The French chose to ignore the warning, with dire consequences for the Vietnamese, who led the fight for independence in French Indochina. Defeat at Dien Bien Phu in 1954 confirmed France's colonial bankruptcy, but the surprising success of Vo Nguyen Giap's young communist soldiers caused panic in Washington, where Cold War fears got the better of common sense. Only the British succeeded in achieving a dignified retreat from empire, in large measure because of Clement Attlee's determination to grant India early independence. Chapters 6 and 7 follow the tortuous process of decolonisation through the second half of the twentieth century. Also described are the two great transformations of this period: the recovery of Chinese strength through the founding of the People's Republic, and the emergence of a defeated Japan as an economic superpower. That they were both entwined with Cold War rivalry was an inevitable result of US intervention in Asia, the salient feature of the final stage of Western withdrawal. The last section of this study deals with post-colonial conflicts in India, Pakistan, Sri Lanka, Indonesia, Malaysia, Burma, Vietnam, Cambodia and East Timor.

Photo Credits

Cover   *HMS Bulwark* docking at Singapore naval base in 1961 © British Crown Copyright IMOD. Reproduced with the permission of the controller of Her Majesty's Stationery office.

Chapter 5

Pg 216   The signing of the Tripartite Pact between Germany, Italy and Japan in 1940. *Source: Getty Images*

Pg 224   *USS Arizona* going down in flames at Pearl Harbour, Decemeber 1941. *Source: Getty Images*

Pg 231   *HMS Prince of Wales* sinking off the coast of Malaysia. Courtesy of the Trustee at the Imperial War Museum

Pg 237   A Japanese victory parade at Singapore in early 1942. Reproduced with permission from Robert Hunt library

Pg 255   At Cairo in 1943, Franklin D. Roosevelt, Winston Churchill and Chiang Kai-shek. *Source: Getty Images*

Pg 260   After a kamikaze attack, *USS Bunker Hill* retires from Okinawa. *Source: Getty Images*

Pg 263   The second atomic bomb exploding above Nagasaki, 9 August 1945. *Source: Getty Images*

Chapter 6

Pg 270   The Japanese arrive for the surrender ceremony aboard *USS Missouri*, 2 September 1945. *Source: Getty Images*

Pg 272   British internees leaving Stanley Camp on Hong Kong Island. Reproduced with permission from Imperial War Museum

Pg 275   Premier Attlee with Aung San in London, early 1947. *Source: Getty Images*

Pg 278   Manila after the American Liberation. *Source: Corbis*

Pg 285   The two political rivals, Nehru and Jinnah, at a 1946 conference. *Source: Getty Images*

Pg 294 Parachute regiment soldiers on patrol in Batavia. Courtesy of the Trustee at the Imperial War Museum

Pg 301 On 1 October 1949 Mao Zedong proclaims the People's Republic in Beijing. *Source: Getty Images*

Pg 315 A less than comfortable Japanese Emperor with Douglas MacArthur. *Source: Getty Images*

Chapter 7

Pg 322 US troops were shocked by the Korean winter in 1950. *Source: Getty Images*

Pg 335 French soldiers take cover at Dien Bien Phu. *Source: Getty Images*

Pg 339 Tunku Abdul Rahman signs the agreement for Malayan independence. *Source: Corbis*

Pg 343 One-man air-raid shelters in Hanoi during the Second Vietnam War. *Source: Getty Images*

Pg 346 Richard Nixon is greeted at Beijing airport by Zhou Enlai in 1972. *Source: Getty Images*

Pg 350 Deng Xiaoping and Gerald Ford inspecting troops in 1976. *Source: Getty Images*

Pg 362 Australia meets Indonesia: Sir Robert Menzies and his wife with Sukarno. National Archives of Australia: Indonesia; AA1972/341; 322.

Pg 367 The Saviour of East Timor, Bishop Carlos Ximenes Belo. *Source : Getty Images*

Special thanks to Imperial Images © and Ray Dunning for all the older illustrations featured in the book.

Part 1

The Slow Rise of Western Imperialism

Chapter 1

Iberian Expansion Overseas 1415–1647

> Then, we entered the land, and no one was spared, neither male, nor female, pregnant women and droves of infants. And this because this land. . . had always been an enemy of the Christian name, and above all of the Portuguese; and the land which was wholly put to sack and fire, is called Goa.

Piero Strozzi's account of the Portuguese capture in November 1510

Portuguese and Chinese Maritime Exploration Compared

At the beginning of the fifteenth century, on the extreme ends of the Old World, two powers simultaneously were conducting a series of maritime expeditions. In 1415, King João of Portugal descended on the Moroccan port of Ceuta with a crusader fleet and siezed the city, a project long in the preparation. That same year, the Chinese admiral Zheng He sailed back to the imperial dockyards in Nanjing after his fourth voyage to the "western and southern oceans", which included visits to Vietnam, Cambodia, Malacca, Java, Sumatra, Sri Lanka, India, east Africa, and Hormuz, near the mouth of the Persian Gulf. Neither of these two countries were at this time aware of their mutual interest in the sea, although a century later marauding Portuguese ships would be in virtually undefended Chinese coastal waters. So very different were the outcomes of the Portuguese and Chinese expeditions that there is no better place to begin an account of the Western power in Asia than a consideration of their motives, as well as their means of navigation.

The great fleet commanded by the Moslem eunuch Zheng He undertook between 1405 and 1433 seven major seaborne expeditions, which caused the authority and power of the Ming emperor to be acknowledged by more foreign rulers than ever before, with even Mamluk Egypt sending an ambassador. The renown of the restored Chinese empire, after the expulsion of the Mongols in 1368, was increased by these voyages, in which the foremost navy in the world paid friendly visits to foreign ports; and states that acknowledged the sovereignty of Beijing were guaranteed protection and gifts were bestowed on their kings. "Those who refused submission," we are told

> they were over-awed by a show of armed might. Every country
> became obedient to the imperial commands and, when Admi-
> ral Zheng He turned homewards, sent envoys with him to
> offer tribute. Emperor Yong Le was delighted and before very
> long ordered Zheng He to go overseas once more and scatter
> largesse among the different states. On the second expedition
> the number of ambassadors who presented themselves before
> the dragon throne grew ever greater.[1]

The maritime expeditions had another purpose besides the reassertion of Chinese authority in the southern and western seas after liberation from Mongol rule. They restarted a system of state-sponsored trading, first introduced to protect the precious metals of the empire. The import of luxury items such as ivory, drugs and pearls had been a severe drain on the limited supply of bullion available, and a regulation issued in 1219 specified the commodities to be used instead of coin to pay for foreign imports—silk, brocades and porcelain. The Southern Song Emperor Gao Zong had already remarked in about 1145 how "the profits from maritime commerce are enormous. If such trade is properly managed, the revenues earned amount to millions of strings of cash. Is this not better than taxing the people?" The loss of the northern provinces to the Jin, nomad precursors of the Mongol invaders, had made the Chinese sea-minded for the very first time. Though the immediate cause of this new interest was pressure from the warlike peoples of the northern steppe-lands, the economic and political centre of the Chinese empire had been shifting for many centuries from the north to the south, from the great plains of the Yellow River to the Yangzi delta.

By the Southern Song period, the southern coastal provinces were both the richest and most populous parts of China. A consequence of the southward movement of the imperial capital to Hangzhou and the unavailability of northern overland routes for trade was a remarkable increase in seaborne commerce, an expansion that was to impress Marco Polo when he visited Zaiton, modern Zhangzhou, in Fujian province. To this port he tells us, "come all

The Ming emperor Yong Le, who sent Zheng He to explore the "southern and western oceans" from the imperial dockyards in Nanjing

the ships from India laden with costly wares and precious stones of great price and big pearls of fine quality. . . And for one ship that goes to Alexandria or elsewhere to pick up pepper for export to Christendom, Zaiton is visited by a hundred."[2] Southern Song officials had deliberately encouraged overseas contacts by sending out trade missions laden with gifts, which were gratefully received at foreign courts. So pleased was the sultan of Malindi with Zheng He's presents that he sent an embassy to the Ming capital of Nanking in 1415 bearing exotic gifts of his own, among them a magnificent specimen of a giraffe for the Imperial Zoo. At the gate of the palace, the third Ming emperor Yong Le personally received the animal along with a "celestial horse" and a "celestial stag"; the giraffe was regarded as "a symbol of perfect virtue, perfect government and perfect harmony in the Empire and the universe".[3] To mark his appreciation, the ambassadors were taken all the way home to east Africa on Zheng He's fifth voyage of 1417.

Exceptionally powerful though they were, Ming expeditions had a very different character from those of the Portuguese: instead of spreading terror, slaving and planting fortresses, the Chinese fleets engaged in an elaborate series of diplomatic missions, exchanging gifts with distant kings from whom they were content to accept merely formal recognition of the Ming emperor as the Son of Heaven. The intolerance of the crusader was entirely absent. Indeed, the arrival of the Portuguese in the Indian Ocean in 1498 abruptly ended the peaceful oceanic navigation that had been such a marked feature of Asian trade. Arab and Chinese sources speak of the hazards of the sea, of storms and shipwrecks, but they are silent about violence, other than brushes with pirates. What the Portuguese and their European successors brought with them was the notion of exclusive rights to maritime trade, something entirely alien to the tradition of long-distance commerce in Asia.[4]

No greater contrast could be drawn between the trading activities of Zheng He at Calicut, on the western coast of India, and the atrocities practised there in 1501 by Pedro Alvares Cabral and by Vasco da Gama on his second visit two years later. There was no Chinese equivalent of the Portuguese habit of sailing into port with corpses hanging from the yards. On only three occasions did Zheng He have to resort to force of arms. In 1406, he crossed swords with a pirate chief who attempted to surprise his camp at Palembang: the buccaneer was duly returned to China for punishment, since he hailed originally from Guangdong province. Eight years later, again on the island of Sumatra, Zheng He was ordered by Emperor Yong Le to restore a deposed sultan to the throne of Semudera. The third clash of arms occurred in 1411 near Colombo, where Zheng He's troops were attacked by those of the Sinhalese ruler Alagakkonara. The Chinese won a complete victory, and the captured king, along with his family, went to China as hostages when the fleet set sail from Sri Lanka for Nanjing.

Archaeological evidence for the pacific tenor of Zheng He's diplomacy ironically comes from Sri Lanka, where a stele, dated 15 February 1409, has been found at Galle with a trilingual inscription. The Chinese text explains how the voyages were intended to announce the mandate of the Ming to foreign powers, the inscription ending with a list of the presents offered to the Buddha: gold, silver, silk and so on. Here we have a Moslem ambassador from China dedicating at a Buddhist shrine in the Indian Ocean gifts from the Son of Heaven, the One Man of Confucian philosophy. More fascinating still is that the other two inscriptions do not exactly translate the Chinese one; the Tamil text praises Tenavari-nayanar, an incarnation of Vishnu, and the Persian one invokes Allah and the great saints of Islam. But while the texts are thus different, they all agree about the list of gifts.[5] Hardly surprising then was the relaxed attitude taken by the Chinese over the conversion of the sultan of Malacca to the Moslem faith. The nodal position of Malacca, at the meeting point of several major Asian trade routes, was understood by Emperor Yong Le, who entertained its ruler and granted him a war junk, so that he could return to his capital and protect his country. Between this state visit to China in 1411 and Zheng He's fourth voyage two years later, Malacca had adopted Islam, a faith then being spread throughout Southeast Asia by the permanent settlement of Indian traders. Ma Huan, an official interpreter on the voyage of 1413 and a Moslem himself, noted with sympathy how "the King of Malacca and all the people follow the new religion, fasting, making penance, and saying prayers".

Such urbanity has nothing in common with the religious fanaticism of the Portuguese, whose own sense of identity had been largely shaped in a struggle against Islamic domination. "Whenever the treasure ships arrived from China," Ma Huan goes on to tell us, "their crews at once erect a stockade, like a city wall, and set up towers for watch-drums at four gates. At night there are patrols of policemen carrying bells. Inside they erect a second stockade, like a small city wall within which are constructed warehouses and granaries. All the valuables and provisions are stored in them. Later the ships which have gone to other ports return with foreign goods and, when the south wind becomes favourable, the whole fleet puts to sea and returns home."[6] With the consent of the local ruler, Malacca obviously acted as a temporary naval base during each of Zheng He's expeditions.

From the beginning of an empire overseas, Portuguese belligerence was legitimised by successive popes as a continuation of the crusades. In 1502, King Manuel demanded of the ruler of Calicut that all Moslems should be expelled from his kingdom, because they were enemies of Christ. The chronicler João de Barros puts the issue bluntly in his *Décadas de Asia*, written in 1539.

> It is true that there does exist a common right for all to navigate the seas, and in Europe we acknowledge it fully. But this right does not extend beyond Europe, and so the Portuguese as lords of the sea by the strength of their fleets are justified in compelling all Moors and Gentiles to take out safe-conducts under pain of confiscation and death. For the Moors and Gentiles are outside the law of Jesus Christ, which is the true law that all must keep under pain of damanation to eternal fire. If then the soul be thus condemned, what possible right has the body to the privileges of our laws? It is true that the Gentiles are reasoning beings, and might if they lived be converted to the true faith, but as they have not revealed any desire to embrace it, we Christians have no duties towards them.[7]

Just how matter of fact this chilling statement is about the unlimited scope for violence enjoyed by the Portuguese may seem strange now, but Barros was simply stating the obvious to his Catholic contemporaries. Responsibility for relations with non-Christians was believed to rest solely with the Pope, and in return for bearing the costs of the work of their conversion, papal bulls granted to Portugal a monopoly of trade in Asia. The closeness of papal support can be judged from the very first venture overseas: King João's surprise attack on Ceuta. This expedition received indulgences, although preachers did not mention that it was a crusade until after the fleet had left Portuguese waters, so as to keep secret its destination as long as possible.[8]

Perhaps an even greater contrast between the deep-sea navigation of the Chinese and the Portuguese, however, is to be found in the relative sizes of their fleets. Populous and powerful Ming China dispatched Zheng He abroad with a veritable armada. On his first voyage, in 1405, he took 317 ships to Java, Sumatra, Malacca, Sri Lanka and India: 27,870 men in all were under his command. Some of Zheng He's vessels possessed as many as nine masts and his so-called treasure ships displaced 1,500 tonnes. Arguments over the tonnage of Chinese oceangoing junks were settled in favour of such a large figure by the discovery of an actual rudder post in 1962 at the site of one of the Ming shipyards in Nanjing. It once turned a rudder blade of at least 100 square metres, large enough to steer a vessel between 130 and 190 metres in length. Had Vasco da Gama rounded the Cape of Good Hope 70 years earlier, he would have found his own tiny squadron sailing alongside ships belonging to a Chinese fleet with an average displacement three or four times heavier than his own.

The advanced state of Ming nautical technology derived from a tradition of invention already over a millennium old. The steering oar, used in the West until the late Middle Ages, put a severe limitation on the size of ship that could safely be constructed, besides giving the steersman a hazardous task of control in rough weather. In China, it was replaced in the first century of the Christian era by the stern-post rudder, the prototype of Zheng He's impressive oceangoing steering system. Other early Chinese advances in shipbuilding were the watertight compartment, which allowed junks to become large deep-sea craft, and the aerodynamically efficient mat-and-batten sail. These improvements fascinated Marco Polo, who felt it necessary to provide shipbuilding details for the benefit of his Venetian compatriots. The bulkhead-built hull, divided into separate watertight compartments, really caught his attention, since it permitted repairs to be carried out at sea. But it was the mat-and-batten rig that allowed junks to make headway to windward, something the square-sailed ships of Europe simply could not do.

For this reason Portuguese shipwrights had turned to Arab models when developing long-distance craft. The famous *caravo* or *caravela* (from the Arabic word *karib*) had a wide hull displacing little water, with three masts hoisting triangular sails, hung from very long spars. This permitted greater mobility in manoeuvring as well as better use of the wind. By the time Vasco da Gama left Lisbon for India with four vessels, the dhow-like caravels in his tiny fleet had still only increased their displacement from 50 to 300 tonnes. A Chinese invention of direct use to him was undoubtedly the magnetic compass, which had passed westwards through Arab hands. The magnetic compass, along with accurate star charts, allowed Zheng He's fleet to reach southern Africa, touch the northern coast of Australia, and sail widely in the Pacific Ocean.

What Vasco da Gama found on rounding the Cape of Good Hope was an almost empty Indian Ocean, because after 1433, the Ming emperors discouraged maritime activities and ran down the imperial fleet, a policy of indifference to sea power that would eventually expose China to the unchecked depredations of European navies. Not all the causes are apparent for this crucial reversal of policy, which left a power vacuum in the southern and western oceans—into which the Portuguese, the Spaniards, the Dutch, the English and finally the French sailed. A combination of circumstances seems to have been responsible. Chinese scholar-officials, strongly against the ocean voyages from the beginning, were even more opposed to the prestige Zheng He and the eunuchs derived from their success. The grip that the eunuchs gained over state policy was to worry the imperial bureaucracy greatly as young or weak emperors were manipulated one after another. So influential did they become that the Manchus, who overthrew the Ming dynasty in 1644, regarded eunuch power as the chief reason for their victory. Under the Qing, their own dynasty, the management of the imperial household passed into the hands of the emperor's own kinsmen. The eunuchs were once again restricted to duties in the imperial harem. But the despatch of fleets overseas was anyway becoming less profitable as trading ventures and the cost of mounting them pressed hard on the imperial exchequer.

Another consideration was the removal in the 1420s of the capital from Nanjing to Beijing, the site of the former Mongol seat of power. The laying out of a city and a palace there shifted the centre of imperial gravity northwards and concentrated attention on the Great Wall. This line of defence was bound to rank as the top priority, once strong leaders re-emerged among the nomadic peoples living to its north. Ming preoccupation with this new threat culminated within a hundred years of Zheng He's death in 1433 in a series of anti-maritime edicts that made it a capital offence to own or build craft with two or more masts. Even the administrative records of the great voyages were destroyed in the 1470s on the grounds that they contained "deceitful exaggerations of bizarre things far removed from the testimony of people's ears and eyes".[9] Yet this lack of interest in the rest of the world was part of a more general attitude in East Asia. The inward-looking societies of pre-modern China, Korea and Japan chose to concentrate on their own affairs, and as far as possible ignore the arrival of Western power and influence. Though the Japanese were initially fascinated by the Portuguese, and as many as 200 Catholic churches were built, in 1614 missionaries were summarily expelled. Even more commerce with Europe was soon ended, except for a very limited exchange with the Dutch, who had conveniently arrived to replace the zealous Portuguese. The Dutch managed to trade by eschewing all missionary activity, a calculated policy that was condemned by their European rivals as nothing more than a cynical accommodation with Japanese superstition.

No such compromise was ever countenanced by the Portuguese crown, the driving force behind the expansion overseas from Ceuta onwards. For it was from the aristocrats who actually attended court, or who were the monarch's representatives outside the capital, that the impetus for overseas conquest and exploration nearly always came. War with Spain had sharpened interest in seapower—the city of Seville was attacked in 1369 by a fleet of 32 Portuguese ships—and so encouragement was given to shipbuilders in the form of tax-free timber from the royal forests, and to merchants by means of maritime insurance. Ships paid 2 per cent of the value of their cargoes into the royal treasury and received insurance against losses in war or against unexpected taxes. Anti-Spanish sentiment was behind the foundation of the Avis dynasty in 1385.

11

In alliance with the English duke John of Gaunt, whose daughter he married, King João managed to turn back a full-scale Spanish invasion at the battle of Aljubarrota. Learning from English experience in France, the outnumbered Portuguese army remained on the defensive behind a makeshift barricade of stakes and brushwood, which was intended to break Spanish cavalry charges. From the safety of this position, longbow shot could be directed against attackers either on horseback or on foot. Some 700 English soldiers were among the 7,000 men at Aljubarrota who fought for King João I. Their surprise victory prevented any permanent merger of Portugal with Spain, although during a temporary union under the Habsburgs from 1580 until 1640, the old alliance with England did not exempt it from attack by English forces.

The marriage on 14 February 1387 of King João and Lady Philippa symbolically united England and Portugal. Because Dona Filipa, the name given by the Portuguese to the Lancastrian bride, took delight in chivalry, she would have enjoyed the ten days of tournaments that were held after the wedding. And we are aware that she wholeheartedly approved of King João's wish that their sons "should be knighted in splendid fashion".[10] According to the chronicler Gomes Eannes de Azurara, this was what the monarch wanted above all else. A great expedition was therefore secretly arranged: an attack on Ceuta, a city situated on the Moroccan side of the Straits of Gibraltar. King João found himself in much the same position as his Lancastrian relations in England. His possession of the throne was also due to a usurpation, and he had to find employment for a quarrelsome nobility now that Portugal was at peace with Spain.

The capture of Ceuta in 1415 actually coincided with Henry V's invasion of Normandy and the resumption of the Hundred Years War. Rather like the youthful English monarch, João thought that young men must practise the arts of war or they would waste the best years of their lives, for it was only through fighting that knightly ambitions could ever be fulfilled. Honourable though this medieval notion was as a means of maintaining status, the Portuguese king could not quite disguise an obsession over plunder during the overseas expedition. Besides regular trading with Norway, Flanders and Genoa, his own ships are known to have participated in the piracy that customarily took place between Moslems and Christians. Arguably, it was this characteristic Mediterranean mixture of commerce and conflict that Portugal later transferred to the Indian Ocean. At a time when the value of rents steadily fell, ransoms were as useful a way of supplementing income as trading profits. Portugal was, as were many other European countries, very short of gold, and Moroccan coins were in general circulation as a result of Moslem purchases of fruit from the Algarve. Their high quality, plus knowledge that Ceuta handled a large proportion of the west African gold trade, was the economic spur behind the expedition, Portugal's first overseas crusade. The large loans raised by King João from bankers in Portugal and elsewhere to finance it would not have been forthcoming without an expectation of their ready repayment.[11] That it was the royal treasurer, João Alfonso, who acted as the chief advocate of the Ceuta attack can be taken to reflect the confidence felt about its prospects by the merchant community.

Six years were spent in making preparations for the expedition. The king of Granada, the last Moslem holding of any size on the Iberian peninsula, sent an embassy to inquire about its purpose. But the secret was so well kept that when the Portuguese fleet dropped anchor off Gibraltar, before turning south towards Morocco, in alarm the Moslem authorities there sent out to King João "the best and most precious things they could find, while asking him to assure them of peace. The Portuguese king, however, would make no promises and confined himself to accepting their presents."[12] An outbreak of plague in the expeditionary force failed to deflect King João's purpose, and tactical surprise was achieved on its arrival at Ceuta. Recording the events in the 1450s, when fresh Moroccan expeditions were being planned, Azurara was at pains to present the capture of Ceuta as the logical first step in conquest overseas, and to elevate the role played by Henry the Navigator, third youngest of the Portuguese princes. Henry was always keen on a forward policy in Morocco, and to him fell the difficult task of holding Ceuta on behalf of the Portuguese crown. His extended governorship of the Algarve makes sense as the person officially responsible for the fate of this African city. Yet its possession was a drain on the royal treasury for the reason that, once the Moslems realised recapture was impossible, the trade they controlled across the Sahara was diverted to other cities.

For Azurara, there was no question about the correctness of King João's actions. Celestial signs lent their support before the assault, in which the Moslems were shown no mercy at all. Fighting raged in the streets and in Moorish houses that made "our poor homes look like pigsties". Ordinary Portuguese soldiers, Azurara had to admit, were less interested in glory than gain.

> But theft was dangerous in houses with low and narrow doorways, like those of the Moors. Men who were carried away by covetousness entered without caution, which often led to their destruction, for many of the Moors had taken refuge in their houses and were defending them to the end, preferring to lose their lives rather than preserving them by flight. . . . Seized by grief, they hid themselves behind doors in order to kill their enemies when they crossed the threshold; but from this the Moors had little advantage, for behind the foremost were others, and they were all armed.[13]

The fall of Ceuta permitted King João to dedicate its great mosque to Christian worship, and under the newly consecrated dome make his three oldest sons into knights. For the dubbing ceremony, the king had brought along three special swords that Dona Filipa had provided. She died just before the expedition set off. Then, leaving behind a garrison of 2,700 men, the Portuguese sailed away after a stay of just 13 days.

Although the attack on Ceuta was the beginning of a century and a half of warfare in Morocco, the limited advantage gained through this initial foothold weakened for some years the alliance formed between Portuguese commercial interests and the Avis dynasty. Relations were hardly improved by the disastrous attack of 1437 on Tangier, under the command of Prince Henry. It was thought that occupation of the city would give support to Ceuta and facilitate progress inland, a move still effectively thwarted by Moslem arms. The expedition seems to have been poorly supported, so that the capture at Tangier of King João's youngest son, Fernando, came as a considerable embarrassment. Henry found himself in the unenviable position of having to argue against the ransom of his captured brother, for whom the Moslems demanded the surrender of Ceuta. Whilst Prince Fernando died as a prisoner of war, hard-nosed Henry established himself at Sagres on the south-western tip of the Algarve and sponsored exploration along the African coast.

Once again it was the lure of wealth that motivated Henry as much as his hatred of Moslems: the ships he sent against them in the service of the Catholic faith were expected to seek plunder, slaves and ransoms as well. Although privateering had become increasingly the favoured economic activity of the Portuguese nobility, Henry's captains were little different from the followers of the Lancastrian invaders of France. To maintain support, Henry V of England had from the start of the new campaign against the French made it his policy to share the profits of war.[14] Finding employment and opportunities for young retainers to prove their skills and abilities was a constant problem for European rulers at the close of the Middle Ages, and Portuguese monarchs largely solved it by overseas adventures, although very few of them proved immediately profitable.

Chivalry might well be used by Azurara as a manifesto for the Avis dynasty's foreign policy, but beneath the chivalric veneer of his narrative the reality of hit-and-run raiding is visible. In 1441, the first black slaves were brought back to the Algarve, and two years later, Henry obtained from the Pope a bull confirming his rights to their homeland in Guinea. The prince had every right to be pleased, according to Azurara, because "though their bodies were captive, this was small matter in comparison with their souls which would enjoy freedom for eternity". It did not seem to worry anybody at Lagos, the Algarvian port at which African slaves were landed, how families were usually split up on purchase, with parents and children being sent to places far apart. In the Algarve itself, slaves came to make up 10 per cent of the population, in Lisbon the proportion was even higher. By the time Henry died in 1460, slaving had become a staple of Portuguese trade.

The Sea Route to India Discovered

Rivalry with Spain for control of the African coast stimulated the Portuguese to push their claims by making new discoveries. In 1474,

Prince João, the future João II, was at the age of 19 charged with responsibility for overseas expansion. To him, rather than Henry the Navigator, credit should be given for the creation of a deliberate plan of discovery. Once on the throne, King João II tried to direct the financing and planning of an overseas empire himself, in contrast to Spanish monarchs who tended to restrict themselves to an indirect role through granting licences to conquistadors. It earned his equally energetic successor, Manuel, the title of "grocer king". The expedition King João II sent southwards in 1482 was perhaps the most important of all, because its discovery of the eastward trend of the African coast to the north of the equator appeared to promise the chance of reaching India by sea. Intelligence gathered by Pero de Covilham a decade later revealed the existence of a maritime route to the east coast of Africa from India. Fluent in Arabic, Covilham had travelled in the guise of a Moorish merchant as far east as Calicut and Goa. His report to the Portuguese king contained details of the spice trade, including both its origins and routes of exchange. Covilham died in 1526 in Ethiopia, where he had gone to make contact with the legendary Christian ruler Prester John.

It was the voyage of Bartolomeu Dias to the Cape of Good Hope in 1487–88 that finally located the passage from the Atlantic to the Indian Ocean. In all probability a professional mariner rather than a member of the nobility, Dias had been sent southwards with three vessels to discover where the African continent ended. It took him a good seven months to sail back home after the discovery. Another explorer watched Dias' return to Lisbon, for the Genoan Christopher Columbus was still trying to enlist the support of the Portuguese crown for a scheme of his own: basing his calculations on the work of Italian mapmakers, he argued for a westerly sea route to India.

It could well be the confusion caused by Columbus' apparent success on behalf of Spain in 1492, which brought about a pause in Portuguese exploration. What news of his discovery of the "Indies" certainly did was to oblige the Holy See to redefine the spheres of influence belonging respectively to Spain and Portugal. A bull issued in 1493 placed the dividing line west of the Azores, or the Cape Verde Islands. With the exception of Brazil, which Portugal had yet to discover, it remained in force until Ferdinand Magellan, a Portuguese in Spanish service, arrived off the Philippines in 1521. By sailing there in a westerly direction via Cape Horn, he invalidated the papal bull and forced another revision in 1529, when the Spaniards gave up any claim to the Moluccas in exchange for a Portuguese undertaking to allow the Spanish conquest of the Philippines.

The resumption of Portuguese exploration in 1497 thus took place in the shadow of Spanish exploits. Even the size of Vasco da Gama's expedition belied King Manuel's claim to lordship over the Indian Ocean. Four vessels and fewer than 200 men hardly matched the expedition's declared intentions: these were sailing direct to India, the establishment of Portuguese control over the spice trade by force of arms, and the making of alliances with Christian rulers who supposedly lived there.

While Lisbon could see the long-term financial gain of breaking the Venetian–Moslem monopoly over the supply of spices to Europe, King Manuel may not at this stage have been ready to stake a great deal of his personal prestige on the venture. Another possibility is that da Gama was not his own choice for the command, but had been

Vasco da Gama was the first Portuguese commander to sail to India, reaching Calicut in 1498

forced upon him by nobles who feared the increased power that would gather to the crown from the diversion of Asian trade round Africa. Except for a few years in the 1460s, it had already exercised a monopoly on all imports of gold and slaves from West Africa. Royal licences were needed by well-born people who wished to take part in this profitable trade, and Azurara tells us they included noblemen, churchmen, high officials, as well as members of the military orders. The government even tried to set the price for imported pepper, but it was naturally forced down as supplies increased. By the last decade of the fifteenth century, however, increasing demand for spices in general pushed prices upwards and stimulated further Portuguese exploration.[15]

For Vasco da Gama's epoch-making voyage, we are fortunate to possess a chronicle, most likely a personal diary kept by a certain Alvaro Velho on board the *São Rafael*. Little is known about the author, whose account of the expedition covers the period from July 1497 to June 1498, the month the tiny fleet of four ships left Calicut for the return voyage to Lisbon. Beforehand, Velho may well have spent some time in Guinea. Having travelled more than half the distance of the outward journey, da Gama's ships came on 25 December 1497 to the farthest point reached by Bartolomeu Dias: it is still called Christmas, or Natal. Continuing up the coast of east Africa the condition of the crews became pitiful, as scurvy took its toll. "There were many with swollen hands and feet, the gums growing over their teeth to such an extent they could not eat."[16] After a month restoring their health and making repairs to their vessels, da Gama made for Mozambique, Mombasa and then Malindi, from which he eventually set sail for Calicut in late April.

Mozambique was the first direct contact made by the Potuguese with the Indian Ocean trading network. This is how Velho reports the encounter:

> The people of this country are dark and well-built. They are Moslems, and their language is the same as the Moors. Their clothes are made of fine linen or cotton, with coloured stripes and rich embroidery. All of them wear caps decorated with silk tassels and gold thread. They are merchants, and trade with the White Moors, four of whose vessels were at the time in port, laden with gold, silver, cloves, pepper, ginger, and silver rings, as well as quantities of pearls, jewels and rubies, all of which articles are used by the people in this country. We understood them to say that all these things, with the exception of the gold, were brought here by the Moors.[17]

The distinction drawn between black Moslems and White Moors, in other words between "native Moslems" and "Moors from Mecca", indicates that the Portuguese explorers saw the last as their principal adversaries. But they realised from the start how they lacked adequate manpower to engage in an all-out war against Islam. Unlike Ming China, with a population approaching 200 million, Portugal was inhabited by barely 1.5 milion people. The total number of Portuguese at any time in Asia is reckoned never to have topped 10,000 men.[18]

It was fortunate then for da Gama that at this time Egypt, Persia and Vijayanagar in southern India had no armed shipping in the Indian Ocean, if indeed they ever owned navies at all. And later this stroke of good luck continued with the foundation of the Mughal empire in India, a land-oriented power with little concern for the sea. Its third ruler, Akbar, responded with puzzlement when in 1586 he stood on a beach and first saw waves. In desperation, Venice had requested in 1502 that the Mamluk sultan of Egypt should take action over the Portuguese incursion into the spice trade, but he was in no position to stop the newcomers from blocking trade along the Red Sea. The sultan asked the Pope to intervene instead, on pain of Egyptian harassment of Christians and destruction of sacred sites in Jerusalem. Not until the Ottoman Turks had conquered Egypt, and extended their power into the Persian Gulf with the capture of Basra in 1546, would the Portuguese become really stretched at sea.

But da Gama's visit to Mozambique did not pass off without violence. After the local sultan promised to provide pilots, two of the Portuguese vessels came under attack and a three-hour engagement ensued. Blame was placed on the White Moors here and at Mombasa, where once again there was fighting. Henceforth, Velho refers to them as "dogs". It was a stroke of luck that the Moslem ruler of Malindi was willing to lend da Gama a Gujarati pilot, who guided his fleet straight across the Indian Ocean to Calicut, the expedition's destination. There anti-Moslem sentiment among the Portuguese crew got the better of common sense and they worshipped at a Hindu temple a goddess said to be the Virgin Mary, in part because no sign of Islam was in evidence. "Many other saints were painted on the walls of the church, wearing crowns. They were painted variously with teeth protruding an inch from the mouth, and four or five arms. Below this church was a large masonry tank, similar to many others, we had seen on the road."[19] In his dealings with the powerful ruler of Calicut, da Gama proceeded with caution and decorum. The first person sent ashore had been an ex-convict named João Nunes, who on meeting two Tunisian merchants in the city made the famous remark about how the Portuguese had come to Asia in search of "Christians and spices". No animosity is apparent in Velho's account of the exchange, which points to the peaceful transaction of trade at Calicut.

Face-to-face with the king himself, da Gama discovered to his dismay that relations were far less easy, in all likelihood because of the poor gifts sent by King Manuel. He felt that the Indians were deliberately drawing him into a trap, when he was told to bring his ships closer inshore and hand over the rudders and sails. Leave-taking was also complicated by the holding of hostages, although da Gama departed at last with a letter from the ruler of Calicut, in which he offered the Portuguese monarch cinnamon, cloves, ginger, pepper and precious stones in exchange for gold, silver, coral and scarlet cloth. The feelings of the expedition were summed up by Velho, who wrote that "we were saddened to think a Christian king should treat us so badly".

The expedition's return to Lisbon in 1499 helped to strengthen King Manuel's hand. At very little cost, Vasco da Gama had fulfilled a royal dream of direct trade with India. On the way back, the *São Rafael* had to be abandoned and burnt after passing Mombasa, because death and disease had reduced the expedition's crews so much that it was impossible to sail all the ships. The goods on board were, however, transferred to the remaining vessels. And against his noble detractors, King Manuel could now declare that there were populous Christian kingdoms in India, potential allies against any Moslem interference with Portuguese trade. Even more telling was the intelligence that very little naval opposition could be expected in the Indian Ocean. So confident was the Portuguese court that it joked how the Venetians would soon turn to fishing for their livelihood because they had no future as international traders. Without hesitation, Manuel added to his title of "King of Portugal and the Algarve and beyond the sea in Africa, and Lord of Guinea" this ambitious extension of authority: "Lord of the Conquest, Navigation and Commerce of Ethiopia, Arabia, Persia and India".

Although Manuel and his successors never termed themselves emperors in Asia, unlike British monarchs were to do in India, the extent of the authority claimed by the Portuguese crown seems immense as a result of a single expedition. But with a speed surpassing even Spain's lightning conquest of the New World, the Portuguese were about to spread along the eastern trade routes of the Old World, and by 1517 drop anchor off distant Guangzhou in southern China. These voyages were quite different in character from da Gama's first expedition, for the lukewarm welcome he had received at Calicut determined Manuel to show off Portuguese power in Asian waters. He had already announced plans to modernise and develop Lisbon's commercial facilities in anticipation of a massive increase of overseas trade. Within a century, it had brought immense wealth to the Portuguese crown, the net profit on pepper alone having risen to 152 per cent.

The firm conviction of King Manuel about the possibilities of Portuguese power in Asia explains the second expedition which he dispatched in 1500. It comprised 13 ships, ten of which belonged to the crown and the rest to syndicates of noblemen and merchants. For the expedition's commander, the king passed over Vasco da Gama and instead chose Pedro Alvares Cabral. He was a member of the Order of Christ, a military organisation that had been active in the Portuguese penetration of Africa. As early as 1433, the Order of Christ had received a royal grant of authority over Madeira, Porto Santo and other islands, which was confirmed by papal bulls. So favourable were their terms that by 1455 it could claim "all power, dominion and spiritual dominion" over the whole area of Portuguese expansion.[20]

A contemporary even went so far as to maintain that Manuel was an instrument of the divine will, since "the King is not King of his own self, or for his own self. . . The King's heart is in the hand of God, and God inclines it where he will, as the Holy Scripture says."[21] The Portuguese monarch gave Cabral detailed instructions on what he was to buy and how he was to deal with local rulers. Believing its king to be a Christian, he was told to insist at Calicut on the expulsion of all Moslems, a policy that Manuel under intense pressure from Spain had already put into force in Portugal. But his decree of 1496 was lax in comparison with those of Spain: conversion for Jews and Moslems was largely symbolic, because these prominent traders were given 20 years to instruct themselves in the Catholic faith. Only with the Counter-Reformation would Portugal come to match the fanaticism of Spain, the Inquisition establishing itself in Lisbon in 1536. Cabral's instruction for Calicut can therefore be seen as essentially a commercial device intended to disrupt the flow of spices to the great Moslem terminals for Asian trade at Hormuz and Aden.

En route the second expedition was blown off course and in April 1500 made landfall in Brazil. The discovery was believed to be a sign of divine providence, and one ship was sent back with the news. Manuel responded by dispatching three vessels to Brazil in 1501, before Cabral returned from India. Meanwhile, the elaborate

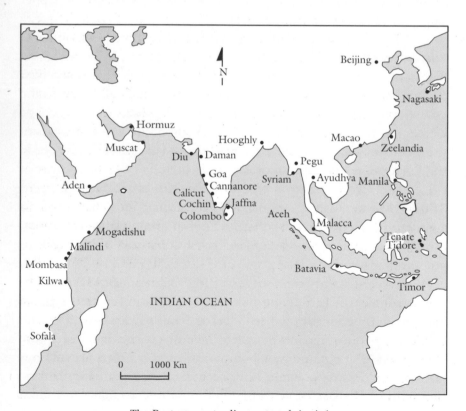

The Portuguese trading network in Asia

gifts carried by Cabral got him off to a much better start with the king of Calicut than da Gama had achieved. At this stage of the negotiations, the Portuguese still thought the people of Calicut followed a deviant form of Christianity, for Manuel proposed sending "clerics and also church ornaments, so that you may be able to see the doctrine of the Christian faith which we hold".[22] Even though this view turned out to be incorrect, there was no reason to expect Cabral to resort so quickly to arms, unless he connected the slowness of negotiations with Moslem influence at the Calicut court. But with more than 1,000 men on board, he could afford to take a tough line and, in reply to local intransigence, a bombardment of the city was ordered. Afterwards, the Portuguese fleet sailed to nearby Cochin, where the ruler received Cabral warmly and allowed him to load a cargo of pepper. Before leaving for Lisbon, he also visited Cannanore, a city to the north of Calicut, because he had heard that it would also welcome good relations with Portugal.

On his return home Cabral justified his use of force by reference to Islam. His dispelling of any lingering illusions about Christian powers being situated around the Indian Ocean added to the gloom felt in the Portuguese court. As Barros noted, it was realised how on the Indian coast "there were more Moors than all those facing us on the coast of Africa between Ceuta and Alexandria. . . All of whom plotted our downfall."[23] The king's counsellors urged caution, but Manuel refused to be down-hearted and a third expedition was launched under the command of da Gama, not Cabral. It seems very likely that the setting aside of Cabral reflected court intrigue. Though less well connected and well born than Cabral clearly was, da Gama had his supporters at court, who were only too ready to point out Cabral's inability to make Calicut into a firm ally of Portugal.

At a solemn ceremony held in Lisbon cathedral on 30 January 1502, da Gama was awarded the rank of admiral and handed the royal standard to carry on his voyage. If the change of command was intended to mark a less belligerent approach in India, the outcome was no different from Cabral's because the third expedition subjected Calicut to another bombardment. Da Gama additionally slew several hundred innocent fishermen who were caught up in the action. The era of peaceful trading in the Indian Ocean was over. Even Mamluk Egypt was stirred to revive its navy, and at Diu unsuccessfully challenge the Portuguese with Gujarati support in 1509. By then, Manuel had no option but to go onto a permanent war footing. It is impossible to be sure of the exact purpose of da Gama's second voyage, because the instructions he received were not recorded. But the Portuguese monarch may have already decided on a robust approach, for in 1503 a small fort, the first in India, was built at Cochin, and another fort at Cannanore followed two years later.

The Formation of the Portuguese Empire

A new policy seems to commence with the appointment of Francisco d'Almeida in 1505 as commander of the fleet for three years. His title was viceroy of Portuguese Asia, and his brief was to trade where possible, to make war where necessary. The continuity of leadership was meant to secure the Portuguese presence in the Indian Ocean, for Almeida was ordered to capture and fortify Sofala and Kilwa in east Africa as staging posts for shipping, while a third fortress was to be built on the Angediva Islands, southwest of Goa. Another instruction suggested that Sri Lanka and Malacca might be occupied as well. Already Manuel appreciated the importance of controlling the Red Sea trade, although an attack on Aden was not launched by Alfonso de Albuquerque, the second viceroy, until 1513. Its failure was the only setback for the Portuguese in their plan of domination. According to his son, Albuquerque

> often used to say that for the preservation of India, and for the prevention of troubles arising from that territory to the Kings of Portugal, there were four main things, of which their possession by the Portuguese must be made very strong and very sure. These were: Aden, in order to have dominion over the Straits of Mecca, before the Grand Sultan could forestall them in seizing it; Hormuz, so as to have supreme rule over the Straits of Bacora; and Diu and Goa, for sovereignty of all the other districts of India. And with these four places assured to Portugal, and fortified with very strong fortresses she could avoid many other unnecessary expenses to which she was now subject.[24]

Under the tireless command of Albuquerque, the Portuguese secured their hold over much of the spice trade. In 1510, he captured the Moslem stronghold of Goa, the future capital of the Estado da India, or "State of India".

A keen participant in the assault was Piero Strozzi, an extract from whose letter to his father heads this chapter. Along with other Florentines granted a licence by the Portuguese king to trade in Asia, Strozzi was enrolled by Albuquerque in his attacking force, which took Goa in November. The place Strozzi describes as "very strong, and popu-lous, and large, where there is a castle and fortress; where in guard of it were eight to ten thou-sand persons, with more than 200 pieces of artillery, where, by the grace of God, we entered by force of arms, and to enter it we killed around two thousand per-sons who resisted us. And these

Alfonso de Albuquerque, whose aggressive policies laid the foundation of Portuguese power in Asia

were almost all Turks, and renegade Christians of every sort; among whom were Venetians and Genoese in the largest numbers". Having disposed of the garrison, the Portuguese laid waste the town, killing men, women and children without distinction. Strozzi's only regret was an arrow wound that prevented him from looting anything, unlike his fellow Florentines. In his remarkable letter home, there is a curious mixture of hatred and admiration for the Moslems, whose merchants "can do better calculations by memory than we can do with the pen. And they make fun of us, and it seems to me they are superior to us in countless things, except with sword in hand, which they cannot resist."[25]

A year later, Strozzi sailed with Albuquerque's fleet of 17 ships against Malacca, the eastern entrepot for spices. The second viceroy clearly felt that he had a mandate for aggression. Yet Albuquerque, like his fellow countrymen, drew equal strength of purpose from celestial portents. Sailing in the Red Sea he was deeply moved to observe a cross in the sky, "very clear and resplendent. When a cloud tried to pass across it, the cloud was rent into several parts without touching the cross, or reducing its brightness. The cross was seen by the whole fleet, and all the crews knelt and worshipped it, with tears in their eyes." Despite this favourable portent, no one would agree with Albuquerque's recommendation that the fleet should put about and seek out Prester John because, unlike the viceroy himself, they were "men of little faith".[26] A strong streak of messianism also resided in the breast of Manuel, to whom a report of this incident was immediately sent. The king managed to combine a belief in crusading against the enemies of Christ with a shrewd commercial instinct, even after the disappointment of

The Portuguese fortress at Malacca. Some 4,000 foreign merchants resided in the town outside its fortifications

discovering that Hindus were not religious brethren. His own miraculous elevation to the throne after the death of six better-placed candidates served to reinforce an idea of his reign as being one of great deeds against unbelievers.[27] Never entirely abandoned at court was the hope of recapturing Jerusalem as the final stage of Portuguese expansion overseas.

At Malacca, in 1511, Albuquerque had the personal satisfaction of delivering a powerful blow against the infidel while simultaneously advancing Portugal's commercial interests. In a conference held a few days before the assault, he told his captains that the expulsion of the Moors from the city would destroy Islam locally. As for trade, the construction of a fort at Malacca must bankrupt Cairo and Mecca, and oblige the Venetians to buy spices in Lisbon. On St. James' day, a saint to whom Albuquerque was particularly devoted, the fierce fighting began. Despite the Malaccan sultan being well supplied with canon and Javanese mercenaries, the Portuguese force of 1,100 men triumphed within two weeks and looting rivalled in quality the booty taken by the Spaniards in the New World, even though most of the city's wealth remained in the hands of its original owners, because Albuquerque had issued flags of protection to residents who did not oppose his coming. Chinese merchants had even loaned him a junk to overwhelm the bridge in the centre of Malacca.

After the capture of the city, the Portuguese worked round the clock to build a fortress strong enough to resist a counter-attack. They were fortunate that the nominal overlord of Malacca, the Ming emperor, was disinclined to offer the deposed sultan any assistance at all. Having received complaints from Chinese merchants about their unfair treatment by the sultan, he was gratified to learn of the restraint shown by Albuquerque towards them and their property.[28] But it is unlikely that China still possessed the naval capacity for imposing its political will in Southeast Asia anyway.

Courage and faith aside, Portuguese success at Malacca depended upon a concentration of firepower. Their cannon would have even outgunned the Chinese, who for centuries had led the world in the use of gunpowder. Portuguese muzzle-loaders were less likely to burst, their trajectories were longer and more accurate, and their shot was heavier than most Asian cannon of equivalent weight. For the Chinese imperial armies, the new weaponry was to come as a rude shock, when in 1592 they exchanged fire in Korea with the Japanese invasion force sent there by the warlord Toyotomi Hideyoshi. The samurai were armed with superior guns based on the Portuguese musket. The possession of better guns was at this time giving the Russians an advantage on the steppes too, as they pushed eastwards over the Urals in pursuit of their Tartar enemies. Russia had always been vulnerable to attack from Asia: Moscow was burned to the ground as late as 1571. The Russians only won control of the lands on the European side of the Urals in 1552, when they took the fortress-city of Kazan. With superior artillery, plus the services of a Danish sapper who supervised the mining of the walls, Ivan the Terrible was able to storm it and then overrun the whole Kazan khanate. Vast numbers of prisoners were taken; some were deported to Russia and forced to convert, whereupon they were enrolled in Ivan's army; others were simply killed on the spot.

The Cossacks who crossed the Urals into Siberia in the 1580s also made effective use of firearms to expand eastwards, reaching the Pacific within half a century in their pursuit of furs. This rush to the ocean soon brought about conflict with China, which in 1689 concluded at Nerchinsk its first treaty ever with a European power. Even though signed by a Manchu emperor, the Treaty of Nerchinsk was the first occasion on which the Chinese empire accorded diplomatic equality to another signatory. Emperor Kang Xi appreciated the settlement reached with the Russians for the good reason that he was now free to deal with the Mongols, the perennial enemies of China. One of the great military achievements of the Manchu conquerors for the security of the Chinese empire was to remove once and for all the nomad threat to its civilisation of settled agriculture. It is important to keep the Western technological edge in warfare in a proper perspective, however. Not till after the end of Portuguese supremacy in Asia would the European advantage become a significant factor, as the military revolution in Europe during the late seventeenth century fed through to colonial warfare. The string of early Portuguese victories may have been in part due to the application of concentrated firepower at specific strategic targets, but such an innovation was not on such a scale that some Asian states were unable to emulate it themselves.[29]

Leading Indian states understood the need for artillery, not least the Mughal empire, whose southward drive the Portuguese viewed with grave alarm. The Venetian Nicolao Manucci, a doctor in the service of the Mughals, noted the early recruitment of an English gunner from Surat, at the staggering rate of

five hundred rupees a month. However, the English race, like other European peoples, being fond of drinking wine, a thing they cannot procure in Hindustan owing to its prohibition under Mohamedan law, the gunner, in spite of all those rupees, was most unhappy. One day Akbar directed the Englishman to fire at a target for which purpose a great sheet had been erected in front of the palace on the bank of the river. The gunner intentionally fired the ball into the air, so that it disappeared. On this account was the emperor much put out, thinking that the gunner had no skill taking aim. He asked the man the reason for such a great error in his aim, when he had such repute in the art of discharging canon. The Englishman replied that the mistake arose from his not being able to see; if he had drunk wine he could aim straight at the target. The king commanded that they should bring him spirits (of which there was no shortage in the imperial household, where it was made for giving to the war-elephants to increase their courage). When he saw the spirits, the Englishman was highly delighted; he seized the bottle, putting it to his mouth with the same eagerness that a thirsty stag rushed to a crystal spring. At one go he drank the whole, and then licked his moustache. The king was amazed and astounded to see the pleasure that the Englishman had in drinking spirits. Purposely the Englishman made all sorts of gestures to show his satisfaction; then, turning towards the target, he rubbed his eyes, and asked them to take away the sheet and replace it with a pot stuck upon a stick. So said, so done. He discharged the piece and knocked the pot to bits. At this the king and his courtiers were all lost in amazement at such a good shot. It was on account of this fact that Akbar conceded to Europeans the permission to distil spirits for their own consumption, and would not allow anyone to interfere with them. He said that as Europeans must have been created at the same time as spirits, and if deprived of them were like fish out of their element, unless they had drink they could not see plain.[30]

How much European mercenaries in the pay of Moslem states owed to this artful gunner it is impossible to tell, but the presence of these military experts was recognised over a wide area by "their eyes rolling from drinking liquor".[31] Akbar's successor, Jahangir, may have recalled the service rendered by the thirsty Englishman when in 1608 he gave the English East India Company permission to set up a factory at Surat. Realising later that trade with the English would jeopardise good relations with the Portuguese, the Mughal emperor withdrew permission for the factory and expelled the English. Jahangir did not wish to offend officials of the Estado da India in Goa, lest they direct their fleet to disrupt vessels carrying pilgrims to Mecca, a destination he was bound to ensure that Moslems could safely reach.

All ships in the Indian Ocean were required by the Portuguese to have a *cartaz*, or "pass". It stated who was the captain, how big

An island at the entrance of the Persian Gulf, Hormuz was captured by the Portuguese in 1515

was the ship, and what crew it carried. Usually issued at a fort, a pass required that a ship should trade with the Portuguese or call in to pay customs duties on its cargo before proceeding to its final destination. A cash deposit had to be left at the place where the pass was issued. Any vessel sailing without such an official safe conduct could be taken as a prize. Central to the system of passes was Hormuz, an island at the mouth of the Persian Gulf: Albuquerque captured it in 1515, two years after his repulse at Aden. He achieved this conquest in spite of strong opposition from his captains, who preferred the much easier task of plundering merchant vessels at sea.

Mixed Portuguese Success in Southeast Asia

Because very few forts were ever established to the east of India, Albuquerque's hope of extinguishing Islam in Southeast Asia came to nothing. An unforeseen consequence of the capture of Malacca by the Portuguese was the further spread of Moslem belief, as the local population worked hard to keep the spice trade from falling into Christian hands. Utterly beyond Portuguese strength was retention of distant outposts at Ternate and Tidore in the Indonesian archipelago. They had been set up there in the 1520s among "the spice islands" so as to check Spain, but they collapsed as much through mismanagement as opposition from local rulers. The vicious and corrupt Lopes de Mesquita, captain of the Ternate fort, precipitated a crisis that ended the Portuguese presence altogether. This greedy official tried to expropriate a large part of the clove crop for his own personal benefit, and stabbed the friendly sultan to death when he pointed out the blatant injustice of this action. Mesquita even had the body cut into pieces and cast into the sea. Sultan Baab Ullah, the vengeful son, called the people to arms and in 1576 forced the surrender of Ternate: the Portuguese hung on for a while at Tidore, but the arrival of the Dutch soon encouraged the local inhabitants to drive them out as well.

But the grip of Portugal was already loosening elsewhere in Southeast Asia, in large measure through the energies of Aceh, a

31

fanatically Moslem state situated in northern Sumatra. Fourteen times the Acehnese launched attacks on Malacca. From the 1530s, they also shipped pepper and other spices to the Turkey-dominated Red Sea without apparent difficulty. There is indeed evidence of military cooperation between the Ottoman Turks and the Acehnese against Portugal. A chronicle composed in Aceh reveals how its aggressive ruler, Alau'ddin Ri'ayat Syah al-Kahar sent "a mission to Istanbul in order to strengthen the Moslem faith. The sultan there sent back craftsmen and experts who knew about making guns. It was at this time that large guns were cast. It was also he who first built fortifications at Aceh, and he who first fought all unbelievers, to the extent of going to attack Malacca in person."[32] By the 1560s, the idea of a pan-Islamic counter-crusade against the Portuguese had taken root in Southeast Asia. When Aceh sent a succession of envoys to Istanbul, Turkey responded by sending not only technicians capable of casting cannon but even more soldiers to serve as artillerymen.

At the height of its military power in the 1620s, Aceh boasted 5,000 large and small cannon. For the attack of 1629 on Malacca, an enormous ship was specially built, known as "the Terror of the Universe": it may well have been one of the largest wooden vessels ever launched, since its armament comprised 100 guns, according to the Portuguese who captured the vessel.[33] Frequent though the assaults were on Malacca, the Portuguese never countered with any blow directly on Aceh, a sign of the increasing weakness of the Estado da India.

Even in the Bay of Bengal a manpower crisis had forced the announcement of a general amnesty for those Portuguese who had deserted for trading and raiding on their own account. The Estado da India hoped that they would return to the service of the crown. Right around the Bay of Bengal, unofficial Portuguese settlements had sprung up in the major ports as private initiative came to the fore. About 1551, some 240 Portuguese were living in Pegu, the capital of the Toungoo dynasty in southern Burma. Their choice of residence connected with its traditionally profitable relations with Malacca. Once the Achenese moved against Malacca, and disrupted the supply of foodstuffs from Java, the trade with Pegu became vital as the city came to rely on Burmese rice. Trade was not, however, the only activity with which unofficial Portuguese residents concerned themselves. Reports were received at Goa about their involvement in warfare both as mercenaries and suppliers of firearms.

The Portuguese traveller Fernão Mendez Pinto tells us how news of an impending Burmese attack on Ayudhya, the Thai capital, resulted in a general call-up. Foreigners were given three days to quit the country or rally to the colours. He records that

> with regard to the Portuguese, who had always been shown the highest respect, the Siamese king sent a minister, the governor of the kingdom, to ask them to voluntarily join his army, in view of the reputation they had, for he was most desirous of having them serve as his personal guards since, from what he knew about them, they were better suited for it than all others. Considering the nature of this message, which was accompnied by liberal promises and expectations of high wages, favours, honours, and above all, permission to build churches in his kingdom, we felt so deeply obligated to him that, out of the 130 of us Portuguese who were there at the time, 120 agreed to go with him.[34]

The Thai monarch whom these volunteers served was Naresuan. On two occasions before Naresuen became king in 1590, the Burmese had sent forces to intimidate Ayudhya but, as the heir apparent, he saw off both these threats. The decisive moment came in early 1593 at the battle of Nong Sarai, for which the Portuguese contingent was hastily recruited.

Although outnumbered by the Burmese invasion force, a Thai chronicle relates how Naresuan found comfort in the appearance of auspicious signs such as relics of the Buddha, which glowed in the sky as they moved slowly northwards. But he placed his hope of victory in the effectiveness of "the lotus array", a military formation using a vanguard supported by powerful wings. His army was thus deployed when a small force he had sent forward to reconnoitre the enemy's position was driven back in disorder. Instead of coming up to its aid, Naresuan decided to stand firm and let the Burmese advance in the belief that the whole army of Ayudhya was retreating before them. The uncoordinated approach of the Burmese units gave Naresuan's soldiers the advantage in the general engagement that ensued, although they had to fight very hard to avoid envelopment. Pinto mentions how the Thai king cleverly adjusted his tactics after the initial contact, but he does not record the encounter between him and the Burmese commander, in which Naresuan slew his opponent with a long-handled sword from the top of his favourite elephant. And, more important still, there is no mention of a singular Portguese success: a shot fired by one of the volunteers killed the chief contender for the Burmese throne atop his elephant, and contributed to a succession struggle that for a generation weakened the Toungoo dynasty.[35]

The aftermath of Nong Sarai, according to Pinto, was a determined effort to strengthen the Thai position, since "the king attended with great haste to the fortification of the city of Ayudhya and to everything else that was necessary for its security. To determine his losses in battle he ordered a review of his troops and found that he had lost only 50,000 men. . . whereas for his enemies, it was learned on the following day that 130,000 of them had died."[36] The Toungoo dynasty eventually recovered from this reverse, and in Anaukpetlan and his successor Thalum produced great kings, but these two rulers had to accept the independence of Ayudhya, and to overlook the sanctuary it provided for Burmese dissidents.

It was Anaukpetlan who brought to an end the most remarkable example of Portuguese enterprise in the Bay of Bengal, the private kingdom of Filipe de Brito e Nicote at Syriam in the Irrawaddy delta. Before taking up service as a mercenary with the ruler of Arakan, de Brito was a salt merchant resident at Chittagong. Even though affairs on the eastern side of the Bay of Bengal interested Goa very little, it was a region into which many underpaid, indeed unpaid, Portuguese soldiers had drifted in search of personal wealth. Pinto places the number of Portuguese mercenaries fighting for the Toungoo dynasty at 700: this figure may be as exaggerated as his claim that outside the city of Prome there were among the dead "500 Portuguese whose only burial then was in the bellies of the vultures and crows that tore them apart bit by bit as they lay scattered in the fields."[37] This earlier encounter between the Burmese and the Thai was complicated by disease arising from contaminated water, which carried off most of the Portuguese soldiers of fortune in the

Toungoo camp. De Brito's own opportunity for independent power came after the disastrous Burmese invasion of Ayudhya in 1593.

In the turmoil after the battle of Nong Sarai, the Arakanese succeeded in taking Pegu, the capital of Burma, and despoiling the city of its famous treasures. With members of the Toungoo royal family fighting among themselves for the Burmese throne, there was nothing to stop the Arakanese invasion force from leaving a garrison of Portuguese mercenaries under de Brito's command behind at Syriam. Possibly, the Portuguese commander gave up his share of the spoils from Pegu, or paid the ruler of Arakan cash, for the privilege of building a wooden fort there in 1601. In the following year, de Brito arrived in Goa with an interesting proposition for the Portuguese viceroy. He pointed out the absence of the fortresses belonging to the Estado da India in the area and suggested that a customs house at Syriam would be ideally placed as a counterpart to Malacca. A Portuguese squadron stationed there could easily supervise the trade between Burma and the Indonesian archipelago.

De Brito's motive seems to have been a desire to rejoin mainstream Portuguese society. Therefore, he sought to link his holding in Syriam via Goa with both Lisbon and Madrid—two capital cities, because between 1580 and 1640 Portugal was under the Spanish crown. While Philip II had decided that the two overseas empires of Spain and Portugal should remain separately administered entities, de Brito could not have been unaware of joint Luso-Spanish efforts in Cambodia during the 1590s. So anxious were Cambodian kings about pressure from Ayudhya and Laos that one of them seriously contemplated Christianity as a means of securing military aid. A Portuguese adventurer named Diogo Veloso received permission to construct a fortress on an island from King Ton, the son of the legitimate king, in gratitude for his help in succeeding to the Cambodian throne. The grant of land to Veloso provides an insight to the difficulties besetting the Cambodian kingdom at this time.[38] With the aid of Spanish troops from Manila, Veloso had deposed a usurper and placed Ton on the throne. But this new ruler was assassinated in 1599, the year that Spanish soldiers were also massacred. Veloso died in a separate altercation in peninsular Malaya, possibly over a dispute on trading rights. Useful though this fleeting foreign support may have been in introducing firearms to an embattled

Cambodia, the strategic weakness of the kingdom remained its position, wedged between the Thai, Laotians and Vietnamese.

Because the political situation in lower Burma seemed more favourable to the Estado da India, de Brito was well received in Goa by the viceroy, who lent him support in his dealings with Lisbon, and married one of his daughters to him. In return for Syriam coming under the formal control of the Estado da India, which decided to maintain a customs house there, de Brito was given ships, men and supplies. He was also ennobled and given the title to the captaincy of the Syriam fortress for life. Should he have a legitimate son, then this entitlement would be inherited by him. For Goa, the endorsement of de Brito's enterprise held the distinct possibility of dominating the commerce of Burma. Until Syriam fell to a resurgent Toungoo dynasty in 1613, de Brito was allowed to behave like a semi-independent ruler with jurisdiction and authority over the Portuguese living along the eastern shore of the Bay of Bengal. He had the power to pardon their crimes, even when deserving a death sentence.[39]

Although his enclave enjoyed some indigenous backing through the recruitment of Indian and Burmese mercenaries, de Brito's conspicuous patronage of the Catholic church ensured that he was always looked upon as an outsider. In any case, the local population was never really large enough to sustain a state with territorial ambitions, for the prolonged period of civil war and invasion had laid the Irrawaddy delta waste. When Anaukpetlan besieged Syriam, de Brito probably had no more than 400 Portuguese and Indian followers, and perhaps five times that number of local auxiliaries, to face a Burmese army of 100,000 men. Once he ran out of gunpowder and was unable to use his cannon effectively, his local troops stole away till de Brito's remaining followers could no longer man the defences. As a punishment for looting Buddhist temples, de Brito was impaled on an iron stake, where he lingered for two days in full view of his men. However, Anaukpetluan decided to spare the lives of these cowed professionals, and for well over a century their descendants were responsible for Burma's artillery.

What the fate of Syriam demonstrated was the limits of European power when confronted by the manpower resources of organised Asian states. Only in disunited Sri Lanka would the Portuguese become rulers of extensive territory for any length of time, and benefit from a monopoly of cinnamon. Colombo had been seized as a stronghold in 1518, but after gaining control of the coastal lowlands where this spice grew, Portugal never formally claimed possession of the island.[40] The Estado da India was content to manipulate instead the once-dominant kings of Kotte, who embraced the Christian faith from 1557 onwards. This conversion did not impress the predominantly Buddhist population and the Portuguese were obliged to move the puppet dynasty to the safety of Colombo in the 1590s. Already, the costs of dealing with the restless vassals of the Kotte kings was proving a liability for the Portuguese, and policy wavered dangerously between a landward advance and complete evacuation.

Indian converts in Goa, the headquarters of the Estado da India. The Inquisition arrived there in 1560

In the event, the Dutch solved the dilemma for Portugal, its last fortress falling to the new arrivals on the northern coast of the island at Jaffna in 1658. With the notable exception of Sri Lanka then, the Portuguese always accepted that they were too weak on land to defeat a determined Asian enemy. So they tended to come to terms with local rulers and commercial interests so that they could hold on to their initial gains. On the eastern periphery of the Estado da India, this cautious approach was even more marked, although the refusal of Ming China to allow its merchants to trade with Japan gave the Portuguese the lion's share of Sino-Japanese trade. Along with the Malaccan spice trade, revenues drawn from it made up a substantial proportion of Goa's already declining receipts.

Missionaries swiftly followed on the heels of merchants. The Society of Jesus sent Francis Xavier to preach Christianity in Asia. A disciple and friend of Ignatius Loyala, the order's founder, Xavier made many converts in Sri Lanka, before staying for six months at Malacca in 1547. There the future saint asked his congregation to pray for victory over the Acehnese, a recommendation all could support. More controversial was his urging of the Portuguese "who were living with female slaves either to sell them or marry them".[41] Abuse of domestic slavery was not of course restricted to Malacca, but there it seems to have especially flourished with one man having "twenty-four women of all races, all of whom were his slaves, and all of whom he enjoyed".[42] With a chronic shortage of Portuguese women in the Estado da India, there was a sexual problem which the authorities simply could not ignore. Quite likely thinking of future manpower needs too, Alfonso de Albuquerque had inaugurated an intercommunal marriage policy, when in 1510 he encouraged his men to marry the "white and beautiful" widows and the daughters of Moslem defenders of Goa whom they had slain in battle or subsequently burnt alive. The viceroy was quite frank about his disdain for dark-skinned Indian women, who seemed little removed from the slaves so readily traded in Africa. Many of his men did not share this racial prejudice, but there were many others who did and the offspring of such marriages often found themselves poorly regarded.

A later viceroy, Antonio de Mello de Castro, lamented in 1664 how "our decay in these parts is entirely due to our treating the natives thereof as if they were slaves or worse than if they were

Moors".[43] A reinforcement of prejudice came from the attitude of the religious orders, as they tended to uphold white supremacy. Clerics indeed pointed out how it was divinely ordained that black people should be enslaved; they bore the burden of Noah's curse as the supposed descendants of his son Ham. This insidious notion of racial inferiority provided a convenient cloak for the slave trade. Whereas Noah's other two sons Japhet and Shem were believed to have settled in Europe and West Asia respectively, Ham dwelt in Africa. One of the descendants of Shem was none other than Jesus Christ, a circumcised Jew, whose life and death brought about the conversion of Japhet's offspring, the uncircumcised Europeans. Entirely outside the Catholic church, and the protection of Christ, were the heretical descendants of Ham. For St. Augustine, the ancient interpreter of the Christian world, the division between Japhet, Shem and Ham, between European, Hebrew and African, was not a question of ethnicity, but rather a matter of those who lived according to divine will and those who lived according to human desires. This is hardly an unexpected interpretation of the biblical story when it is remembered that Aurelius Augustinus was of Berber stock himself.

That Noah's curse was evoked at the very moment of Iberian expansion overseas should not come as a surprise, for the disdain it justified towards African peoples was a useful device for aggressive imperialism. As yet, this attitude was not the fully fledged racism of the late nineteenth century, when pseudoscientific evidence was adduced to shore up Western dominance in world affairs. The English travel writer Samuel Purchas could still hold in 1613 that the diversity of mankind was evidence of God's wondrous handiwork: "The tawney Morre, black Negro, duskie Libyan, ash-coloured Indian, olive-coloured American should with the whiter European become one sheepe-fold, under one great shepheard, till this mortalitie being swallowed up of life, wee may all be one, as he and the father are one. . . Without any more distinction of colour, Nation, language, sex, condition al may bee One in him that is ONE, and only blessed forever."[44] For Purchas, the apparent differences between people had more to do with custom than intrinsic qualities.

It was not a view shared by Xavier, who in persuading Portuguese settlers to marry their local concubines, imposed a definite colour bar. "When the woman was dark in colour and ugly featured, he employed all his eloquence to separate his host from her. He was even ready, if necessary, to find for him a more suitable mate."[45] Although Xavier was genuinely shocked by the moral laxity of the Estado da India, his response was no more saintly than that of other Jesuits who welcomed measures taken in Goa against Hinduism. Xavier even asked the Portuguese king to transplant the Inquisition as soon as possible: it arrived in 1560, eight years after his death. An estimated 30,000 Hindus were subsequently obliged to quit Goa, leaving the majority of the population with mixed parentage.

An Indo-Portuguese wedding. In spite of official disdain for Indians, many Portuguese men took local wives

During the last quarter of the sixteenth century, Alessandro Valignano, the dominant figure among the Jesuits in Asia, proved to be less tolerant still. Already he had decided that Indian converts were unsuitable candidates for admisson to the Society of Jesus, before he left Goa for his mission in Japan. The "dusky races" were condemned as "stupid and vicious, and of the basest spirits".[46] Senior officials and members of the aristocracy had little interest in most Indians, whatever their social standing, but the humbler soldiers who followed them from Portugal seem to have been less disdainful, in spite of religious admonishment. In the Philippines, a similar pattern of relations pertained between the ordinary Spanish settlers and the indigenous peoples. But in comparison with that of the Portuguese, the Spanish enterprise in Asia was a modest affair, not least because the Philippines always remained an offshoot of Spanish dominion in the New World, being under the direct jurisdiction of the viceroy in Nueva España, present-day Mexico. The death of its "discoverer", Fernão de Magalhaes, better known as Magellan, hardly acted as an encouragement for settlement, despite the cargo of spices loaded in the Moluccas on the homeward voyage more than covering the cost of this first expedition. Trying to elevate one local chieftain over others as a client ruler of Spain, Magellan had overestimated the advantage of European arms, and fell in an engagement against more than a thousand warriors on the island of Mactan.[47] While few Spaniards were actually killed in the attacking force of 50 men, the aura of invincibility was lost, and a tactical withdrawal became necessary.

Born about 1480 in northern Portugal, Magellan had fought in Africa, India and the Indonesian achipelago before he returned to Lisbon seeking a reward for this period of service. Having two petitions turned down between 1514 and 1516 in Lisbon, he decided to try his luck with the Spaniards instead. By sailing to Asia in a westerly direction and rounding Cape Horn, he led his tiny Spanish fleet to the Philippines in 1521. On its return to Spain, the failure was conveniently blamed on the impetuosity of the dead commander. But other expeditions fared no better until in 1564 a fleet of five ships and more than 400 men under the command of Miguel Lopez de Legazpi set sail from Mexico, with instructions about "the conversion of the natives and the discovery of a safe route back to Nueva España, that the kingdom may increase and profit from trade".[48] On the site of a Moslem stockade at Manila the expedition constructed the first stone fortress in the Philippines. By 1650 its walls had been extended to surround the settlement which rapidly developed close by.

Because there was no single political or religious authority in the Philippine archipelago, the Spaniards were able to exploit island rivalries for their own advantage, once the healthy climate attracted enough permanent settlers at Manila. The brutality of these immigrants was to some degree mitigated by intermarriage with Filipino converts. The effect of conversion in lowering barriers between the rulers and the ruled would have been even greater had not the Spanish authorities decreed that for security reasons only priests were allowed to live in the interior. Missionary activity was increasingly seen as a sure method of preparing the indigenous peoples for acceptance of the Spanish state. Thus Portuguese and Spanish settlers in Asia were unlike later Dutch and British arrivals, who tended to view themselves as only temporary residents.

China and Japan

In East Asia, the strength of the major powers restricted the Portuguese solely to business. Neither China nor Japan ever perceived the fleets of the Estado da India as a major threat, notwithstanding the restriction placed on trade by the former and the general exclusion the latter eventually pronounced against missionaries and traders. The first Portuguese vessels from Malacca reached Guangzhou in 1517. Others followed without mishap but relations with the Chinese were strained by Simão Peres d'Andrade's construction of a fort downstream from Guangzhou, from which he proceeded to hinder the movements of rival merchant vessels. This typical Portuguese method of coastal domination so annoyed the Ming emperor Wu Song that he denied the king of Portugal's envoy an audience. But the cool reception accorded Tomé Pires at Beijing in 1521 may have been the consequence of other factors than Simão Peres d'Andrade's high-handedness. Adverse reports about Portuguese rule in Malacca seem to have prompted several ministers to recommend a complete rejection of Pires' overtures.[49]

The sudden death of the 31-year-old Wu Song meant that the imperial court had to observe a period of mourning in any case. The Portuguese envoy was ordered to return to Guangzhou, where he was arrested at the same time that Chinese troops destroyed the fort downstream. Pires did not survive imprisonment and his fellow countrymen were forced to trade at Chinese ports by subterfuge. They had to remain below decks while hired Malays or Thai dealt with the exchange of goods and paid customs duties. Ming China even revived its coastal protection fleet to deal with Portuguese smugglers and pirates. The unsatisfactory situation was only resolved when a small Portuguese settlement at Macao, near present-day Hong Kong, received Chinese toleration. But its swift growth soon caused the local Chinese authorities some uneasiness, and in 1574 they constructed a wall right across the isthmus connecting Macao with the mainland, posting soldiers to guard a single gateway, above which was written: "Fear Our greatness, and respect Our virtue." Movement through the gate was henceforth denied to foreigners lacking official Chinese passes.

Although Macao was an admission that foreign trade could not be prohibited, the imperial government ensured by this arrangement that contact between Chinese and foreigners was kept to a minimum. Above all else, Beijing feared that unregulated coastal trade would disturb the social life of China's countryside, the place where the overwhelming majority of its people lived. What happened in the Macao enclave was of no concern to the Chinese, who were uninterested in the efforts made by its residents to keep Spaniards out, even after Philip II seized the Portuguese throne. In 1567 the Ming dynasty lifted its ban on Chinese participation in foreign trade and within a decade Portuguese residents were permitted to travel from Macao to Guangzhou to purchase Chinese products. The more relaxed approach also encouraged Chinese merchants to venture abroad with the result that large numbers settled in the Philippines. Violence dogged the Chinese community there almost from the

Portuguese Macao. The cross on the gateway (bottom left) is fanciful because this barrier was built by the Chinese authorities

beginning, as Spanish records give the number killed in 1603 alone as 15,000. Earlier, Philip II had rejected a suggestion by the governor of Manila that Spain should attack China. This proposal to open up the Chinese market by force, if it had been carried out, would have anticipated the First Opium War by two and a half centuries.

Tiny though Macao was in comparison with other Estado da India holdings, merchants living there conducted the most lucrative of all Portuguese trading operations in Asia. Even more remarkable is the circumstance that the impetus for the Macao–Nagasaki exchange came neither from the Portuguese court nor its overseas representatives, but traders and missionaries who stumbled upon an untapped market. Because of Japanese pirate raids, China forbad all direct trade with Japan. The exchange of Chinese silk and gold for Japanese silver was naturally something the Portuguese were delighted to handle.

At first, this very profitable commerce was open to all, but the Estado da India moved to extract the maximum return for the crown by allowing just a single ship to make the Goa–Macao–Nagasaki run. Its hold was hired out by the person who held the concession for each round trip. Spanish merchants at Manila were also drawn into Macao's trading network, as they purchased Chinese silk with American silver and sent it back to Europe via Mexico. When in 1641 the Dutch captured Malacca and closed the straits to Portuguese vessels, the Manila trade helped to save Macao from commercial extinction. Well before the last Portuguese were expelled from Japan in 1638, this eastbound trade so greatly surpassed Macao's business with the Japanese that the movement of silver from the New World became a headache for Spain. Its scale genuinely shocked Spanish officials visiting Mexico and the Philippines.[50]

On the southernmost Japanese island of Kyushu the Portuguese found a ready market for firearms as well as Chinese products. But that peculiarly Japanese talent for imitation quickly put a local version of the musket into production so that there was "not a village or hamlet, no matter how small, where they do not produce a hundred or more, and in the important cities and towns they speak of them in nothing less than thousands". It was evident to Pinto that the people of Japan took naturally "to military exercise, which they enjoy more than any other nation that is known to date".[51] This disposition suited the Portuguese, who could relate to the

Portuguese traders in Japan, where their clothes soon set the fashion for city dwellers

sword-wearing samurai as well as the large numbers of foot-soldiers fighting in the interminable civil wars. With their own military religious orders of Santiago, Avis and Christ, they found no difficulty in understanding the regiments of warrior-monks maintained by Buddhist monasteries. The paradox that wars between monasteries devoted to the worship of the gentle Buddha should be part of the contemporary turmoil entirely passed them by. They showed no curiosity over battle flags bearing the legend: "The mercy of the Buddha should be recompensed even by rending flesh. One's duty to the Sage should be recompensed by smashing bones!"

For Japan seemed such a relief to the Portuguese after China, where a brush-wielding bureaucracy had relegated the military to a subordinate role in government. Responding to the chivalry and pride of the samurai, to the traditional way of the warrior, Xavier believed that the Japanese were the best people so far discovered in Asia. His single reservation was homosexuality, a widespread phenomenon among warriors and monks alike. He was amazed that monks "had many boys of prominent families in their monasteries, where they taught them to read and write and abused them for sinful purposes, as they openly admitted. The laymen agreed with Xavier and his companions when they condemned these unnatural sins as a severe offence against God. But the vice was so general and so deeply rooted that the monks were not reproached for it."[52] Never able to reconcile himself to this practice, Xavier tried without success to get the Buddhists in Japan to condemn monastic homosexuality. In addition to this mini-crusade, he sought out the Japanese emperor, admission to whose presence was secured by payment of an entrance fee. As baffled by the destitution of the imperial court as he was by the corruption of the monasteries, Xavier learned that the emperor lived in a village near Kyoto because he could not afford to repair his palace in the city. Power had long since shifted to the great warrior families, who owed allegiance to the shogun, the supreme military commander, a post held in theory by permission of the throne. In practice, even this quasi-feudal order had almost broken down, leaving the way open for the rise of all-powerful warlords such as Oda Nobunaga and Toyotomi Hideyoshi.

On his return to Goa in 1552, Xavier reported favourably on the prospects of mission work in Japan, and spoke highly of the character of the Japanese people. He urged the dispatch of missionaries without delay, and they had considerable success on the island of Kyushu, where local rulers always welcomed the arrival of Portuguese merchant ships. One of the Jesuits active then was Luis Frois, who had travelled to Japan after nine years in Malacca. In 1569, this Portuguese missionary impressed Oda Nobunaga when the warlord was inspecting the construction of a bridge at one of his castles. Asked about his purpose in coming to Japan, Frois explained about Christianity while disparaging the Buddhist faith. As the great Buddhist monasteries remained a thorn in his side, Oda Nobunaga was more than willing to protect the Jesuits against Buddhist hostility, which Frois said was the result of exposing the sins of the monks. This did not mean the warlord was a likely convert: Frois reported to his Jesuit superiors in Europe that Oda Nobunaga "states unequivocally that there is no Creator, no immortality of the soul, and no life after death".[53] He was a straightforward soldier who disliked the rigmarole of both religious observance and court etiquette. So plain

A Japanese and a Portuguese merchant. During the sixteenth century Portugal dominated Japan's international trade

were his own clothes, except for a tiger skin that he wore round the waist, that no one dared to appear before him in expensive robes.

Within two years of their meeting, Frois witnessed Oda Nobunaga's most notorious single act, the complete destruction of the Enryakuji temple complex on Mount Hiei near Kyoto. Long the most belligerent Buddhist foundation, its warrior-monks had sided with the warlord's enemies in 1570. The immediate cause of the quarrel between Oda Nobunaga and Enryakuji was his confiscation of some estates owned by the monastery. The sudden assault on the temple complex was meant to quell once and for all military opposition from the Buddhist monasteries. Oda Nobunaga's men destroyed every building and killed every person they encountered at Enryakuji. Here is how Frois described the event:

> On the following day, which was the last of September, the day of the glorious Saint Jerome, the great temple. . . located on the top of the mountain was first burned down, and thereafter, Oda Nobunaga sent many harquebusiers into the mountains

and woods to hunt for monks who might be hiding there. The soldiers were to spare nobody, and they executed this order promptly. This victory did not satisfy Oda Nobunaga, however. As he wanted to quench his thirst for revenge still more and thus strengthen his reputation, he ordered his whole army to immediately devastate the remaining houses of the monks, and to burn the four hundred or so temples. . . I have been told that 1,500 monks died, as did an equal number of men, women and children. . . Praise be to God's providence and ultimate goodness, for he has ordered such a great hindrance to be punished by extinction, so that one day His holiest law will be propagated in these parts in abundance.[54]

In 1587 the followers of a subordinate surprised the residence of Oda Nobunaga early one morning in Kyoto. After exterminating the warlord and his next of kin, the rebels dithered over their next move, giving Toyotomi Hideyoshi ample scope to avenge Oda Nobunaga's assassination.

As ruthless as his assassinated overlord, Toyotomi Hideyoshi dominated all Japan by 1590, ending more than a century of civil wars. Of peasant origin, he reduced the feudal lords to obedience through a spectacular series of victories. Unlike Oda Nobunaga though, Toyotomi Hideyoshi dealt generously even with those he had overcome in battle and did not tolerate the unnecessary slaughter of prisoners, before the frustration of the expeditions which he sent against Korea. They were intended to divert the restless energies of the samurai into conquest abroad, starting with Korea as a first stage of an invasion of China. His rage in 1596, when Chinese ambassadors offered him recognition as the king of Japan in return for peace in Korea, reputedly caused "vapour to rise from his head". A decade earlier a Catholic embassy had better luck, since Alessandro Valignano succeeded then in preserving a degree of toleration for mission work.

When it was later announced that Toyotomi Hideyoshi would pay a visit to Kyushu, the Jesuits still decided to disguise churches, take down crosses and send novices to remote areas.[55] This was prudent because in matters of religion Toyotomi Hideyoshi differed from Oda Nobunaga. Although his own personal beliefs remain unknown, he was less hostile to Buddhism than Christianity, and he disliked the influence exercised by the Jesuits over Kyushu leaders.

Toyotomi Hideyoshi had no sympathy for Christianity and
deplored everything foreign

He was also displeased by the adoption of Portuguese fashions in
clothes: at Kyoto there was a vogue for everything foreign.

This was obviously a different world from Goa, where Valignano
exhibited a profound distrust of the indigenous population. He even
reproved Francisco Cabral, a leading Jesuit, for calling Japanese
converts "blacks", and insisted that any of them who entered the
Society itself should have the same treatment as other recruits.[56] For
Valignano appreciated the strength of Japan, positively discouraging
any wild Luso-Spanish ideas of dominion. He knew that Toyotomi
Hideyoshi had dispatched an army of 100,000 men against Korea.
The king of Ayudhya, Naresuan, offered to send his nominal overlord naval assistance against the Japanese, but the Ming emperor
had no need of the Thai navy for the good reason that in the Korean
admiral Yi Sunsin the defenders were blessed with a strategic genius.
Not only did he design and build the first fully armoured warship
in the world, but during several engagements Yi Sunsin sank one

Japanese fleet after another. The Korean admiral's "turtle boats" were invincible in close combat.

Toyotomi Hideyoshi was beside himself with anger, threatening to attack Manila after conquering Korea and China. In 1583, an engagement had been fought between Japanese and Spanish ships in Filipino waters. And Toyotomi Hideyoshi executed seven Franciscans from Manila, who were less tactful than the Portuguese Jesuits in their dealings with him. Yet the willingness of the Jesuits to become involved with Japanese affairs of state led to their undoing: it was soon to become apparent that the teachings of the gospels did not quite square with the harsh code of the Japanese warrior. Refusal by Japanese converts to follow this pattern of traditional loyalties could be construed only as treason.[57] As a result of such occurrences, after his triumph over all rivals at the battle of Sekigahara in 1600, Toyotomi Hideyoshi's successor, Tokugawa Ieyasu, issued an edict that stopped samurai from professing the Christian faith.

The arrival of the Dutch in 1609 conveniently brought the Portuguese monopoly of international commerce to a close. The ensuing rivalry between them was advantageous to Tokugawa Ieyasu, who desired to curb Catholic evangelism without disrupting trade. In retaliation for the severe punishment of riotous Japanese sailors in Macao, he destroyed the Portuguese vessel *Madre de Deus* in 1610 and executed its crew. Macao merchants continued to trade under growing Japanese pressure, which in 1636 meant the removal of remaining Portuguese residents to the artificial island of Deshima in Nagasaki harbour, until an edict issued two years later barred them altogether, leaving Deshima in the sole possession of the Dutch. The political consequences of the Spanish takeover of Portugal had reached the farthest-flung outpost of the Estado da India.

It is one of the ironies of history that the country in which the Portuguese commenced their expansion overseas at Ceuta in 1415 should have witnessed a defeat that led to this disastrous union of crowns, for it was in Morocco that the childless Portuguese king Sebastian fell at the battle of Alcazar in 1578, the victim of an ill-conceived and ill-prepared crusade. The fanatical king led 10,000 poorly armed men deep into the interior, where a Moroccan army routed them in a six-hour engagement. One of the cannons fired by the Moslems had been supplied by the English, something Habsburg propagandists did not fail to point out in 1580, the year in which Philip II of Spain was able to occupy a disorientated Portugal with the loss of very few men. The bungled crusade cost the Portuguese dear: previously on friendly terms with all Europe, they acquired Spain's enemies, notably the French, the English and the Dutch, who preyed upon their shipping and their overseas empire.

The Dutch were indeed already in rebellion against Philip II, and in 1598 they took their war of independence abroad. Within seven years Dutch warships had reached the Moluccas, from which they expelled the Portuguese with local help. A Spanish counter-offensive from the Philippines had to be repulsed by the Dutch, before they could gain the upper hand in the Indonesian archipelago over intruding English ships and in 1641 take the greatest prize of all, Portuguese Malacca. In India and Sri Lanka, Portuguese losses were just as great, for they lost control of pepper and cinnamon supplies. But at Macao the Dutch were in 1622 decisively repulsed, much to the disgust of the Dutch governor-general Jan Pieterszoon Coen, by "many Portuguese slaves, Kaffirs and the like, [who] having been made drunk, charged fearlessly against our muskets, that it was a wonderous thing to see".[58] Another eastern possession that escaped capture was East Timor, the main source of sandalwood for India as well as China. After the fall of Malacca, some Catholics of mixed parentage joined existing settlers there and formed a group called by the Dutch the Zwarte Portuguesen, or "Black Portuguese". The ethnic mixture actually comprised people of Dutch, Portuguese and Timorese ancestry. A backwater of the Dutch East Indies, the Portuguese colony was left largely undisturbed until the middle of the twentieth century.

By 1700, the Estado da India was reduced to no more than a collection of territorial niches and trading networks, the latter populated by merchants who were anxious to keep officials at arm's length. Positioned between piracy and capitalism, between the late medieval and the early modern, the Portuguese empire in Asia had been at its height an incredible instance of opportunistic endeavour which somehow managed to overlook its own obvious shortcomings and weaknesses. An amazing achievement was its creation of a global system of seaborne exchange, which the Dutch and the English in particular were about to transform into the present-day pattern of world trade. But unlike the Spaniards in the Philippines, the Portuguese did not hold on to extensive Asian territories, their chief possessions being confined to Africa and South America. Not that the successors of Philip II possessed a valuable asset in the Philippines, an archipelago singularly short of the natural commodities attractive to early international commerce. The export business of the Manila Company was never very buoyant: the first shipment to Spain of tobacco and indigo dates from as late as 1784, and represents a transfer of tribute in kind rather than the beginnings of commercial agriculture. For though the brief absorption of Portugal gave the Spanish crown authority over the largest colonial empire in the world, the defeat of the Armada by the English in 1588 and the independence of Holland in 1648 spelt the end of any global strategy.

It signified little that Philip II sent out his best military engineer to strengthen Portugal's chain of fortresses overseas. His enduring monument today is Fort Jesus at Mombasa. Built around a rock core with solid foundations, the new fortress was impervious to the greatest danger faced by all fortifications: mining beneath the walls to make a breach.[59] But this did not stop Fort Jesus changing hands on more than one occasion. As Philip II's envoy in Lisbon had prophetically written to his master: "The gain or loss of Portugal will mean the gain or loss of the world."[60] What he failed to foresee in the heady days of 1580 was that the Spanish link would cost the Estado da India an Asian world of its own.

Chapter 2

The Struggle for Supremacy 1647–1815

See what an Augean Stable there is to be cleansed. The Confusion we behold, what does it arise from? Rapacity and Luxury: the unreasonable desire of many to acquire in an instant, what only a few can, or ought to possess. Every Man would be rich without the Merits of long Service.

Robert Clive's view in 1765 of English East India Company corruption

Early Dutch Power

Except for Britain at the start of the nineteenth century, no power ever approached the global reach of early Dutch trading ventures. Even before the ratification in 1647–48 of the Treaty of Münster, by which Spain acknowledged Holland's independence, Dutch ships had already disrupted Portuguese commerce throughout Asian waters. The fact is that Portuguese possessions were the chief target of attack rather than those belonging to Spain during the period when Portugal fell under Spanish domination. Lack of success against the Spaniards in the Philippines—the Dutch suffered a disastrous defeat at Manila Bay in 1617—was one reason for this strategy; the other was a realisation that more could be gained by breaking the *cartaz* system. Goa was blockaded for two years until 1623 and again for six years until 1644, while on one occasion a Dutch squadron prevented any vessel sailing from Lisbon. Merchants' losses to enemy shipping mounted year by year and commercial traffic hitherto centred on Goa migrated to other Indian ports, mostly outside Portuguese control. The situation was made worse by the loss of Hormuz, although the Estado da India retained control of Muscat and a chain of fortresses on the Arabian peninsula. But Portuguese naval patrols from Muscat found it impossible to bar unlicensed traffic from the Strait of Hormuz after 1622.

The Dutch did not easily wrest control of the spice trade from the Portuguese, who fought hard to defend their stake in Asian commerce. Before the establishment of the United East India Company, the VOC (Vereenigde Oost-Indische Compagnie) in 1602, Dutch ships had simply scrambled for a share of the Indonesian spices. Many failed to return but those who got back to Amsterdam showed a 400 per cent profit, enough to persuade shipowners that they needed to secure this lucrative market by means of a coordinated assault on Portuguese holdings. Because there was already a rival in the English East India Company, to which Elizabeth I had granted a charter two years earlier, it was considered advisable to set up a permanent eastern base. The VOC made its first, and lasting, inroads into Asia in the Indonesian archipelago, which contained the most far-flung Portuguese outposts. Several locations were tried before a permanent foothold was gained in Java. The occupation of Jakarta, restyled Batavia in 1619 after the ancient name for Holland, was opposed by English traders, who enlisted the support of local Malay rulers. Once provided with fortifications though, Batavia was able to resist attacks by the Muslim state of Bantam in western Java, so that ships sailing direct from the Cape of Good Hope reached a safe anchorage on landfall.

This route was to remain the preferred one, even though the Straits of Malacca were soon to pass into Dutch hands. Lodgement on the island of Java had profoundly different consequences for the

Dutch because, unlike the Portuguese in Southeast Asia, it eventually turned them into a land-based colonial power. The VOC initially made little headway against the Portuguese outside the Indonesian archipelago. Its first embassy to the Mughal court, carrying letters of introduction from the Moslem sultan of Aceh, was intercepted by a Portuguese patrol before it could land in India, and its members were executed at Goa. What the ambassadors sought was access to Indian textiles so that they could be exchanged for spices, because

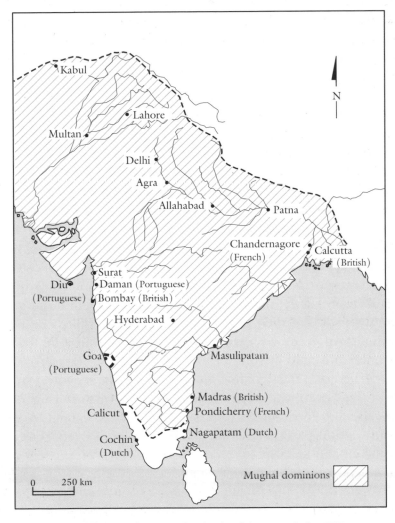

The Mughal empire on the death of Aurangzeb in 1707

the VOC had discovered that silver purchased fewer spices at less favourable prices than a consignment of cotton from India did.

Goa's position in India was threatened by more than the Dutch, however. Well before the Mughal emperor Shah Jahan fell seriously ill in 1657 and his son, Aurangzeb, imprisoned him and usurped the throne, relations between the Mughals and the Portuguese had become less amicable. In 1632, Mughal forces had destroyed the Portuguese factory at Hooghly, giving the Dutch an unexpected opportunity in Bengal. After Aurangzeb's usurpation, Goa was kept at a deliberate distance from a Mughal court increasingly preoccupied with an austere version of Islam. Ornament was proscribed along with music and poetry: Aurangzeb seems to have spent most of his time off the battlefield copying the Koran, something he achieved twice.[1]

Religious differences were not of course absent from the confrontation between the Portuguese and the Dutch. The officials of the VOC were convinced Calvinists, who regarded their opponents as the followers of Anti-Christ, a compliment returned in kind by the Portuguese condemnation of them for apostasy. In 1624, Lourenço Coelho de Barbuda succinctly remarked: "The Hollanders are merely good gunners, and are otherwise fit for nothing save to be burnt as desperate heretics."[2] It has to be said that high-minded Calvinism was not the motive that drove men to enlist in eastern expeditions against the Portuguese for, though the VOC was a Dutch organisation, the lure of personal gain attracted European adventurers of all nationalities. So brutal were they in dealing with those who fell into their power that the Chinese called the Dutch "Ocean Devils", a view that may have stemmed in part from an encounter at Macao in 1601.

That year, a fleet commanded by Jacob van Neck was so battered by storms in the South China Sea that two surviving vessels made for the Portuguese concession. Van Neck's logbook notes Macao's striking silhouette, "a great town spread out before us, all built in the Spanish style, and on a hill a Portuguese church crowned by a large blue cross". To his dismay, the Portuguese not only captured the people he sent ashore, but later they executed most of them as pirates. He could not contact the Chinese authorities for the good reason that a local fisherman informed Van Neck

A Chinese illustration of a Dutch vessel, whose crew were termed "Ocean Devils"

how handling a communication from a foreign country was punishable by death. Clearly, the two Dutch ships were looking for more than shelter in a friendly port, because they asked the Portuguese for permission to trade. They were investigating the commercial possibilities of the Pearl River estuary, a venue long reserved by the Chinese empire for the import of goods brought by foreign merchants. The Portuguese were afraid that the Chinese would grant the Dutch a trading beach: the Spaniards of Manila had been given one three years before Van Neck's arrival but failed to develop it. Therefore, they ensured that the Chinese authorities failed to learn anything about Holland, other than that it was a pirate lair, which seemed to be confirmed by the seizure of the *Santa Catarina* in 1603. This Portuguese vessel was captured by the Dutch en route to India, an event immediately reported in China.

The *Santa Catarina* was a galleon of 1,400 tonnes, a huge and cumbersome transport carrying goods to Goa from Macao. Whereas the Portuguese employed smaller vessels for coastal trading, the ships in their oceangoing fleets tended to be as large as Spanish galleons. Against the slow *Santa Catarina* the Dutch deployed fast, heavily armed ships, relying on their ability to swiftly change course during action. An Arab commentator wrote:

> When the guns on one side of the ship have been discharged, they swing the ship round so as to fire those on the other side, for they have the ability of manoeuvring for the purpose of fighting just as a horseman can wheel his horse on land.[3]

Even though the Portuguese had foundries at Macao and Goa, their output of guns was inferior to Dutch cannon. At Trincomalee, the Portuguese fort dominating its fine harbour was taken in 1639 after a bombardment made a wide breach in the walls. Unable to resist Dutch firepower, the Portuguese hold on Sri Lanka was steadily loosened: loss of Trincomalee, Batticaloa, Negombo and Galle seems to have convinced them that they would soon forfeit all their Asian bases. Only a truce between Holland and Portugal, now separated from Spain, offered a respite for the Estado da India. It was grasped by the hard-pressed Portuguese with both hands until they realised that Batavia had no intention of ending its encroachment in Sri Lanka. Possibly Goa imagined that the Dutch at Batavia lacked the authority to renew hostilities in Asia, but the VOC had come to the conclusion that the sole means of preventing Portugal from competing in the European spice market was a resumption of hostilities. By 1652, the Dutch ruled a considerable territory in Sri Lanka and had gained control of the trade in cinnamon.

Cinnamon trees grew wild along the sea coast, which was very fortunate for a European naval power. Their inner bark, when dried in the sun, produces a fragrant smell that can be used in several ways to spice food. The Portuguese had succeeded in controlling virtually all the cinnamon-producing lands, something the Dutch tried to emulate by dominating the coastline. The VOC always remained worried about native Sri Lanka rulers selling cinnamon to other European powers and a strict watch was kept on ports to see that no ship carried the spice out of the country. Quite unexpected by the Dutch was the extent of intermarriage between the Portuguese and the Sinhalese. They discovered that men of mixed descent had fought alongside the Portuguese in large numbers and were partly responsible for the prolonged resistance to Dutch arms. Although they were also perturbed by the power of the Catholic priesthood, their Calvinist outlook was most offended by Buddhism, the majority religion.

The Dutch harried Portuguese priests, with the result that many of them left, but they stopped short of attacking Buddhist beliefs even though they did not allow new temples to be built.[4] And their missionary activity was in the main directed at the 250,000 indigenous Catholics they now ruled in Sri Lanka. Johan Maetsuyker, governor-general from 1645 until 1650, made the best of the situation by following the Portuguese practice of integration. He encouraged Dutch settlers to marry Asian women, arguing that their children would be better acclimatised than those born of European parents. But he stipulated that the daughters of such unions should be married to Dutchmen, "so that our race may degenerate as little as possible".[5] What would ensure the loyalty of these children to Holland was religious education, a carefully supervised part of the curriculum in schools. Maetsuyker's colonial experiment foundered despite offering a bonus of three months' pay to any Dutch soldier or sailor who would take a local wife. The few tempted to settle down in Sri Lanka could not earn a decent living unless they became tavern keepers, since heavy drinking was a notable feature of Dutch colonial life.

The problem Maetsuyker faced was the composition of the lower levels of the VOC. Most of its soldiers and sailors were mercenaries, so that there were more Germans, Scandinavians, French and English among them than there were Dutch. They might have been fitter than Portuguese troops, some of whom were half-starved boys, but this did not make them suitable settlers. Additionally, there was the aloofness of higher VOC officials, a superior attitude that would culminate in *apartheid*. Not until the late nineteenth century could the Dutch evince any feeling of moral obligation towards their colonial subjects: in the absence of a positive approach, everything was therefore driven by commercial gain. While non-interference with Sri Lankan social life was normal to minimise unrest and the disruption of trade, official dispatches reveal the profound distrust of the Dutch for individual Sri Lankans, who were often termed "evil Moors" or "unfaithful heathen".[6]

Indifference to everything but profit also typified relations in Southeast Asia, where in early 1641 the VOC seized Malacca from the Portuguese. The news was received with jubilation at Batavia.

> Thus falls into our hands this important fortress, generally recognised as impregnable, with its canon and all other war materials. Henceforth it will be under the rule of the States General of the Free United Netherlands, and His Royal Highness the Prince of Orange. Further it will be considered as private territory and a dominion of the United East India Company.[7]

Impressed though the Malay rulers were by the Dutch capture of Malacca, they soon came to appreciate how its new occupiers were intent on monopolising trade and paying unrealistically low prices into the bargain. Supplies of tin were withheld and the VOC resorted to force. In Perak, then a subject state of Aceh, 27 Dutchmen who manned an outpost were killed in a surprise attack. In spite of a blockade of Aceh and Perak, the attackers escaped punishment and the attempt to isolate both from international trade came to nothing, because the Dutch were unwilling to turn back English ships lest relations were strained to breaking point in Europe. As the VOC spread out and took control of more areas of the Indonesian archipelago, Malacca lost its initial significance for the Dutch. Elsewhere they firmly established themselves as a major trading force, and even secured a foothold in Japan.

Dutch ambitions to dominate Asian trade received encouragement from the difficulties that the Portuguese encountered in Japan. The union of Spain and Portugal had led to Japanese reprisals in the form of an embargo and the detaining of Portuguese vessels on arrival. This action was provoked by a Spanish captain's seizure of a Japanese ship. An embassy from Macao made little headway and in 1640 a final effort ended in disaster: four leading Macao citizens, together with 57 members of their entourage and crew, were summarily executed at Nagasaki. Behind the exclusion policy was the increasing dislike of Japanese leaders for the missionary activities of Catholic priests. As the Dutch studiously avoided advancing the cause of Christianity, the VOC was soon the only foreign trader left in Japan. It was allowed a single trading station on a secluded island of Deshima at Nagasaki, where its staff were provided with food and women. No other contact was permitted. This tiny Dutch outpost was the only channel through which the Japanese kept themselves informed of events in Europe, and through it received the Dutch books that a few Nagasaki interpreters could read.

Deshima island at Nagasaki, the VOC's sole point of access to the Japanese market

The unique advantage of the VOC in having sole access to Japan was at first difficult to exploit because the Japanese market required Chinese silk, a commodity still largely controlled by the Portuguese. Because China was annoyed by how the Dutch interfered with Chinese traders buying pepper and spices in Java and

61

Sumatra, it preferred to deal with the Portuguese and the Spaniards. Attacks on Manila and Macao were followed by raids on the southern coast of China, which paralysed international trade until the Chinese court agreed to the Dutch handling of silk. Already on Taiwan the VOC had constructed a trading station near present-day Tainan, Fort Zeelandia, which served as a depot for trade with China, Japan, India and Iran. By the 1630s, the volume of goods handled at Fort Zeelandia was greater than any other Dutch outpost.

It is ironic that in 1662, when the VOC was at the height of its power in Asia, the Dutch should be expelled from the island of Taiwan by Zheng Chenggong, a Ming patriot who shifted his base of operations there after failing to recapture Nanjing from the Manchus. Coxinga, as the Dutch knew Zheng Chenggong, refused to accept that Taiwan was not entirely Chinese territory. Heavy losses did nothing to deter the besiegers and, after a severe blockade, Fort Zeelandia surrendered. As Zheng Chenggong died shortly afterwards, his followers held onto Taiwan for a mere 20 years. On its acceptance of Manchu rule in 1684, his successor was made a minor noble and enrolled as an officer by Emperor Kang Xi. The timely submission ended opposition to the Qing dynasty, China's last imperial house.

Although it had European and Indian competitors, the VOC met no determined opposition in India, where a factory was established as early as 1606. From there cloth went eastwards to the Indonesian archipelago, China and Japan, and westwards to Europe and the West Indies. Southeast Asian markets accounted for an overwhelming proportion of the total Asian market for Indian textiles, because the VOC used cloth as a medium of exchange for spices.[8] Its near monopoly proved almost counterproductive because the price put on the cloth was so high that the supply of spices dried up. By the 1630s, more reasonable trading arrangements had evolved and VOC profits ranged from between 40 and 100 per cent. VOC business with Gujarat, a long-established supplier of Indian textiles to Southeast Asia, also rested on the spice trade. The principal spices it sold there, in the port of Surat, and much farther inland at Agra, where the VOC had an outlet close to the Mughal court, were cloves, nutmeg and mace. The willingness of the Moslem aristocracy to pay inflated prices for cheaply procured Indonesian spices baffled VOC representatives, who considered lowering prices to widen the market. Batavia blocked this move, and stamped out smuggling, so that the cost of Asian spices should never be allowed to fall to a level that would be worth their while for the English to buy spices in India and take them to Europe. The English East India Company already had a factory of its own in Gujarat, although it did not reach Bengal until the 1650s. There the VOC was well entrenched in pursuit of two commodities: raw silk for Japan and opium for Southeast Asia. More than half of its Bengal trade went to the Nagasaki market before the arrival of the English.

Besides Portugal, Holland and England, the only other European power active in Asian trade at this time was Denmark. But the Danes allocated neither the capital nor the manpower that was necessary for a successful trading venture in Asian waters. By the 1680s therefore, the chief traders were the Dutch and the English, the former having been challenged by the Royal Navy in European waters. To English merchants, the VOC's outlook seemed little different from Iberian claims of overseas sovereignty: they were both intent on restricting international trade. To counter Dutch maritime supremacy, the Navigation Act was passed in 1651. Among other things, it banned the import of goods except in English or specified ships. A successor piece of legislation in 1660 was more practical and less rigid, but it had the effect of stimulating English trade and shipping. Tension between Holland and England over commercial issues arising from these acts led to a naval arms race, the Dutch deciding to add 150 warships to their navy. In addition, they insisted that crews for merchant vessels took second place to the sailors required to man warships. Instrumental in developing the Dutch navy was John de Witt, a powerful civil servant, who saw how it could be deployed for Holland's benefit abroad. He was right in the Baltic, where Dutch warships restored the balance of power between Denmark and Sweden, but wrong as regards England and France.

De Witt would never have been so successful as he was in naval matters if his policy had not served Amsterdam's commercial interests. What its merchants overlooked in their ready support for war was the fact that most Dutch trade routes passed close to English shores, and Holland was completely dependent on seaborne trade for food and livelihood. England, by contrast, was self-sufficient in food and hardly engaged in overseas trade at all. "The English are going to attack a mountain of gold," one Dutch diplomat remarked, "we have to face one of iron."[9] Until 1665, the Dutch navy lacked good leadership at sea, but with the appointment of the popular Michiel de Ruyter it found an admiral capable of taking the war to the English. Two years later, he entered the Thames, captured an unfinished fort at Sheerness, and then forced the Medway. At Chatham dockyard, six English warships were set ablaze and the flagship *Royal Charles* towed away. As at Pearl Harbor in 1941, the attack could have been more devastating had the shore installations been totally destroyed; they would have taken a generation to rebuild. Samuel Pepys wrote in his diary "that in all things; in wisdom-courage-force-knowledge of our own streams and success, the Dutch have the best of us, and do end the war with victory on their side."[10] The Dutch triumph was short-lived because de Witt's foreign policy fell apart through a joint attack by England and France. The Treaty of Westminster, which concluded the third Anglo-Dutch War in 1674, was really an admission that neither the English nor the Dutch could decisively prevail in battle. They simply had to tolerate each other on the high seas.

Before the War of the Spanish Succession, Holland remained a major European power. That conflict was to cripple its public finances through expensive campaigns on land and sea. Although peace was agreed at Utrecht on Dutch territory in 1713, the exhausted state of Holland meant that it was not strong enough to play much of a role in the final treaty negotiations. Yet contemporaries were amazed that the Dutch had been able to exercise the sway they did for so long. The VOC monopolised the spice trade while its ships virtually ran intra-Asian trade from the Red Sea to Japan. Nothing like this single trading network had ever existed before. As late as 1715, the VOC could send 3,000 troops against Calicut, the largest display of European military might in India until the onset of the Anglo-French struggle in the 1740s. As one English commentator put it:

> For it seems a wonder to the world that such a small country, not fully so big as two of our best shires, having little natural wealth, victuals, timber or other necessary ammunitions, either for war or peace, should notwithstanding possess them

all in such extraordinary plenty that besides their own wants (which are very great) they can and do likewise serve and sell to other Princes, ships, ordnance, cordage, corn, powder, shot and what not, which by their industrious trading they gather from all quarters of the world: in which course they are no less injurious to supplant others (especially the English) than they are careful to strengthen themselves.[11]

Not at all untypical is this mixture of admiration and envy for the world emporium that Holland became in the late seventeenth century, the first occasion on which economic power was concentrated at a single point in the world. London would eventually succeed Amsterdam in this role, although not until the United Kingdom (as it was known after union with Scotland) had beaten France. Holland managed to achieve its earlier supremacy by innovation in manufacturing, combined with new techniques in stockpiling commodities, buying ahead and speculative trading.[12] That and a willingness to risk sailing anywhere for the sake of commercial advantage.

New Rivals: the French and the English

In comparison with Dutch activity, French and English participation in Asian commerce was still modest in 1713, because the VOC remained the most effective of the East India companies. Its authority went unquestioned in Holland through the maintenance of close links with government, while in Asia its representatives exercised firm control from one centre, the stronghold of Batavia. Despite republican institutions at home, Dutch officials overseas were as autocratic as the Portuguese in their dealings with Asian peoples, but without sharing Portugal's religious zeal. No systematic attempt was ever made to propagate the Calvinist faith, unlike the support given to Portuguese missionaries whose efforts did so much to spread Catholicism in Asia. The VOC always remained preoccupied with making money.

The English East India Company was less well placed. In the eyes of contemporaries, it was simply one of several trading companies with its headquarters in Leadenhall Street, not far away from the docks. Improve as its administration might in London, the voyages that the English East India Company sponsored were ventures dependent on short-term borrowing. Returns were sufficient for rival merchant interests in Bristol and Liverpool to attack its monopoly, with the result that the government extended the company's existing charter until 1766 in return for a payment of £200,000 and a reduction in interest on a sum of money it owed to the company. Afterwards, the English East India Company's stock was regarded as a gilt-edged investment, with the result that its finances were more securely based. Soon it felt confident enough to dispense with insurance altogether and write off losses by shipwreck as they occurred. Already a change in company policy is discernable in the shift from peaceful to armed trading.

First the Portuguese, then the Dutch, had developed the idea of the fortified settlement as a haven for shipping. Whereas Portuguese forts concentrated on taxing seaborne traffic, those of the Dutch were used to dominate local trade, in particular the production and distribution of spices. In the case of the English, the commitment to fortified settlements was slow to evolve and had much to do with the decline of Mughal power in India from the 1720s onwards.

Bombay became English in 1661 as a result of Charles II's marriage to Catherine of Braganza

Situated in a location close to the area disputed by the Mughals and the Marathas, Bombay could not be left without adequate defences. This settlement had been ceded by the Portuguese in 1661 as part of Charles II's marriage settlement: it was rented to the English East India Company for £10 a year. Bombay was to become the centre of the British empire in Asia because it provided a safe anchorage, a dockyard and a locally raised squadron to supplement the Royal Navy. Yet Charles' Portuguese queen, Catherine of Braganza, brought more than the island of Bombay with her to England, as her taste for tea set a fashion that would transform the English East India Company into the world's foremost trader.

The problems experienced by English merchants in India were obviously complicated by the Mughal–Maratha conflict. Hardly surprising then was the view of the governor of Bombay, Charles Boone. In 1718, he told London that in company relations with India, the threat of violence was essential: "no naval force no trade, if no fear no friendship". Later Robert Clive took the same view of Siraj-ud-daula, the young *nawab* of Bengal, who in 1756 seized the company settlement at Calcutta. His "deep resentment against the English", averred Clive, meant that his previous "compliances" had arisen "solely from fear".[13] Although the English East India Company remained uninterested in more than recovering Calcutta and containing the French, its local representatives had sufficient strength at hand to take the French Bengal settlement at Chandernagore, as well as depose Siraj-ud-daula in favour of another prince, who bribed Clive and his fellow officials. By then, the English East India Company, like it or not, was well on its way to becoming a political power on the subcontinent.

Very different was the situation in France, where several companies vied for a share of Asian trade. Not until the involvement of the French government at the beginning of the eighteenth century would a French organisation of any worth, the Compagnie des Indes, come into existence. But the company's directors were mere servants of the French monarch, who controlled trading operations via an appointed council of courtiers, naval officers and prominent merchants. It seems likely that Louis XIV imagined that he could merge this new organisation with the VOC once he had annexed Holland to his realm. In the event, the Compagnie des Indes, had to manage on its own and twice fight in India against the English East India Company before it disappeared in 1793. Competition between the Dutch, the English and the French was most intense in Bengal, from which the VOC drew 40 per cent of the total value of its imports from Asia into Europe. The region also played a vital part in VOC's intra-Asian trade, although there was a steady decline in the Japanese demand for raw silk.

So greatly did the activity of the English East India Company increase that in 1700 Parliament forbad the import of "all wrought silks, Bengals and stuffs mixed with silk or herba of the manufacture of Persia, China or the East Indies and all calicoes painted, dyed or printed or stained there".[14] Because this piece of legislation only sought to protect the English market, it had no impact on the growing re-export trade in Asian textiles. Because it usually did not own the ships in use, unlike the VOC, the English East India Company had to tolerate a degree of private trading, a circumstance that was to lead to conflict in China. To protect its trading position there, the company was content to sell opium in Calcutta so that private shipowners could peddle the drug in Chinese waters. The pretence of non-involvement was designed to protect the English East India Company's reputation with the imperial authorities in China. In 1827, company officers were ordered to have no communication with English ships unloading opium on Lintin Island, to the south of the Pearl River estuary.

English East India Company officials were allowed to trade as individuals, and two governors of Madras made their fortunes through diamonds. Governors often organised syndicates that invested in one or more ships sailing from this southern settlement, first occupied by the English in 1639. Within a couple of years, its Fort St. George housed all the company's storehouses and merchant accommodation, while a thriving town of Indian cotton workers grew up outside the walls. The presence of an English mint was the engine that drove commerce because its silver rupees were not only used locally but sent in large numbers to Bengal as well. Coined money constituted a key element in Indian trade, without which it would have been difficult to conduct any large-scale transaction. The Mughals let both the Dutch and the English convert bullion or foreign coins into local currency because it simplified the purchase of

Fort St. George, the English East India Company's stronghold at Madras

Indian products and spread wealth through the Mughal empire. As a result, mints turned trading ports into financial centres, such as Surat in Gujarat, where the United East India Company raised extra capital at a low rate of interest.

   The Mughal empire was a shadow of its former self in the eighteenth century. One of the largest Asian powers in premodern times, its population exceeded 100 millions and was spread over most of the Indian subcontinent. Its network of client states had been held together by the determination of successive emperors, who combined military prowess with exceptional administrative skills. Their advisers consolidated imperial authority and dealt with the new dimension of European trade. After a brief civil war brought about by rivalry between Aurangzeb's sons, the eldest one, Muazzam, was acknowledged as emperor Bahadur Shah in 1707. Despite unrest on the recently conquered Deccan, the Mughal empire still seemed to be militarily and financially sound. The treasury at Agra then contained 240 million rupees, much more than Akbar, its third and greatest ruler, ever had at his disposal.

But a series of rebellions were about to undermine Mughal rule the most unexpected of which was that of the Sikhs, who sought to avenge the execution of Govind Singh's two youngest sons. He was the tenth Sikh leader, whose spiritual authority was believed to stretch back to the deity by means of a message imparted to Nanak, the original guru. Unable to obtain redress from Bahadur Shah, whom Govind Singh had supported in the war of succession, the Sikhs overran the Punjab and defeated in a pitched battle the imperial forces sent against them. Mughal reinforcements pushed the Sikh rebels from the plains into the hills, but they had no chance of ending a guerrilla war sustained by wide popular support. Fighting was still going on in 1712, when Bahadur Shah died at the age of 70.

Another war of succession left his weakest son Jahandar Shah dominated by Zulfikar Khan, the most powerful member of Bahadur Shah's court. The new Mughal emperor sat on the throne in name

The Mughal emperor Shah Jahan, creator of the Peacock Throne and the Taj Mahal

only as Zulfikar Khan decided on appointments and imperial policy. Unable to influence affairs, Jahandar Shah took to drink along with his favourite concubine, Lal Kunwar. Court extravagance drained the imperial treasury to the extent that unpaid soldiers refused to march against the inevitable rebellion. In desperation, the palace was stripped of its finery as precious cups, jewels, even wall decorations were put on sale. Defeat at Agra in a day-long battle saw Jahandar Shah and Lal Kunwar seek refuge in its fort, while Zulfikar Khan retreated with the surviving troops to Delhi. The rebel leader Farrukhsiyar, the governor of Bengal, declared himself emperor and marched on Delhi, where he executed Jahandar Shah, Zulfikar Khan and their chief supporters. His reign lasted until 1719, the year that a grandson of Bahadur Shah was installed as a puppet ruler.

A demoralised and dispirited aristocracy refused to rally to the new Mughal emperor and paralysis at court put the empire into steep decline. As outlying provinces and subject rulers asserted heir independence, state revenues decreased and commerce was disrupted. So vulnerable did the Mughals become that in 1739–40 an Iranian army captured Delhi, looted the city, slaughtered its inhabitants and carried away the famous Peacock Throne. This ostentatious imperial seat had been commissioned by Shah Jahan, the builder of the Taj Mahal. Even though they lost their power, the prestige of the Mughal emperors lived on in the imitation of their ways at other Indian courts, since palaces and gardens in the Mughal style appeared in Hindu as well as Muslim states. And in 1857, the last Mughal emperor, Bahadur Shah Zafar II, was still thought important enough to legitimise the Indian Mutiny. Exiled to Rangoon for this reluctant action, he was in 1862 buried there in a simple grave at the back of a prison. Not until 1943 would any ceremonial parade be held at his graveside. Then Subhas Chandra Bose, Japanese ally and renegade Congress leader, invoked Zafar's memory as "the man under whose flag fought Indians from all provinces, Indians professing different faiths. . . [in] the first war of independence".[15]

One of the ominous features for the freedom that Bose wished to restore to India was the tendency of rival princes to enlist foreign aid. In the 1740s, both the English and the French gave assistance to warring rulers in southern India, which was funded by cessions of land and taxation. By now Dutch authority in Asian waters had already passed its zenith, since the Dutch navy had slipped into being a second-rate force through lack of investment: this was evident in the age and unseaworthiness of so many of its warships. Even newly built vessels were found to be too slow to tackle Barbary privateers.[16] Realisation that the Dutch were now without a powerful navy came as a surprise to the British in 1744. A squadron sent to Portsmouth to cooperate with the Royal Navy was in such poor condition that its ships leaked. Corruption and mismanagement had served to compound problems encountered at sea. In 1761, the Amsterdam dockyard was discovered to be rife with malpractice, not least of which was the embezzlement of monies earmarked for shipbuilding. More fundamental a weakness, however, was the absence of experienced commanders such as de Ruyter from the deliberations of the Dutch admiralty. In contrast to the situation in London, seafaring knowledge was never integrated into naval administration, with the result that poor decisions were taken. In the 1780s, Holland doubled its warship strength as part of a general European rearmament, but it was the United Kingdom that won out in 1815, with a Royal Navy equal in size to all other navies combined. Although its worldwide supremacy might have been seen as inevitable at that moment of triumph, the rise of British power was by no means smooth in the late eighteenth century. Setbacks were as common in India as they were in Europe and America.

The Battle for India

It has been argued that the English owed their dominion in India to the French. Rivalry there certainly led to conflicts, which ended with the English East India Company becoming the major power, yet at the start of these wars its eyes were fixed on quite limited and immediate objectives. When in late 1744 news reached India that England and France were fighting each other, few were surprised. In Germany, French and English soldiers had opposed each other for months on behalf of their respective allies in the War of the Austrian Succession. Because pursuit of profit was uppermost in the minds of all European traders, they sought initially to prevent hostilities from spreading to Asia. From Pondicherry, the administrative centre of

French factories in India, Françoise Dupleix sounded out the English at nearby Madras with a view of reaching a local agreement on neutrality. Though he had the support of Paris for his proposal, and moreover the defences of Madras were then in a poor condition, the English replied that they lacked the authority to enter into such an agreement. In spite of inclining to accept governor Dupleix's proposal, their caution was justified because at the headquarters of the company in London there was a belief that sending four Royal Navy warships would be adequate protection for its activities in India. Possibly, there might even be advantages for the English East India Company in a confrontation with the French.

Fearful that his province would become a battlefield, the newly installed ruler of Karnataka, Anwar-ud-din, urged both the French and the English to keep the peace. He had just been appointed as the Mughal emperor's governor at Hyderabad to restore order in southern India. Anwar-ud-din's instruction was ignored by French and English naval commanders, who felt duty bound to enter the conflict. It was indeed the initiative of Bertrand de la Bourdonnais at Mauritius that brought matters to a head. When he heard of the Royal Navy attacks on French trading vessels, he improvised a fleet out of ships belonging to the Compagnie des Indes and to private merchants, supplementing their crews with African slaves. In 1745, captured French ships returning from China had yielded the Royal Navy £92,000 in prize money. Because Dupleix suffered personal loss through this seizure, he invested Madras while de la Bourdonnais drove off the Royal Navy squadron.

In the meantime, Anwar-ud-din had taken the field to enforce his prohibition on fighting. His 10,000-strong army, commanded by his son Mahfuz Khan, met a French force of 230 Europeans and 700 Indians on the banks of the Adyar River. They were on their way to help in the siege of Madras and, when Mahfuz Khan tried to stop them, the French commander ordered his men to open fire; the decision was a turning point in colonial history because it demonstrated how successive volleys from a small but disciplined force could disperse a larger Mughal army. We are fortunate that Dupleix's Indian secretary Ananda Pillai recorded the event in his diary. Arriving at the governor's residence, he was told of the engagement by Dupleix.

Tidings have come from Madras. When on the march with his troops, M. Paradis encountered the army of Mahfuz Khan, who had drawn up in his men in four parties around the four sides of the bungalow on the sea-shore, near the estuary [of the River Adyar] at Mylapore, and had marshalled his matchlock-men, cavalry, and artillery, in battle array. On approaching this force, M. Paradis constructed a breast work of palmyra-trees, formed the soldiers and the Mahe sepoys who accompanied him into four divisions, and ordered each to engage a separate body of the enemy. He placed himself at the head of the foremost party. On this, three Rachur rockets and four cannons were fired by the Muhammadans. Their contents fell in the sea and river, and caused no damage. The French opened a fire of musketry on the enemy, killing numbers of them. The Muhammadans threw down their arms, and fled, with dishevelled hair and dress. Some fell dead when in the act of flight. The loss caused to them was immense. Mahfuz Khan also ran on foot, until he reached his elephant, and mounting this, made his escape. He and his troops did not cease their flight until they reached Kunattur. The rout was general, so much as that not a fly, not a sparrow, not a crow was to be seen in all Mylapore. M. Paradis remained there an hour, and then permitted his soldiers and sepoys to sack the town. After it had been pillaged, he marched with his men to Madras.

So few casualties were sustained on the French side, with only two sepoys wounded, that Pillai assured the governor that "Providence completely protects your interests. . . It is by the grace of God that you are able to congratulate yourself on having vanquished such a man as the Nawab."[17]

The significance of the battle at Adyar River was not missed: a musketry salvo fired by European-trained Indians was as effective as one fired by Europeans. All the European powers in Asia, from the Portuguese onwards, had attempted to compensate for their numerical weakness by recruiting local troops, but the French were the first to systematically train these recruits to fight in a European manner. After 1751 they supplied them not only with muskets but European officers as well.[18] The lead was followed by the English East India Company, which in the process founded the British Indian Army. As early as 1762, a detachment of some 600 sepoys was sent to assist in the capture of Manila, despite their marked dislike of a sea voyage.[19] Indian military resources, once firmly under the control of the United Kingdom, gave its empire in Asia and elsewhere an undoubted manpower advantage that lasted until its voluntary dissolution after the Second World War. Encouraged by the fall of Madras, Dupleix decided to capture the English East India Company settlement of Fort St. David as well. Situated closer to Pondicherry than Madras, Fort St. David was defended by barely 300 troops. But among them served Dupleix's nemesis, the 21-year-old Robert Clive, who had escaped Madras and been granted an ensign's commission on his arrival at the beleaguered fortress. To aid the garrison Anwar-ud-din sent 2,500 men and they were sufficient to hold off the French who retired to Pondicherry. Dupleix realised that he had

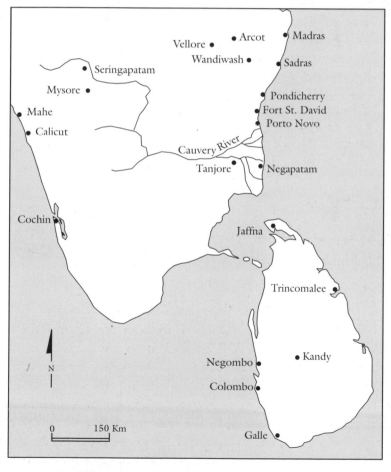

South India during the period of Anglo-French rivalry

come to an understanding with the Mughals, and with the plunder of Madras at his disposal, he was able to bribe Anwar-ud-din to abandon the English. He even allowed the Mughal flag to be hoisted over Madras for one week. The arrival of more Royal Navy ships carrying troops forced Dupleix on the defensive, but he was saved by a bungled assault on Pondicherry in 1748. The event deeply upset Clive, who distinguished himself in the fighting there. As had other former English East India Company clerks, he learned the art of war the hard way, on the battlefield. Since he enjoyed the praise he received for his display of courage, Clive determined to improve his public standing through a military career, which he correctly divined would gain him financial rewards far greater than those he could ever expect to get from penpushing.

News of peace from Europe did not immediately halt military operations, since there was a desire to redeem the Pondicherry failure by intervening in southern Indian politics. A short and successful campaign ensued, in which Clive's conduct attracted further praise. Not to be outdone Dupleix intrigued against Anwar-ud-din, whose aid to the English at Fort St. David still rankled. He encouraged other local contenders for power and at the battle of Ambur another Indian army was defeated once again by a smaller Franco-Indian force using European weapons and tactics. Anwar-ud-din himself fell along with hundreds of his men: his opponent's losses were 24 Europeans killed or wounded, and 300 casualties among the sepoys. A grateful successor to Anwar-ud-din is believed to have presented Dupleix with a personal gift of £77,500, while the Compagnie des Indes received a mere £22,000. Now the powerbroker in southern India, Dupleix devised more schemes to increase French influence, his ambition stretching onto the Deccan where the Mughals were under severe pressure from the Marathas. In 1751 he even installed a compliant ruler in Hyderabad, once a powerful Mughal stronghold. Though the Compagnie des Indes acquired a substantial tax revenue as a result, Dupleix got for himself a fortune estimated at £200,000. Shortly afterwards he informed Paris that all his efforts were directed to attaining for the benefit of France the vast revenues belonging to India.

Alarmed by the growth of Pondicherry's network of Indian allies and client rulers, the new governor of Madras came to the conclusion that something must be done. A stern man, Thomas Saunders did not possess the agility of Dupleix, but he was determined to protect the English East India Company's interests against the ambitious Frenchman. Saunders informed London that:

> We must recognise that if Europeans had not intervened in these affairs and had left Indian princes to resolve their own quarrels, that might have been infinitely beneficial to trade. But since the French have put themselves in possession of extensive domains and have raised their flag at the bounds of our territory and have striven to constrain our settlements to such an extent that they can neither receive supplies nor goods, it has been judged essential to thwart their designs lest their success render our situation worse during peace than in time of war . . . We shall oppose them to the greatest extent which we are capable.[20]

The governor of Madras was therefore ready to listen to Muhammad Ali, the younger son of Anwar-ud-din, who had fled to Trichinopoly to escape Chandra Sahib, the puppet ruler whom the French had installed in his place. Muhammad Ali may have suggested to Clive a diversionary attack on Arcot, Chandra Sahib's capital a short distance inland from Madras. With a force of 210 European and 300 Indian soldiers, Clive took possession of Arcot by surprise and survived a two-month siege before Muhammad Ali's Maratha allies came to its relief. At one point Chandra Sahib launched an all-out assault: his men tried to scale the walls, force their way through two breaches, and knock down the city gates with pikes fastened to the heads of elephants.

With a small reinforcement from Madras and the Marathas, Clive went after Chandra Sahib and caught up with his army at Arni. Clever tactics and good use of artillery won Clive a victory, the French soldiers with Chandra Sahib putting up a very poor show; but his opponent lived to fight another day, so that it took a second battle to finish him off. Encountering the enemy strongly posted in an orchard at the village of Kaveripak, not far from Arni, Clive carefully studied the ground before launching a night attack. Half his forces fell on the enemy's unguarded rear as he led a daring frontal charge. In the ensuing panic Chandra Sahib's men abandoned their guns, ammunition and animals. Captain Clive's heroic defence of Arcot, and his swift victories afterwards, decisively checked French power in southern India, with the result that Dupleix's dream of overlordship came to nothing. According to Pillai, he was so depressed that he could neither go to church nor eat his food. For the English East India Company, however, Clive's triumph had been costly since military expenditure cut into the proceeds of its sales by doubling overheads through the purchase of ammunition and supplies. As yet, the company did not realise how its China trade could support its activities in India. Tea had still to become the commodity in highest demand: it would increase one-hundredfold in value from £8,000 in 1701 to £848,000 in 1774. Almost all was consumed in Britain and its American colonies. Because the Compagnie des Indes suffered an even greater loss than the English East India Company, Dupleix was recalled to Paris. Clive also went home for a rest as a wealthy man: he had amassed a small fortune from prize money, private trade and, above all, the profit he derived from responsibility for military supplies.

In England, the hero of Arcot was lauded for his discomfiture of the French. Aware that another war with France was imminent though, Clive soon returned to India as deputy-governor of Fort St. George, with the rank of lieutenant-colonel. He was additionally promised the governorship of Madras when the post became vacant. Events were now to give the English East India Company a chance to create an Indian client state in Bengal, a major financial prop of the Mughal empire. Less taxation was being remitted to Delhi through the increased independence of its provincial governor, Allahvardi Khan, but the flow of funds remained an important source of imperial income.

In early 1756, immediately before the outbreak of the Seven Years War, Allahvardi Khan died, leaving the province to his 20-year-old grandson Siraj-ud-daula. Headstrong and determined to hang on to his inheritance, the new governor was highly suspicious of the English at Calcutta and the French at Chandernagore, upstream on the River Hooghly. When both trading settlements strengthened their defences against each other, Siraj-ud-daula thought that they might be preparing to aid one of his rivals. Considering what had recently happened in southern India, his suspicion was not entirely groundless, and the offhand reply from the governor of Calcutta to his request to stop work on its fortifications only served to deepen the anxiety. Unlike the French who sent Siraj-ud-daula a customary gift of 350,000 rupees on his accession, the English seem to have underestimated the tactlessness of their refusal to take account of his wishes. First, Siraj-ud-daula seized the English factory at Kasimbazar to the north of Calcutta and imprisoned its occupants including Warren Hastings, a future governor-general of Bengal. He then marched on Calcutta with 50,000 men. The English took to their ships, leaving behind a token garrison, whose surrender was followed by the incident of the "Black Hole", the notoriety of which was largely the work of a survivor named John Holwell.[21]

So as to cover the shame of the rush to the ships and the virtual abandonment of the settlement, the horror of the night's incarceration in a tiny cell of nearly one hundred people provided a convenient story with which to blacken Siraj-ud-duala's name. Ignorant of the cruel imprisonment at the time, Siraj-ud-daula was nonetheless personally blamed for the atrocity, and Clive was conveyed along with 600 European and 900 Indian troops on two Royal Navy ships to exact vengeance. Augmenting his army with the surviving two companies of Bengal European infantry and volunteers from the company's employees who had escaped from Calcutta and its outposts, Clive not only restored the English position in Bengal but intervened with decisive effect in the internal affairs of the province, bringing about the deposition of Siraj-ud-daula after the battle of Plassey in 1757. Less fighting probably occurred at Plassey than at any other eighteenth-century battle, for the issue was decided by an attack late in the day on the Bengali camp. Much time had been taken up by an exchange of artillery fire, and, believing after a downpour that the English would undertake no further action that afternoon, Siraj-ud-daula's troops began moving back to their camp. Seeing the opportunity to attack, Clive advanced his troops at the double, and, fearing for his life, Siraj-ud-daula disappeared on a fast camel. Once again, a small Anglo-Indian army had routed a larger Indian opponent, in all probability 30,000 strong.

Thoroughly rattled, Siraj-ud-daula offered to make peace and restore the English East India Company's privileges. Within days, a peace treaty was signed, much to the annoyance of Calcutta merchants, who said that the compensation agreed would not cover their losses. Clive brushed their objections aside for the good reason that he intended to expel the French from Bengal next. A motive for action was news that Siraj-ud-daula had sought an alliance with France in the hope of revenging himself for Plassey. Clive had already surrounded Chandernagore and demanded its surrender. Receiving no answer, he closely besieged the French settlement, which was soon subjected to such a terrific Royal Navy bombardment that it gave in after three hours. The French defeat did not please Siraj-ud-daula, who still burned for vengeance against Clive. Aware of this continued animosity, Clive came to believe that "there can be neither peace nor security while such a monster reigns".[22] He had not long to wait for the fall of Siraj-ud-daula. Alienating his courtiers and his allies, the young governor was stabbed to death by servants of his successor, Mir Jafar, a relation by marriage to Allahvardi Khan. Clive had already gained the backing of local English East India Company representatives to recognise Mir Jafar as the new governor of

Robert Clive with the Great Mughal, whose authority was then in steep decline

Bengal, something the Mughal emperor had no choice but to accept. For his support Clive received £240,000, a drop in the ocean for Mir Jafar whose treasury dazzled his English ally. Later Clive was to say how amazed he was at his own moderation.

But the lazy and luxury-loving Mir Jafar soon found his vast wealth inadequate for his needs, in part because the English East India Company gained control over the internal trade of Bengal. It stretched its exemption from taxation to undercut local competitors by describing every product handled as British. So widespread was this practice that in 1761 Warren Hastings was "surprised to meet with several English flags in places which I have passed; and on the river I do not believe that I passed a boat without one".[23] Mir Jafar was powerless in preventing the decline of his tax revenue and, sorry for the parlous state into which his candidate had fallen, Clive refused to abandon him to his enemies. Thus he became active in the politics of Bengal as well. Even though Clive knew Mir Jafar was a poor ruler, he saved him from overthrow and endeavoured to provide guidance in handling difficult subordinates. Mir Jafar was irked by the constraints that were put on his rule, but he seems to have understood how weak his position really was.

By 1760, costs in Bengal were crippling the English East India Company and Clive's successor demanded a cession of territory from Mir Jafar to supplement its income. When Mir Jafar refused, he was replaced by his son-in-law Mir Kasim. The cession was readily agreed by Mir Kasim, whose plan was to abandon lower Bengal to the English East India Company while he strongly established himself farther inland. He remodelled his army in the European manner and manufactured arms at his new capital of Monghyr. He was particularly concerned to dominate Bihar, well away from foreign interference. Meanwhile, Clive turned his attention to southern India to oppose the French, who had been reinforced from Europe. In 1758, they captured Fort St. David. Incensed by this loss, Clive felt he must immediately do something to counteract French pressure, and he launched a diversionary campaign in the Northern Circars, the coastal area of present-day Andhra Pradesh. The local rajah had called upon the English East India Company for help.

In the Northern Circars, the French met total defeat as sepoys fighting for the English East India Company proved to be better trained and more disciplined than those in French employ. At Masulipatam, to which the French had withdrawn, the fortifications were carried through the steadiness of the sepoys when European troops broke under fire. The French had no choice but surrender, so that in early 1759 the English East India Company was ceded a considerable territory around Masulipatam. By then, the course of the war in southern India had turned against the French. Unable to besiege Madras without an effective naval blockade, they were obliged to fight a conventional battle at Wandiwash, southeast of Arcot. This was just what the English commander Eyre Coote wanted. Each side had about 2,000 European troops and a similar number of sepoys. Better discipline won the English another great victory; for Wandiwash was to southern India what Plassey had been in Bengal. It sealed the fate of the Compagnie des Indes, for without relief from the sea, Pondicherry had to surrender at the beginning of 1761.

The English East India Company's position was further strengthened in the following year when Manila was occupied by an expedition sent from Madras on receipt of the news of Spain's entry into the war. For a few months, the expedition tried to establish company rule over the Philippines, until news of peace arrived from Europe, and then for more than a year it tried to collect the ransom promised on the surrender of the city. Half the ransom was collected from the residents of Manila on threat of pillage, but the rest never appeared, to the anger of Dawsonne Drake, who assumed control of affairs there.

Born at Madras, Drake had a chequered career with the English East India Company before his election as chief councillor in Manila. After the brief occupation, Drake was accused of abusing his authority to extort money from anyone who came into his power, not for the purpose of completing the ransom, but for his own personal gain. Although he was censured by his employers, he remained a not insignificant figure at Madras, possibly because he was well regarded in the United Kingdom.[24] Yet Drake's actions were thought corrupt by some of his contemporaries: he had apparently enriched himself by threats. Somehow this was deemed to be different from deposing a ruler and accepting a payment from his grateful successor as Clive did. Speaking about his acceptance of presents, Clive said:

> When presents are received as the price of services to the Nation, to the Company or to that Prince who bestowed those presents; when they are not exacted from him by compulsion; when he is in a state of independence and can do with his money what he pleases; and when they are not received to the disadvantage of the Company, he holds these presents not dishonourable . . . Was I, after having resigned my life so often in the Company's service, to deny myself the only honourable opportunity I ever had or could have of acquiring a fortune, without prejudice to the Company, who it is evident would not have had more from my having less?[25]

Such modesty was of course contrived, given Clive's willingness to bribe and be bribed, not to mention the greed of other employees of the English East India Company.

In 1773, the whole question of conduct in India was debated in Parliament. Under the spotlight, Clive could only argue that private gain and public good were not incompatible, least of all when the national interest was being advanced overseas. Members agreed with him and passed this resolution: "That Robert, Lord Clive, did at the same time, render great and meritorious services to his country." Though he narrowly escaped his critics, Clive's vast fortune was not easily overlooked and new legislation sought to check the rampant corruption in India. Warren Hastings was actually appointed governor-general with a special mandate to introduce reform.

How heavy the burden of gift giving had become was evident in 1763, when Mir Kasim marched on the English factory at Patna, which was situated higher up the Ganges than Monghyr. Squeezed by private trade, territorial losses and expensive presents, Mir Kasim's financial crisis pushed him into a war with the English East India Company. A force was sent to defeat him, but Mir Kasim fled to nearly Oudh and found an ally in its ruler. Mutinies among the company's European and Indian troops delayed the final reckoning, which came when Oudh was temporarily overrun. During the campaign, enough booty was taken to provide £12,000 in prize money for the soldiers, who had been brought back to order by a new commander, Hector Munro. His firmness seems to have convinced the Europeans under his command that he would never tolerate insubordination, a correct conclusion in the light of the treatment of a subsequent sepoy mutiny.

Major Munro sentenced the ringleaders of the mutinous sepoys to be blown from canons. Four of the condemned were tied to the muzzles and were about to be blown away when four others stepped forward and claimed that they should have the honour of being the first executed. Granted their request, they were blown away before another four men were tied to the guns. When the sepoys threatened to intervene, the determined major had the cannon loaded with grapeshot and pointed at them. Realising his resolve, they obeyed the order to ground arms, and the 24 executions continued to the end. The mutinies had arisen through serious arrears of pay and poor prospects of plunder. In this regard, Clive had been meticulous and, though he termed the sepoys "blacks", he always gave the impression that he considered them the equal of European troops, which of course they were on the battlefield. And they always responded positively whenever he led them into action himself.

Munro's terrible punishment had the desired effect. The rebellious spirit that had bedevilled operations for months was stamped out, and all resistance to the English East India Company crumbled. In return for an annual payment of three million rupees, the Mughal emperor made the best of a bad situation by granting the company the land revenue of Bengal, Bihar and Orissa. Clive commented: "We must become Nabobs ourselves."[26] The consolidation of the English East India Company's control of Bengal was the work of Clive's successors, although little was accomplished before Warren Hastings' tenure of office. Hastings had a distinguished record as a Bengal civil servant, having fought at Plassey as a volunteer, and he gained a reputation for honesty in all his dealings. He spoke Bengali and Urdu and had some knowledge of Persian, the official language of the Mughal court. In 1773, Hastings stopped payment to the Mughal court on the grounds that it was funding the Marathas, then the most powerful people in the subcontinent.

Inspired by Hindu warrior traditions, the Marathas evolved from a collection of warring clans into a powerful military confederacy that was capable of taking over the rump of the Mughal empire. In 1784, Mahadaji Sindhia, the Maratha maharaja of Gwalior, was invited to administer the imperial lands as the Mughal emperor's regent. There was never a head of any Maratha state because five separate dynasties held sway: the Raos at Poona, the Sindhias at Gwalior, the Holkars at Indore, the Bhonsles at Nagpur and the Gaikwads at Baroda. Their disputes frequently disturbed the peace and, in 1802, a bitter quarrel would cause Baji Rao to ask for the assistance of the English East India Company. It was a rare opportunity to intervene for Arthur Wellesley, Napoleon's future adversary, who exploited it to splinter the Maratha confederacy.

Hastings had set out to eradicate embezzlement and corruption, but reform was one of the many tasks from which he was often distracted. On assuming office as governor-general in 1772, he described Bengal as "a confused heap of undigested materials as wild as Chaos itself".[27] He did succeed in preventing officials involved in the collection of taxes and the administration of justice from private trading. And the preparation of opium, which made enormous profits for the factors at Patna, was put out to contract. So important did the drug become for the English East India Company, once it formed the basis of its trade with China, that its value in India was second only to that of the land tax. What distracted Hastings most was war. Robert Clive had predicted that the French would seek to reverse the verdict of the Seven Years War and try to regain their former power in coalition with discontented Indian princes. His prophecy was fulfilled by an alliance between France and Haidar Ali, the ruler of Mysore. As soon as Hastings learned of renewed conflict with the French, he ordered the reduction of their remaining outposts in India. Haidar Ali took grave offence at the capture of Mahe, on the southwestern coast, because the settlement was leased by the French from Mysore. Though no stranger as an opponent of the English East India Company, Haidar Ali's easy defeat of its forces did come as a rude shock. A master of intrigue, Haidar Ali had risen from the ranks of the Mysore army and made himself ruler of this Hindu kingdom. He seems to have been intent on conquering the whole of southern India.

Hastings sent Eyre Coote, the victor of Wandiwash, with every rupee and soldier he could spare, to take charge at Madras. In 1781, Coote gained a victory over Haidar Ali at Porto Novo, to which the Portuguese had moved after the VOC evicted them from nearby Negapatam a century earlier; but he could not prevent Mysorean forces from moving freely about company territory. An army 70,000 strong was difficult to contain because it included battalions of European-trained sepoys commanded by French officers. By 1782, Haidar Ali had discovered that without control of the sea he could not bring the war to a satisfactory close. A year later, Haidar Ali was killed by a gangrenous ulcer on his neck, which he would not allow a French surgeon to remove, which left his son Tipu Sultan to continue the war.

Admiral Pierre-André de Suffren, the only serious opponent faced by the Royal Navy in Asian waters

As luck would have it, Tipu Sultan found himself with an unexpected naval ally in the French admiral Pierre-André de Suffren, who arrived with five ships of the line. Four were copper bottomed, a new technique that prevented the accumulation of barnacles, preserving the ships' sailing speed. Confronting Suffren were nine Royal Navy ships under Rear-Admiral Sir Edward Hughes, a quite different commander. Whereas Suffren was foul mouthed and popular on the lower deck but hated by his captains, Hughes displayed a cool detachment that impressed everyone who met him. Two days after Suffren's arrival off Madras, he attacked Hughes in what proved to be the first of a series of battles. That February in 1782 at Sandras, to the south of Madras, Suffren was denied victory by the failure of several captains to attack the enemy when ordered to engage more closely. In April, Suffren might have caught Hughes at a disadvantage had all his ships been copper bottomed, since he possessed the advantage of numbers: his squadron now comprised 12 to Hughes' 11. But the opposing squadrons gained equal honours.

Beside himself with fury, Suffren said: "If in this squadron we do not change five or six, that is half of the captains, we shall never achieve anything and perhaps miss every opportunity that offers."[28] In July Suffren's aggressiveness almost brought disaster in a savage encounter off Negapatam but, even though Hughes claimed to have won, the Royal Navy squadron had sustained great damage. It took 12 days to repair the mainmast of Hughes' flagship sufficiently to sail the vessel back to Madras. Even its rudder had to be rehung so as to replace the ironwork, which had been shot away by enemy fire. Suffren's capture of Trincomalee in August was another setback for Hughes, because it gave the French admiral a convenient anchorage in northeastern Sri Lanka. Hughes got there too late to save Trincomalee, then garrisoned by English East India Company troops after the expulsion of the Dutch, who had also joined in the hostilities. Batavia indeed sent supplies to Suffren during his fight against Hughes. The naval encounter off the captured town at the start of September ended as inconclusively as previous battles and fighting was suspended during the winter. It is to Suffren's credit that through improvised repairs he was able to face Hughes again in June 1783. In what the latter termed "a heavy cannonade", the dead and wounded were about equal in number on each side. Shortly afterwards, Hughes sent under a flag of truce the news that peace had been agreed in Europe.

The Treaty of Paris between the United Kingdom and the United States of America, along with related treaties ending the United Kingdom's wars with France and Spain, truncated an overseas empire but left the position of Britain as a world power unchanged. If anything, the loss of the North American colonies turned British imperial interests eastwards, where India received the most attention. China was soon to be seen as an adjunct of growing dominion in the subcontinent through the expanding trade of the English East India Company, no matter that it involved pushing opium to maintain tea supplies.

Britain's Triumph

The trigger for the extraordinary surge in the English East India Company's trade was the reduction of duty on the import of tea in Britain. Increased demand for tea underwrote the company's expenditure during the period that India was embroiled in the conflicts of Clive's immediate successors. This period witnessed rising British power as well as French and Dutch decline. By siding with France, Spain and the rebellious American colonies, the Dutch sealed the fate of their maritime empire in Asia: the VOC sustained such losses that it could hardly postpone the bankruptcy that overtook it in 1795. The run-down state of the Dutch navy and the neglect of VOC garrisons were the principal causes of defeat, which was acknowledged in a peace settlement agreed with Britain just before the Treaty of Paris. Worse was to come in 1806, when Napoleon replaced the Dutch Republic with a compliant monarchy, which led to the British takeover of South Africa, Sri Lanka, Surinam and Java. Although the last two annexations were returned in 1814, a Dutch empire thereafter existed on sufferance. Perhaps realising the limits of British power, London then chose not to exclude the Dutch from the Indonesian archipelago and adopted a policy of collaboration overseas with both European and Asian states.

   In India, Warren Hastings had seen that his country's possessions were preserved. He received little thanks for this on his return home. Considering the corruption and incompetence that had recently lost the American colonies, it seems incredible that Hastings should be in the dock for seven weary years at Westminster Hall. Fortunately for him, fashionable interest fell away as the trial dragged on and the terrors of revolutionary France gave London society other things to talk about. When news of Hastings' complete acquittal in 1795 reached Calcutta, the city celebrated with illuminations. Even though Parliament took the view that "to pursue schemes of conquest and the extension of dominion in India, are repugnant to the wish, the honour, and the policy of this nation", Hastings' successor as governor-general behaved like a thoroughgoing imperialist.

By shrewdly arranging for £500,000 to be paid each year to the exchequer in London, and maintaining an upright image in the United Kingdom, Lord Cornwallis got away with policies that

Governor-general Richard Wellesley, who transformed Calcutta into a colonial capital

eventually led to territorial acquisitions on a par with those made by Clive. Unlike the politicians, King George III was keen to see the map that depicted each of the English East India Company's territorial gains.[29] The monarch was also pleased to learn how Cornwallis kept down the costs of the campaign against Tipu Sultan by making his troops live off the land. Yet victory in 1792 left a reduced Mysore with a ruler smarting for another war. Possibly, for Cornwallis, the harshness of the terms he then imposed on Tipu Sultan represented some compensation for those he had had to accept from George Washington at Yorktown. Not that the loss of the American colonies would have been seen by Tipu Sultan as more than an irrelevance to the struggle in southern India, which was soon renewed by Richard Wellesley, the second earl of Mornington in the peerage of Ireland.

On his appointment as governor-general in 1797, Richard Wellesley indicated that the company's role would extend well beyond trade. India ought be "ruled from a palace, not a counting house", he said, "with the ideas of a prince, not those of a retail trader in muslins and indigo".[30] He was more than fortunate in having on hand his younger brother Arthur, who was commanding the 33rd Foot in Bengal. Yet the international situation at this moment could not have been worse for the British. They were at war with revolutionary France as well as Holland and Spain; their last remaining ally, Austria, had just been defeated by the rising French general Bonaparte, and compelled to agree to peace; while mutinies at the Nore and Spithead seemed to indicate that morale in the Royal Navy was breaking down. Undaunted by the prospect of French intervention in Indian affairs, the new governor-general set about improving as well as preparing to strike at Tipu Sultan. He had Government House and 16 other buildings torn down to make room for a great Palladian residence set in an extensive park. The public rooms, as fine as any in Europe, were to be graced in 1799 by Tipu Sultan's looted throne of crimson and gold.

Richard Wellesley reacted to information received from Mauritius with an immediate decision for war against Mysore. On that French island, its governor was reported to have called for volunteers to serve under the colours of Tipu Sultan in cooperation with a force of French regulars. Napoleon had already landed in Egypt, and Wellesley was not alone in thinking that his next move might be an advance on India, either overland or by ship from the Red Sea. To Napoleon, India was always more than a British possession. It inspired in him a vision of conquest crowned by Asian wealth and splendour.

Richard Wellesley transferred his brother Arthur's men to southern India, where the invasion of Mysore began. Although Arthur Wellesley was subordinate to Sir George Harris, the commander-in-chief of the English East India Company army, who kept him at a polite distance, he saw action before Seringapatam, Tipu Sultan's stronghold. Ordered to attack an outpost at night, Arthur Wellesley had to commit his soldiers without reconnaissance, an omission that he never forgot. The attack was a miserable failure and it looks as though he fled on horseback. He saved himself by admitting sole responsibility for what happened to the 33rd Foot, which sustained casualties. Had his brother not been the governor-general, Arthur Wellesley might not have survived as an officer. But Harris did not hold the reverse against him, and he learned two valuable lessons: the necessity of properly observing the terrain and the importance of self-control

Tipu Sultan's Seringapatam, where in 1799 Arthur Wellesley almost ruined his military career

in the thick of battle, both of which were to serve him well during his ultimate test against Napoleon at Waterloo. Seringapatam was taken by assault early one afternoon in 1799. Its defenders were literally caught napping during the hottest hours of the day. Tipu Sultan's body was found amid a heap of dead and wounded Mysorean soldiers. He had been stabbed and then shot through the head by a grenadier, anxious to remove the gold buckle from his sword belt.

The death of Tipu Sultan placed in Richard Wellesley's hands a substantial kingdom, from which he annexed territory for the English East India Company. Another annexation went to the ruler of Hyderabad, Mysore's enemy and a company ally. The remainder was left as a small state but not under the control of any of Tipu Sultan's sons. Knowing that the British public would welcome his forestalling a French bridgehead in India, Richard Wellesley went as far as to suggest that a supposedly independent Mysore was tantamount to English East India Company territory. In Tanjore, a tiny southern India state with a troubled succession, he actually ordered outright annexation, pensioning off one of the claimants with £40,000 a year.

Another "peaceful" acquisition was the Gujarati port of Surat, where Indian Moslems going on pilgrimage embarked for Mecca. It was one of the largest cities in India, with a population of nearly half a million. Arguments over defence costs persuaded Richard Wellesley to displace the Mughal emperor's governor and install his own city administration. His treatment of Oudh, Bengal's western neighbour, was even more high-handed. Unable to get its ruler to abdicate in favour of the English East India Company, Arthur Wellesley obliged him to increase the amount he was required to pay for the upkeep of the company's troops and, then in 1801, he demanded the cession of half of Oudh. Threatened with a takeover of all his possessions by force, Oudh's ruler caved in and signed a treaty to this effect. The new annexation, far up the Ganges and Jumna rivers, was a complete reversal of Calcutta's policy, for Oudh ceased to be a barrier for the protection of Bengal against the belligerent Marathas.

One reason for this change of policy was that the Marathas were no longer viewed with such alarm as they had been during the inconclusive First Anglo-Maratha War of 1775–76. Richard Wellesley considered that the time had arrived for bringing their confederacy under Calcutta's control. In this aim, he was inadvertently helped by the British government, which directed him to expel the remaining French from India. Because most of these soldiers of fortune were in the employ of the Marathas, the directive was seen by the governor-general as giving him a free hand to take such action as he thought fit. On this occasion his younger brother was to render exemplary service as a general, a rank to which he had just been gazetted. During the 1803 campaign against the Marathas, Arthur Wellesley ensured that the daily ration of locally distilled spirits was unadulterated with ingredients that could cause permanent damage to his men. He also made certain that they had plentiful supplies of clean drinking water, essential to health in the hot Indian climate. To guarantee the supply of rations and forage for cavalry horses, he organised well-protected convoys, which proceeded along roads specially widened by gangs of labourers. And he ordered officers and other ranks to jettison unnecessary luggage. By these simple but then innovative measures, Arthur Wellesley was able to pursue the lightly armed and mostly mounted Marathas at the rate of 25 kilometres a day. Harris' army in the invasion of Mysore could not top seven kilometres.

The Second Anglo-Maratha War began as a response to an appeal from Baji Rao, who was the nominal head of the Maratha confederacy. Ousted from Poona by another Maratha leader named Jeswant Rao Holkar, a humiliated Baji Rao requested the English East India Company to help him regain power. Because he was prepared to cede territory and accept vassal status, Richard Wellesley was only too pleased to help. Marching from Madras, an expeditionary force under the command of Arthur Wellesley reached Poona without difficulty and reinstated Baji Rao. Besides the improved logistics, its passage was smoothed by the absence of looting, an unheard of occurrence in India, whether the army on the march was friend or foe. Arthur Wellesley's Indian army was more receptive to such an order than ever his British forces were during the Peninsular War. Given sole discretion by his elder brother, he was able to move swiftly against those who chose to oppose the intervention and win at Assaye a very great victory indeed.

The battle took place near present-day Jafrabad, where Arthur Wellesley located the enemy encampment after questioning two merchants who were intercepted on their way to sell corn to the Marathas. He galloped off at once with only a few men as escort, so that he could see its exact position himself. There was to be no second Seringapatam. The Marathas were camped at the confluence of the rivers Juah and Kaitna, which gave protection for their tents on three sides. Because they seemed to be in the process of breaking camp, Arthur Wellesley decided upon an immediate advance to catch them off guard. It seems that the Marathas were not unaware of his presence but assumed that he would not dare to attack an army of 40,000 men with such a small force. Their English opponent led no more than a tenth of that number: 1,200 European and Indian cavalrymen, 1,300 European infantry and 2,000 sepoys. A larger English East India Company force had still to link up with him. Arthur Wellesley's staff argued that because the Maratha infantrymen would stand their ground, it would be better to await the expected reinforcement, but they could not dent his determination for immediate offensive action, and he ordered a direct infantry assault on the Maratha infantry and its artillery. This decision stands in stark contrast to his defensive strategy at Waterloo. Possibly believing that a decisively delivered blow against his enemy's elite troops would scatter the rest of the Maratha army, Arthur Wellesley focused on the enemy's infantry battalions, which were still close to the confluence of the two rivers. He personally reconnoitred the bank of the Kaitna, found a ford, and then waved his own infantrymen across the river about one o'clock in the afternoon.

About 11,000 Maratha infantrymen turned to meet them under their French officers. Arthur Wellesley was convinced that "the defeat of [this] corps of infantry would be most effectual".[31] On the tongue of land between the Kaitna and Juah rivers, the two opposing lines of infantry engaged, after the English East India Company troops fording the river had been subjected to harassing artillery fire. By moving against the Marathas at the narrowest end of the battlefield, Arthur Wellesley was positioning himself in such a way that enemy numbers would count for less if they should attack. "While we were forming up," wrote Mounstuart Elphinstone in a letter afterwards, "the enemy's infantry and guns advanced on us, and their cannonade was very destructive."[32]

Mounting casualties might have deterred a less resolute commander, but Arthur Wellesley was going to fight to the finish and he kept his troops in position while artillery support was being brought up. Its arrival distracted the Maratha gunners until it was overwhelmed by their superior fire. Owing to the number of men and draught animals killed, Arthur Wellesley had to abandon the artillery duel and advance with bayonets at the ready. By ordering his infantry forward, he hoped to regain the initiative, rather than continue to take heavy casualties where he stood. His soldiers in the southern and central part of the battlefield advanced at a steady pace, fired a volley and then killed the enemy gunners in hand-to-hand combat. After this, they pressed on with bayonets into the Maratha infantry who were posted behind the guns. But these experienced opponents rallied when they noticed how surviving Maratha gunners had swung their guns round to fire into the backs of Arthur Wellesley's men. These gunners had merely pretended to be dead. The English East India Company infantry were now caught between musketry in front and artillery in the rear.

In the northern part of the battlefield, the Marathas were also giving a good account of themselves. From the village of Assaye, Maratha gunners laid down a devastating fire in support of their own infantry. So severe were the casualties inflicted that Arthur Wellesley was forced to adopt the desperate expedient of a cavalry charge. Cavalry could be lethal against disordered infantry but it had little hope of overcoming artillery as long as the gunners remained steady. If they did not lose their nerve and run away from their guns, the attacking horsemen would get a hot reception. The cavalry charge on the village, in which Arthur Wellesley took part, was credited with saving the day. Even though losses were great, the Maratha guns here fell silent, leaving Arthur Wellesley free to restore order elsewhere, something he did by retaking the guns from those Marathas who had risen from a feigned death. During this action, he was briefly dismounted when a pike was driven into his horse's flank. Once on a new horse, he issued orders for an attack on the reformed Maratha infantry: a fierce struggle with sword and bayonet ensued. At last, the Marathas gave way, leaving Arthur Wellesley to count the cost of this hard-fought triumph, with one-third of his men killed or wounded. That the sepoys paid

Arthur Wellesley about to be unhorsed at Assaye in 1803

a heavy price is evident in Arthur Wellesley's personal appeal for a pension claim by an Indian officer wounded at Assaye. Nearly two years after the battle, bone splinters were still being removed from his shoulders. The Marathas lost 7,000 men.

Too exhausted to pursue the enemy, Arthur Wellesley's troops slept where they were. He bedded down on a pile of straw in a mud hut. The English East India Company reinforcements set off northwards after the retreating Marathas, who, beaten though they were, remained a dangerous opponent. Every effort had to be made to stop them preparing for a second battle. Having seen to the dead and wounded, Arthur Wellesley swiftly joined the chase. News of the fall of Agra and Delhi, Mughal cities occupied by the Marathas, confirmed his view that this was the moment to assert the company's authority on the Deccan. Learning that a Maratha army was in the vicinity of Argaum, Arthur Wellesley drew all the English East India Company forces together for a final contest. There another 5,000 Marathas fell, against a loss of 346 killed, wounded or missing among his men. The last Maratha army of any consequence was thus destroyed.

These two victories finally established Britain as the major power in India. Within a decade, the Wellesley brothers had increased its territorial holdings fourfold. Over time, the warlike Marathas would become firm friends of the British and they remained loyal during the Mutiny of 1857. Arthur Wellesley's task was now over, since another English East India Company army had already overcome Maratha resistance elsewhere. A factor in the Maratha defeat was the desertion of many European officers. At the outbreak of hostilities, Richard Wellesley had ordered all British subjects to leave Maratha employ, offering them service with the English East India Company. Those soldiers of fortune who obeyed brought with them invaluable military information, while those who chose to ignore the order were dismayed at the number of French officers soon deserting. Arguably, the Marathas might have fared better if they had relied on their traditional method of hit-and-run cavalry tactics. By copying European infantry formations, they pitted themselves against English East India Company sepoys as well as British regulars, but there is no question that Maratha artillery was the best in India at this time.

Both the Wellesley brothers returned to England shortly after the Second Anglo-Maratha War. Arthur Wellesley went first and found that there was war again with France. In October 1805, Napoleon had triumphed on land at the battle of Austerlitz, but Britain had not done badly at Trafalgar the same month: although it cost him his life, Nelson utterly routed the French and Spanish fleets, a victory that gave the Royal Navy command of the ocean for the next century. This dominance allowed Arthur Wellesley to sap French strength in what became known as the "Spanish Ulcer", a relatively cheap way for the United Kingdom to weaken Napoleon. His brother Richard was fully aware of the cost of warfare. Without informing London, he had diverted bullion intended for the China trade to pay for his expansionist policy in India. The resulting shortfall in cash helped to stimulate opium production, an increasing source of revenue for Calcutta. Prime Minister Pitt was so annoyed with Richard Wellesley's handling of Indian affairs that he described him as acting so "imprudently and illegally that he could not be suffered to remain in the government".[33] On his return home, Richard Wellesley was coolly received and not until 1808 did Parliament finally drop charges against him.

That Richard Wellesley's displacement of so many Indian princes would cause trouble for the English East India Company was not foreseen, in spite of change coming so quickly to such a large area of the subcontinent that it was bound to spread unease amongst its sepoys, who were jealous of their own beliefs and customs. When these soldiers were ordered to don a European-style uniform and shave off their beards, a mutiny broke out at Vellore, a fortress close to Arcot. Especially hated was the shako, a cylindrical hat with a peak and a leather cockade. It was rumoured that dressing sepoys like British regulars was the first step to making them become Christians. At Vellore in the summer of 1806, the sepoys suddenly attacked the European troops stationed there, killing and wounding nearly 300 men. The few survivors shut themselves in a bastion above the main gateway. They were relieved by a contingent of English East India Company soldiers from Arcot. Some mutineers were executed, others discharged from service; all the battalions to which they belonged were disbanded.

Afterwards it was considered that the Vellore mutiny was purely a military matter, but the incident had serious implications for British power in India: Indian officers as well as other ranks had responded to a prophecy that its end was at hand. When a Moslem sepoy warned that there was a plot to murder the Europeans in the garrison, his story was referred to a committee of Indian officers, most of whom were sympathetic to the conspiracy. They reported that his allegation had no foundation, and the sepoy was jailed as a troublemaker. Without Indian officers acting as its eyes and ears, the English East India Company was entirely ignorant of what was happening among the sepoys. A no less worrying aspect of the disturbance was the first mention of religion as a grievance.[34]

East of India there were also territorial acquisitions connected with the struggle against France. The English East India Company had been looking for years to find a suitable base to protect its China-bound ships passing through the Straits of Malacca, a vital bottleneck for trade with East Asia. A Dutch campaign in central Sumatra had disrupted free passage through the straits in 1784 and, to the consternation of Calcutta, it was learned that the French had obtained permission to refit vessels at Aceh in northern Sumatra. Strong northeast monsoon winds prevented Royal Navy ships from finding a sheltered harbour on the company-controlled east coast of India during the winter months, forcing them to anchor off Bombay on the west coast. By contrast, the French could use Aceh to dominate the Bay of Bengal at this season. A base was therefore urgently needed close to the Straits of Malacca. It was found on the island of Penang by Francis Light, a naval officer who had lent support to the sultan of Kedah in 1785, when he was attacked by Indonesian pirates.

A Calcutta street, with the masts of trading ships showing the city's purpose

A grateful sultan offered to rent Pulau Pinang as a base, believing perhaps that a Royal Navy presence there would deter Kedah's enemies. The English East India Company called it Prince of Wales Island, but the new name did not take. Known as Penang throughout the colonial period, the hilly island kept its association with the betel nut palm, *pokok pinang* in Malay. Light built a stockade and a dock in 1786 and encouraged settlement by giving away land. To have the land cleared, he ordered a cannon to be loaded with silver coins and fired into the jungle: whoever cut down the vegetation and recovered the coins was deemed to be the owner. Before Light died there in 1794, the new colony was several thousand strong, many of its residents Chinese seeking to escape Dutch domination of trade. As Singapore was to be later on, Penang was an open port that levied negligible duties on commerce.

Although the island settlement weakened the trading position of Malacca, it was a less satisfactory base than the Royal Navy had hoped. Not until Thomas Stamford Raffles founded Singapore in 1819 would a first-rate harbour become available. That year, he persuaded the sultan of Johore to grant permission for English East India Company occupation of the island. When Holland fell under the sway of Napoleon, the Dutch ruler William V had fled to England and taken up residence at Kew. In what are known as the "Kew Letters", he instructed Dutch colonial officials to surrender their territories to Britain, so that they would not fall to the French. Armed with this authority, the English East India Company moved to take over the Dutch East Indies, but at first Batavia refused to comply. Once under English East India Company control, there was some discussion about whether this sizable territory should be added permanently to Britain's Indian empire. Richard Wellesley's large acquisitions of territory were by then bearing fruit, and along with the new revenue derived from the occupied Dutch territory, Calcutta was able to remit £10 million annually to London over and above the provision of funds for company investment in Asian trade. To administer the Dutch East Indies, Raffles was appointed to the governorship of Java.

While few of the measures Raffles tried to introduce there outlasted his stay, he is remembered in the annals of colonial history as a great reformer, except by the Dutch. In rejecting what he termed the "perverted liberalism" of Raffles in the 1830s, governor-general Johannes van den Bosch imposed the *cultuurstelsel*, or "culture system", in which Javanese farmers had to devote one-fifth of their land or 66 working days each year to the cultivation of export crops for the Dutch authorities. Profit was once again the order of the day, as an impoverished Holland attempted to recover from Napoleon. Raffles had fully understood the weaknesses of Dutch rule: the lack of a money economy and the alienation of the Javanese from the colonial government. His introduction of a land tax encouraged the circulation of coin, and his recognition of the village as a primary unit of administration drew, however reluctantly, the native inhabitants into a relationship with Batavia. Quite unexpected was the rebellion that one of Raffles' officials caused shortly after the return of the Dutch. Brusque treatment of the ruler of Yogyakarta, Java's second city, ended in the destruction of his court, a slight that was never forgotten by the Javanese aristocracy, who responded in 1825 to the attempted arrest of Pangeran Dipanagara by a call to arms. Of royal descent, Dipanagara defied Batavia for almost five years, some 200,000 Javanese and 8,000 Dutchmen losing their lives in the uprising.

With the return of peace in Europe after Napoleon's exile to St. Helena, the British government had allowed the Dutch to reoccupy their Asian territories, but it was agreed that Holland would cede Malacca and recognise the British claim to Singapore in return for an undertaking that London would never enter into any treaties with rulers south of the Straits of Malacca. Without a rival, Britain could now afford to dictate the shape of colonial Asia. France had ruined itself and much of Europe too, leaving the United Kingdom as the dominant world power. Only one Asian country refused to recognise Britain's unique position: the Chinese empire remained annoyingly indifferent towards the lure of international trade.

A Chinese Rebuff

Trade with China was important to Britain. But much was felt to be unsatisfactory through its concentration at Guangzhou, by tradition the place where foreign merchants had access to Chinese products. This southern port was China's sole point of diplomatic contact with European countries as well. English East India Company traders were obliged to deal with a guild of merchants there, and the silver that they were expected to hand over in exchange for tea was already posing a major problem. To check the outflow of bullion, Lord Macartney was dispatched from London to establish friendly relations between Britain and China. When he set out on his long voyage in late 1792, Macartney also hoped to obtain a commercial treaty that would open up other Chinese ports to international trade. That he would fail to regularise diplomatic relations through the acceptance of a British representative in Beijing was something no one then considered a possibility. Other European powers had sent envoys to the Chinese capital, but none of them had succeeded in opening permanent embassies there. The British government was more confident of being well received because the English East India Company carried away the bulk of China's exports. What was not properly grasped in London was the attitude of China towards international trade.

Guangzhou, the southern Chinese port known to Europeans as Canton

From the Chinese point of view, it was never envisaged that foreign merchants should come to China and transact business wherever they chose. The reason for this lack of interest in external commerce was twofold: the sheer extent and wealth of the Chinese empire, and the so-called tributary system that governed its relations with other Asian countries. As the Qing emperor Qian Long was to intimate to Macartney, China was a world in itself and quite capable of managing on its own. Though the British ambassador was astute in connecting this exclusion policy with the maintenance of Manchu supremacy, and in particular a fear of what effect outside contact would have on the Chinese, the reluctance of the emperor to end restrictions on seaborne trade tallied with a policy already centuries old. A compromise of sorts had been the imperial decree of 1757, which ordered all such transactions to take place at Guangzhou, a port remote from Beijing. Apart from the violent behaviour of Europeans, there was another reason for imperial disdain of foreign traders: the ancient system of tributary relations.

Because China was both the Greece and Rome of East Asia, it is not surprising that its civilisation was regarded by its neighbours with awe. Korea, Vietnam, Siam, Burma, Indonesia and even Japan had all sent embassies bearing gifts. And because this tribute was of no real importance to the imperial treasury, while the items given to foreign envoys in return either balanced or outweighed its value, the whole system was seen as a symbolic recognition of the Chinese ruler's supreme role as the Son of Heaven. By acknowledging the suzerainty of China, tributary nations were officially recognised and, when the occasion arose, aided against their enemies. Thus a Chinese army went to Korea's relief during Toyotomi Hideyoshi's invasion of 1592–98. In the event, the country was saved by the great Korean admiral Yi Sunsin, who cut off the invaders from Japan. At most, the tributary system might take the form of state trading when the eunuch admiral Zheng He explored the southern oceans in the fifteenth century; at its least, the exchanges of gifts amounted to no more than the maintenance of friendship between Asian courts.

All this was beyond Macartney's comprehension when he arrived in the summer of 1793. He would have probably regarded it as hyperbole anyway. In his journal, he complains about the oriental tendency to exaggerate, quite misunderstanding one of the Chinese emperor's titles. When addressed as Ten Thousand Years, which may be translated as "forever", the ruler was simply being wished a long and joyful reign. Directed northwards to Jehol, the summer residence of the Qing court beyond the Great Wall, Macartney believed that there was a good chance of fulfilling his mission. It never occurred to him that he was regarded by Qian Long as no more than an ambassador bearing tribute from afar. A hint of the imperial attitude should have been picked up in the argument over prescribed court ritual.

The British ambassador refused to kowtow, insisting that he should show the emperor the same respect that was due to his own sovereign. A kowtow consisted of three separate kneelings, each one followed by a full prostration with the forehead knocking the ground three times.[35] There were intense negotiations before it was accepted that Macartney would be excused. The following year, members of a Dutch embassy kowtowed readily on every occasion. Once its leader made a fool of himself in the eyes of Qian Long when his wig fell off while kowtowing at a frozen roadside as the emperor passed. Naturally, it was a blow to Manchu pride if an envoy did not kowtow, but Macartney's refusal was attributed to barbarian ignorance.

Emperor Qian Long being carried to an audience tent to receive Lord Macartney's embassy in 1793

More to the point was the comment of Father Amiot, a French Jesuit then resident in Beijing. He told Macartney that the imperial court regarded embassies as temporary ceremonies and that it saw no reason to conclude a treaty with a distant power. Father Amiot also said that the British embassy "would have met with fewer difficulties at its outset if it had arrived before the Government had been alarmed by the news of great troubles in Europe, the inhabitants of which are indiscriminately considered by them as of a turbulent character".[36] Though the Jesuit went on to advise a regular exchange of letters between the rulers of Britain and China as the best means of building profitably on this initial contact, Macartney came away with very little to show from his embassy.[37]

The frustration in London was palpable. If only the imperial frontiers could be forced, and a convenient island seized as a secure trading base. This was of course to be Hong Kong, which was ceded to Britain in 1842. As Macartney had confided in his journal, how could the Manchus

> possibly expect to feed us long on promises? Can they be igno-
> rant that a couple of English frigates would be an overmatch
> for the whole naval force of their empire, that in half a summer
> they could totally destroy all the navigation of their coasts and
> reduce the inhabitants of the maritime provinces, which subsist
> chiefly on fish, to absolute famine?[38]

Yet the inability of Qian Long and his officials to appreciate the danger of a seaborne attack was not so shortsighted as it seems to us now. In the 1760s, his armies had completed the conquest of the Mongols and finally overcome the threat of nomad invasion. Having rid the Chinese empire of its most troublesome enemies, the land-oriented Manchus felt that they had no reason for further defensive measures, and certainly not from any seaborne threat.

Although Macartney never ruled out a demonstration of Britain's naval strength in Chinese waters, he was conscious of how its "settle-ments in India would suffer most severely by any interruption of their China traffic which is infinitely valuable to them, or as connected with their adventures to the Philippines and Malaya. To Great Britain the blow would be immediate and heavy." On a personal note, Macartney added that "we should lose from China not only its raw silk, an indispensable ingredient in our silk fabrics, but of another indispensable luxury, or rather an absolute necessary of life: tea".[39]

Chapter 3

Imperial Heyday
1815–1905

It was duly enjoined on me as a matter of vital importance that I should insist on all outward and visible signs of deference and respect which Orientals with a leaning to sycophancy, resulting from generations of subjection and foreign rule, are only too willing to accord.

Advice given to Henry Cotton in 1867 on his appointment as a civil servant in Bengal

The Opium Wars

Strategy had not been a notable feature of Britain's handling of Napoleon. The British government did little more than respond to the French emperor's moves until, almost by chance, it was able to focus on a single campaign in Portugal and Spain. Victory at Maida in southern Italy—the first over French troops on the European mainland—excited Britain in 1806, but the cause was not immediately grasped: the effectiveness of British volleys fired at close range. Not until Arthur Wellesley had the opportunity of perfecting their use against French columns during the Peninsular War would the tide begin to turn against Napoleon. But this particular campaign might never have been fought had the French emperor not misjudged the temper of the Spanish people and then chosen to compound his mistake by a marked reluctance to withdraw. Even though it was his adversary from the Peninsular War who delivered the knockout blow at Waterloo, Napoleon's advance towards Brussels caught his opponents by surprise. To the very end, he remained the master of strategy if not tactics. As Arthur Wellesley wrote after the battle: "Napoleon did not manoeuvre at all. He just moved forward in the old style, in columns, and was driven off in the old style."[1] The French emperor's plan of battle was nothing more than head-on fighting.

In its dealings with the Chinese empire Britain showed a similar lack of strategic thought. An inability to comprehend the stance of the Qing emperors on international commerce combined with a laissez-faire attitude towards the opium trade to bring about a situation in which conflict was inevitable. It only needed a belligerent foreign secretary like Lord Palmerston to ensure that war broke out, since his usual solution to intractable foreign issues was the dispatch of a gunboat. Yet the Royal Navy frigate, the *Andromache*, which dropped anchor at Macao in the summer of 1834, was not expected to open fire on the Chinese. That it did so had much to do with William Jardine, a former ship's surgeon, who befriended his fellow Scot William Napier on his arrival as superintendent of British trade at Guangzhou. *HMS Andromache* brought the newly appointed official to fill the vacuum left by the abolition of the English East India Company monopoly the previous year. Jardine made sure from the start that he had Napier's ear. Given that he dared to send his own heavily armed clippers to sell opium off their decks at small coves on the south China coast, Jardine was not a person to urge caution on his inexperienced guest when dealing with the Chinese authorities.

Baffled by his inability to make progress, and annoyed by an unwillingness to accept him as a representative of the British government, Napier issued a proclamation entitled "State Relations between China and Great Britain at Present", had it translated into Chinese, then printed and distributed around Guangzhou. In it, he accused the city governor of gross incompetence, even suggesting that he had no conception of the value of commerce. The double offence of the criticism and its general address to the Chinese public not surprisingly led to an order for Napier to quit Guangzhou. At this point, even Jardine seems to have favoured a compromise, but Napier believed he was facing savages and only force would improve matters. Though he ordered *HMS Andromache* and another frigate upriver from Macao, their captains were instructed to hold their fire unless attacked. Already exceeding his authority as a superintendent of trade, Napier was finally obliged to quit Guangzhou because a Chinese blockade even threatened the frigates. Only two British sailors were killed but hostilities had in reality started.

Napier died shortly afterwards and was buried at Macao. The indignity of his journey downriver on a Chinese vessel may have aggravated a raging bout of fever: it was deliberately tedious, the slow passage in the hot weather being marked by fireworks and the beating of gongs. Even though Palmerston saw the ludicrous side of Napier's escapade, he was sympathetic to a call for stern measures against China, something Jardine's partner, James Matheson, was quick to urge on reaching London. All that was

Commissioner Lin Zexu. In London, his destruction of £2,500,000 worth of British property at Guangzhou was rarely acknowledged to have been opium stocks

needed was a pretext for action, which Lin Zexu provided in 1839. Commissioner Lin had been sent to curtail opium imports, then running out of control. A member of the Spring Purification party, a group of senior officials concerned among other things with the adverse effect the smoking of opium was having on Chinese society, Lin Zexu argued in a memorial to the emperor that measures against pushers should be intensified and foreign traffickers treated as harshly as native ones. As a result of giving this advice, he was charged with the suppression of the opium trade and allowed unlimited powers to accomplish the difficult task.

First, Lin Zexu broke up the network of Chinese importers and distributors; next he destroyed the opium stocks of Western merchants without compensation; and finally he obliged them to promise to end the odious traffic in the drug. The Chinese action was exploited by Jardine, who financed a London pamphlet that referred to the siege of the British merchant community in Guangzhou as another "Black Hole of Calcutta". War was formally declared on the Chinese empire and what became known as the First Opium War lasted from June 1840 until August 1842. Profit swept every objection aside in Parliament, although William Gladstone said:

> A war more unjust in its origin, a war more calculated to cover this country with permanent disgrace, I do not know of and I have not read of. The right honourable gentleman opposite spoke of the British flag waving in glory at Canton. That flag is hoisted to protect an infamous contraband trade; and if it were never hoisted except as it is now hoisted on the coast of China, we should recoil from its sight with horror.[2]

Cleverly, Palmerston had insisted that it was national pride, rather than commerce, that was the issue: the freedom of British citizens abroad had to be guaranteed at all costs. The Qing dynasty was about to discover exactly what it would have to pay in consequence.

News that Lin Zexu had excluded the British from Guangzhou was considered reason enough to send an expeditionary force of 20 ships with some 4,000 troops on board. Quite overlooked was the specific cause of the exclusion: a drunken brawl in which sailors had killed a Chinese man. When none of these men were handed over for justice, Lin Zexu compelled British residents to live on their ships off Hong Kong, the rocky island that Napier had urged London to seize six years earlier. There they awaited the expeditionary force, which was about to humble the Chinese empire because the British were overwhelmingly superior in arms. Their possessions in India provided ready troops and supplies, and their shallow-draught warships could easily bombard upriver cities and towns. The steamer *Nemesis*, armed with two pivot-mounted 32-pounder guns, was quite capable of blasting a hole in any fortress wall. Additionally the steamer had five six-pounders, ten smaller cannon and a rocket launcher. The largest iron ship built thus far, *Nemesis*, allowed the British to capture the forts protecting the approach to Guangzhou, easily sink Chinese war junks and then threaten Guangzhou itself. Her captain William Hall noted that the Chinese called her "the devil ship and say our shells and rockets could be only invented by the latter. They are more afraid of her than all the Line-of-Battle ships put together."[3]

The assault was not of immediate military significance for the British, but it was to have serious consequences for the Qing dynasty. The disorder in and around Guangzhou was a forerunner of the Taiping uprising of 1850, which for nearly 15 years afterwards troubled the southern provinces of the Chinese empire. The decisive phase of the First Opium War only occurred when British ships sailed northwards. The great port of Amoy, present-day Xiamen, fell at the cost of two dead and 15 wounded. Leaving a garrison behind, the expeditionary force transferred its area of operations to the lower Yangzi river valley, where Ningbo was quickly taken, there being hardly any resistance. A bemused group of Chinese residents watched the bandsmen of the Royal Irish Guards playing *God Save the Queen* on the city walls. Shortly afterwards, Shanghai surrendered without a fight.

Manchu soldiers were handicapped in resisting the British by a fear of the Chinese siding with the invaders. And there is indeed some evidence that the declining popularity of Qing rule was a factor in Britain's military success. Documents were found on a dead official that expressed serious worries about the barbarians getting into the good books of the Chinese population. No longer the

The British capture of Ningbo

splendid imperial house it had been in the eighteenth century, the Qing dynasty was increasingly seen as a foreign imposition and, during the British seaborne attack, one quite incapable of defending China. That the Yangzi campaign took place in one of the most densely populated parts of the Chinese empire meant that dynastic weakness could no longer be hidden.

After Shanghai, the next target was Nanjing, once an imperial capital and still the most important city in south China. Because its fall would destroy the prestige of the Qing emperor, a peace treaty between Britain and China was in 1842 hurriedly signed on *HMS Cornwallis*, anchored off the city. The Treaty of Nanjing awarded Britain a large indemnity, opened five ports to international trade and ceded the island of Hong Kong as a sovereign base. Most obnoxious to Chinese sentiment was the "most favoured nation" clause, which established the divisive principle of extra-territoriality. The total immunity this gave British residents from Chinese law was to become deeply resented, especially when they carved out for themselves privileged enclaves in the so-called Treaty Ports.

The opium trade went unmentioned because the British negotiators took the view that it was a matter for the Chinese authorities to sort out. Made transparent was the British intention of keeping drug traffickers out of Hong Kong and its waters, but at the same time British subjects were to remain exempt from Chinese regulation. They could not be molested by Chinese officials, nor would British officials have any obligation to enforce Chinese laws against them. A recipe for total misunderstanding, this ambivalent attitude was soon to bring about the Second Opium War of 1858–60. By then, opium sales had made the drug the most valuable commodity in the world, as the growth of British trade with China continued to depend on opium imports as the means of paying for tea and silk exports. Matheson told his leading captain not to be conspicuous and "make every effort. . . to please the mandarins, such as moving from one anchorage to another when they require it, and not approaching too near to their towns. The opium trade is now very unpopular in England, that we cannot be too cautious in keeping it as quiet and as much out of the public eye as possible."[4]

Renewed conflict between Britain and China predictably began at Guangzhou, but on this occasion it had no direct connection with opium. British policy had settled upon non-intervention but, with Palmerston's return to power, the Hong Kong merchants perceived an opportunity to further their interests through treaty revision. They clamoured therefore in 1856 for a stern response to the *Arrow* incident. The *Arrow* was a *lorcha*, a schooner rigged with a junk's batten sails, and by registration in Hong Kong it was entitled to fly the British flag and claim British protection. A skirmish with Chinese pirates led to the intervention of Guangzhou's port authorities, who boarded the *Arrow* and took into custody both the crew and the pirates. The nominal Irish captain was not there when the police arrived. Yet this Chinese action over a Chinese-built boat, owned by a Chinese subject, manned by a Chinese crew, and sailing in Chinese waters was treated as "an insult of a very grave nature" by the British consul Harry Parkes. That on sailing into Guangzhou, the *Arrow* would have lowered its flags in accordance with British nautical practice, and could be mistaken as a Chinese vessel was ignored, even though the officer in charge of the marine police said on their arrival that no flags were displayed and no foreigners were on board. *Arrow*'s registration had actually expired, but this technicality was not sufficient to stop armed action.

Consul Parkes had just returned from Britain, where Palmerston agreed that the Chinese should be made to pay for any insult, no matter how trivial it might seem. Sir John Bowring, the governor of Hong Kong, backed Parkes because he also deemed the near-affront to the British flag justified a resort to arms. In concert with Britain over the Crimean War, France decided that the execution of a Catholic missionary in south China, where he had been stirring up rebellious feelings among the inhabitants, entitled it to any benefits that might derive from a new assault on the Chinese empire. Riding a wave of national enthusiasm for his gunboat diplomacy in 1857, a 72-year-old Palmerston appointed as special plenipotentiary for China the experienced James Bruce, the eighth earl of Elgin. As did Napier before him, this Scottish peer needed money to support his family and his estate: his father had run up serious debts through the expense of acquiring the Parthenon friezes. Lord Elgin was not keen about fighting the Chinese, and confided to friends that the *Arrow* affair was

> a scandal to us, and so considered. . . by all except the few who are personally compromised. Nothing could be more con-temptible than the origin of our existing quarrel.[5]

Yet he was a professional administrator, having been governor-general of Canada, and considered that it was his duty to accept Palmerston's orders. They were brief: he was to demand, by direct negotiation with the imperial government in Beijing, the establishment of a permanent British ambassador there; the opening of new ports to trade; and a Chinese promise to comply with the provisions of the Treaty of Nanjing.

At his disposal was an Anglo-French force of 5,700 men. It took almost a year to reach Guangzhou because some of the soldiers had to be diverted to suppress the Indian Mutiny. The entire expedition was ready for action in January 1858, when Guangzhou was captured and Parkes found himself its governor. For three-and-a-half years, the triumphant consul was in charge of the city, although a puppet imperial official was installed in the old governor's palace for the sake of face. The Qing emperor Xian Feng tolerated this arrangement, while secretly encouraging the local population to rise against the British. He was to be disappointed, for the single assault that was made on Guangzhou by the local militia in July collapsed under British artillery fire. It has to be said that an earlier move might have had a chance of success, because the city was the scene of unrestrained looting. As Elgin noted in his diary

> My difficulty has been to prevent the wretched Cantonese from being plundered and bullied. There is a word called "loot" which gives unfortunately a venial character to what would, in common English, be styled robbery. Add to this that there is no flogging in the French army, so that it is impossible to punish men for this class of offence.[6]

Not that Elgin himself could resist loot, a Hindi word with which British soldiers were very familiar. As special plenipotentiary for China, he restricted his own looting to the city treasury, confiscating its silver and gold in lieu of official reparations.

Making no impression at all on the Qing court by the capture of Guangzhou, Elgin directed the expedition northwards and anchored off Dagu, the stronghold that guarded the estuary of the river leading to Beijing. An attack on its fortresses was soon followed by the passage of eight gunboats up the river to the port of Tianjin, some 40 kilometres from the imperial capital. A peace treaty named after the threatened port was quickly agreed and Elgin sailed off to inaugurate Anglo-Japanese relations. Although Royal Navy vessels had visited Japanese waters in search of Dutch ships under Napoleonic control, the task of opening up the country to international commerce fell not to Britain, but to the United States. In 1853, a quarter of the US fleet, eight frigates in all, had sailed to establish diplomatic relations with the Japanese government.

Commodore Matthew Perry forced the Japanese to accept a letter from his president to the emperor of Japan and then weighed anchor, promising to return in a year for an answer. On his return in 1854 Perry secured the "most favoured nation" treatment for the United States but no guarantee for starting trade. Townsend Harris, US consul at the port of Shimoda, persuaded the Japanese to agree

Lord Elgin signing the Treaty of Tianjin in 1858. Chinese reluctance to implement its terms resulted in the attack on Beijing two years later

to international commerce as well as a schedule of tariffs. The first embassy from the Tokugawa shogunate travelled to Washington in 1860, the same year a trade agreement was signed with Britain.

The Treaty of Tianjin was still not working by this date. Neither Elgin's demand for the Chinese market to be opened more widely to international trade nor his demand for China to enter into diplomatic relations with other countries had been fully met. Diehards in Beijing simply could not countenance the equality between Britain and China that these arrangements implied, especially as regards diplomatic representation. Though impressed by British power, the Qing court was no more prepared to acknowledge state-to-state equality now than it was during Macartney's abortive embassy. Learning that the fortifications at Dagu were being strengthened and booms placed across the river, the British had tried to force them in 1859 with disastrous consequences. Six gunboats were stranded and 500 men killed or wounded. Emperor

Xian Feng only made matters worse. He was now a hopeless opium addict, dominated by his harem ladies; one of them was Ci Xi, who was also addicted to opium herself, despite keeping her dosage to a level that prevented physical damage. A fierce xenophobe, Ci Xi persuaded Xian Feng to defy all the foreigners then threatening the Chinese empire.

The encouragement that Xian Feng gave to officials who flouted the terms of the treaties was of course unwise. It was only a question of time before retribution would arrive in the form of Elgin, whom an exasperated Palmerston directed to intervene. With 10,000 British and Indian troops plus a contingent of 5,800 Frenchmen, he set off to accomplish his mission. Having forced the river mouth at Dagu, the British and French troops occupied Tianjin, where negotiations with senior officials representing the imperial government took place. As soon as Elgin became convinced that Xian Feng was still uninterested in reaching an agreement, he declared that in future negotiations would be conducted at Tongzhou, a city less than ten kilometres from Beijing. The proposal was rejected outright by the imperial government and Manchu cavalrymen were sent to block any further advance. The allied envoys sent ahead to Tongzhou included the zealous Harry Parkes.

When they and their escort fell into the hands of the Manchus, Parkes insisted that under a flag of truce he and his colleagues should be able to move with freedom. An infuriated Manchu general told the British consul that he was personally responsible for China's woes. On the general's order, Parkes was dragged from his horse and ordered to kowtow. When Parkes refused, Manchu soldiers banged his forehead three times on the ground. After the envoys were imprisoned in Beijing, an all-out assault was prepared on the imperial capital, from which the emperor had already fled.

Ci Xi had dissuaded Xian Feng from fighting a face-saving battle outside Beijing's walls, and leave instead his brother Prince Gong to treat with the invaders. When this prince refused to release the captives as a preliminary to proper negotiations, Elgin felt he had no choice but to commence hostilities, and siege guns were readied to breach the ramparts of Beijing. The threat caused a negotiator to be lowered in a basket so that the city gates did not have to be opened. In return for keeping the majority of his troops out of the imperial capital, Elgin got the prisoners released, or rather those who were still alive. A timely surrender by Prince Gong saved Beijing from bombardment and Elgin was admitted with a few soldiers.

It is not a little ironic that Elgin, the son of the self-styled saviour of the Parthenon friezes, should have chosen to avenge the 20 persons who had died in captivity by ordering the destruction of the Summer Palace, the great walled pleasure-ground that Qian Long had laid out before Macartney's arrival. One senior British officer remarked that its sack was like "having the run of Buckingham Palace and being allowed to take away anything and everything you wanted. Things were plundered and pulled to pieces, floors were literally covered with fur robes, jade ornaments, porcelain, and beautiful wood carvings." After this decision, Elgin insisted on being taken to the Purple Forbidden City, the imperial palace at the centre of Beijing, in a litter carried by eight porters, the number reserved for the highest officials. There Prince Gong ratified the Treaty of Tianjin and through the Conventions of Beijing agreed a lease on Kowloon, the peninsula opposite Hong Kong.

China's humiliation. Lord Elgin's triumphal entry to Beijing in 1860

British policy thereafter concentrated on sustaining the peace party led by Prince Gong, although after Xian Feng's death in 1861, it was Ci Xi who dominated the Qing court. Four years later, the prince was accused at her behest of disrespect for the emperor, obstructing the imperial will, and secretly fostering discord. Because foreign ambassadors now permanently resident in Beijing had a great respect for Prince Gong, the charges were dropped but the damage to the prince's prestige was done. He was never again the force he had been in political circles. It made little difference to the survival of the Qing dynasty. The Russians had taken advantage of its differences with Britain to appropriate vast territories along the Amur river, traditional Manchu possessions. The dismemberment of the imperial system then proceeded apace: Burma in 1885 passed into British hands, Vietnam the same year into French, and in a short campaign during 1894–95 Japan sought to dominate Korea, the Liaodong peninsula and the island of Taiwan. European and American pressure denied the Japanese ownership of the Liaodong peninsula, which the Russians occupied instead. But they were ejected by the Imperial Japanese Army in 1905 and Korea was annexed by Tokyo in 1910.

In 1860, the fall of Beijing to the Anglo-French expeditionary force was not expected to inaugurate such a process of disintegration. To his personal dismay, the world's press condemned Elgin's casual plunder of the priceless Chinese treasures housed at the Summer Palace. The British government ignored the chorus of criticism and a delighted Palmerston commented: "It was absolutely necessary to stamp by such a record our indignation at the treachery and brutality of these Tartars, for Chinese they are not."[7] One of the looters, Charles Gordon, stayed on with his artillery corps to help the Qing dynasty deal with the Taiping rebellion. A tragedy for this modernising movement, despite its professed Christian belief, was the coldness of most Europeans living in south China, especially those with commercial interests at stake or missionaries anxious about doctrinal differences. Painfully, the Taipings learned that Europeans were neither co-religionists nor allies against the Manchus.

Having wrung more concessions from Beijing, the British believed there was nothing to be gained by supporting the Christian rebels. They were content to leave the humbled Qing imperial court as it was: an anachronism in an increasingly modern Asia. Manchus such as Ci Xi might cling to power there, blocking any attempt at reform, but she could not prolong Qing rule indefinitely. As soon as Japan demonstrated the value of Western technology against the Chinese army in Korea, it was obvious that China would have to change as well. Ci Xi's imprisonment in 1898 of the ninth Qing emperor Guang Xi, who 23 years earlier she had placed on the Dragon Throne, thwarted his Hundred Days of Reform: what it could not do was banish the ideas that informed his proposals from the public agenda.

The Indian Mutiny

The uprising in India to which Elgin diverted troops bound for China took the British by surprise. With the notable exception of Afghanistan, where in late 1841 the entire British garrison of 16,000 men at Kabul was destroyed and civilians dragged off to domestic slavery, Britain had few dangerous enemies in either India or Central Asia. The prisoners were liberated on the recapture of Kabul in 1842 but, the difficulties involved in occupying such a remote land once appreciated, Afghanistan was then evacuated in an orderly fashion. The new governor-general, Lord Ellenborough, arrived in time from London to welcome the relief expedition back. Buoyed by this success and intoxicated with the power of office, Ellenborough annexed Sind the following year without bothering to consult the British government. What most upset English East Indian Company officials working in India was not so much his high-handedness as the undisguised contempt he displayed towards them. Adverse reports of the governor-general's behaviour reached London where there were many who desired his recall. Writing to Queen Victoria offended ministers while his disregard of the company policy as regards patronage was equally disliked by its directors.

Lord Ellenborough had long argued for the British government to assume direct responsibility for the English East India Company's foreign possessions. He saw the need for public works and was shocked at the little that had been done. Yet his self-conceit so annoyed everyone who knew him that Ellenborough's early recall was unavoidable. The "wild elephant", as *The Times* aptly described him, made way for Sir Henry Hardinge, Arthur Wellesley's liaison officer with Blücher at Waterloo. The blow was less painful to the outgoing governor-general perhaps for the reason that Hardinge was his brother-in-law. Almost at once, Hardinge found himself at war with the Sikhs, whose great leader Ranjit Singh had built up his kingdom in the Punjab shortly after the British defeat of the Marathas. Appreciating the need for improved military organisation, Ranjit Singh disguised himself and visited a British encampment to observe training methods. His rare achievement in uniting the Sikhs was for the most part due to his reorganisation of his army along European lines.

After his death in 1839, the Punjab descended into chaos as rival commanders scrambled for power: Ranjit's only son proved quite incapable of emulating his famous father, and the bitter civil conflict eventually led to an appeal for the Punjab to become a British protectorate. What remained of the Sikh army anticipated this move, invaded English East India Company territory and threatened Ferozepur, south of Lahore. But it was handicapped by a distrust of several commanders, whose desire to win could be questioned, while on the British side, the commander-in-chief was hampered by the presence of the governor-general. Hardinge had volunteered to serve on his staff, but could not resist interfering with strategy. Three bloody battles were fought before the Sikhs were finally driven back to Lahore, Ranjit Singh's former stronghold. As far as the Sikhs were concerned, the struggle was not over and another war occurred before the end of Sikh independence. It was not, however, an ennobled Hardinge who annexed the Punjab. Instead his successor, the 35-year-old Lord Dalhousie, ordered its annexation: he believed that this was the right course of action for Indian states that had shown that they could not govern themselves. Had the Punjab remained a separate power in 1857, then the British fate during the Indian Mutiny could have been very different indeed. Well-trained Sikh soldiers might have decisively bolstered the strength of the mutinous sepoys rather than, along with the Gurkhas, filling the depleted ranks of the English East India Company's own forces.

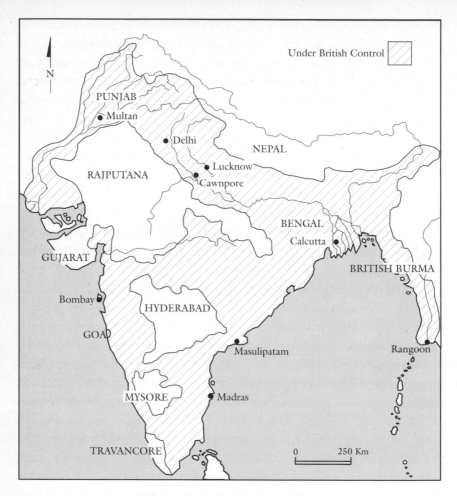

Under British Control

N

PUNJAB
● Multan

● Delhi
NEPAL

RAJPUTANA
● Lucknow
Cawnpore

BENGAL
Calcutta ●

GUJARAT
BRITISH BURMA

Bombay ●
HYDERABAD

GOA

Masulipatam ●
Rangoon

MYSORE
● Madras

TRAVANCORE
0   250 Km

India under Lord Dalhousie in 1856

Undoubtedly one of the most energetic governor-generals, Dalhousie did much to improve administration and continue with a programme of public works. Yet his eight years in office were not marked by any real understanding of his Indian subjects. Because he held that British government, laws, customs and manners were the best in the world, no concession was offered to Indian sentiment. At some distant point in the future, India might possibly prove capable of governing itself, but for Dalhousie the present state of affairs suggested that the whole of the subcontinent would be better off coloured red. No attempt at all was made to cultivate the friendship of the Indian people. As Syed Ahmed Khan, a judicial officer in 1857, tellingly remarked: "The Hindustanees fell into the habit of thinking that all laws were passed with a view to degrade and ruin them." Though an anglophile Moslem himself, Ahmed Khan noted how "the Muslims were in every respect more dissatisfied than the Hindus, and hence in most districts they were comparatively more rebellious, though the latter were not wanting in this respect."[8] Trouble appeared within months of Dalhousie's arrival. At Multan, once an outlying province of Ranjit Singh's kingdom, a dispute about taxation involved the killing of one young British officer and the wounding of another. Without warning they were attacked by a soldier in their escort. Even though the incident allowed Dalhousie to take over direct control of the Punjab, it revealed how vulnerable British officers and their families were to sudden attack, a danger missed in a Calcutta busy with Dalhousie's reforms.

The Punjab was not the only province that Dalhousie added to the English East India Company's possessions by conquest. Complaints from merchants trading at Rangoon gave him in late 1851 the opportunity to impress upon the Burmese the need to recognise British superiority. Naval forces seized the ports of Rangoon, Bassein and Matapan. In 1852, even the upriver city of Pegu was taken, despite spirited resistance. The king of Burma did not formally acknowledge the loss of a large stretch of coastline but, after a dignified period of time, he informed the British that they could stay there without Burmese interference. This was not the only territory to be lost to the English East India Company. The First Anglo-Burmese war had added in 1826 Manipur, Arakan and the Tennasserim at some cost: the deaths of 15,000 British and Indian soldiers as well as tens of thousands of Burmese. The protection of Bengal was the ostensible cause of the conflict, which Calcutta considered to be endangered by the Burmese occupation of the upper Brahmaputra river valley.

In 1852, the acquisition of new territory in Burma gave the English East India Company an immediate problem, that of finding enough troops to garrison it. Hindu sepoys were unsettled by sea voyages, so Dalhousie decided that future recruitment to the ranks of the Bengal army would involve the unavoidable obligation of service overseas. Moslem sepoys, who had no religious scruples about going to sea, were also adversely affected by this decision,

Britain's seizure of Rangoon added to the grievances of Hindu sepoys, who hated sea voyages

because they had benefited equally with their Hindu comrades from the bounties offered to those who would embark for duty abroad. To those Hindus who could never be enticed by money to sail, the new regulation caused their sons to be denied military employment altogether. Though the duty of overseas service could not be imposed on them, they were still apprehensive about being forced to undertake it in an emergency.

Thus the scene was well and truly set for a military mutiny among the sepoys. What brought matters to a head was the introduction of the Enfield rifle. Muzzle-loaders like the smooth-bore muskets they replaced, Enfields used ammunition that came in the form of paper cartridges. The cartridge was opened by the soldiers using their teeth, since one hand was required to hold the weapon upright while the other held the cartridge. Because the cartridges were greased using animal fat, the composition of the grease was an issue that concerned both Hindus and Moslems. Discontent at Dum

Dum, the great arsenal close to Calcutta, was revealed in January 1857 when two-thirds of the sepoys stationed there expressed religious objections to the greased cartridges. Beeswax or coconut oil was believed to be a suitable alternative, and each was later authorised, but it soon became obvious that the Enfield rifle would not be accepted without great difficulty. Even the new shiny paper of the cartridges was believed to be manufactured from either cows or pigs. How hysterical the situation became can be judged from an apocryphal story of the time. When an untouchable labourer at Dum Dum was refused a drink by a high-caste sepoy, he told the Indian soldier that the barriers of caste that informed his lack of courtesy were about to fall, because the English East India Company was already grinding pig and cow bones into army flour.

As rumours and complaints proliferated, it should have been realised that one of the chief props of British power in India was about to collapse. The Bengal army could no longer be relied on. Though its troops alone rose in revolt, and then not in every regiment, the extent of the disruption in northern India was nonetheless staggering. Northeast of Delhi the largely Moslem garrison at Meerut started the mutiny in May, when sepoys released comrades imprisoned for refusing to handle the new cartridges. They attacked their British officers, and anyone who seemed to oppose them, before marching to Delhi and putting themselves under the command of Bahadur Shah Zafar II, the Mughal emperor. Forced to speak directly to the mutinous sepoys, he told them he had no troops, no armoury and no treasury to support them. They replied, "Only give us your blessing. We will provide everything else." Fearing for the safety of his court as well as his city, Zafar reluctantly allowed the mutineers to rally under his standard, the green flag of Islam. At 82 years of age, he was never a war leader, and his own lack of ambition combined with an otherworldliness to make him little more than a convenient figurehead. So powerless was he that he failed to expel the horses of rebel cavalrymen from the palace gardens.

Paradoxically, it was the recently conquered Sikhs who prevented the mutiny from gaining a really firm grip in the northwest. They had no great reason to support the British but even less to throw their lot in with the sepoys who had so conspicuously helped to defeat them. The Sikhs had in addition a settled hatred of the Mughal dynasty whose rulers had persecuted their leaders. The murder of the tenth Sikh guru Govind Singh's two sons was not forgotten, nor was the great rebellion against the Mughal emperor Bahadur Shah that followed in 1709. Another incentive to side with the English East India Company was the prospect of loot, when rebellious cities like Delhi were retaken. In north India, this rare opportunity for personal gain also drew into the ranks of its depleted forces a variety of fierce hillsmen. As Indian princes remained aloof from the mutiny, the sepoys occupying Delhi soon discovered that they were in an uncertain position. Yet they were in a less precarious fix than Calcutta, whose patent weakness was due to the small number and poor distribution of British troops: the largest concentration was in the Punjab, where 10,000 men faced 50,000 mutinous sepoys.

News of the Meerut uprising had reached Calcutta by telegraph, before the mutineers cut the wire. After the fall of Delhi, every effort was made for its recapture. British troops were summoned from other parts of India and reinforced by those destined to help Elgin take Beijing. Another mutiny at Lucknow, between Delhi and Calcutta, was barely stopped by loyal sepoys. Elsewhere, mutinies sometimes spared British officers and their families, but this was not usual when civilian rioters joined in. At Allahabad, to the southeast of Delhi, many Hindus and Christians were killed in the city by a mob of Moslems, while British officers and civilians who took refuge in the fort there were at first in grave danger. Four hundred Sikhs under British command saved the situation, although the consumption of looted alcohol somewhat undermined their effectiveness. Timely relief by the Madras Fusiliers prevented a massacre but failed to prevent their colonel from ordering one of his own. When these actions became known in Calcutta, a report noted how

the indiscriminate hangings not only of persons of all shades of guilt, but of those whose guilt was at the very least doubtful, and the general burning and plunder of villages, whereby the innocent as well as the guilty, without regard to age or sex, were indiscriminately punished, and, in some instances, sacrificed, had deeply exasperated large communities not otherwise hostile to the Government.[9]

The executions at Allahabad were not untypical of the British response to the Indian Mutiny. Irrational though the killing of people who had no connection with the uprising undoubtedly was, it was the product of a deep sense of betrayal made worse by exaggerated tales of torture, violation and murder.

At Delhi, the hapless Mughal emperor was appalled by the violence of the rebellious sepoys. Having already resisted a demand from one of his courtiers to issue a *firman* against all unbelievers, Hindu, Sikh and Christian alike, the Mughal emperor tried to prevent the rebels from killing the British prisoners he was keeping in safe custody in his palace. Their number had grown to 52 after several more families were found to be hiding in the city. Not without reason, the sepoys accused the emperor's staff of holding the prisoners so that when the English East India Company returned in strength, they could use them as a bargaining chip with its soldiers. By this time, however, Bahadur Shah Zafar was thoroughly tired of the looting and killing. The fact that many of the would-be executioners were Moslems accorded the Mughal emperor little influence over the prisoners' fate. With tears in his eyes, he told them to beware of divine judgement for shedding innocent blood. It made no difference: the helpless men, women and children were put to the sword. Afterwards, the bodies were taken in two carts and thrown into the river. When the event was discussed throughout Delhi, the conclusion of its Hindu residents was that this cruel action ensured that the sepoys could never be victorious over the British. In his heart, Bahadur Shah Zafar almost certainly agreed with them. And he knew that his inability to prevent the slaughter had already condemned his dynasty to extinction, because the British would never forgive him for the mass execution.

The British counter-attack threw up a number of unlikely heroes, one of whom was Sir Henry Havelock. This 62-year-old colonel had spent most of his 42 years of service in India, where he had learned several of its languages. That he had married the daughter of a Baptist missionary, and become a pious Baptist himself, probably slowed his promotion in spite of obvious military skills. He spent much of his spare time at prayer meetings and he conducted Bible classes for his own troops. Lord Hardinge said he was "Every inch a soldier, and every inch a Christian."[10] Such was Havelock's appeal to the Victorians that within a year he had streets, roads and squares and named after him. With the temporary rank of brigadier-general, he was sent off to Allahabad to relieve nearby Cawnpore and support Lucknow. It was his first independent command. At Lucknow the mutineers had been driven off by loyal sepoys, but the city was still not safe from attack.

At Cawnpore, there were fewer British troops to stiffen sepoy loyalty, and its commanding officer, Sir Hugh Wheeler, prepared for a siege by unostentatiously placing a shallow trench and a low mud wall around two disused barracks. There he moved 59 British artillerymen with their six guns, plus 75 convalescents from the British regiment stationed at Lucknow. Wheeler also laid in sufficient supplies to feed a thousand people for one month. It is possible that he believed this makeshift refuge, which was locally called "Ford Despair", offered defence enough against civil rioters, as reports suggested his sepoys would not mutiny unless provoked. The intelligence proved to be wrong and at the beginning of June the 3,000 sepoys rose in revolt. Their attack was not at first very determined but towards the end of the month they pressed very hard indeed. With casualties mounting, supplies running low, and no relief force in sight, Wheeler accepted an offer of safe passage in return for the surrender of his guns. Merely a trick to get the British into the open, they were ambushed when about to leave by boat. About a hundred surviving women and children were imprisoned in Cawnpore. Later it was learned that two British officers and two rankers got away in one of the boats. They drifted downstream under fire from pursuers on each bank, until friendly Indians gave protection and escorted them to safety.

It was at Allahabad that Havelock heard of the atrocity, but the monsoon delayed his start for Cawnpore, so that it was not until mid-July that he approached the city. On the way, his small force of 1,000 British soldiers, 130 Sikhs and six artillery pieces defeated the mutineers and their allies on four separate occasions. Just short of Cawnpore, he outflanked a force of 5,000 men and drove it away in disorder. On entering the city, Havelock was disappointed to find that he had arrived too late. The women and children held prisoner had been hacked to death, and their remains thrown into a well. Havelock's troops were so enraged by the coldblooded killing that they went on the rampage themselves. For the Sikhs, it was yet another excuse for plunder. Even though Havelock quickly halted the violence, reporters sent off lurid accounts of indiscriminate slaughter. Having no time to argue the facts of the case, he pressed on towards Lucknow, where a similar situation to Cawnpore existed. The presence of a British battalion helped some of the sepoys to resist the call to mutiny, but it could not hold the city on its own. As in Cawnpore, earthen defences had been made ready and concentrated within them were the British soldiers along with nearly 700 Indian troops—loyal sepoys, even sepoy pensioners who volunteered their services, and a small contingent of Sikhs. In all, there were 1,600 soldiers and armed civilians. As many as 2,000 others, British, Anglo-Indian and Indian, were within the defensive perimeter as well. At the end of June, the protracted siege began. The mutineers acknowledged as their leader the son of the last ruler of Oudh, whose capital had been Lucknow: still a child, his father's ex-advisers represented him in the rebel councils. Despite the 7,000 mutinous sepoys being reinforced by numerous freelance insurgents, they were initially content as at Cawnpore with artillery fire and sniping in the hope of an early surrender. Only towards the end of July did they launch the first of four all-out assaults, which were repulsed.

Havelock's men literally had to fight their way there. They never made it in the monsoon heat: casualties from heatstroke were as high as those from combat. With no choice but to preserve his tiny force, Havelock fell back on Cawnpore. His gallant attempt to reach Lucknow was applauded in a Britain unsure about the outcome of the Indian Mutiny. By August, the worst was in fact over. The spate of mutinies had reduced to a trickle, and the centre of the rising was still lodged in the northwestern provinces. Had Havelock pressed on to Lucknow and suffered an inevitable defeat, then British rule in India would have most probably ended. As it was, he remained threatened in Cawnpore, around which city his opponents operated at will. What he did not realise was that the main concentration of sepoys at Delhi were now much less confident of their survival. In mid-September, siege guns blew two holes in the city walls and a few days later the British succeeded in getting three columns inside. Savage street fighting ensued, the attackers suffering over a thousand killed or wounded by the evening of the assault, but the next morning revealed that the now despondent mutineers had fled.

Delhi before the Indian Mutiny. Its fall marked the end of Mughal rule

Among those who ran away was the Mughal emperor himself, who took refuge with his family at the great marble-domed tomb of Humayun, the dynasty's second ruler. It was the first monumental tomb to be built by the Mughals some 300 years earlier. When his place of hiding became know to the British, Bahadur Shah Zafar agreed to surrender in return for a promise that his life would be spared. Two of his sons and a grandson discovered at the tomb were shot there out of hand. Far worse than this was the wholesale plunder of Delhi and the massacre of many of its inhabitants by the English East India Company soldiers. Hangings became a form of public entertainment, with the result that the suspended corpses gave the city the look of an aerial necropolis. The poet Ghalib, the sole member of the Mughal court to remain in Delhi, had a lucky escape. Asked by a British interrogator whether he was a Moslem, Ghalib replied "Half." When he was asked to explain, he said, "I drink wine but I don't eat pork." The humour was enough to save him, but he never recovered from the destruction wrought in his beloved city. His friends were dead, his patrons gone, his muse lost forever. "People are going mad with sorrow," he wrote, "would it be surprising if I were to lose my mind?"[11] The Mughal emperor himself was quietly removed by bullock cart, a humiliating end to a once great dynasty. He died an exile at Rangoon in 1862, and seven years later Ghalib, still a Delhi resident, followed him to the grave. With their passing Moslem India ceased to exist.

The recapture of Delhi was followed a few days afterwards by Havelock's relief of Lucknow. Bitter hand-to-hand fighting took place in the city itself, where desperate sepoys battled to the last. But the four-and-a-half-month mutiny was all but over. It seemed that the English East India Company had survived intact until the British government decided to place its Indian possessions under the Crown. Instead of its directors' rule, there were to be in future two sources of authority: the Secretary of State for India, who answered to Parliament, and the Viceroy, who oversaw everyday administration and lawmaking in Calcutta. This radical change was in effect an admission that Britain had only just got through the Indian Mutiny. Turning point though the crisis undoubtedly was in colonial affairs, the gap between the rulers and the ruled had been widening for a long time, as more and more of the subcontinent came under British control. This fundamental change in social relations had contributed to the military uprising, no matter that the specific grievance was greased cartridges.

A case in point was the deteriorating status of the Anglo-Indian community, which came to occupy a no-man's-land between the Indians and the British. As early as 1786, Anglo-Indian children of deceased British officers were prevented from travelling to Britain to complete their education. To no avail, it was protested that there was no law to prevent a serving British officer with Anglo Indian children from sending them there. Why discriminate against orphans? In 1795, Anglo-Indians were no longer permitted to serve as English East India Company soldiers. Thrown out of soldiering, the only profession many of them knew, there was nothing but to transfer their services to Indian princes. "It was a sad spectacle—the father in the Company: his son a mercenary in the pay of a late enemy Chief."[12] Keeping the Anglo-Indian community at a distance from lucrative employment was one reason for the restrictions, another might well have been an anxiety about the emergence of a local interest group with a voice in Indian affairs. At this stage there was no suggestion of racial antagonism. Servants of the English East India Company readily took Indian wives or mistresses. Richard Wellesley's wife, who in 1798 had chosen not to come to India during his governor-generalship, agreed that he might keep an Indian mistress. He had written to say that the climate so aroused his senses that he could not live without regular sex. His well-born Sikh mistress not only satisfied this pressing need but she also bore him three sons before he returned home in 1805.

Disarming sepoys at Barrackpore in Bengal, where one of them had wounded two officers

Ordinary British soldiers were not allowed to marry in India. Concerned about the impact of venereal disease on the low numbers stationed there, the military authorities tried to make available a supply of prostitutes subject to medical inspection. This did not stop individual soldiers from supporting favourite girls, but the prohibition on marriage drove a wedge between the rankers and Indian women. Some army surgeons took the view that the best way to keep men out of the syphilis ward was to encourage a soldier to stick with one partner. Because the status of prostitutes, like that of mistresses, carried no social opprobrium in India, supply always met sexual demand. Not until the arrival of larger numbers of British women, from the 1850s onwards, would the moral climate change. Then Victorian prudery began to inform colonial behaviour and attitudes. By 1905 nearly every Indian woman was viewed as a carrier of venereal disease in "a horrible, loathsome and often fatal form". This was because, Lord Kitchener told his troops, "the common women as well as the regular prostitutes in India are all more or less infected with disease". Its prevalence was in fact a symptom of a "diseased" society.[13]

Already the Indian Mutiny had come to be regarded as a reaction to British efforts to improve India, their "over-eager pursuit of Humanity and Civilization". For as long as the English East India Company ruled in the interests of commerce, and the Mughal emperor still sat on his feeble throne, the British could not easily claim the moral high ground. After the deposition of Bahadur Shah Zafar and the transfer of power to the Crown, it was possible to present their Indian empire as a natural historical consequence of the decay of Indian institutions, both Moslem and Hindu. A consequence was the proclamation of Queen Victoria as empress of India in 1877, and the adoption of an "Indianised" style for public buildings. Pseudo-Mughal verandas, colonnades and minarets were suddenly the order of the day. A less attractive side of this self-glorification was social separation: the senior officials' aloof reserve, the memsahibs' petty snobbery, the colour bar at clubs, and the studious avoidance of Indian passengers on trains.

All this was less tolerable for Indians than the earlier brashness of the English East India Company because it was almost everywhere in a subcontinent dominated the British. They did not know it at the time but this imperial era was not destined to last. For the same year that Ghalib died, a Gujarati boy named Mohandas Karamchand Gandhi was born. It would be the political agitation led by Gandhi, rather than the uprising that the last Mughal emperor was forced to endorse, that pointed the way to an independent India.

France's Colonial Revival

Not to be outdone by the British, the French pushed their way into mainland Southeast Asia, the last remaining colonial prize. British private enterprise in the shape of James Brooke had already accounted for what was left of Borneo. Born in India, the son of an English East India Company official, Brooke tired of commerce and bought a schooner, arriving at Singapore with a crew of 20 in 1839. His inspiration was Raffles' governorship of Java during the Napoleonic Wars.

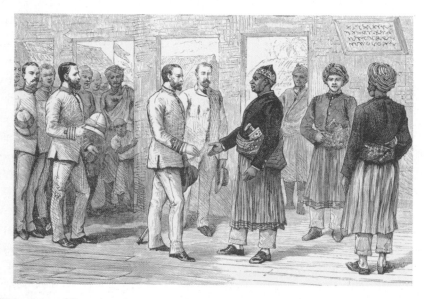

The sultan of Brunei with British officers. In 1844, he gave the island of Labuan to the Royal Navy as a coaling station

The arm's-length policy of the English East India Company outside the Straits Settlements gave scope for Brooke to carve out a kingdom for himself in Sarawak. He went to what was to become his capital, Kuching, and helped put down a rebellion against the sultanate of Brunei by Land Dyaks and local Malays. Raja Muda Hassim, the heir apparent to the sultanate, welcomed this assistance and in 1843 Brooke was confirmed as governor. From the start there was a notably relaxed atmosphere about Brooke rule, which had much to do with the new governor's liking for the people. Early on he noted how intermarriage with Chinese settlers had strengthened local population.

> The mixed breed of the Chinese with the Malay and the Dyak
> are a good-looking and industrious race, partaking more of the

Chinese character than that of the natives. . . This mainly arises from education and early formed habits, which are altogether Chinese; and in religion and customs they likewise follow, in great measure, the paternal stock. The race are worthy of attention as the future possessors of Borneo.[14]

Further Chinese settlement was encouraged as a means of developing agriculture beyond the native slash-and-burn technique. Charles Brooke, the nephew and successor of James, arranged for large numbers of Chinese immigrants to settle around Sibu, in central Sarawak, since in the 1880s he saw the country's future as an exporter of rice.

Support from British warships in the suppression of Sea Dyak pirates allowed James Brooke to consolidate his own position and overawe Brunei, which in 1844 presented the island of Labuan to the Royal Navy as an anchorage and coaling station. A permanent British garrison was installed within two years. James Brooke's own lucky survival of an uprising of Chinese tin miners in 1857 allowed the continuation of his dynasty, which steadily encroached on Brunei. London was never comfortable with Sarawak as an independent kingdom but, because its coastline commanded one of the two sea routes to China, the Royal Navy insisted upon its protection. After remarkable exploits during the First Opium War, the *Nemesis* had helped James Brooke defeat the Sea Dyaks at the battle of Beting Marau in 1849. *Nemesis'* paddles literally churned to pulp the wooden craft of the pirates. An outcry in Parliament over the £20,700 of "head money" paid to the ship's captain and crew by the naval authorities in Singapore hardly registered in Kuching. Because so many of the "pirate" heads were taken back to longhouses by James Brooke's own headhunters, his wars were always very popular. Royal Navy support for the Brooke regime remained a fundamental element in its Asian strategy, and especially after the French occupation of Saigon meant that another European power controlled the only other sea route to China.

"Indochine", the name by which the French knew the countries they occupied on the Southeast Asian mainland, well described the two distinct historical traditions they endeavoured to amalgamate in a single empire. At its two extremes were Vietnam and Cambodia: the former, despite its long resistance to Chinese domination, was a

The moonlit battle of Beting Marau in 1849. The steamer *Nemesis* made short
work of the pirates who opposed Charles Brooke

country profoundly influenced by Confucianism; the latter, though
a shadow of its former glory, was the lineal descendent of an Indian-
inspired kingdom. French authority was first established in the
Mekong delta shortly after the Anglo-French capture of Beijing.
Even before the Second Opium War, the French admiral Rigault de
Genouilly had attacked the port of Danang, intending to capture it
as a prelude to taking the Vietnamese capital of Hue. Ignorance of
the terrain and a lack of flat-bottomed boats restricted the attackers to the occupation of an offshore island. Heavy casualties from
tropical disease rather than fighting obliged de Genouilly to transfer
his gunboats southwards to Saigon, where French missionaries were
firmly installed. He boldly announced:

> The laws and customs of the country will be respected, but
> the courts and the police will act under French authority. The
> measures which I will take will bring commerce to the city.

> The justice of our administration, which will fairly protect the interests and rights of all, will attract numerous residents.[15]

Not until 1862 did France reach a formal agreement with the Vietnamese emperor Tu Duc: sickly and pessimistic by nature, he was almost resigned to French domination of his country. The Treaty of Saigon ceded three southern provinces, Bien Hoa, Dinh Tuong and Gia Dinh, as well as the island of Poulo Condore. A later treaty, signed in 1874, gave France control over all six provinces of Cochinchina, the name by which this French colony in Vietnam's southernmost region was known.

The French wasted little time in drawing up plans for the transformation of Saigon from a minor Vietnamese port into an elegant colonial city. It was to be the Paris of the East, an ambition evident today in its faded squares and boulevards. During the city's construction public squares were deliberately increased in size so that each district could enjoy a spacious garden, while an abundance of fountains were introduced to cool the air and provide drinking water. As there were no natural springs, water had to be brought by pipe from sources outside the city. The French governor's residence alone drew adverse criticism as it was said to look more like a railway station than a palace. It is possible that the absence of charm explains the location of a ball held in honour of Nicholas II, the tsar later killed by the Bolsheviks. It took place on a warship anchored in the Saigon River.

Although the French colonial authorities hoped that their rebuilt city would become a second Hong Kong, they were also intent on expanding beyond Cochinchina, and finding an inland route to China. In 1866, a young lieutenant by the name of Doudart de Lagrée was sent up the Mekong in order to see if it was navigable as far as the Chinese province of Yunnan. Lagrée and his five companions conceded defeat in mid-1867 at the Tungho rapids, which extend along the river for more than a hundred kilometres. Although the Mekong expedition may have failed in its prime objective, it gave the French a handy excuse to claim rights over adjacent Cambodia and, later in 1887, over landlocked Laos, a loosely organised kingdom lying east of the Mekong and next to Vietnam.

Thai pressure had caused the Cambodian monarchy to abandon the monumental splendour of Angkor and in 1431 found a new capital at Phnom Penh. Apart from the greater distance from the Thai border, the suitability of the new site lay in its location at the confluence of two rivers, the Mekong and the Tongle Sap, thus enabling a diminished Cambodia at least to maintain itself as a commercial state. Despite the loss of great ceremonial buildings, the position of the throne was not altered: powerful families might combine to oppose the ruler's wishes, but the loyalty of the people was never in doubt. As late as 1906, on the coronation of the 66-year-old Sisowath as king of Cambodia, the ruler was considered to be an embodiment of universal order. Sisowath's right eye represented the sun, his left the moon, his arms and legs the four cardinal points, the six-tiered umbrella above his head the six lower heavens, his pointed crown the top of thunder god Indra's palace on Mount Meru, the home of the gods. No matter that his kingdom was so overshadowed by France that it was the French governor-general of Indochina who handed Sisowath his royal regalia, the hallowed throne remained the focus of Cambodian political thought. Shortly afterwards the king attended the Colonial Exhibition at Marseilles, in the company of his royal dancers, perhaps without appreciating how he was something of an exhibit himself. There Sisowath's dancers made a tremendous impression and reminded Europe that Cambodia, and not Thailand, was the true custodian of Indian cultural traditions in mainland Southeast Asia. The recently arrived Thai had appropriated Cambodian traditions as late as their final capture of Angkor.

The practice of taking Thai and Vietnamese princesses as royal consorts in Phnom Penh inevitably produced two factions—one pro-Thai, another pro-Vietnamese. It was in fact the former that blocked a treaty with France in 1856, correctly guessing that the French would help Cambodia to recover the Thai-occupied provinces of Battambang and Siem Reap. In 1863, the French persuaded King Norodom to sign a treaty according France a protectorate over Cambodia. Later on they even got him to name his pro-French step-brother Sisowath as heir. Thus the French colonial era began without a shot being fired. But shots were fired on Norodom's behalf in the mid-1880s, when he faced a nationwide rebellion.

Already the French governor-general Charles Thomson exerted a tight control over Cambodian affairs. He had sailed from Saigon to Phnom Penh and forced Norodom to sign a new treaty, in which he accepted "all the administrative, judicial and commercial reforms which the French government shall judge, in future, useful to make their protectorate successful".[16] Doubtless a gunboat anchored within sight of the royal palace had an effect. Over the next decade, there was a steady increase of French influence, which in 1892 extended to taxation to cover the costs of what was actually a colonial administration. In 1916, thousands of peasants were to march through Phnom Penh, requesting Sisowath to reduce taxes, because, though the French determined their level, they were still collected by Cambodian officials. In spite of coinciding with more drastic anti-French protests in Cochinchina, the demonstration changed little because on Sisowath's orders the marchers quietly returned to their villages.

France's progress as a colonial power in Vietnam was inevitably slowed by the Prussian defeat of 1870–71. The capture of Napoleon III at Sedan, then the Commune in Paris, left the colonial authorities at Saigon uncertain about the policy they should adopt towards the ailing Vietnamese emperor Tu Duc. Because they were concerned to head off any competition by European rivals, especially Britain which was about to open an overland route to China via Burma, no restraint was placed on Brooke-like enterprise in the Red River valley. There the French trader and arms seller Jean Dupuis discovered this river was navigable all the way to Hunan, the province on which British traders from Burma had set their sights. He also realised that north Vietnamese salt fetched 30 times its price in Hunan. When the Vietnamese authorities in Hanoi tried to prevent Dupuis from towing upriver stolen junks filled with salt, he ordered his band of Chinese ruffians to seize a part of the city and run up the French colours. In a somewhat halfhearted fashion, the French authorities in Saigon came to Dupuis' aid and in 1874 it was agreed with Tu Duc that there would be concessions for France in Hanoi as well as Haiphong.

The Qing court regarded Vietnam, and in particular the northern province of Tonkin, as vital to the security of the empire's southern border. Not only had this area once been Chinese territory for a thousand years, but almost for the same length of time it formed part of the imperial tributary system too. Now the French were behaving as though China's suzerainty had come to an end. When Saigon reinforced its garrisons in the north, fighting broke out, and in 1883 a French relief force was ambushed and its commander was killed outside Hanoi. In response to a Vietnamese request, China sent troops to aid its vassal, but the French prevailed because their opponents could not match the weapons they used. Although on his deathbed Tu Duc had refrained from declaring war on France, his officials in Tonkin had issued proclamations that called on the people to take up arms against the French and even offered bounties for French heads.

In 1884 this French action in Tonkin ended Chinese suzerainty over Vietnam

The pro-colonial premier Jules Ferry embraced the enthusiasm of France for conquest, and additional troops were sent to humble both the Chinese and Vietnamese. Disarray in the Vietnamese court after Tu Duc's death, where in rapid succession a nephew, an uncle and a cousin came to the throne, ensured that there was no difficulty in imposing a protectorate over the whole country. Jules Ferry seems to have assumed that the acquisition of Vietnam would open up for France vast economic possibilities in the Chinese provinces adjacent to Tonkin. He said that

> the creation of the outlet with which we are now concerned will give us, in a certain future, free and even privileged exchange with China and, with that, markets of four hundred million inhabitants. . . not poor blacks like the inhabitants of equatorial Africa, but. . . one of the most advanced and wealthy people in the world.[17]

Though these commercial expectations were to be disappointed, because France was never able to seriously penetrate the Chinese consumer market, French industry came to rely on China for raw materials such as silk.

An immediate problem for the French was how to bring about a decisive victory over the Chinese. A two-pronged attack was tried, with mixed success. After a bombardment of the south China coast, 1,800 men were landed on Taiwan. This ridiculously small force had no chance of overcoming the island's garrison, even without an outbreak of cholera decimating its ranks. In Tonkin though, there was a chance of ending the war and in 1885 a defeated China signed a treaty with France expressly abandoning its long-standing tributary relationship with Vietnam. Hue accepted the severance of the historical link in the hope of retaining some prestige for his own Chinese-style government.

Examinations in Confucian learning were still the means of official preferment, although the father of the future revolutionary Ho Chi Minh refused an appointment in 1900 after gaining the highest qualification. He could not bring himself to serve a puppet emperor of the French. Ho Chi Minh himself was taught the Confucian classics by another scholar who rejected an official post, but he chafed over the lack of books written about Vietnamese history. He soon came to believe that traditional learning, the Chinese heritage of Vietnam, stood in the way of national renewal. In 1905, the year a modernised Japan defeated the Russians, Ho Chi Minh started to learn French, better to understand the colonial enemy. His impoverished father had had to take up imperial employment in Hue, where now there was no disguising the ineffectiveness of the throne. As far as Ho Chi Minh was concerned, the liberation of Vietnam from French colonial rule was the only goal that deserved proper study.

France's last addition to its possessions in Indochina was Laos, a landlocked kingdom at the mercy of Thai, Burmese, Vietnamese and Chinese arms. The Thai never made any bones about their interest in Laotian affairs and often placed a garrison in the royal capital, Luang Prabang. Their battles with Lan Na, a power centred on Chiang Mai, and Lan Sang, the original name of Laos, can be viewed as a struggle for leadership of the migrant Thai. Lan Sang was virtually a Thai kingdom, one of its early rulers calling himself Samsenthai, meaning king of 300,000 Thai.[18]

The re-emergence of Anglo-French colonial rivalry encouraged the movement from informal domination to direct control. There was for a time some talk of Laos acting as a buffer between the two imperial powers; an idea that came to nothing through the activities of Auguste Pavie. He offered the Laotian king French protection against Bangkok, whose troops had intervened in northern Laos shortly before France's victory over the Chinese. Pavie had great personal sympathy with the peoples of Laos and Cambodia and he worked actively to end Thai influence in both countries. The killing of a French officer by Thai troops in Laos conveniently brought matters to a head. French gunboats forced the defences of Bangkok in 1893 and threatened the city until Pavie gained his objective: a treaty that agreed to the whole of Laos east of the Mekong becoming a French protectorate and to the establishment of a 25-kilometre demilitarized zone on the river's west bank and along the western border of Cambodia.

Further territorial losses were conceded to France and Britain down to 1909, when these colonial powers decided that a shrunken Thai kingdom, rather than Laos, could act as a useful buffer between their holdings. The arrangement meant that the Thai were the only Southeast Asian people to avoid colonial rule. By aligning with Japan in 1942, Thailand could well have suffered

Western occupation at the end of the Second World War had the United States reciprocated the declaration of hostilities. As luck would have it, the Thai ambassador in Washington had already mentioned the likelihood of the military dictator Luang Phibunsongkhram in Bangkok supporting the Japanese. Because he insisted that Thailand had been betrayed "by one or two men, chiefly the Prime Minister", the ambassador was able to persuade the Americans to back the Thai people against the military dictatorship and its Japanese allies.[19]

In 1900, the French chose Vientiane as the administrative capital of Laos, from which they hoped to accelerate economic development. But the small population of the country, as did that of Cambodia, precluded the growth of a sustainable consumer market, for such trade as there was remained tied to the needs of subsistence farmers. Efforts to persuade Vietnamese immigrants to increase agricultural production were soon regarded as a failure, since those who moved to Laos preferred to be traders or hold positions in the French administration. Food supply has remained a persistent problem, the government of an independent Laos being forced as late as the 1970s to import rice because of drought. Apart from the vagaries of the weather, Laotians lack the rich alluvial soils of Cambodia and Vietnam.

In British Burma, public works were deliberately used to stimulate the economy, notably the building of railways and irrigation projects. Interestingly, it was a French offer to construct a railway between Mandalay and Hanoi that finally ended Burmese independence. Seeking the friendship of France was a high-risk strategy for the Burmese king Thibaw, who in 1878 seized the throne in a bloodbath. Neither Calcutta nor London was willing to countenance foreign involvement in what was perceived as a British sphere of influence. As earlier in India, Britain responded to a French threat by yet another war and outright annexation. Burma formally became a colony in 1886, although the resistance to direct rule tied down 30,000 British and Indian troops for more than four years. Large numbers of Burmese died in a series of uprisings throughout the country, but the imposition of a colonial government ended French penetration of a valuable market and abolished monopolies previously enjoyed by the Burmese nobility. A consequence was British exploitation of increased trade in timber as well as rice. Of all the

A British attack on Borneo pirates, a policy endorsed by the Americans

rice sold worldwide in 1914, mainland Southeast Asia supplied 90 per cent, of which 60 per cent came from Burma.

The American Colony of the Philippines

Perhaps the oddest Western colonial venture in Asia was the American occupation of the Philippines. Just as Britain had not acquired an empire there by accident, but through intense competition with France, so the United States could not reasonably claim that its annexation of the Philippines occurred in a fit of absentmindedness. Although it suited President William McKinley to portray the event as an unforeseen result of American intervention in the Spanish Caribbean, the truth is that he had already decided to advance his country's position in the Pacific by means of the acquisition of key islands.

In 1899, McKinley disingenuously told Methodist church leaders how he had appealed for divine guidance about the future of the Philippines:

> I walked the floor of the White House night after night until midnight; and I am not ashamed to tell you, gentlemen, that I went down on my knees and prayed to Almighty God for light and guidance. And one night it came to me in this way. . . that we could not give the islands back to Spain—that would be cowardly and dishonourable. That we could not turn them over to France or Germany, our commercial rivals in the Orient— that would be bad business and discreditable. . . That there was nothing left to do but take them all, and educate the Filipinos, and uplift and civilize them, and by God's grace do the very best by them as our fellow-men for whom Christ also died. And then I went to bed, and went to sleep and slept soundly.[20]

American missionaries were soon to be disconcerted by the discovery that the Filipinos were Christians already, having been forcibly converted to Catholicism by Spain. Worse still there remained in the south of the Philippines a sizable Moslem population whose determination to resist conversion was by no means weakened by the ousting of the Spaniards. Even in post-colonial times, a powerful separatist movement among the Moros on the southern island of Mindanao continues to trouble the Filipino democracy.

When McKinley took the presidential oath in early 1897, a revolution was in progress on the island of Cuba, barely a hundred kilometres from the US coast. Popular support for the rebel cause among Americans, who saw Spain as a weak colonial power from which they had already taken vast territories on the mainland, failed to persuade the new president to officially recognise the rebels. He preferred to hold Madrid fully responsible for protecting US lives and property, while behind the scenes pushing for enough Cuban autonomy to stop the rebels fighting. Spain refused point blank. It saw no reason to liquidate what little was left of a once-mighty empire that had spread right round the globe.

The Spanish choice of Valeriano Weyler y Nicolau, a tough professional soldier, as the commander-in-chief was a mistake, however.

He tried to break the back of the revolution by rounding up thousands of Cubans and placing them in barbed-wire concentration camps. Implementing the policy effectively was beyond the means of the Spanish military, and inadequate housing, food and sanitation carried off some 100,000 internees. Nicknamed "the Butcher" in American papers, Weyler ignored the bad publicity and pressed on with a brutal campaign. Reinforcements from Spain seemed to give him the upper hand over the rebels, who were compelled to operate in small guerrilla bands, but as the Liberal Party leader, Práxedo Mateo Sagasta, observed in Madrid: "After having sent 200,000 men and having spilt so much blood, we are masters in the island only of the land upon which our soldiers stand."[21] Such trenchant criticism ought to have brought about a change in policy: instead the Spanish government hoped for a military solution to the Cuban conflict until it was too late to influence events. An eventual offer of home rule was seen by the rebels as a means of undermining their will to fight, while loyalists regarded the concession as proof of Spain's inability to win the war.

With Weyler relieved of his command and efforts being made to treat with the rebels, loyalists were joined by soldiers in riots at Havana in early 1898. There was even talk in Spain of Weyler staging a military coup against the new Liberal government of Sagasta, the advocate of Cuban autonomy. McKinley did nothing except move a warship, the *Maine*, into Havana harbour to protect US interests. When on 15 February an explosion sank the *Maine* and killed more than 200 sailors, the United States concluded that a bomb had been placed on board by saboteurs. More likely it was an explosion in the engine room, but the sinking of the warship through an unfortunate accident was not something an agitated American public then chose to consider possible. Because he remained convinced that the United States was unready for war, McKinley was content to wait two months before its declaration. Another reason for the delay was worry about the foreign entanglements that might follow after defeating Spain.

One casualty might well be the traditional US open-door policy towards a tottering Chinese empire, because Japan's easy victory over China in Korea during 1894–95 had unleashed fresh demands for territorial concessions. Though Japan was stopped from occupying the strategically important Liaodong peninsula, Russia took its place and constructed naval facilities at Port Arthur, while in 1897 Germany seized Qingdao in nearby Shandong province. At pains to reassure the Germans that a new British base at Weihaiwei, on Shandong's northern coastline, was intended to counter Russia rather than Germany, the lease gained in 1898 greatly strengthened Britain's position in north China. The Royal Navy used the unfortified port until the British government gave up the lease in 1930. Thwarted on the mainland, the Japanese added to their empire Taiwan and the islands of the Pescadores, which lie between Taiwan and the Chinese coast.

Aware of the threat to stability posed by Japanese aggression, McKinley thought he had found a solution to American weakness in Asia with the acquisition of the Philippines. There Spain was facing a parallel uprising to that in Cuba. Commodore George Dewey was ordered by Washington to prepare his squadron, anchored off Hong Kong, for an attack on Manila. Once hostilities between the United States and Spain commenced in Cuba, Dewey steamed south and, passing Subic Bay en route for Manila, commented on its suitability as a future US naval base. Had the Spaniards bothered to prepare its natural defences against assault, the Americans would have not won so easily. As it was, the Spanish admiral responsible for Manila's defence could not make use of Subic Bay: no heavy guns had been mounted and only five mines were positioned to protect the harbour. He was obliged to keep his ships close to Manila, where they were placed in a defensive position ready for the American attack.

Dewey's fixed intention was to do battle with the Spanish fleet on arrival, despite the dangers from guns and mines at the entrance to Manila Bay. At night, five American cruisers and a gunboat successfully entered the bay in single file and at dawn opened fire on the Spanish fleet, which surrendered just after noon. On hearing the news of the great victory, McKinley promoted Dewey to admiral, while Congress presented him with a jewelled sword designed by Tiffany's.

Less concerned about the loss of Cuba than the Philippines, Spain despatched in mid-June a squadron consisting of two battleships, two cruisers, three destroyers and two troopships carrying 4,000 soldiers, along with four colliers. No ships or reinforcements were sent to the Caribbean. To avoid early contact with US warships, the Spanish squadron headed for Manila via the Suez Canal. Dewey was therefore faced with a repeat of his own attack unless he moved his ships elsewhere. In the event he did not need to redeploy because utter defeat in Cuba persuaded Spain to negotiate an end to the war. An American expeditionary force under the command of Wesley Merritt, a Civil War veteran like McKinley, had already landed to join forces with Dewey and capture Manila. The president instructed Merritt to establish in place of Spanish colonial rule an American military government, since McKinley realised that he would have to control all the Philippines if Manila was to become a permanent American base.

Adroit handling of the Senate and Congress allowed McKinley to consolidate American influence in the Asian Pacific. He annexed Guam, the chief island of the Spanish Ladrones, the present-day Marianas. Guam was in fact the first American conquest of the Spanish-American War. Its governor had mistaken three shots fired by an American warship as a naval salute, apologising for not returning the courtesy because he lacked any cannon. No news of hostilities had reached the island's tiny Spanish garrison. Another McKinley acquisition in 1898 was Hawaii, whose mid-Pacific location provided a vital base for American warships heading towards the Philippines. He was spurred into action by Japanese interest, whose imperial government envisaged some kind of union between Hawaii and Japan. The idea anticipates the aim of the Greater East Asia Co-Prosperity Sphere 60 years later, when its imperialist propaganda called for Hawaii's reunion with Asia.

Notwithstanding the development of naval facilities at Pearl Harbor, the greatest asset to the United States, as Dewey foresaw, was Subic Bay, still a key naval base today. It gave McKinley a lodgement in Asia from which he could conveniently use force to maintain the cherished open-door policy. He must have been gratified to read in the *Presbyterian Banner* how the United States had been "morally compelled to become an Asiatic power. . . America and Great Britain will see to it that China is not Russianized".[22] After the Russo-Japanese War of 1904–05 though, it was much less certain that Washington could keep Japanese encroachment on the Chinese mainland in check. As the radical critic of Tokyo's drive for empire Kotoku Shusui realised, American intervention would only serve to strengthen Japanese determination to guard their own interests. For Japan looked upon the American colony of the Philippines with a mixture of fascination and frustration. How could the first people to escape from the clutches of European colonialism presume to restrain other imperial powers while becoming imperialists themselves?

In 1901, Kotoku Shusui wrote *Imperialism, the Monster of the Twentieth Century* to highlight the evil of colonial expansion. His standards were part Confucian, as he quoted the Chinese philosopher as saying the people should be made comfortable before teaching them. The imperial government, he insisted, was using imagined foreign glory to distract the Japanese people from their domestic ills. And he was deeply depressed by the fashion of imperialism spreading to the United States. Frightened by the first large-scale strike in Japan, a decade later the imperial government hanged Kotoku Shusui and eleven others for conspiring to assassinate the emperor. The trumped-up charge was intended as a warning to social reformers, whose writings were thereafter subject to official scrutiny before publication: intellectual freedom was an early casualty of Japan's drive for an overseas empire. Although Kotoku Shusui was right in anticipating that a conflict between the United States and Japan would have to precede the emergence of his own country as a major economic power, he failed to envisage how this industrial

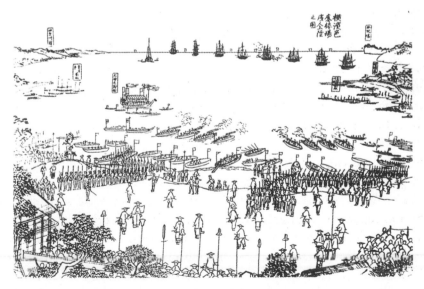

A Japanese view of the Perry's arrival at Yokohama in 1853. US interests in the Pacific made the Philippines an inevitable colonial acquisition

transformation might occur in post-colonial Asia. In 1901 he had pointedly asked the question: "If the United States truly fought for freedom and independence in Cuba, why does it try to deny the freedom and independence of the Philippines?"

It was something the Filipino rebels pondered as soon as American intentions became clear. The rebel leader Emilio Aguinaldo had originally welcomed the US force that defeated Spain, but McKinley paid little attention to Aguinaldo until he declared a Philippine republic in January 1899. The fighting that began the next month continued for three years because, realising that conventional tactics would fail against the United States, Aguinaldo ordered his army to dissolve into guerrilla bands and to take to the countryside. At first, Washington believed its forces could subdue the rebels without difficulty. As in a number of wars fought in Asia during the twentieth century, and most notably in Vietnam, this assumption proved to be completely wrong. Thousands of US soldiers struggled to contain Aguinaldo's guerrillas and, in despair, a policy of concentration was adopted along the lines of "the Butcher" Weyler. The use of concentration camps inflamed anti-imperialist opinion in the United States, where a Baltimore journal could not decide whether it was more ironic or tragic that "we have actually come to do the thing we went to war to banish".[23]

Not even the Gatling gun, whose hand-cranked multibarrel had just dealt such destruction to equally barefoot opponents during the American Indian campaigns, could overcome the hit-and-run tactics of the Filipino insurgents. The final advance in gun manufacture in the colonial era, the machine gun allowed an infantryman to fire from a concealed position, in any weather, 15 rounds of ammunition in as many seconds at targets a kilometre away. The Maxim gun, which superseded the Gatling, was light enough to be carried by hand: its lethal discharge was to change warfare forever after 1914, when Western nations chose to turn the weapon against each other.

That American military technology was totally inadequate for the task of conquering the Philippines finally dawned on Washington. Treating the Filipinos like "Red Indians" was bound to increase the savagery of the conflict, a racial dimension not lost on Arthur MacArthur, the father of the Second World War general

Douglas MacArthur. Appointed military commander in 1900, the older MacArthur rapidly came to the view that only devolution of power to a civil government would quell the insurrection. Cultivating wealthy landowners, who stood to gain from cooperation with the Americans, he managed to isolate the rebels from mainstream Filipino politics. The capture of Aguinaldo by means of a ruse was an absolute godsend. At Manila in 1901, the rebel leader swore an oath accepting the authority of the United States over the Philippines and pledging his allegiance to the American government. Even though his call for an end to hostilities was not heeded by all his followers, the rebellion was beaten and the Philippines became the US equivalent of Hong Kong.

An aggrieved Aguinaldo had to await the coming of the Japanese for his revenge, yet independence within the Greater East Asia Co-Prosperity Sphere was not the exciting prospect of freedom for which Filipinos had fought Spain as well as the United States. An American campaign to end the embarrassment of colonial rule had already succeeded in getting Congress to pass the Philippines Independence Act, which prescribed a preparatory period during which the colony was to be a semi-autonomous commonwealth under a government of Filipinos. The date for independence was actually scheduled for 4 July 1946. The contrast between the resistance shown to the Japanese in the Philippines and the Dutch East Indies was noted by President Franklin D. Roosevelt, who at once began to consider new political arrangements for a post-war settlement. With the active support of a Labour government in Britain, they were to bring down the final curtain on Western colonial power in Asia.

The Russo-Japanese War

The first serious challenge to Western supremacy in Asia came with the Japanese defeat of Russia in 1905. Relations between the Russians and the Japanese had deteriorated badly after the Boxer crisis of 1900, since Tsar Nicholas II had been encouraged by his advisers to use the anti-Christian movement in China to occupy the whole of Manchuria. By 1902, there were more than 100,000 troops to protect an influx of Russian colonists. The following year, full Russian authority was established at Port Arthur and Evgeny Ivanovich Alekseyev arrived as the first viceroy. The 60-year-old uncle of Nicholas, Alekseyev managed to upset not only his own senior officers but, by his arrogant manner, also provoke Tokyo into a war for which Russia was ill prepared. It is possible that the Russians believed that Japanese cooperation during the Boxer uprising was a sufficient guarantee of peace. Of the 45,000 troops sent by the countries whose diplomats were besieged by the Boxers in the Legation Quarter at Beijing, half were Japanese. They were instrumental in putting down this latest outburst of protest at the continued dismemberment of the Chinese empire. By foolishly backing the Boxers, the Manchu empress Ci Xi had in effect declared war on Britain, Germany, France, Russia, Austria-Hungary, Belgium, Holland, Italy, Spain, Japan and the United States. From Manila 5,000 US troops were ordered to China, where McKinley used their presence to reaffirm an open-door approach designed to preserve Chinese territorial and administrative integrity.

For Tokyo this policy seemed a convenient means of getting the Russians to evacuate Manchuria, long an objective of Japanese imperialism. When they ignored diplomatic pressure and behaved as if it were now an integral part of the Russian empire, Tokyo determined on war. In St. Petersburg, the Russian minister of finance, Sergei Yulievich Witte, feared the outcome of such an event, but he was powerless against the hard-liners who thought Russia could obtain whatever they liked in Asia because the Japanese would not dare to fight. Witte also concluded that the tsar "in his heart thirsted for glory that would come from a victory". Recalling a meeting with the Japanese ambassador, he recognised how Russian procrastination only served to provoke Japan still more. The envoy

> told me how my country was dragging out negotiations while his was acting with dispatch. Japan would make a proposal, Lamsdorff (the Russian foreign minister) would say that matters were in Alekseyev's hands, while Alekseyev and Rosen (the Russian ambassador to Japan) would say that their hands were tied because the Tzar was away. To Japan this sort of tactic meant that we want war, and he felt it a matter of honour to do what he could to prevent conflict. Time was short, he argued. Japanese public opinion was becoming increasingly aroused and was

therefore difficult to keep under control. After all, he declared, Japan was a sovereign state, and it was humiliating for her to have to negotiate with some sort of "viceroy of the Far East", as if the Far East belonged to Russia and Japan was but a protectorate.[24]

When a delayed series of Russian responses merely brushed aside the Japanese proposals, which included formal recognition of Japan's interests in Korea, Tokyo concluded that hostilities were inevitable. That they opened without a prior declaration of war by either side surprised the world.

On 6 February 1904, ten Imperial Japanese Navy destroyers, all built in Britain between 1898 and 1902, staged a night attack at Port Arthur against Russian ships, badly damaging two battleships and a cruiser. Admiral Togo Heihachiro knew that Japan's hopes in the war depended on total control of the sea. Lacking enough ships to blockade the two Russian naval bases of Vladivostok and Port Arthur at the same time, he struck at the latter without warning. Togo Heihachiro devised his mini-Pearl Harbor because he dared not expose the few ships under his command to the extremely powerful coastal forts there.

The treaty port of Amoy, present-day Xiamen. The Japanese attack on Port Arthur followed the aggressive British approach to China

Japan had two new battleships nearing completion in British yards but, once fighting began, Britain prohibited their delivery. Tokyo still remained deeply mistrustful of Britain, the strongest naval power in Asia waters, but in 1902 it had secured an Anglo-Japanese alliance. Then with the Boer War not quite over, the British Army in India was short of 11,000 men and the defence of the northwest frontier seemed perilous in the event of a Russian invasion. Should this happen, Britain hoped for relief through a Japanese attack on Russia's Pacific coast. An alliance with Britain was equally attractive to Japan for the good reason that it did more than ensure British neutrality: apart from denying the Russian fleet assistance from the ubiquitous facilities of the Royal Navy, there could be no question of a British loan to finance St. Petersburg's war effort.

The Imperial Japanese Navy moreover enjoyed the benefit of close liaison with the Royal Navy, which kept it informed on the movements of the Russian Baltic Fleet during its fateful voyage eastwards. In the company of other officer cadets, Togo Heihachiro had gone to Portsmouth and Cambridge in the 1870s for training. Even the bricks that built Japan's own naval academy at Etajima on the Inland Sea were imported from Britain. Etajima laid emphasis on the offensive, a Royal Navy doctrine which Togo Heihachiro was about to exemplify best at the battle of Tsushima.[25] During the First World War, when Japan sided with the Allies, the Imperial Japanese Navy actually joined forces with the Royal Navy, sending in 1917 a squadron of 12 ships to the Mediterranean, where they earned an excellent reputation operating out of Malta against enemy submarines. The British government was grateful for their assistance in the protection of convoys, just as in the opening months of the war it had welcomed Japanese willingness to chase German raiders from the high seas.

Viceroy Alekseyev refused at first to credit the disaster of the night attack at Port Arthur. Not until the three torpedoed warships limped back into the inner harbour, and settled one by one in its shallows, was his confidence shaken. An attempt to put on a brave face by parading in full uniform around the town on horseback was undercut by an order that stories about Port Arthur's lack of preparedness must cease immediately and that rumourmongers would be severely punished. Had the inhabitants known how Japanese soldiers were already using Korea as a staging post for an overland attack, then no amount of bluster or censorship would have prevented outright panic.

A second attack launched by Togo Heihachiro, on this occasion in broad daylight, completed the naval blockade of the port on 9 February. About 30 heavy shells fell on the town itself, but the damage was restricted to the waterfront. International reaction to the attacks was coloured by a deep disdain for Nicholas' government, whose belligerence abroad was matched by an indifference to violence at home. Little was done to curb the murder of Jewish citizens, the most notorious instance being the massacre at Kishinev, a town close to the Black Sea. Of the ten men subsequently charged in 1902 with the killings, six were acquitted, and the four who were found guilty were sentenced to four years' imprisonment. As a result of the general antipathy towards Russia, *The Times* was unmoved by the unannounced Japanese attack on Port Arthur. In an editorial it declared:

> Our ally put her navy in motion with a promptness and courage that exhorted the admiration of the world and her action in doing so before war had been formally declared, so far from being an international solecism, is in accordance with the prevailing practice of most wars in modern times.[26]

Although American newspapers were less generous in their praise, there was support for Japan, and a war loan was easily raised in New York. One prescient American, the conservative Henry Adams, advised caution. He wrote to a friend how "all are anti-Russian, almost to a dangerous extent. . . I am half-crazy with fear that Russia is sailing straight into another French revolution which may upset all Europe and us too".[27]

St. Petersburg grossly underestimated the difficulty of supplying an army on a war footing by means of the single-track Trans-Siberian railway, and even more the tremendous voyage that any naval reinforcement would have to undertake to sail from the Baltic or the Black Sea. Within weeks of Togo Heihachiro's night attack the Imperial Japanese Army had an expeditionary force of 300,000 men opposing the Russians, who were soon besieged at Port Arthur. By the spring of 1905, when the battle of Mukden was fought, the Japanese had almost one million soldiers in the field, a total somewhat below the Russian strength. Casualties at Mukden were 70,000 Russians killed or wounded against 75,000 Japanese; another 20,000 Russians were taken prisoners. These figures reveal the ferocity of the action, an aspect of the fighting that impressed the military observers who flocked to witness this first "modern" war. The large number of Russian prisoners baffled the Imperial Japanese Army. After offering stiff resistance, the Russian infantrymen suddenly gave up the fight. Discipline collapsed as troops turned against their own officers, rifled their baggage, stole their horses and tried to flee.

Port Arthur had already surrendered at the start of January. As at Mukden, the courage of the Imperial Japanese Army led to substantial losses: 57,000 dead or wounded out of a total force of 90,000 men. Ignoring the tactical advantage of prepared positions, the Japanese commander Nogi Maresuke ordered his troops into costly frontal attacks. In spite of the poor construction of Port Arthur's defences, the Russians were able to concentrate a deadly fire against their suicidal attackers. Capturing one strongpoint alone cost the Japanese 16,000 casualties. Reprimanded for the rising casualty rate, Nogi Maresuke was neither relieved of his command nor expected to slacken his efforts. On the death of his second and favourite son in action, he told a member of his staff that now he knew how to apologise to the Japanese emperor for losing so many men: he could say that the Nogi family had suffered too. Yet it was not Japanese courage, but the spread of scurvy among the defenders that brought the siege to a close. When Nogi Maresuke committed suicide after Emperor Meiji's death in 1912, the overwhelming majority of Japanese people believed that he had been moved by remorse over the soldiers who were so unnecessarily slain at Port Arthur, a comforting thought for the bereaved. Unknown at the time was that the fanatical general's ritual disembowelment was not the only occasion on which he had attempted suicide. Twenty-five years earlier he tried to kill himself after losing a regimental flag in a campaign against opponents of the restored imperial government.

Then the emperor had ordered him to desist, but the shame never left him and its burden may explain his repeated orders for all-out attacks at Port Arthur.

A final disaster at sea had still to be inflicted upon Russia. In an effort to break the Japanese naval blockades of Vladivostok and Port Arthur, the Russian Baltic fleet left Europe in November 1904. After sailing around Africa, because the British refused permission to pass through the Suez Canal, the Russian armada passed through the Straits of Malacca and headed north, still 3,500 kilometres short of Vladivostok. Reaching French Indochina, its commander, Zinovy Petrovich Rozhestvensky, loaded welcome food supplies and fresh water while awaiting orders from the tsar. When the admiral suggested that it was too late to proceed, Nicholas would hear nothing of a withdrawal and he instructed the naval authorities to prepare Vladivostok for Rozhestvensky's belated arrival.

Thus a course was set for a battle in the Straits of Tsushima, between Korea and Japan. The 50 warships in the Russian armada composed one of the biggest fleets that had ever sailed together, but its superior numbers did not mean it surpassed Togo Heihachiro's. It is true that the Russians possessed more battleships, but the Japanese were much stronger in destroyers and cruisers, and these faster vessels were to prove invaluable when Togo Heihachiro out-manoeuvred Rozhestvensky during the two-day engagement in what were after all home waters for the Japanese admiral. On 14 and 15 May 1905 he annihilated the Russian fleet, Rozhestvensky's flagship *Suvorov* being disabled after barely half an hour, so accurate was the Japanese gunnery. The *Suvorov* lost masts, funnels, guns and all electrical power. As its decks blazed it was like "a peasant hut on fire", according to Nikolai Ivanovich Nebogatov, who took over command from Rozhestvensky. He ordered the surrender to Togo Heihachiro, who generously congratulated him on bringing his ships without harm from the Baltic to the Pacific.[28]

The naval defeat was decisive in persuading Russia to negotiate for peace. The tsar had no option but let President Theodore Roosevelt mediate and send Witte to the United States as negotiator. That Witte had always opposed the war was a last ironic twist in the sorry tale of Nicholas' Asian misadventure. The Treaty of Portsmouth left Japan in a perfect position to pursue its imperialist aims on the Asian mainland, although Washington remained convinced that China could be saved from Japanese interference. It was a pious hope. Well before the Russo-Japanese War there were calls in Japan for an imperial mission aimed at checking Western influence. The manifesto of the ultra-patriotic Black Dragon Society declared that it was "the urgent duty of Japan to fight Russia. . . and then lay the foundation for a grand continental enterprise taking Manchuria, Mongolia and Siberia as one region".[29] After 1905, it was easy to add north China to the wishlist.

The resounding victory at Tsushima was of course won by warships built outside Japan. But the alacrity with which Japanese firms responded to the tide of patriotic fervour that flowed from Russia's dramatic humiliation can be seen in the subsequent figures for naval construction. More than 200 major vessels were built before Pearl Harbor, including Japan's first aircraft carrier, the *Hosho*. The 7,500-ton *Hosho* was the second warship after *HMS Hermes* to be designed from the keel up as a carrier and in 1921 the first to be completed. During the Pacific War, the *Hosho*'s aircraft complement was restricted to fighters because of the short length of its flight deck. The tiny aircraft carrier's chief role then was providing defensive cover for the fleet.

Part 2

An Asian Challenge

Chapter 4

The Advent of Imperial Japan 1868–1941

It seemed very strange to me that the Japanese army should be mobilized because of a rebellion in Korea, and that they should be dispatched to the peninsula to fight another army from China. The Shimizuya bookshop in the meantime was busily stocking three-leaf coloured prints of the war . . . (which) were immensely popular with us boys, who would stand gazing at them almost daily.

Tanizaki Junichiro's childhood memories of Tokyo

The Meiji Restoration

The second half of the nineteenth century in Japan witnessed great changes. In the 1860s, the country was still divided politically into many feudal domains under the ebbing authority of the Tokugawa shogun in Edo, present-day Tokyo. By 1900, imperial Japan was the only modern state in Asia, having abolished feudalism and imported from the West the institutions, finance and technology necessary for the establishment of an industrialised economy. Recognition of this new international status led Britain in 1902 to sign an alliance with Japan. The Japanese government warmly welcomed the British initiative as an admission of its rightful place in Asian affairs. Popular enthusiasm for an alliance with the world's leading naval power stemmed from memories of the humbling of Japan by American warships.

Commodore Matthew Perry set sail in 1853 for Japan with orders to open up the country by force if necessary. So ill prepared were the Japanese that along the shore they had installed false batteries made from black canvas, which the American sailors dubbed "dungaree" forts. Fully appreciating the weakness, Perry refused to communicate through either Dutch or Chinese intermediaries and insisted that the letter he carried from the American president be received and replied to by the Japanese themselves. A compromise of sorts was agreed, whereby Perry would land and hand over the letter to a nobleman on a quiet beach with the minimum of ceremony. Afterwards, a witness wrote how the American officers treated the Japanese "in such a polite and friendly manner as to win their good will, while not a single point to which we attached importance was yielded. There was a mixture of firmness, dignity and fearlessness on our part, against which their artful and dissimilating policy was powerless."[1] The task completed, the Americans returned to their ships and weighed anchor. No sooner had the smoke from the funnels of the steamers cleared than argument broke out over the best course of action that the supreme warlord, the shogun, should adopt.

Shogun Tokugawa Iemochi was at a total loss. In theory the emperor's commander-in-chief, he was actually the last in a line of military dictators. It had long been the policy of such warlords to isolate the emperor from current events, and encourage the idea that he was some sort of a living god involved in an endless round of ceremonies. The policy backfired shortly after Perry's return for an answer to the president's letter because a group of reformers were able to exploit the supposed divinity of the emperor to push through radical changes. At the time of the abolition of the shogunate and the imperial restoration, the coup seemed little more than a shift of power from one section of the aristocracy to another. But the events of 1868, which Perry's intervention in Japanese affairs had provoked, were to inaugurate a thorough transformation of the country's economy and society. The motive power for change came from the samurai, warriors who like the emperor himself had little more than a ceremonial role. Their attention was focused on the problem of remaining financially solvent, rather than the finer points of swordplay, because their stipends could not provide a reliable income in a money economy. Although samurai might carry two swords, and have the right to behead a peasant on the spot for an insult, it was the town dwellers who now owned Japan's wealth.

On Perry's return in early 1854, the Japanese response to American requests was limited. They agreed to give protection to shipwrecked sailors and opened two relatively inaccessible ports for obtaining coal and provisions. There was no commitment to international trade. In 1858, Townsend Harris, the US consul at the isolated port of Shimoda, succeeded in getting more ports opened to American traders, but the continued mismanagement of the

Sir Harry Parkes with the shogun at Osaka. The emperor-shogun relationship was then still troubling Japan

Japanese economy hampered commerce. Time was fast running out for warlords, however, and after a brief civil war in 1868, the whole country acknowledged the rule of the new young emperor. That year, he had selected a slip of paper from among others placed before him. It bore the two characters "bright" and "rule", and thus gave his reign its name, Meiji.

For the British ambassador, the imperial restoration was a relief, because he considered that until the emperor–shogun relationship was satisfactorily resolved, Japan could never attain a stable government. The envoy was none other than the ubiquitous Parkes, now Sir Harry. It was he who took the lead in finally settling the commerce issue, which the Emperor Meiji accepted by means of a treaty with Britain, France, Holland and the United States. The American author, John Russell Young, contrasted the US ambassador John Bingham with Parkes in these terms:

> Mr. Bingham, whose keen face grows gentler with the frosty tints of age, is in talk with Sir Harry Parkes, the British minister, a lithe, active, nervous, middle-aged gentleman, with open, clear-cut Saxon features, the merriest, most amusing, most affable gentlemen present, knowing everybody, talking to everybody. One would not think as you followed his light banter, and easy rippling ways, that his hand was the hand of iron, and his policy was the personification of all that was hard and stern in the policy of England.[2]

This was in 1879. Young was then accompanying Ulysses S. Grant and his wife on a round-the-world tour. Of equal interest are the remarks that the ex-president of the United States addressed to the Japanese emperor. "European powers have no interests in Asia, so far as I can judge from their diplomacy, that do not involve the humiliation and subjection of Asiatic peoples," Grant said. "The diplomacy is always selfish, and a quarrel between China and Japan would be regarded as a quarrel that might ensue to their own advantage."[3]

The dispute to which Grant referred was over the ownership of the Ryukyu Islands, the largest of which is Okinawa. Equidistant from Japan, Korea and the Chinese province of Taiwan, the tiny Ryukyu kingdom sent tributary missions to Beijing, although its people spoke a language closer to Japanese than Chinese. The Meiji government had no hesitation in placing the kingdom under Japanese rule in 1871, a move that China described as an act of extreme contempt not only towards itself but all other countries. Perhaps the cool reception that Grant's remark received was not such a surprise to the ex-president, who already had been obliged to review the Japanese army. He told Emperor Meiji that he was a reluctant soldier and disliked nothing more than military parades. So fond was the emperor of the army, however, that he indulged his commanders, exercising little control over their decisions in the field, a habit that was to suit very well the more aggressive generals who were to serve his grandson, Hirohito. Not that this meant that Emperor Hirohito bore no responsibility at all for the Second World War spreading to Asia: he agreed in late 1941 to the surprise attack on Pearl Harbor and similar plans for British Malaya.

In 1872, the custom of celebrating the emperor's birthday was instituted by government order as a religious festival. Two years before this elevation of the throne, all households were required to register with a local Shinto shrine, whose purpose was the worship of the Japanese gods and showing respect to the emperor. With Buddhism rudely pushed to one side, and its ceremonies entirely banished from the imperial palace, the way was open for the rise of emperor worship as an integral part of Japanese nationalism. Emperor Meiji was even declared a direct descendant of the sun goddess Amaterasu. On his accession Emperor Meiji had transferred his place of residence to Tokyo, where a new palace arose on the site of a Tokugawa stronghold. His presence was a great political asset for the reformers, who renamed Edo: it became Tokyo, meaning "Eastern Capital".

Preoccupied with material progress through national prosperity and defence, the Meiji government strove to develop the strategic industries on which modern military power depended. It took the lead, too, in developing modern communications, the extraction of raw materials and the mechanisation of textile manufacture. But the strain on the imperial exchequer proved too great, and in the financial retrenchment during the 1880s, most of the government holdings were sold cheaply to supporters in the business community, even to officials. This expedient had the accidental effect of concentrating much of Japan's nascent industrial sector in the hands of the few people with enough money to buy factories and mines. Once the initial difficulties of industrialisation were overcome, and the national economy put back on a steady course, their energetic new owners came to dominate nearly all production. By the 1920s, they had created financial combines such as Mitsui and Mitsubishi, each of which encompassed a great variety of enterprises, including banking, extractive industries, manufacturing companies, transportation and trading firms. Mitsui began as brewers in the seventeenth century, turned to money lending and became the official banker for the Tokugawa family, besides opening shops in Edo, Kyoto and Osaka. The company's rare ability to make the transition from feudalism to the modern world owed much to Minomura Rizaemon, the first non-family appointment to the post of general manager. He moved the firm's headquarters from Kyoto to Tokyo, and then sent members of the Mitsui family and employees to the United States to study modern business methods.

Yet it was Mitsubishi, Japan's second-largest combine, that would help create a powerful navy, because it possessed shipyards at Yokohama, Kobe and Nagasaki: they were able to supplement the hectic pace of warship construction being undertaken at imperial navy yards. With the evolution of carriers, from the miniature *Hosho* to the mighty *Akagi*, the company moved into the production of carrier aircraft, its most notable fighter being the Zero. The plane's agility and speed combined with a phenomenal range of 1,200 kilometres to make the Mitsubishi Zero the master of the Asian skies before the advent of more powerfully engined US aircraft from 1943 onwards.

The Meiji transformation was unique. The swiftness of its modernisation of Japan took the European colonial powers by surprise. What they underrated was the peculiarly Japanese talent for absorption and imitation. Some Japanese leaders were of course worried about the pace of change, because they believed that Japan was fundamentally different from other countries and should preserve its own values to avert the social dislocation so evident in European nations. As the soldier–premier Katsura Taro commented in 1908:

> We are now in an age of economic transition. The development of machine industry and the intensification of competition widens the gap between rich and poor and creates antagonisms that endanger social order. Judging by Western history, this is an inevitable pattern. Socialism is today no more than a wisp of smoke, but if it is ignored, it will some day have the force of a wild fire, and there will be nothing to stop it. Therefore, it goes without saying that we must rely on education to nurture the people's virtues; and we must devise a social policy that will assist their industry, provide them work, help the aged and infirm and, thereby, prevent a catastrophe.[4]

In retrospect, it can be seen that this conservative social programme was really an extension of the feudal practice of keeping the people under firm control. Its urgency was fear of what imported ideas might do to the Meiji restoration.

After the heady days of learning exciting new things from the West, the Meiji government had moved step by step to rein in Japanese excitement over foreign ideas, so that standardised textbooks, ethics courses and uniforms soon prevailed. The school system acted as the means of getting the official message across. By 1900, nearly every child received a basic education, and its state-approved instruction stamped a uniform outlook on most Japanese minds. Beyond elementary school, the government had less influence on the curriculum, although military virtues were deliberately inculcated during the Russo-Japanese War. In 1917, military training was formally introduced into secondary schools. An education commission declared that its object was

> to create a strong and healthy people by improving physiques through training and to develop knowledge and skills in military matters and thereby cultivate loyalty by moral discipline, and to lay the foundation for future military training, an essential element of education in Japan today that cannot be slighted.[5]

Starting in 1925, serving military officers were assigned to boys' schools as the Imperial Japanese Army sought to deepen its pool of recruits. What had begun under the Meiji government as a quest for national security had by then turned into preparation for a showdown with the West. Anti-war books such as Kotoku Shusui's *Imperialism, the Monster of the Twentieth Century* were already banned and the American film *All Quiet on the Western Front* was severely cut before it could be shown in Japanese cinemas. Not much of this anti-war classic remained after the censors put away their scissors.

A New Balance of Power

The Sino-Japanese War of 1894–95 first galvanised the Meiji government into giving serious thought to the purposes of education. It was realised that a well-behaved population was not enough for an imperial power. Education also needed to inspire support for the drive to empire and, among boys, a willingness to die for the emperor in time of war. A piece prepared by teachers in one elementary school famously met the bill. Displayed on the school noticeboard, it read:

> September 22, 1894. Battle report. Japanese troops defeat Chinese at Pyongyang and win a great victory. Chinese corpses were piled up as high as a mountain. Oh, what a grand triumph. Chinka, Chinka, Chinka, Chinka, so stupid and they stinka.[6]

The easy victories obviously fed a sense of national superiority, which increased by leaps and bounds after the Japanese defeat of Russia a decade later. The conscription law of 1873, introduced at the insistence of Yamagata Aritomo, laid the foundations of the Imperial Japanese Army. Universal male conscription represented a critical change in Japanese attitudes to war, as it dispossessed the samurai of their monopoly of arms and with it their status as a military elite. Since the samurai had never approached 10 per cent of the population, and their skills revolved around swordplay and archery, they were in Yamagata Aritomo's eyes quite inappropriate for an up-to-date army.

Nineteenth-century Hong Kong, the envy of the European colonial powers

Yamagata Aritomo had studied military organisations in Britain, France and Germany before his appointment to a senior post in the Japanese military department. He was insistent that conscripts were to be drilled in Western tactics and organised into units regardless whether they were samurai or commoners. Former samurai disdained their fellow soldiers, especially if they remained in the ranks themselves. Their unease was not just a question of snobbery though, for many conscripts were unhappy about their forcible recruitment as soldiers. Drunkenness among soldiers was so prevalent in Tokyo on the eve of the Sino-Japanese War that a newspaper lamented how "the martial spirit has greatly declined in our country of late and there are even those who . . . escape conscription!"[7] Yamagata Aritomo was concerned, too, because he saw the conflict as the first test of Japanese patriotism.

Intervention in Korea, the scene of the Sino-Japanese War, came about through the Tonghak rebellion. While small in comparison with the Taiping uprising in China, the Tonghak rebels were imbued with the same sense of frustration at a remote and corrupt government. Its founder, Ch'oe Che'u was another Confucian scholar denied of an official career. Unlike the Taiping leader Hong Xiuquan however, he did not resort to arms and lead a rebellion, possibly because the Korean dynasty was one of great age and not a foreign house like the Manchu one in China.

Having burned his books and left his well-to-do home in quest of understanding, Ch'oe Che'u was convinced after wandering the Korean peninsula for a decade that the end of the traditional world was at hand. Mystical experiences added to a conviction of his own destiny in remaking society, as the appointed agent of the supreme deity on earth. In all probability, shamanism moulded Ch'oe Che'u's basic view of god and man as inseparably linked. Slogans such as "all men are sages and princes" were bound to frighten an entrenched aristocratic order, and in 1864 the visionary was beheaded for propagating false doctrines.

After Ch'oe Che'u's death, the Tonghak went underground but membership continued to rise till it felt sufficiently strong to demand tolerance. Before the gates of the royal palace in Seoul, several thousand members petitioned in 1893 for an end to suppression and a posthumous exoneration of Ch'oe Che'u. When the Korean king refused, the Tonghak movement became a revolutionary peasant uprising. In desperation, officials let it be known that they were willing to listen to grievances, but the Tonghak reform programme was now far too radical for acceptance. It demanded the punishment of corrupt officials, the ending of noble immunity for misconduct, the abolition of slavery, the right of young widows to remarry, fair examinations for recruitment to the civil service and, not least, the imprisonment of those who collaborated with the Japanese. This last demand turned out to be the significant one, because it branded the Tonghak as an anti-Japanese organisation at the very moment Japan wished to assert its suzerainty over Korea.

In a state of panic, the Korean government hastily appealed to China, the traditional protector of Korean kings. Within a month, a Chinese force landed at Asan Bay, to the south of Seoul. When Japan also sent a contingent of troops, the two powers faced each other in an increasingly tense situation. After the Tonghak rebels withdrew to southern Korea and the threat to Seoul was removed, China proposed to Japan that as the reason for stationing Chinese and Japanese troops in the peninsula no longer existed, there should be a joint withdrawal, a proposal that had the support of the Korean

Japanese conscripts about to embark for Korea, where their effectiveness reassured the Meiji reformers

government as well as the European colonial powers. Determined to expel the Chinese once and for all from Korea, Tokyo ignored this suggestion and declared war on 1 August 1894. Engagements on land and sea had already taken place. At Songhwan, a short distance from Seoul, a clash cost the Imperial Japanese Army 82 dead and wounded: Chinese casualties ran into the hundreds.

Off the Korean coast the Imperial Japanese Navy had also gone on the offensive, intercepting Chinese reinforcements and inflicting damage on an enemy cruiser. It was on this occasion that a British merchant vessel, the *Kowshing*, transporting over a thousand Chinese soldiers, was deliberately sunk by Togo Heihachiro. The Japanese admiral had ordered the *Kowshing* to stop and, when this order was disregarded, he opened fire. The captain and two other British officers were rescued, but the Chinese crew and troops were left to drown. This assault on the British flag was not treated in London as more than an unfortunate event: not wishing to fight Japan on China's behalf, the *Kowshing* failed to rouse the same level of indignation as the earlier *Arrow* incident. But Togo Heihachiro's brutality undoubtedly helped the Imperial Japanese Army retain the initiative as it denied to the Chinese the shortest route for dispatching reinforcements to Korea.

Having taken control of Seoul, the Imperial Japanese Army provoked a confrontation with Korean guards and used this as a pretext to occupy the royal palace. The queen and her children were taken as hostages to the Japanese embassy while the king was kept virtually as a prisoner in his own capital. The treatment of King Kojong by Japanese army commanders deeply offended the Korean people, who thereafter looked upon the Tonghaks, not as rebels, but loyalists pledged to rid the country of an uncouth invader. Even though Japan gained enormously after the Sino-Japanese War from its greater control over Korean affairs, the hatred of the Koreans towards the Japanese was to be a permanent feature of future relations.

The Japanese advance into Manchuria after retreating Chinese forces revealed their prime target as Port Arthur, a strategic prize at the tip of the Liaodong peninsula. Finding the mutilated remains of Japanese prisoners within the port's defences, the captors rampaged on 21 November 1894 through the nearby city, killing and wounding thousands of civilians. This outrage was regarded by Japan's admirers in the West as nothing more than an aberration, a naïve response to the cruelty for which the Imperial Japanese Army was to become notorious later on. The massacre of Chinese civilians at Nanjing in 1937 and the murder in 1942 of staff as well as patients at Alexandra Hospital in Singapore were but two of its better-known acts of barbarity.

Perhaps a late realisation in Tokyo that the West would never permit a Japanese occupation of Beijing helped to bring an abrupt end to hostilities. As the Japanese were about to discover, even the terms they wanted to impose on a defeated China greatly displeased the European colonial powers. As a result, they were obliged to evacuate the Liaodong peninsula, but in compensation allowed to annex Taiwan and the Pescadores Islands. When the Russians instead of the Japanese occupied Port Arthur and extended its naval facilities, it became clear that Russia and Japan were heading for conflict. Yet Japan's victory over China served to raise its international standing. A firm supporter of the conflict, the Japanese foreign minister Mutsu Munemitsu noted the advantages as well as the disadvantages of winning:

> The effects of our military successes against the Chinese . . . enhanced our position and our influence in the eyes of our countrymen and observers abroad, and permanently disabused the Western powers of the degrading notion that Japan was little more than a superficial imitator of civilization. No longer did they conceive of Japan as simply a beautiful Oriental garden . . . we now commanded the world's respect (but) we had also become an object of some envy.[8]

A Chinese warship sinking at the start of the Sino-Japanese War

Mutsu Munemitsu had always argued that a protectorate over Korea would be the best outcome for Japan, because economic benefits must flow from imposed reforms.

There were indeed some Korean officials who acknowledged Japanese progress and hoped through a close relationship to gain from their experience of modernisation. One was Kim Hong-jip, a key member of the pro-Japanese government installed after the detention of King Kojong. For a time, Kim Hong-jip enjoyed the king's favour and a concerted attempt at reform was tried in the face of strong opposition. King Kojong in early 1895 had visited the royal ancestral temple and vowed to his ancestors that he would push forward with the task of modernising Korea. Yet the increasing Japanese pressure encouraged those Koreans who disliked the drift towards Tokyo to look elsewhere for external support, finding a ready ally in Russia. A pro-Russia faction quickly formed in the Korean government, in spite of Kim Hong-jip remaining its head. As this arrangement did not suit the Japanese, they assassinated the Korean queen, the person whom they held responsible for this political realignment. Queen Min had in fact moved against one of Kim Hong-jip's closest allies when she heard that he was plotting to force her abdication. A party of Japanese civilians and policemen, some of them dressed in Korean uniforms, cut down the queen in the royal palace. No mercy was shown to her, alive or dead: the queen's corpse was carried on a plank to a courtyard, where it was doused in kerosene and set alight. King Kojong and his son had already been badly manhandled for failing to divulge Min's hiding pace. Despite the attempt of the Meiji government to distance itself from the murder of Kojong's consort, its sheer audacity did more harm to the reputation of Japan than the Port Arthur massacre. Fearing that he was next in line for either deposition or assassination, the king took refuge in the Russian embassy at Seoul for a whole year.

Anti-Japanese protests continued until the outbreak of the Russo-Japanese War. Once Russian opposition to Japanese encroachment ceased after defeat in 1905, there was no power prepared to save Korea: Britain and the United States quietly acquiesced in the tightening of Tokyo's grip over the country, for they were more interested in preserving China intact than any of its tributary states.

Outright annexation was not yet on the Japanese agenda as the resident-generalship of Ito Hirobumi illustrates. Three years before he took up office in 1906, the Meiji government concluded that Japan would secure "national defence through the protection of Korean independence". Looking at Lord Cromer's informal domination of Egypt as a model suitable for Korea, Ito Hirobumi had restrained those in Tokyo who would have denied the Koreans any say in their own affairs. Having forced a protectorate upon Korea though, Ito Hirobumi was as little trusted by the Koreans as he was by his more belligerent Meiji colleagues. Japanese soldiers had accompanied him in 1905 to the royal palace in Seoul and restrained Korean officials who objected to the "agreement" that they were made to accept.

Adopting Lord Cromer's approach to the Egyptians, Ito Hirobumi felt that true independence for the Koreans was necessarily a long way off. Whether the resident-general would have relished the view Cromer took of modernisation outside the West is less certain, because the British proconsul held that educated colonials retained all the customs and prejudices of their own people under a top-dressing of Western learning.[9] It may be that this observation was too close to the mark for a Japan that made no pretence that modernisation would ever lead to Western-style democracy. The political system the Meiji reformers had established came from above: it was granted by the emperor himself. What no one foresaw at this time was how easy it was going to be for the Imperial Japanese Army to hijack the constitution for its own purposes. In 1909, the resident-general was killed by a young Korean nationalist. Ito Hirobumi's last words were "What a fool!" The next year Japan annexed Korea.

General Terauchi Masatake, Ito Hirobumi's successor as resident-general and the first governor-general, was an entirely different man. He compelled the Korean government to agree to annexation, forced Kojong's son to issue a proclamation yielding both the throne and the country to Japan, and inaugurated a repressive colonial regime that lasted for 35 years. Terauchi Masatake declared the maintenance of law and order to be the highest priority of his administration, and to achieve this end he employed the dregs of Korean society as his bully boys. They were to become infamous as camp guards of Allied prisoners during the Second World War. After an initial reign of terror, Japan's newest colony settled down to effective and sustained passive resistance, which hoped to gain from the principle of self-determination that the US president, Woodrow Wilson, proposed in 1918. It was on the basis of this principle that the old empire of Austria-Hungary was broken up and new countries such as Czechoslovakia came into existence. Even though defeat for the Democrats in the 1920 presidential election turned the United States towards isolationism, Wilson's radical ideas were never quite forgotten, either at home or abroad. The Japanese would go on crushing with apparent impunity peaceful Korean demonstrations, in 1919 burning protestors alive in a church at Sunron, near Seoul; but the logic of this aggression would lead in turn to the nemesis that streamed from Pearl Harbor. In the fullness of time, it liberated the Korean peninsula from Japan, albeit as two states, rather than as a single country.

In 1910, the leading position of Japan in Asia went unquestioned. The defeats inflicted on China and Russia had brought about a new balance of power in which the Japanese were recognised as a major force. Tokyo's attempts to exclude Manchuria from the scope

The Audience Chamber at Beijing. Empress Ci Xi's unwillingness to accept change ensured the collapse of the Chinese empire

of the open-door policy towards China had damaged relations with both Britain and the United States, but not yet to the extent that these two powers were moved to take any action. However, major events soon were to provide Japan with ample scope for a further imperial advance: first, the overthrow of the Qing dynasty in China and, second, the outbreak of the First World War in Europe. The end of the Chinese empire in 1912 left the country in the hands of warlords, notwithstanding Sun Yatsen's declaration of a republic. For the next two decades these provincial commanders exercised virtually independent authority over large areas of China. Not until the troops belonging to the leader of the Guomindang, the premier warlord Chiang Kai-shek, reached Beijing in 1928 was there any semblance of unity. Even then the so-called Northern Expedition had to bypass Japanese units stationed in Shandong province, before driving the forces of the Manchurian warlord Zhang Zoulin from the old imperial capital. His assassination by the Japanese, who blew up the armoured train in which he fled, may not have been so opportune for the Guomindang as it first seemed. Eight years later, it was his son, Zhang Xueliang, commander of the anti-communist expedition in Shaanxi province, who devised the Xi'an Incident, when at the point of a gun Chiang Kai-shek agreed to a truce with the Chinese Communist Party and a united front against the Imperial Japanese Army.

In 1914, the outbreak of the First World War seemed to Tokyo an ideal chance to establish Japanese rights and interests in Asia. As an active ally of Britain, the conflict opened the way for the pursuit of a more vigorous foreign policy unimpeded by the restraining hand of the European colonial powers. Besides the assistance given to the Royal Navy, Japan's main contribution to the Allied war effort was the seizure of German bases on the Shandong peninsula and in the Pacific. In spite of allied requests for the dispatch of troops to Europe, Tokyo limited its military cooperation outside Asia to sending units of the Imperial Japanese Navy as convoy escorts in the Mediterranean. Unusually for most participants in the First World War, Japan was strong enough and remote enough from the main theatre of operations to remain secure whoever won.

Prime objectives for the Japanese were the territory of Qingdao, held by Germany on a long lease from China, which comprised the

Jiaozhou naval base and a railway line into mineral-rich Shandong province, and Germany's islands in the northwest Pacific: the Mariana, Palau, Caroline and Marshall groups. Qingdao surrendered without much resistance after being surrounded by the Imperial Japanese Army, while the defenceless Pacific islands were seized by the Imperial Japanese Navy without bloodshed. Another objective, which only became clear to the Allies during the course of the war, was the ousting of the anti-Japanese president of China, Yuan Shikai. After the Japanese capture of Qingdao, Yuan Shikai had cautiously asked the Imperial Japanese Army to withdraw its soldiers within the boundaries of the leased territory. In response Japan presented the Twenty-One Demands, which amounted to a virtual Japanese protectorate over the new Republic of China. Yuan Shikai made great efforts to involve other countries in opposing these demands, but it soon became apparent that the war against Germany was the Allies' top priority. Only the still nonbelligerent United States expressed its disapproval and forced Japan to moderate some of them. The outcome was nonetheless a considerable expansion of Japanese interests in China, most notably in Manchuria.

As the war in Europe approached its end, the situation became ever more favourable to the advancement of Japan's imperial ambitions. The United States had entered the war in 1917, and the Russian Revolution erupted the same year. Now prime minister, Terauchi Masatake tried to improve Japan's chances of getting international recognition of its rights in China by placating Britain, and so he ostentatiously endorsed Winston Churchill's policy of intervention in Russia. Premier Lloyd George warned his war minister against committing the country to a "purely mad enterprise out of hatred for Bolshevik principles" and urged Churchill to consider the domestic consequences of such action.[10] The Allies were already in occupation of Vladivostok, because it was feared that military stores landed there by Britain and the United States might be transferred to Germany. Throughout 1918, Germany had looked to a defeated Russia for the supply of foodstuffs, fodder, oil and minerals.

President Wilson had at first refused to involve the United States in Russia until strong pressure from Britain and France made him relent. The Australian leader Billy Hughes, while in Washington on his way to London, found members of the Senate foreign affairs committee "distinctly in favour of intervention, provided the operation was a joint one and not conducted by Japan alone".[11] Vladivostok and its environs were therefore declared to be under Allied protection, and 9,000 Japanese troops arrived with a similar number of Americans. Within two months, Terauchi Masatake had increased the Japanese contingent to 70,000 men. Even though they stayed in Vladivostok the longest, Tokyo was lukewarm about joining any anti-Bolshevik crusade, because Terauchi Masatake preferred a joint-defence treaty with China aimed at preventing revolutionary influences spreading from Russia. Its inestimable advantage was the right of the Imperial Japanese Army to move freely throughout northern China.

During 1919, the Red Army expanded to more than three million men, and the logistical and political obstacles to operations against it were enormous. What is more, some 30,000 of its officers previously had been commissioned under the tsars. Leon Trotsky, the creator of the Red Army, had succeeded in portraying intervention as an attack on Holy Mother Russia, rather than on the Bolshevik regime. In addition, the propaganda he put out to Allied troops usually began with the question: "The war is over, why are you not returning home?" There were mutinies among British and French conscripts drafted to Russia. In August 1919, a group of British sailors mutinied on learning they were to return to the Baltic. When 45 made their way to London to present a petition of protest, they were arrested at King's Cross railway station. Faced with such a level of discontent and too financially stretched to sustain a long campaign against the Bolsheviks, Britain scaled down Churchill's dream of intervention to the provision of military advice and equipment.

By 1920, the civil war in Russia had moved decisively in the Bolshevik regime's favour, with the result that the Allies wrote off the Whites. Only on Russia's Pacific coast was a non-Bolshevik state still in existence: the Far Eastern Republic. The Soviet-Polish War of 1919–21 had forced the Red Army to redeploy units from Siberia. That reduction in strength, plus the continued presence of Japanese forces, persuaded Moscow that the sovietisation of Russia's Pacific provinces would have to be postponed. Better a buffer between Moscow and Tokyo than providing the Japanese with an excuse to entrench themselves on the Russian mainland. As soon as the last troops of the Imperial Japanese Army quit Vladivostok in summer 1922, the Red Army overran the Far Eastern Republic. A White resurgence there could not be tolerated, notwithstanding the "last of the White Mohicans" being such a motley bunch. They were so undisciplined that one commander dismissed 10,000 men from the ranks, as well as hundreds of officers.[12] Having served its purpose, the Far Eastern Republic was absorbed into Soviet Russia on 15 November 1922.

Thwarted though Japan was in Russia, it had gained a great deal from participating in the First World War. At the peace conference in Versailles, it received equal representation as a great power, less than 20 years after negotiating an end to its unequal treaties with the West. Britain had given up the right of extra-territoriality long before concluding the Anglo-Japanese Alliance of 1902. And, along with France and Italy, Britain endorsed Japan's claim to German rights in Shandong province, leaving the United States in lonely opposition. Because the Chinese wanted to regain complete sovereignty over the leased territory, they withdrew their delegation from Versailles without signing the peace treaty. Popular indignation over the news of the award of Qingdao to Japan compelled this unprecedented action. In Beijing, the May Fourth Movement, spearheaded by about 3,000 university students, had spread from Tiananmen Square to the American embassy, where concern was expressed to the ambassador, and on to the houses of pro-Japanese ministers, which were burned to the ground. The impact of this spontaneous demonstration upon China was out of all proportion to its size: in towns and cities, meetings were held and a boycott of Japanese goods inaugurated.

This anti-Japanese outburst took Tokyo less by surprise than the row that broke out at the peace conference when Japan proposed a clause in the treaty concerning racial discrimination. Britain and the United States allowed the Australian premier Billy Hughes to take the lead in opposing this proposal. The British government thought that imperial unity might be threatened unless Australia and New Zealand retained the right to exclude Japanese immigrants. President Wilson was afraid, on the other hand, that the Senate might reject his plan for a League of Nations if the Pacific coast states were forbidden to discriminate against them as well. In 1900, California had passed an Asian exclusion bill and, in San Francisco, a city ordinance actually segregated Asian and non-Asian children at school. Without much success in 1907, Japan offered to no longer allow labourers to emigrate to California, provided the state stopped discrimination against its existing 24,000 Japanese residents. For Billy Hughes, the maintenance of "White Australia" was actually a war aim: he said that Australia had gone to war "to maintain those ideals, which we have nailed to the very top of our flag-pole".[13] Fear of the "yellow peril" in Australia was to be converted into the "red rash" after the Second World War, when the People's Republic of China became the new Asian bogeyman. Political pamphlets appeared showing Australia festooned with red spots, a symptom of dangerous ideological contamination.[14]

The argument at Versailles created the impression that the Japanese were good enough to be asked for help yet not good enough to be recognised as an equal in the white man's imperial club. Nonetheless, it was disingenuous of Emperor Hirohito to suggest much later that a cause of Japan's entry to the Second World War was the rejection of the racial equality clause: he knew only too well how the Japanese had a pecking order of their own for Asian peoples. As did European colonialists, they tended to regard their subject peoples as inferior. The Koreans were categorised as backward and lazy, an attitude reflected in the lower pay scales of Koreans in the colonial administration and a marked reluctance to employ qualified Koreans in Japanese banks, firms and factories. In 1938, Korean businessmen appealed for a greater share in the colony's economy. Pro-Japanese Hyon Chunho said:

> In the area of business too, indeed, in each area of business, especially where lucrative, profitable business is possible, I would like to ask you to apportion shares—and beyond that, apportion, for example, even directors' shares—among Koreans as well as Japanese.[15]

Possibly the plea fell on deaf ears because Hyon Chunho spoke the Japanese language poorly in spite of a university education in Tokyo. He was regarded as being still insufficiently assimilated to a higher culture. This attitude was even more stark in Manchuria, where it was announced that the role of Japanese settlers was to "lead and enlighten" the Chinese inhabitants, who lacked "moral guidance". Belief that technological advance was a result of racial superiority justified Japan's ruthless exploitation of Manchuria and other parts of north China. One commentator even cited smell as an important measure of racial difference, by describing his utter revulsion at the body odour of "a crowd of Chinese coolies".[16]

Revolution in China

Whereas Japan's response to the West was modernization, that of China was revolution. On 1 January 1912, the world's oldest and most populous empire became a republic. Sun Yatsen and his followers were delighted with its up-to-date governmental machinery, quite overlooking the massive jump that the Chinese people would have to make to turn the Republic of China into a democratic reality. Between these republicans and the majority of the Chinese people there was only one point of agreement: the correctness of overthrowing the Qing dynasty. Within a decade of its foundation, the Republic of China was the plaything of warlords, regional commanders who converted their provinces into virtually autonomous areas. Not that this really mattered because Cao Gun, who had left his forces to take up a government position in Beijing, had already debased politics. A photograph published in 1923 showed nationwide the 5,000 yuan cheque with which he had bribed one elected representative so that he could become president.[17]

Cao Gun wasted his money. The following year, the Manchurian warlord Zhang Zoulin occupied the ex-imperial capital and remained there until the Northern Expedition arrived in 1928. It was indeed the rivalry of the warlords that convinced Sun Yatsen that he needed to resort to force if republican institutions and national unity were to be preserved. In the south of China, far away from the fighting among the northern commanders, Sun Yatsen set up a base for the country's reconquest, thereby converting the Guomindang from a political party into an armed movement. This alteration would allow his successor Chiang Kai-shek to end up as China's supreme warlord. Mao Zedong had reached a somewhat different conclusion to Sun Yatsen.

He told Edgar Snow that warlord suppression of a student demonstration at Changsha in 1920 made him "more and more convinced that only mass political power, secured through mass action, could guarantee the realisation of dynamic reforms".[18]

The prelude to the Guomindang and Chinese Communist Party's resort to arms was the uneasy transfer of power from an imperial to a republican system of government. Prince Zaifeng, the father and regent of the last Qing emperor Pu Yi, had tried to return power to the central government and in particular to the imperial court. Too much authority had leaked out to provincial governors and army commanders during the period of Empress Ci Xi's ascendancy. She had a weakness for powerful men and indulged her favourites, one of whom was Yuan Shikai. Sidelined by Zaifeng for most of Pu Yi's short reign, Yuan Shikai was recalled when news reached Beijing in late 1911 of the uprising at Wuchang, one of the three cities which form the Yangzi river port of Wuhan. The reinstated general slowly advanced to the Yangzi: his pace was politically motivated, as he was secretly negotiating with the rebels. With China's only really modern force under his command, there was nothing the Qing imperial house could do to stop Yuan Shikai.

On 12 February 1912, Pu Yi was obliged to abdicate in Beijing and the general was declared president by an unanimous vote of the provisional assembly in Nanjing, Sun Yatsen stepping aside so as to prevent civil war. It was unfortunate for China that the European colonial powers preferred the regime which Yuan Shikai ran in Beijing, and floated enormous loans for its benefit, when so many of Sun Yatsen's southern revolutionaries were such uncritical admirers of Western democracy. Europe hardly batted an eyelid when, as his enemies predicted, Yuan Shikai tried to restore the Chinese empire with himself as ruler.

Yuan Shikai encouraged the idea of an imperial restoration throughout 1915 and he celebrated the winter solstice in the Temple of Heaven at the close of the year. He was driven in an armoured car down Beijing's great central avenue to the 90-minute ceremony. The entire route was covered with yellow sand, as was customary for an imperial progress. At the Temple of Heaven, Yuan Shikai changed his military uniform for a robe embroidered with dragons. The first emperor of the Great Constitution, as Yuan Shikai's dynasty was

The imperial palace's main entrance at Beijing. The deposed Qing emperor, Pu Yi, remained in residence until 1924

rather ambiguously styled, was announced on 1 January 1916. At once the Japanese openly encouraged Yuan Shikai's subordinates to reject this seizure of power. And it has to be said that the move was seen by a large number of Chinese as the final betrayal of the would-be dynast, who had successively betrayed the reforming emperor Guang Xu and the child-emperor Pu Yi. Within months his imperial ambitions were finished, and asylum in the United States was under consideration when Yuan Shikai died in June, after a collapse brought on by nervous exhaustion.

But the Republic hardly enjoyed a breathing space because, at the request of several ministers tired of the political wrangling in Beijing, the warlord Zhang Shun then intervened. The "Pigtail General", as Zhang Shun was called for his retention of the queue as a sign of loyalty to the deposed Qing dynasty, decided that only a return to imperial government would work, and on 1 July 1917 he announced the restoration of Pu Yi to the Dragon Throne.[19] According to Pu Yi,

> the excitement was intense and citizens who did not have any flags handy made them out of paste and paper. Qing court attire which had disappeared for a few years appeared on the streets.

184

It was as if the dead had stepped from their coffins in their burial clothes. The press brought out extras about the restoration . . . Taylors made and sold dragon flags; secondhand clothing shops found that Qing court dress became their best-selling items since the newly appointed officials all wanted them; and theatrical supply shops were besieged with requests for artificial queues made out of horsehair . . . But it all lasted little more than five days. Everything changed when an aeroplane from the forces stationed at Tianjin dropped some bombs on the palace. Then there were no longer people to kowtow to me and there were no more imperial edicts to read. Furthermore, most of the high officials who had a hand in government matters disappeared.[20]

The air raid was a warning to the 11-year-old Pu Yi, and it worked. He realised that "the pilot did not really mean business", because the three small bombs he dropped caused little damage and injured a single person. A week later, Zhang Shun's troops were defeated close to Beijing and Pu Yi was deposed once again.

The luckless Pu Yi was not expelled from the imperial palace until 1924. Then Zhang Zoulin drove him to seek safety in the Legation Quarter, where Japanese diplomats welcomed Pu Yi with open arms. Later, they persuaded him to head the puppet state of Manzhouguo, which covered most of Manchuria. In 1934, he received the title of emperor once again, not from a Qing relative but from Emperor Hirohito of Japan. Impotent though he was in his second empire, Pu Yi paid for his collaboration with the Japanese after the establishment of the People's Republic. Branded a "war criminal", he had to undergo a thorough self-examination of his past actions before his rehabilitation in 1959 as a gardener.

Arguments over the legality of the governments that followed Zhang Shun's abortive restoration of Pu Yi bedevilled politics down to Chiang Kai-shek's capture of Beijing in 1928. Well might the Guomindang present the Northern Expedition as an end to the civil turmoil, but its success depended on the acquiescence of other powerful military commanders, with whom the Generalissimo, as Chiang Kai-shek now chose to be called, had to accept alliance. With the assistance of Shanghai financiers, Chiang Kai-shek outwitted them all but still there was no peace: from the early 1930s the Chinese Communist Party emerged as a real threat in the south, and after the death of Zhang Zoulin, the Japanese took over large parts of north China. In 1931, the latter were able to set up in Manchuria a separate state called Manzhouguo, the "Manchu Kingdom".

Skilful though Chiang Kai-shek was in balancing the various forces within Guomindang politics, he conspicuously failed to match the Chinese Communist Party with any programme of popular appeal. For the Generalissimo, uncritical obedience was enough. To many foreign observers though, he seemed a national saviour who ended the chaotic conditions of the early republic and warlord periods, a return to which business interests argued would bring irrevocable ruin to trade and endanger the substantial investments already made in the Chinese economy. They preferred to overlook the uglier aspects of the Guomindang regime. Scant notice was taken of the bullying tactics of the Blue Shirt Society, a parallel of the Italian Black Shirts and the German Brown Shirts, while the spoils of office, the vast fortunes amassed by senior members of the Guomindang, went almost unremarked, even though it was rumoured that Chiang Kai-shek used the craft of the Opium Suppression Superintendence Bureau to traffic in the drug himself.

Although the capture of Beijing had obliged European powers to acknowledge Guomindang rule at last, policy towards China never really advanced beyond the gunboat era. The British were quite typical in their insistence that the Yangzi was an international waterway, the last vessel in their Yangzi River Flotilla, *HMS Sandpiper*, being launched as late as 1933. Britain's continued ambivalence about the Republic of China was adroitly used by Japan to lend a degree of respectability to its own aggression. American fears were already aroused as the Japanese steadily built up Asia's most powerful war machine. This new threat seemed worse in Washington than it really was because Tokyo still enjoyed an alliance with Britain that had been made in 1902, and then renewed in 1905 and again in 1911. If the United States and Japan did fight each other, it was not impossible that at sea the Americans could find themselves fighting against the Royal Navy as well. So the United States in 1920 persuaded Britain to replace its Japanese alliance with the Washington Naval Treaty, essentially a means of maintaining the status quo for battleships in Asian waters.

An early view of Singapore. In 1915 an Indian regiment mutinied there when its Moslem rankers learned that Turkey had sided with the Central Powers

For the British, the treaty was a blessing in disguise. The severe postwar economic downturn gave Britain limited scope for expanding its ageing battle fleet, with the result that London welcomed parity in capital ships with the United States and an advantage over Japan. Most welcome of all was the new focus on cruisers because the Royal Navy possessed the largest number of modern cruisers afloat. By signing the Washington Naval Treaty, Britain saved millions of pounds on constructing warships and the Royal Navy remained superior to any other navy, with indeed a sufficient superiority to send a fleet to Asia while having enough vessels to act as a deterrent in European waters. Because Royal Navy ships permanently stationed in Asia were only capable of a holding action against the Imperial Japanese Navy, it was decided to develop Singapore as a fortress and naval base that could hold out against assault until relieved by a fleet sent from Britain. The Washington Naval Treaty, and other security arrangements that soon followed on from it, were resented in Japan, where many believed that they had been agreed by civilian leaders who had no understanding of imperial defence. Even greater anger was caused when the negotiators, under

Pu Yi, the last emperor of China and the only emperor of Manzhouguo,
in Manchu costume

intense American pressure, allowed the return of Qingdao to China.
Though they had won grudging acceptance from the West, Japanese
imperial ambitions were far from being satisfied, and in 1937 they
plunged Japan into an undeclared war with China which dragged on
until the outbreak of the Pacific War. The unresolved Sino-Japanese
conflict was to be a major factor in Tokyo's rash decision to launch
surprise attacks on Pearl Harbor and British Malaya.

Before the agreement of a truce between the Guomindang and
the Chinese Communist Party in response to Japanese aggression,
Chiang Kai-shek had moved against the bases that Mao Zedong established in south China. The first two Guomindang offensives, in 1930
and early 1932, were repulsed by guerrilla tactics. The third encirclement, directed by Chiang Kai-shek himself, was interrupted by the
Mukden Incident, a Japanese pretext for the creation of Manzhouguo.

The Imperial Japanese Army blew up a railway line near Mukden, in central Manchuria, and then used the incident as a reason for attacking Chinese troops in the area. This unilateral action brought down the Japanese government, the last one in which politicians predominated until after the Second World War. Assassinations of ex-ministers in early 1932 underscored the loss of civilian authority in a country gripped already by ultra-nationalism. Nothing that the Imperial Japanese Army did in China was thereafter considered to be wrong, not even its immediate spread of fighting to Shanghai.

A boycott of Japanese goods in that port-city hit trade hard, while strikes in Japanese-owned factories crippled production. To divert international attention from Manchuria and humiliate Chiang Kai-shek, another incident was touched off in the port-city. It expanded into a full-scale engagement, which involved 30,000 Japanese soldiers. As there were not yet enough men available for a final showdown with the Guomindang, Tokyo was relieved to arrange a ceasefire in Shanghai. Chiang Kai-shek could now turn his attention to the Chinese Communist Party with such effect that by the end of 1934 total defeat stared it in the face. The only hope was to break through the Guomindang encirclement and regroup elsewhere. In October therefore, the Long March began, an epic of human endurance lasting 370 days and covering 8,000 kilometres. Withdrawal to the northeast corner of Guizhou province was the first objective, a move covered through a rearguard action mounted by guerrilla bands, largely comprising men unable to travel a great distance because of wounds. But continued harassment from Chiang Kai-shek's forces made it plain that an overall plan was required. This was devised at the Zunyi conference in January 1935, when Mao Zedong became leader of the Chinese Communist Party. Taking up his slogan "Go north and fight the Japanese", the conference endorsed a strategy of rural conflict and agreed that they should head northwards to Yan'an, the only remaining base in Shaanxi province. Though Chairman Mao, as he was called after Zunyi, had at his disposal a captured horse, the 43-year-old leader walked most of the way during the march. He carried a price of 250,000 yuan on his head.

It is no accident that Chairman Mao came to power at the very moment Japanese forces readied themselves for action. The likelihood that, to avoid a war, the Guomindang might reach a general settlement with Japan was disastrous for the Chinese Communist Party, against whom joint action by the Imperial Japanese Army and Chiang Kai-shek's forces had already been mooted in Tokyo. When the Guomindang indicated no great reluctance over extending diplomatic recognition to Manzhouguo or granting a not dissimilar "autonomy" to other provinces in north China, the Chinese Communist Party became very alarmed and embraced Mao Zedong's nationalist approach. Within the higher levels of the Guomindang, there were those who believed that the liberation of Asia from Western colonial power depended on an alliance between Japan and China. Such a senior colleague of Chiang Kai-shek was the Japanese-educated Wang Jinwei, who at Nanjing eventually headed a puppet government during the Sino-Japanese War. He could never be persuaded that Japan's imperial pretensions made it an unnatural ally for China. Fortified by Wang Jinwei's foreign policy line, Chiang Kai-shek was able to concentrate on internal order, if only because the other reason for not immediately standing up to Japanese pressure was his fear that the main beneficiary of a sustained conflict would be the Chinese Communist Party.

So Chiang Kai-shek concentrated on the destruction of Yan'an. The expeditionary commander was less enthusiastic about this ultimate encirclement. Zhang Xueliang and his Manchurian troops could not understand why the Guomindang was willing to appease Japan, while their native provinces remained occupied and so they were very susceptible to communist slogans like "Fight back to Manchuria". Apparently unaware of the strength of feeling amongst all ranks, Chiang Kai-shek flew into Xi'an to expedite the final campaign against the Chinese Communist Party but found himself instead the prisoner of Zhang Xueliang and Yang Hucheng, commander of the Shaanxi army. At their insistence in late 1936, he agreed a truce that left the communist regime in Yan'an unmolested. Then Chairman Mao and the Generalissimo pledged themselves to resist Japan. Immediately afterwards, the American ambassador in Tokyo noted how:

> The Japanese nation seems to be somewhat thunderstruck by the sudden and unexpected determination of China to yield no

more to Japanese pressure. The nation is, figuratively, scratching its head and wondering what it should do next.[21]

Not appreciating the full significance of the Xi'an agreement, the Japanese Imperial Army soon determined events on Tokyo's behalf. In July 1937, an exchange of shots between Japanese and Chinese troops at the Marco Polo bridge, southwest of Beijing, provided the pretext for the Sino-Japanese War. Time had come for the pledge made at Xi'an to be honoured.

Colonial Unrest

Right down to the Pacific War, a more precise way of describing Japan's extension of the Second World War into Asia, European colonial powers believed in the necessity of empire and their own superiority as governing peoples. To an extent, the United States shared this view of its colony in the Philippines. An anti-imperialist movement had sprung up to oppose President McKinley's foreign policy, but it was not strong enough to deflect White House aspirations in the Pacific. Small though its colonial holdings were in comparison with those of the European colonial empires, victory in the Spanish-American war had admitted the United States into the small, select circle of world powers. The British empire alone extended over one-fourth of the globe and over one-fourth of its population. According to Lord Curzon, the viceroy of India from 1898 until 1905, the British empire was the greatest instrument for good that ever existed. He did not share the view of his country's duty to prepare India for self-government, no matter how far distant this might be in the future. Educated Indians, Curzon insisted, were uninterested in either justice or sound administration. All they cared for was a share of executive power, for which he thought them "as yet profoundly unfitted".[22] That was the reason no Indian had any role in decision making at an important level in Curzon's government.

On a visit to the Persian Gulf in 1903, the single-minded viceroy let slip the real state of affairs. The sovereignty accorded to some of the Gulf sheikhdoms, Curzon said then, was no more than the other side of the coin on which the supremacy of British power was stamped. In India the same kind of sovereignty enjoyed by Arab rulers was allowed to native princes. Because their loyalty during the Indian Mutiny had been one of the factors in saving British rule, Indian princely states were henceforth seen as bulwarks of empire. Guided by British residents, Indian princes were not puppets, claimed Curzon at the end of his period of office, but an integral part of the imperial administration. Unmentioned were the twists and turns of court intrigue, often with sanguinary consequences; the conspicuous consumption for which Indian princes became notorious in Europe; and a marked reluctance to hand over outlaws for British justice. Veritable Toads of Toad Hall, the Indian princes were to be denounced by Gandhi as frauds at the 1931 London conference. They were not representatives of the Indian people, the Congress leader told the assembled delegates, but solely for their own selfish interests.

Growing unrest in India had led to the recognition of Gandhi's pre-eminence within the Indian National Congress, which on its foundation in 1885 had been welcomed by the British as a means of ventilating the views of educated Indians. What in 1914 Gandhi brought from his experience of civil disobedience in South Africa was a method of embarrassing a colonial government, as well as an ability to get Hindu and Moslem Indians to forget their differences in the cause of freedom. Colour prejudice was anathema to Gandhi in all its forms, which he decided in India manifested itself in untouchability. Some Congressmen regarded his campaign to end the discrimination as an irrelevancy during the struggle against the British and others as an assault on Hinduism.

Gandhi's method of civil disobedience, passive resistance, was so effective in disrupting British rule that the Congress leader later suggested that persecuted Jews should adopt the same approach in Germany. In reply, the Jewish philosopher Martin Buber pointed out the different kind of opponent his people faced in the Nazis, whose concentration camps were places of death, not just detention. He also reminded Gandhi of the sheer numbers of Indians who could participate in a protest movement, unlike the relatively small German-Jewish community.[23] Indeed, the sheer size of the Indian protests became as much a problem for the Congress Party as for the British authorities in 1919. Riots broke out in Delhi, Ahmedabad and the Punjab. Although he deplored the looting and the arson, as well as the attacks on Europeans, Gandhi publicly blamed the police for provoking the violence. In private he was dismayed at the ferocity that his civil disobedience call had unleashed. The worst disorder occurred at Amritsar, the site of the Golden Temple sacred to Sikh religion. Rumours of the imminent collapse of British authority excited crowds so much that local officials asked for a reinforcement of its small garrison. Before more troops arrived, the arrest of two outspoken critics of British rule ended in a confrontation that left six protesters dead or wounded. This shooting inflamed the crowd: public buildings were fired, telegraph and telephone lines cut and half a dozen Europeans killed in the street.

General Reginald Dyer came to restore law and order on 11 April. Convinced that the trouble arose from an unholy alliance of Hindu intellectuals and Moslem riff-raff, Dyer was in no mood for the application of moderate measures. He was particularly outraged by a vicious attack on a mission doctor, who was knocked off her bicycle, beaten and left for dead in the gutter. The incident seemed to Dyer to typify the contempt in which the British were now held. When on 13 April the general learned that ignoring an order forbidding meetings and processions, a large gathering was taking place at Jullianwala Bagh, he went there with Indian and Gurkha troops as well as two armoured cars. In the derelict garden, he ordered his troops to open fire on the crowd, killing 379 protestors and wounding over 1,200. Amritsar was cowed.

To signal the restoration of British power in the city, Dyer issued several humiliating orders, one of which required Indians to go on all fours when passing the spot where the doctor had been assaulted. The end of the rioting was appreciated not only by merchants and shopkeepers, who stood to lose most through looting, but even more by the guardians of the Golden Temple. The latter presented Dyer with a turban and a ceremonial dagger as a token of their thanks. Though he remained convinced of the correctness of his military intervention at Jullianwala Bagh, reaction to the massacre was mixed. The British authorities in India were concerned that the "crawling order" would only increase racial tension; Congress roundly condemned all that happened in Amritsar; and the House of Commons was appalled by the undisguised use of force. Churchill described

Dyer's action as "a monstrous event, an event which stood in singular and sinister isolation . . . without parallel in the modern history of the British Empire".[24] Forced into early retirement, Dyer did not lack supporters in Britain: they presented him with £26,000, a not inconsiderable sum of money, and a golden sword inscribed "Defender of the Empire". Gandhi himself thought that the disorder in the Punjab and elsewhere was organised rather than a spontaneous outburst of mob violence. But no ringleaders were ever identified in what must be regarded as the most direct challenge to British rule since the days of the Indian Mutiny.

Throughout the 1920s and the 1930s, Congress kept up pressure for Indian independence. But feeling increasingly unhappy with its policy direction, Gandhi passed the leadership in 1940 to Jawaharlal Nehru. The same year, Chandra Subhas Bose, whose fiery temperament Gandhi profoundly mistrusted, abandoned Congress altogether because of its belief in nonviolent protest. Nehru was equally distressed by Bose's military plan to exploit Britain's wartime difficulties which, he believed, was tantamount to offering a helping hand to Hitler. Once again Gandhi showed his naivety in suggesting that the only way to deal with a Japanese invasion of India was complete nonviolent noncooperation. When an American journalist suggested that the Quit-India campaign, which he had just got Congress to launch against the British, could give victory in 1942 to a now belligerent Japan, Gandhi admitted that an abrupt Allied withdrawal might result in a Japanese conquest of India and China. He said: "I had not the remotest idea of any such catastrophe resulting from my action."[25] The following year Gandhi also confessed that he had never read the India Act of 1935. He now discovered to his surprise that it gave a united India all the essentials of self-government.

An otherworldliness seems to have enveloped Gandhi towards the end of his life. As Martin Buber sagely wrote of Gandhi's ideals:

> There is no such thing as Western civilization, there is just modern civilization which is a purely materialistic one; it, not England, governs India. If the British regime were replaced by an Indian one grounded in modern culture, India would be no better off.[26]

For Gandhi's cherished vision of a traditional Indian way of life was already doomed. Symbolically, its eclipse was marked by the choice of emblem for independent India's flag, an Ashokan chakra instead of a spinning wheel. Renowned though Ashoka was as the first Buddhist ruler of India, he was never adamant in his insistence on nonviolence. He said that he would prefer his descendants to conquer without force, but should it prove necessary he hoped they would conduct a conquest with the minimum of bloodshed. As one of his admirers noted with regret, at his funeral Gandhi's body was not carried on the shoulders of his closest followers, but on a gun carriage. "Gandhi," he commented, "had taken away the tigerish cloak from the Indian people but not their tigerish nature."[27]

A parallel of the 1935 India Act that Gandhi neglected to read was the Burma Act, which separated Burma from India. Burma's powerful Indian community opposed the separation on economic grounds, while the colonial administration valued the link with India for defence and internal security. The Burmese, on the other hand, aspired to an independence that would prevent continued Indian immigration. In the Irrawaddy delta, where the most fertile soil was situated, Indian moneylenders had by stages taken over land previously farmed by the Burmese, and then worked it with cheap imported Indian labour. The Burma Act went some way in curbing this practice, but the degree of self-government permitted by London failed to satisfy the expectations of university students in Rangoon, among whose number was Aung San, the future nationalist leader.

Taking the title Thakins—"the masters" or Europeans—Aung San and these radical students maintained links with anti-colonial groups in India as well as Britain. They were at first prepared to use constitutional means to achieve their aims. In early 1940, Aung San became the general secretary of the Burma Freedom Bloc, an amalgamation of political parties dedicated to the attainment of Burma's immediate independence. Its leader, the experienced parliamentarian Ba Maw, had already argued for this to happen, much to the annoyance of the colonial authorities. In London, there was even an attempt to suppress Ba Maw's proposal in BBC news broadcasts.[28] Nervous over the growing unrest, Sir Reginald Dorman-Smith, the colonial governor, tried to persuade the politicians to amend

WHAT WE OUGHT TO DO IN CHINA.   THE ACCESSION OF THE QUEEN OF INDIA.

These two nineteenth-century British cartoons had by no means become outdated
in their attitudes during the early 1900s

the existing constitution with a view to the realisation of dominion
status at the end of the Second World War. What he did not appreciate was that the Thakins were no longer convinced that Gandhi-
style civil disobedience would work in British Burma. Almost all of
them were hostile to Japan and sympathetic towards the Chinese
struggle against the Imperial Japanese Army, now in its fourth year,
but their frustration with the slow-moving independence movement made them easy targets for Japanese agents. It was only after
the completion of the Burma Road, a thousand-kilometre supply
route that ran from Lashio in northern Burma to the southwestern
Chinese city of Kunming, that the Japanese military started to look
for Burmese recruits. Dunkirk was used to demand the closure of
the Burma Road, which Britain duly did during the rainy season,
but in late 1940, military equipment once again zigzagged along its
tortuous course to Chiang Kai-Shek.

With the Imperial Japanese Army stalled in China, and Tokyo
edging towards a general assault on Western colonial holdings
in Southeast Asia, the strategic position of Burma assumed vital

importance in military planning. Ba Maw had contacts in Japan's embassy at Rangoon through his family doctor, a long-term Japanese resident. Burma's first premier after the enactment of the Burma Act, Ba Maw had no affection at all for the British, who engineered his fall from office in 1939. His close relationship with Aung San and other Thakins ensured that Japan recruited key Burmese figures in the run-up to the Pacific War. In return for organising a rebellion against the British, these recruits were promised independence within the Greater East Asia Co-Prosperity Sphere. After secret military training in Japanese-occupied China, the Thakins came back in twos and threes to Burma where they prepared for an uprising.

After the first Japanese air raids on Rangoon in December 1941, the Thakin organisation covered most of southern Burma, and notwithstanding initial British mistakes in dealing with the Japanese invasion of the colony, the Imperial Japanese Army had the advantage of superior intelligence. Burmese soldiers who deserted colonial units for Aung San's Burmese Independence Army provided devastatingly accurate information and guidance to Japanese commanders in the field. But the honeymoon period between the Imperial Japanese Army and the Burmese Independence Army was short-lived. The announcement of a Japanese military administration for Burma meant that Japan had broken its promise of independence. Switching to the Allied side was unavoidable, Aung San told the commander of the Fourteenth Army, William Slim: "If the British sucked our blood," he said, "the Japanese ground our bones."[29]

In contrast to Burma, Malaya enjoyed calm until the arrival of the Imperial Japanese Army, although there were the first stirrings of discontent with British colonial rule. Well might rural disturbances and strikes in the mines be put down to local grievances, but not the protest from the Malay community that greeted the repeal of a law that restricted grants of land to ethnic Malays. In 1939, Sir Miles Shenton Thomas, the governor of the Straits Settlements and high commissioner for the Federated Malay States, decided that rice cultivation should be opened to non-Malays to reduce the need for imports from Burma. The Malay-language newspaper *Majilis* described the decision as "an outrage of the Malays' rightful preserve and heritage", which would result in them being "swamped out of the padi fields . . . literally deprived of their only certain means of livelihood".[30] Although this prediction proved groundless, the Malays were to be conspicuous bystanders during the Japanese invasion: they did little to aid either side.

Quite different was the response of the Chinese, who perceived the attack on British Malaya as a continuation of the Sino-Japanese War. They had raised large sums of money to support the Guomindang war effort, and now in Dalforce there was an opportunity to fight the Japanese at first hand. Because Shenton Thomas feared the communist element among the Chinese population, no force was mustered until the Japanese besieged Singapore. Called Dalforce after its leader John Dalley, a police officer of the Federated Malay States, its volunteers fought under the Chinese flag and inflicted heavy casualties on the Japanese. Some of them survived the fall of Singapore and the subsequent Japanese slaughter of Chinese residents, disappeared into the jungle and then harassed the Imperial Japanese Army throughout the occupation. Later, these same guerrilla fighters formed the nucleus of the anti-British insurgents during the Malayan Emergency. Had the depth of their anti-Japanese feelings been properly gauged, and even more deployed militarily by the colonial authorities, the racial problems that beset postwar Malaya might have been considerably diminished. The only steadfast opponents of Japan, the Chinese were to find themselves second-class citizens in a colony whose Malay sultans had to varying degrees cooperated with the Imperial Japanese Army. And conveniently forgotten were the great personal risks taken by individual Chinese when they endeavoured to ease secretly the lot of European prisoners of war.

Colonial Malaya was always divided on ethnic lines. Typical in this regard was Sir Frank Swettenham, who rose through the ranks of the colonial civil service to become governor of the Straits Settlements. He was committed to the modernisation through improved communications and shipping facilities, but these American and British financed projects were for the benefit of international capitalism rather than the local people. Other than the nobility, Swettenham argued that English should not be taught to Malays, even though it was becoming essential for any employment outside villages. In 1890, he wrote in an official report that it was inadvisable "to attempt to give children of an agricultural population an indifferent knowledge of a language that to all but a very few would only unfit them for the duties of life and make them discontented with anything like manual labour".[31] Towards the Chinese, whose industriousness was a relief after the laziness of the Malays, Swettenham recommended a friendly but distant relationship that underscored who was the master. After all, most of the Chinese immigrants were either shopkeepers or manual labourers. As for the Indians, who came to work largely on rubber estates, their physical separation from the rest of the population clearly defined their social position. The high mortality rate suffered by Indian estate workers was recognised, however, as a worrying problem. In 1912, one-half of the resident population on a single rubber estate in Selangor died from malaria. It was not until after the First World War that British doctors gained a degree of control over this disease. The wealth of Malaya was based on primary products such as tin and rubber, after the planting of rubber seeds, brought from Brazil via Kew Gardens, cleared vast areas of jungle.

With justification, it was believed by the British community that some of the men who came out as planters would be unemployable elsewhere. Their misbehaviour made an attempt to bar non-Europeans from first-class compartments on trains impossible to enforce during 1904. The *Malay Mail* sent up the attempted segregation with a suggestion that anyone intending to travel first class should carry a genealogy and a birth certificate in case a European pedigree was questioned by a railway porter.[32] In the interwar years, British residents were even more concerned about preserving their prestige than before the First World War. Censorship of the cinema ensured that Asians rarely saw Europeans on the screen as criminals, tramps, clowns or lascivious lovers. Charlie Chaplin was a particularly disliked figure because he showed sides of Western society that were considered better hidden from Asian view.

Race had always been a major issue in the Dutch East Indies, where an unbridgeable gulf was fixed between the Dutch and the Indonesians. Settlers who took local wives were not allowed to return to Holland, other than in exceptional cases. The ban was then extended to Dutchmen who used female slaves as concubines, but this did not stop them chasing good-looking Indonesians because so few Dutch women came out to live in Southeast Asia. Exploitation of Indonesia through the *cultuurstelsel* system had in the 1840s caused widespread famine in Java, an island smarting from the harsh suppression of

Dipanagara's rebellion. But to the amazement of Holland, the Dutch East Indies still produced 19 per cent of all government revenue, a figure that grew to 31 per cent over the next 20 years. After private enterprise in agriculture replaced the colonial monopoly, the Indonesian archipelago remained a crucial source of income for Holland, an entirely different economic situation to that of the Philippines, where substantial US investment underwrote a policy of "benevolent assimilation". After defeating Theodore Roosevelt in the presidential election of 1908, President William H. Taft justified the American colony as being dedicated to the improvement of the Filipino people.

No such notion ever entered the heads of Dutch colonial officials, despite a great deal of soul searching in Holland itself. These colonial administrators were well aware of the need for British support in the maintenance of their Southeast Asian empire. Because London preferred the Dutch to the French as neighbours, the 1871 Anglo-Dutch Treaty of Sumatra was the green light for a Dutch attack on Aceh, the last pocket of Indonesian independence. The war was bitterly fought, the Acehnese holding out in guerrilla warfare until 1904. Just how uncompromising the Dutch colonial attitude was can be glimpsed in the advice offered by L.W.C. van der Berg, a noted specialist on foreign affairs. He recommended that Aceh should be settled by Amboinese, preferably ex-colonial soldiers, in fortified villages. They could gradually take over from the "degenerate" Acehnese "in the same way that savages withdraw from the spreading of civilization . . . and die out".[33]

Such an attitude was not missed in the United States. During the 1930s, prominent newspapers asked how it was that a tiny country like Holland could go on plundering the whole Indonesian archipelago. President Franklin D. Roosevelt openly complained about the living conditions of colonial peoples generally, and the inhabitants of the Dutch East Indies in particular, despite his own forebears. Yet Washington remained anxious about Japan, which it feared might exploit Indonesian nationalism in what was a strategically important area. This gradual shift in American thinking delighted Batavia, which announced that the word "Indonesia" could no longer be used. Relations between the Dutch and the Indonesians then hit rock bottom as police surveillance was stepped up: even the popular village sport of pigeon racing was outlawed to prevent bad news becoming generally known. The fall of the Netherlands to Germany in 1940 could not be kept secret forever, but the feebleness of the Dutch resistance to the Japanese two years later still astonished the local population.

Only in French Indochina did the level of unrest reach Indian proportions. A famous letter written by Phan Chu Trinh in 1906 to Paul Beau explained how dire the situation had become and appealed to the governor-general to live up to the declared French civilising mission in Vietnam by reforming its society along modern lines. Later arrested for supporting a peasant demonstration, Phan Chu Trinh was imprisoned and exiled to France. An advocate of nonviolent protest, the would-be reformer advised the governor-general that:

> Today the Vietnamese mandarins, no matter how high or low, shiver and quake when they meet French officials, fearing above all that they will do something to make the Frenchmen angry. Local gentry in the villages, walking along and unexpectedly meeting a Frenchman, be he French official, French soldier, or French merchant, must bow their heads, droop their ears, and quicken their pace – simply afraid of being disgraced.

It was because the colonial regime "has been contemptuous of the Vietnamese people that this increasing distance has developed".[34] Not that everything, Phan Chu Trinh conceded, could be blamed on France, because it suited corrupt Vietnamese officials to stand between the colonial administration and the Vietnamese people. They spoke to French officials in purposely vague terms about possible uprisings and then managed to frame their enemies or prevent gatherings called to discuss vital issues. It did not matter to the French what the impotent Vietnamese emperor's officials told them as long as they collected taxes.

Apparently Phan Chu Trinh believed that a proper modernisation programme would stabilise the political situation. If the French were prepared to improve the economy, allow the scholar-gentry freedom of expression, open newspapers to stimulate general interest, ban the outmoded Chinese-style examination system for Vietnamese officials, found schools and introduce modern methods of production, then with these reforms under way, the Vietnamese

Saigon cathedral: France transposed to Southeast Asia

people would be more worried about France losing interest in the country than hating its colonial rule. Governor-general Beau apparently thought enough of Phan Chu Trinh's recommendations to have a translation of his letter printed in several Paris newspapers. Approval was not the same as effective action, however, and Beau's administrative response was exactly what Phan Chu Trinh feared—a series of unrelated reform measures.

The year the letter was written, the political situation in Vietnam grew increasingly tense. Emperor Thanh Thai, who had originally been placed on the throne by the French in 1889, was forced to abdicate on suspicion of involvement in rebel activities. His son and successor, the eight-year-old emperor Duy Tan, chose as his reign title a Vietnamese word for modernisation, thereby associating himself with the Meiji restoration. But it was probably too late for the Vietnamese reformers to look for anything worthwhile from the imperial court at Hue. Young Ho Chi Minh certainly expected nothing from the throne. Expelled from school for joining a peasant demonstration there, his father was reprimanded for Ho Chi Minh's behaviour, before being transferred to another post well away from Hue. More serious for the French was a plot hatched by Phan Boi Chau, who tried to stage a coup by poisoning French officers attending a banquet in Hanoi. He hoped that rebels in the vicinity could start an uprising during the ensuing disorder and seize control of the city. When the dosage proved inadequate for its purpose, Phan Boi Chau fled abroad where he had a hand in several assassination attempts, inspired by the killing in 1909 of Ito Hirobumi, the Japanese resident-general for Korea. His targets were Vietnamese collaborators as well as French soldiers. After 20 years on the run, Phan Boi Chau was captured in 1925 while passing through Shanghai. Returned to French Indochina, where he expected a martyr's death, Phan Boi Chau suffered no more than the indignity of permanent house arrest.

The efforts of Phan Boi Chau to ferment full-scale rebellion seemed to have failed until the troubles of 1930. While they could worship in peace at Hanoi's neo-gothic cathedral or listen to Berlioz and Bizet in a scaled-down version of the Paris Opera close by, French officials and colonists who resided in the city were in reality living on borrowed time. For the successors of Phan Boi Chau soon called for a nationwide insurrection. It began at Yen Bay, a small town northwest of Hanoi. The Vietnamese soldiers in its garrison planned to poison their French officers and then start their uprising in the middle of the night. But one of the soldiers lost his nerve and betrayed the plot to the commandant, so that the rebel soldiers were unable to take over the post. Elsewhere, other attacks at outposts failed too. For a moment, the French colonial authorities were able to breathe a sigh of relief; but the lack of a general Vietnamese response to the Yen Bay-led mutiny was deceptive, because it was merely the first in a series of violent events that were to lead to the full-scale rebellion of 1946. Eight months after Yen

Bay, French planes had to bomb 20,000 peasants who were marching on Vinh, the capital of Nghe An province, halfway between Hanoi and Hue. Guided by nationalist activists, these impoverished farmers were protesting against the avarice of both landowners and tax collectors. Imperial Vietnamese troops were dispatched from Hue to bar the way to Vinh, but it was the French air force that dispersed the protesters with devastating effect. A day's bombing left the road littered with hundreds of dead and wounded peasants.

French indifference to the severe punishment inflicted on the Vietnamese is best illustrated by an incident in early 1931 at Nam Dan, a Foreign Legion post situated some distance inland from Vinh. The cruel murder of an unarmed legionnaire, who tried to prevent a crowd of peasants from beheading some village elders, enraged his comrades so much that they shot their Vietnamese prisoners. In the subsequent trial of those responsible for the shootings, the defence counsel argued that the accused were only following orders, since it was common practice to kill one prisoner every day to prevent overcrowding. "That was done in all the posts," he said. Officers too were involved because they "amused themselves by cutting off heads, even with a small regulation knife". After a moving appeal by the local Catholic priest, who insisted that the Foreign Legion was the sole guarantor of law and order, the court marshal acquitted the legionnaires.[35]

The French crackdown after the Yen Bay and Nghe An disturbances was severe. Some 2,000 activists were killed and 51,000 of their followers placed in detention. From then on there could be no compromise with the French, whose colonial rule so transparently rested on naked force. The brutality of the Foreign Legion was especially feared and hated. Shaken by the violent events, the last Vietnamese emperor, Bao Dai, endeavoured to persuade the French colonial authorities to desist in their efforts to run the everyday affairs of Vietnam and return to the looser arrangements that had prevailed immediately after the protectorate treaty of 1884. With the French security service hot on the trail of revolutionaries, real and imaginary, the governor-general was not inclined to distance himself from Vietnamese affairs. Bao Dai was allowed to press ahead with the reform of his own administration, provided it was understood by the young emperor that France alone could take key decisions concerning the colony as a whole. Ngo Dinh Diem, the future president of South Vietnam, resigned in 1933 a ministerial post at Hue when French interference showed no sign of abating.

The Sino-Japanese War

A sense of precarious deficiency was the taproot of Japanese aggression. National resources were certainly stretched by imperial commitments as successive governments struggled with an acute economic crisis, although Japan suffered nothing akin to the runaway inflation of the early 1920s in Germany. In both countries, however, single-minded patriotism and the use of terror by right-wing groups contributed to the rise of authoritarian rule. The assassination in 1921 of Hara Takashi did much to undermine parliamentary government by removing an adroit politician from the system. The prime minister's death also ended any hope of amelioration in colonial rule, for he had promised a modest series of reforms aimed at greater opportunities for Koreans in government, education and commerce. In Taiwan, the assimilation policy he sought to introduce in Korea was to have some effect. Encouragement of integration through the diffusion of the Japanese language and the encouragement of intermarriage gave the Guomindang a headache when they recovered the island in 1945. So unexcited were many of the islanders about liberation from Japan that mainland officials who arrived to help restart a Chinese administration felt obliged to emphasise a common heritage, in particular after the 1947 uprising against the Guomindang. Such an appeal for unity would have been quite unnecessary in the rest of China for the good reason that the savagery of the Imperial Japanese Army had left an indelible impression on the Chinese people. Certain Japanese officers realised the disastrous effects of indiscriminate looting, rape, torture and killing. In 1939 captured documents contained a speech given to officers of the 110th Division in north China by Kuwaki Takaaki, who said that without an improvement in military discipline, Japan would lose the war.[36]

The Mukden Incident of 1931, the overture to the Pacific dimension of the Second World War, was for Japan the beginning of a 15-year conflict. The Japanese challenge to the United States seems now a reckless gamble. However, its unreality was obscured by initial Japanese successes, just as the hopeless task of subduing a country the size of China failed to register in time for any limitation of war aims. The temper of Imperial Japanese Army units already stationed in the Liaodong peninsula and Manchuria allowed little scope for compromise, especially when their officers were determined to detach Chinese provinces and warlords piecemeal from the Guomindang side. In his memoirs Matsuoka Yosuke, who was then vice-president of the South Manchuria Railway, declared that alarm over Japan's position in both Manchuria and Mongolia was deliberately fostered by army officers and leaders of the Japanese community settled in Manchuria. Never in doubt about Japan's entitlement to a dominant role on the Asian mainland, Matsuoka also saw Manchuria as a holy land, "consecrated by the sacrifice of one hundred thousand brothers who shed their blood in the war led by the great Meiji emperor".[37] A career diplomat, he had been a member of the Japanese delegation at Versailles but in the 1920s secured a transfer to the railway company. Later, he stood for parliament and became Japan's foreign minister.

Bitter experience of racial prejudice in the United States, where he graduated as a lawyer, scarcely prepared Matsuoka Yosuke for the role of diplomatic conciliator. Against the expressed objection of Emperor Hirohito, he began his ministerial career by forming an alliance in September 1940 with Germany and Italy, which was directed primarily at the United States. What Matsuoka Yosuke feared most was the danger of Japan "missing the bus" in Asia, since the defeat of France and Holland might presage German control of their Southeast Asian colonies. With tough-minded Japanese residents such as Matsuoka Yosuke behind the scenes, nothing was likely to prevent the Imperial Japanese Army from occupying all Manchuria, where the last Qing emperor Pu Yi was installed as the head of the puppet state of Manzhouguo. Japanese political leaders were by no means unanimous on the question of establishing a new regime there, but the Imperial Japanese Army got its way and on 1 March 1932, Manzhouguo came into existence.

Although Chiang Kai-shek tried to distance himself from the foundation of Manzhouguo, he refused to state publicly that

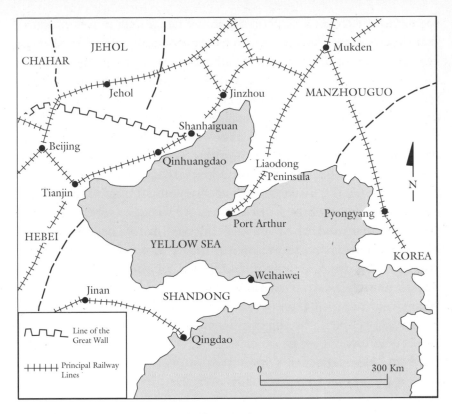

North China in the 1930s

Manchuria was an integral part of China. Even worse was his turning a blind eye to the corrupt warlord regime in Jehol, the province south of Manzhouguo. Because its sole source of income derived from the cultivation of opium, which before the Mukden Incident had been almost entirely exported to Manchuria, this supposedly pro-Guomindang provincial government inclined more to Japan. The Imperial Japanese Army eagerly sought an excuse for the occupation of Manchu-inhabited Jehol, because it always saw it as a part of Manzhouguo. Without Chiang Kai-Shek's approval, the young Manchurian warlord Zhang Xueliang moved his troops to the Jehol border south of the Great Wall. From there he dispatched a "volunteer" force of 40,000 men into Jehol, where it confronted Japanese troops. In late 1932 and early 1933, the strategically situated town of Shanhaiguan, once a key fortress in the Great Wall, was the scene of three skirmishes. The first two were settled locally, with the Chinese offering a prompt apology and the payment of an indemnity. But the third was rigged by the Japanese to develop into a major crisis. Japanese soldiers hurled two hand grenades into an army compound, an action blamed on the Chinese. Reluctant though the United States was to take steps against Japan, Washington recognised the last incident as a sign of the Imperial Japanese Army's intention to invade Jehol and ultimately advance into China. The Americans were unable to persuade the British to join in their condemnation, despite the enormous growth of the United States' influence in world affairs. To defeat Germany during the First World War, Britain had had to enlist first American financial, and then military, strength with the result that there occurred a significant shift in the balance of international power. Acutely aware of its vulnerability in Asia, London still clung to the forlorn hope of reconciliation between Japan and China. Once Jehol was occupied, the Imperial Japanese Army pushed south of the Great Wall into Hebei province.

In Tokyo, there was consternation at the imperial court over this unauthorized southern advance. Emperor Hirohito angrily informed his chief aide-de-camp Honjo Shigeru that commanders in the field had exceeded their orders. As a result, Honjo Shigeru let the Imperial Japanese Army know that

> in future should it become necessary, because of changing circumstances in the battlefield, to make changes in plans submitted to His Majesty, the chief of staff should go to the imperial court in person and explain the situation . . . His Majesty does not necessarily intend to place restrictions on military strategy, but he will not condone infractions against the principle supreme command.[38]

This slap on the wrist did not stop Japanese commanders from advancing all the way to Beijing. For reasons of supply they halted short of the old imperial capital and at Tanggu, near Tianjin, a truce was agreed with the Guomindang. Its terms stipulated the evacuation of both Japanese and Chinese troops from Hebei province, leaving a power vacuum in which Japanese agents could stimulate a separatist movement.

By 1935, there were pro-Japanese governments in autonomous Hebei and Chahar provinces. A change that the Imperial Japanese Army failed to notice was how Chinese resistance was gradually stiffening and, when in July 1937 the Sino-Japanese War began in earnest, it was astonished to hear Chiang Kai-shek declare in Nanjing that the Republic of China had no alternative but to "struggle for national survival". Because Russia was still the principal enemy in the minds of its military planners, Tokyo needed a quick victory over the Chinese. There were indeed battles in 1939 along the northern border of Manzhouguo, and the Japanese fared badly when they encountered Soviet tanks. The unexpected effectiveness of "fire bottles" against armoured vehicles provided only temporary relief for Japanese infantrymen without adequate artillery support. In spite of their heroic efforts, which accounted for more than a

Two Japanese-sponsored posters in the Chinese language. The one showing the Chinese flag, with Wang Jingwei's pennant above it, celebrates the capture of Singapore

hundred tanks, a soft-drink bottle filled with petroleum and sand could never be a substitute for an effective antitank gun, and an engagement at Nomonhan ended as a decisive Russian victory. Losses of more than 8,000 dead and nearly 9,000 wounded had to be concealed from the Japanese public.

Georgi Zhukov, the Russian commander-in-chief, enticed his opponent into an exposed position and then carried out a swift encirclement. In desperation, Japanese soldiers ran across open ground to assault Russian guns in broad daylight, an action reminiscent of the charge of the Light Brigade during the Crimean War.[39] The attack foreshadowed the suicidal handling of troops in the Pacific War. Japanese officers were just as slow against the Americans at Guadalcanal and the British at Kohima in appreciating that bravery was not enough to win a modern battle. Lack of flexibility in tactics became in the end an even more serious handicap for the Imperial Japanese Army than either inferior equipment or a shortage of supplies.

In China, the Imperial Japanese Army at first seemed to have everything its own way. Beijing was captured, then Shanghai and Nanjing, where its troops perpetrated dreadful atrocities. For six weeks, the inhabitants of the Guomindang capital endured the utmost cruelty at the hands of uncontrolled Japanese troops. Hundreds of thousands of Chinese women and children were raped. Even elderly women were shown no mercy. And it was common for a rape by a group of soldiers to end in the slaughter of entire families. A conservative estimate puts the number of people killed in Nanjing during the reign of terror at 260,000, although the Japanese themselves believed at the time of the massacre that the death toll may have been as high as 300,000.[40] There can be little doubt that the figure would have been much higher without the effort made by members of the European community to establish a safety zone in the city.

One of these saviours was a 55-year-old German named John Rabe, head of the local branch of the Siemens electrical company and a member of the Nazi party. Not only did he try to interest Hitler in the fate of Nanjing, but he also kept a diary that details the day-to-day sufferings of the local Chinese. On 28 December, he wrote how "the reports we are hearing from all sides today are so hair-raising that I can hardly bring myself to put them to paper . . . At an empty house . . . the Japanese built a large bonfire, led the groups (of refugees) out one by one, bayoneted the men and tossed them alive on the fire".[41] On his return to Germany in 1938, Rabe publicised the Nanjing massacre by lecturing and showing a film all over Berlin, until the Gestapo forbad him to speak about the Japanese atrocities again. The full extent of Japanese brutality in China is still not squarely faced today. When in 1988 *The Last Emperor* was screened in Japan, the film's distributor arranged for scenes of rape and murder at Nanjing to be cut, lest they annoy Japanese audiences. An equal reluctance to acknowledge guilt is clear in the official Japanese stance on so-called "comfort women", the sex slaves kept by the Imperial Japanese Army. In 2007, Japanese members of parliament were outraged by an American call for an unambiguous apology over the wartime enslavement of hundreds of thousands of women in military brothels.[42]

From the outbreak of the Sino-Japanese conflict in 1937, relations between Britain and Japan went into steep decline, in large measure because London blamed the Imperial Japanese Army for starting the hostilities, while Tokyo believed that the British were aiding Chinese resistance. This did not mean that the two countries were set irrevocably on the road to war. More worried about the European situation, Britain still hoped to avoid a military commitment in Asia, since its only possible ally there was the United States. Given that Washington had recently shown less interest in China's plight, the British government tried to protect its commercial and financial interests in places such as Shanghai and Hong Kong without recourse to arms.

Prime Minister Neville Chamberlain had high hopes of keeping the peace there as in Europe, at least until the Japanese shelled *HMS Ladybird* and *HMS Bee* in December 1937. When the Royal Navy protested, it was told "that firing at the warships was a mistake", although the Japanese "had orders to fire at every ship" on the Yangzi.[43] Less sanguine than Chamberlain, Anthony Eden instructed the British ambassador in Washington to see whether the United States was contemplating "the mobilization of their fleet or part of it" as a result of the sinking of *USS Panay*.[44] He was certain that, as with the earlier attack on the British vessels, Japanese dive bombers had deliberately sunk this American warship. The lukewarm response from the Americans dashed Eden's immediate hope that the crisis would lead to closer ties with the United States. President Roosevelt spoke publicly about the need to quarantine aggression, but he was prepared to accept Japanese apologies and compensation.

Even more galling for the British was that the Japanese attacks had the effect of closing the Yangzi to international trade. The United States seemed to have abandoned its open-door policy in China. This was an incorrect perception because the president soon sponsored the Naval Act of 1938, which took the US Navy above treaty limits for the first time. He also supported Congress in ordering 3,000 aircraft. Eventually, a secret approach from Washington about joint action against Japan was rudely repulsed by Chamberlain, now totally wedded to appeasement.[45] In due course it cost him his foreign secretary, because Anthony Eden tired of the lack of firmness in British foreign policy and resigned.

By mid-1939, the Japanese had occupied many of the large towns and cities in China, the strongholds of Guomindang support. Chiang Kai-shek retreated inland to remote Chongqing in Sichuan province, where he was cut off from the outside world, its only overland communication routes being two earth roads: one ran through the northwestern province of Xinjiang to Russia, while the other negotiated mountainous terrain to connect Yunnan province with the British colony of Burma. Just before this westerly withdrawal, Chiang Kai-shek had won a victory over the Imperial Japanese Army at Tierzhuang, a town near the border of Shandong and Jiangsu provinces. It is possible that more than 20,000 Japanese soldiers were killed or wounded. The Chinese deployed tanks, antitank guns and aircraft, revealing that better equipment could make a difference on the battlefield. Nearly all of it had come from the Soviet Union.

Other than in the urban areas and on stretches of the coastline, Japanese control was restricted to railway lines. This constituted a tactical error because, by the time the Imperial Japanese Army was ready to move into the countryside, the Chinese Communist Party had organised the peasants against it. In the same way that the Imperial Japanese Army tended to misjudge the tenacity of conventional opponents, so the approach it adopted against rural opposition was singularly inept. Communist guerrillas ran circles around the Japanese columns sent to prevent their attacks. On the eve of the Pacific War, the bulk of Japan's troops were tied down by Mao Zedong's poorly armed combatants: only one-fifth of the Imperial Japanese Army took part in operations in Southeast Asia and the Pacific. It was as though the Japanese equivalent of the Panzerarmee Afrika broke the Western colonial hold over Asia. As Emperor Hirohito bitterly complained in 1940, his generals had failed to keep their promise that war in China would not divert scarce resources from Japan's vital air and naval buildup.

Chapter 5

The Collapse of Western Power 1941–45

> Our army and navy working in close cooperation in Malaya . . . have . . . in the teeth of tropical diseases, and enduring heat . . . harried and hunted a strong enemy and broken through his defences at every point, capturing Singapore with the speed of the gods, and destroying Great Britain's base in East Asia.

> *Emperor Hirohito's victory message to the Imperial Japanese Army and Navy in early 1942*

The Outbreak of the Pacific War

By the end of 1939, Japan was living beyond its means. The impact of the European war on the price of key commodities proved disastrous for the Japanese economy, already struggling to keep pace with rising military consumption in China. Planned increases in Japanese output were hit by the doubling in price of scrap iron, and the shortage of good-quality coal for making steel. But the most worrying aspect of the situation was the growing dependence of Japan on imports from the United States. In scrap iron, nickel and oil products, American dominance was so great that Tokyo could not stand any economic pressure from Washington for more than a few months. After the defeat of Japan, Emperor Hirohito said that the focus of prewar discussion was oil.[1] Lack of oil was the issue that led the Imperial Japanese Navy to oppose war initially, while acquiring oil and other strategic materials was the reason the Imperial Japanese Army favoured war. The latter held that a withdrawal from China was an unreasonable price to pay for oil, although President Roosevelt made no secret of his anger at its actions against the Chinese. An oil embargo was therefore a gift to expansionist Japanese generals because it shifted the blame for starting hostilities from Japan to the United States.

In the summer of 1940, spirits in the Imperial Japanese Army were high, because at last the Imperial Japanese Navy was coming round to the view that a southward advance would improve its own reputation and secure a larger allocation of captured resources.

The signing of the Tripartite Pact between Germany, Italy and Japan in 1940

Where the admirals still disagreed with the generals was over the targets for attack. The Imperial Japanese Army hoped that military operations could be confined to Dutch or, at worst, Anglo-Dutch possessions. The United States was not to be involved, the Philippines not to be invaded. Because the Anglo-Dutch naval presence was only token, the Imperial Japanese Navy saw no glory for itself in such a limited advance and argued that the Americans could not be ignored. Japan might well appropriate the oil, rubber and nickel supplies of the Dutch East Indies, but there remained the danger of Anglo-American intervention from Malaya and Hawaii.

The United States was already sending a steady stream of aid to Britain, and both countries would likely join with the remnants of the Dutch forces in Asia to defend the Indonesian archipelago. Only a pre-emptive strike on the US Pacific Fleet at Pearl Harbor could guarantee Japan an opportunity to impose a New Order on Asia. With the two services steadily moving towards an agreed strategy for the Pacific War, the Japanese troops in China were ordered to pacify the whole country. An attempt to force the Yangzi gorges and capture Chiang Kai-shek's headquarters at Chongqing ground to a halt, but behind Japanese lines a political settlement of a kind was reached with Wang Jingwei, a Guomindang defector who declared his "reformed government" established at Nanjing in 1940. Replying with unintended irony to questions from newspaper correspondents about the independence of Wang Jingwei's regime, a Japanese diplomat indicated that there was no need for apprehension, since it was on a par with Manzhougou's.[2]

Yet the terms of the treaty that Japan imposed on Wang Jingwei were far more severe than those Hitler forced the Vichy regime to accept in France. One of its first stipulations was Chinese recognition of Manzhougou, cold comfort for the restored Pu Yi. So frightened had the ex-Qing emperor become of his Japanese advisers that he took his irritation out on his servants in frequent beatings. The "reformed government" at Nanjing was accorded no international standing, and even Japan's two allies, Germany and Italy, did not bother to recognise Wang Jingwei until August 1941.

Wang Jingwei's decision to collaborate was not unlike that of Pierre Laval and Philippe Pétain after the fall of France. In both the Chinese and the French cases anti-British indignation was directed not only at the British themselves but also at their own countrymen for their excessive reliance on Britain and the United States. Chiang Kai-shek was held up as nothing more than a Western stooge. For the Chinese though, there was the added satisfaction that in becoming part of the Greater East Asia Co-Prosperity Sphere they were helping Japan to eject Western colonialists from Asia. A second similarity in the outlook of the French and Chinese collaborators was fear of a takeover by communist parties directed from Moscow. As Wang Jingwei foresaw, the most dangerous challenge to the Guomindang would come not from the Imperial Japanese Army but from the People's Liberation Army. By the surrender of Japan in August 1945, the latter's guerrilla forces were spread over north and central China in defence of nearly 100 million people. At this point, the Chinese Communist Party had merely to sustain the patriotic fervour that it had built up against Japan, and stand back from the corruption of Guomindang, to achieve revolutionary victory four years later. Though Wang Jingwei warned that Mao Zedong would profit most from the war, Chiang Kai-shek held the view that an extension of the fighting might benefit his own position as well. If a Japanese victory could be prevented in China, he was sure that changes in the international situation would eventually create a political climate favourable to the Guomindang. The outbreak of the Second World War, and Japan's subsequent alignment with the Axis powers, seemed to confirm the rightness of offering continued resistance in Chongqing.

In Southeast Asia, the war in Europe had serious repercussions. The only power to which French Indochina could have looked for aid was Britain, but after the Royal Navy had bombarded French warships in North African ports during July 1940 to stop them falling into German hands, all diplomatic relations had been severed. Even an attack on Gibraltar was launched from Vichy airfields in Algeria. The confrontation stirred deep emotions, but it demonstrated Britain's determination to fight on, something Churchill was concerned to impress upon the American public. The British prime minister was reassured by the American presence in the Philippines, although he was not unaware of pressure in the United States for an abandonment of the colony. This view held that "to retain possessions so far from the United States and, relatively, so near Japan is merely to risk entanglement in an area in which the United States could not effectively use its sea power".[3] The attitude of the Americans was important to all European colonial administrations, whether or not they were at war with Germany. Although Churchill welcomed sanctions against Japan, he despaired at the absence of a coherent US economic policy, since Washington seemed to envisage sanctions against Japan as a punishment for specific acts of aggression. The result was that American measures only served to inconvenience Tokyo temporarily.

Resistance was required in French Indochina against two foes, the Thai as well as the Japanese. In Thailand, Luang Phibunsongkham had become a virtual dictator, having been one of the promoters of the 1932 coup that ended an absolute monarchy. An admirer of Hitler, Phibun used France's difficulties in Europe to recover Thai territory incorporated in French Indochina. Having whipped up the Thai people to a state of fury over territorial losses, he sounded out Japan, the only power fully sympathetic to Thailand's quest for a readjustment of its borders. Britain accepted that Bangkok had a case, but not the United States, which cancelled the sale of fighter planes and bombers. In its place, Japan stepped in and offered planes, guns and torpedoes to a grateful Phibun, who was as yet unready to become a military ally of the Japanese.

The stubbornness of the French colonial administration led to the Franco-Thai War of 1940–41. Encouraged by Japan's offer to mediate and German support for its demands, Bangkok had already announced that it "has no wish to disturb the peace of anyone but we will have to wipe out of existence all the injustices that French Indochina has done to us".[4] Because the French could not readily replace their losses in battle, it was only a matter of time before negotiators arrived in Tokyo to sign a peace treaty, although Thai gains fell so short of expectations that Phibun had to deal with severe criticism at home. The Japanese were disappointed, too, because it seemed that Phibun's continued insistence on Thai neutrality was nothing more than a camouflage for covert military cooperation with Britain.[5] So Japan asked Germany to lean on the Vichy regime, because a southward advance on Singapore was considered impossible without going through the Malayan peninsula, and to use this land bridge, Japan had to secure French Indochina and Thailand first.[6] Berlin duly forbad the transfer of aircraft and troops to Indochina, leaving the French colony in no position to refuse Japanese demands for the stationing of units belonging to the Imperial Japanese Army there.

Ostensibly a move aimed at the Guomindang government in Chongqing, the arrival of Japanese forces in northern Vietnam, and later in southern Vietnam, prepared the way for the Pacific War. Foreign Minister Matsuoke Yosuke urged an immediate attack on Singapore, but he was overruled by Tojo Hideki, Oikawa Koshiro and Konoe Fumimaro—the army minister, the navy minister and the premier respectively. Not long afterwards, Prince Konoe resigned in protest at growing support for Matsuoke Yosuke's standpoint. Later, Tojo Hideki denied that from the moment he took over as premier, Japan was totally committed to war. Yet there can be no question that his belligerent outlook pleased Emperor Hirohito: while advocating caution, the emperor was not displeased with the outbreak of the Pacific War. He was regularly informed of war plans before the surprise attack on Pearl Harbor, the details of which were explained to him one month before its actual execution. Even though he was never the decision maker, Emperor Hirohito was a part of the decision-making process.

Japan's grand strategy in Asia and the Pacific relied upon the efforts of Germany and Italy in containing Britain and the United States. Because the Americans were turning their country into a gigantic arms factory and building up their own military strength in Hawaii and the Philippines, Matsuoka Yosuke reinsured his diplomacy by concluding in April 1941 a Soviet-Japanese Neutrality Pact. It was designed to protect Manzhouguo from Russian attack, thereby freeing Japanese troops stationed there for the drive southwards. The volatile foreign minister then suggested on Hitler's invasion of Russia, two months later, that Japan should tear up the non-aggression pact and join the war against the Soviet Union, so convinced was he of a swift German victory. But Tojo Hideki and the Imperial Japanese Army resisted Matsuoka Yosuke's argument, as war with the Russians would require the suspension of operations in China and the abandonment of an advance into Southeast Asia.

On his return from Berlin, Matsuoka Yosuke had already informed his cabinet colleagues that regarding the conquest of Singapore, I made no commitments to Germany, nor did Germany demand any. Germany says that she will let Japan take care of Greater East Asia. Germany says that when she seriously thinks about the problem of Greater East Asia from Japan's point of view, she is convinced that Japan should undertake the conquest of Singapore now. Whether we go ahead or not is our decision, and I have made no promises.[7]

The fact of the matter was that Hitler did want Japan to start the Pacific War as soon as possible. He was disappointed with Matsuoka Yosuke, whom he described as "combining the hypocrisy of an American Bible missionary with the cunning of a Japanese Asiatic". The German dictator would have to manage without Japan for the moment but, as Mussolini's son-in-law Count Ciano noted, "Hitler still considers the Japanese card as extremely important in order, in the first place, to threaten and eventually counterbalance any American action."[8] That is why the neutrality pact that Matsuoka Yosuke negotiated with Josef Stalin came as such an unpleasant surprise to Hitler.

Because Tokyo now knew for certain that Berlin needed Japanese military intervention, it could bide its time. News of the attack on Pearl Harbor would actually reach Hitler when he was handling a crisis on the eastern front, the Russian counteroffensive before Moscow. Despite the seriousness of the military situation there, Hitler immediately ordered German submarines to sink American ships and hurried back to Berlin, where he declared war on the United States. For many months in Tokyo, however, there had been reservations about the feasibility of an attack on Singapore. General Sugiyama Hajime, the chief of staff for the Imperial Japanese Army, warned that operations in Malaya could prove difficult. Only the fear that Hitler might favour France to use its strength against Britain concentrated minds, because the price of Vichy cooperation was bound to include some kind of guarantee for its authority in French Indochina. Tojo Hideki had given a great deal of thought himself to the impact of hostilities on the Japanese empire, for he realised that Japan could never win on its own. The sole solution was to make the United States unwilling to continue as a combatant by defeating China and Britain with the assistance of Germany and Italy. The Russian theatre, Tojo Hideki believed, was solely a German responsibility.

In the months leading up to the Pacific War, the Imperial Japanese Army ruled the roost in Tokyo. The author of the surprise naval attack on Pearl Harbor, Yamamoto Isoroku, lived in fear of assassination for opposing the complete occupation of French Indochina. Tojo Hideki was furious at the breakdown of discipline among senior army circles, although those who angered him most escaped with little more than a dressing down. Admiral Yamamoto was under no illusion about the fate of his country in an extended contest with the United States. "To fight the United States," he said "is like fighting the whole world. But it has been decided. So I will fight my best. Doubtless I will die on board the *Nagato*."[9] The admiral was wrong about this, because in April 1943 he met his death not on the flagship but over Bougainville, when his plane was shot down after radio interception of a message giving details of a tour of inspection.

Catastrophe in Southeast Asia

The Japanese occupation of French Indochina brought relations between the United States and Japan to a head. Last-minute negotiations were in progress at Washington as the task force dispatched to Pearl Harbor closed on its target, the US Pacific Fleet. Admiral Nagumo Chuichi, its commander, had been ordered to leave room for calling off the attack, if the Americans agreed to resume normal trade relations with Japan. In Tokyo a stern Tojo Hideki said:

> We have now reached a point where we can no longer allow the situation to continue, from the point of view of both our national power and our projected military operations. Moreover, the requirement with respect of military operations will not permit an extension of time. Under the circumstances, our Empire has no alternative but begin war against the United States, Britain and the Netherlands.[10]

Southeast Asia in 1941

The Imperial Japanese Army and the Imperial Japanese Navy were instructed to notify all commands that, unless at the last minute the United States agreed to soften its approach to Japan and ease economic sanctions, the Pacific War would commence within a matter of days.

A change of the American stance was an impossibility. The State Department understood Tokyo's real intentions, having six months earlier told its ambassador in Washington that "some Japanese leaders in influential positions are definitely committed to a course which calls for support of Nazi Germany and its policies of conquest and that the only kind of understanding with the United States which they would endorse is one that would envisage Japan's fighting on the side

223

of Hitler should the United States become involved in the European hostilities through carrying out its present policy of self-defence".[11] But American pressure certainly exacerbated an already deteriorating situation. Shortages of almost everything required by the Imperial Japanese Army and the Imperial Japanese Navy caused Tokyo deep concern about its ability to wage war for any length of time. To stockpile vital materials rationing had been introduced as early as 1940.[12]

Admiral Nagumo's 400 carrier-based aircraft still caught the US naval base on Hawaii by surprise. Just after dawn, unbelieving American servicemen watched as bombs rained down on airfields and torpedoes were released against warships. The air attack was a stunning success. Five US battleships sank, another three were put out of action, four cruisers sustained damage along with four destroyers, and six auxiliaries capsized. The principal target was obviously the fleet, but 200 aeroplanes were also destroyed on the ground. American casualties amounted to 2,403 dead and 1,178 wounded. The Japanese lost far fewer men because the number of

USS Arizona going down in flames at Pearl Harbor, December 1941

aircraft that failed to return to the carriers was barely 10 per cent of the entire strike force.

In warfare, however, even the most meticulous preparation cannot always offset the factor of luck. Admiral Yamamoto had hoped to eliminate the American aircraft carriers at a single stroke, because he correctly expected that planes launched from these ships, rather than shells fired from battleships, would be critical during the Pacific War. Not a single one of the three aircraft carriers was in port. Two of them, the *Lexington* and the *Enterprise*, were about to play vital roles in Japanese defeats at the battles of the Coral Sea and Midway. Admiral Chester Nimitz, the victor of the second battle, said it was a blessing for the United States that not only were the aircraft carriers spared but even more that the Japanese hit the battleships at their moorings. If they had been sunk at sea, they would have been a total loss. With a single exception, the *Arizona*, the battleships were rebuilt to modern standards, with enough anti-aircraft guns to supplement the air cover that was henceforth recognised as essential for their safety.

The disparity in losses at Pearl Harbor in no way reflected on the bravery of the Americans. In the confusion there was little panic, which impressed Fuchida Mitsuo, a seasoned pilot who led the second wave of bombers. He recalled how:

> As my group made its bomb run, enemy anti-aircraft suddenly came to life. Dark gray bursts blossomed here and there until the sky was clouded with shattering near misses, which made our plane tremble. I was startled by the rapidity of the counterattack, which came less than five minutes after the first bomb had fallen. Had it been the Japanese fleet, the reaction would not have been so quick, because although the Japanese character is suitable for offensives, it does not readily adjust for the defensive.

But Fuchida Mitsuo was amazed at the shortsightedness of the Americans in not using torpedo nets. Whereas he found that his planes scored few hits by dropping bombs from a high altitude, low-level torpedo attacks invariably found their targets. He noticed that

Utah, on the western side of Ford Island, had already capsized. On the other side of the island the *West Virginia* and *Oklahoma* had received concentrated torpedo attacks as a result of their exposed positions in the outer row. Their sides were blasted off and they listed steeply in a flood of heavy oil. The *Arizona* was in miserable shape, her magazine apparently having blown up; she was listing badly and burning furiously. Two other battleships, the *Maryland* and *Tennessee*, were on fire, especially the latter, whose smoke emerged in a heavy black column that towered into the sky.[13]

Delay in presenting to Washington a note in which the Japanese government conveyed its decision to break off diplomatic relations, whether by accident or design, only served to increase US anger at the Pearl Harbor attack on 7 December 1941. President Roosevelt declared it "a date which will live in infamy".

Relief in Washington that a period of indecision was over has not unnaturally led to conspiracy theories based around Roosevelt's prior knowledge of Japanese plans. It has even been suggested that the president deliberately concealed this information from the naval and army commanders in Hawaii. While Roosevelt was delighted that Japan fired the first shot of the Pacific War, he would have hardly sacrificed the US Pacific Fleet as a bait. In the last two weeks before the Japanese attack, Washington supplied the Pearl Harbor army and navy commanders with enough detail to have put them thoroughly on their guard. What these officers failed to appreciate was the likelihood of a seaborne assault. No effective reconnaissance occurred at sea and on land aircraft were concentrated to deter saboteurs. These planes provided a perfect target for Japanese airmen, who were fortunate that most of the ammunition for anti-aircraft guns remained in guarded stores.

The response in the Philippines to the same information from Washington was altogether different. Admiral Thomas Hart expanded air and sea reconnaissance, although he disagreed with the clandestine nature of the latter: Roosevelt had ordered him to use only chartered vessels. General Douglas MacArthur also readied his troops for a possible invasion and took the opportunity to draw attention to the limited forces available for the defence of the American colony. One of Hart's ships, the two-funnelled yacht *Isabel*, was passed by Japanese warships in the South China Sea, but they steamed on to their various destinations in Southeast Asia. They had no time to investigate the *Isabel*, because Japan's opening move of the Pacific War was a series of simultaneous attacks on Pearl Harbor, the islands of Wake and Guam, Hong Kong, Thailand, Malaya and the Philippines. Surprise was everything, as the US Pacific Fleet so painfully discovered.

The Japanese drive southwards was even more successful than Pearl Harbor, most of the objectives being secured in less time than the planners had allowed. Hong Kong, Malaya, Singapore, Borneo and the Dutch East Indies were all taken over by the end of March 1942. Having captured Rangoon, the Imperial Japanese Army also moved into northern Burma so as to cut the overland supply route for Western aid to the Guomindang. The Americans did not finally surrender in the Philippines until May, but MacArthur had left for Australia in mid-March. Although this Japanese whirlwind amazed the world, nothing in its irresistible path matched the unconditional surrender of 85,000 men at Singapore. The fall of this supposedly "impregnable" fortress was a psychological shock from which British colonial power in Asia never fully recovered.

In Southeast Asia, the first Japanese blows fell on Thailand and Malaya. The former had just changed its name from Siam: yet Thailand, meaning "Freeland", was more a wish than a reality in late 1941. The only independent country in Southeast Asia, Thailand was placed in an intolerable position by powerful neighbours, the Japanese in occupied French Indochina and the British in Malaya as well as Burma. It was the possibility of recovering lost territories from Britain, as had recently happened with France, that finally persuaded Bangkok to side with Japan. Four of the northern states in Malaya—Perlis, Kedah, Kelantan and Trengganu—had been part of the Thai kingdom until 1909, when they were ceded to the British. Tokyo still felt uncertain of Thai intentions right up to the last moment, however.

On 2 December, five days before Japanese troops entered Thailand, Prime Minister Phibun issued a secret order that commanded all troops to fight against a Japanese invasion to the very end.

Tokyo still suspected that Thailand had come to a secret agreement with Britain and the United States over the defence of Southeast Asia, but this was not the case despite increased British and American diplomatic activity in Bangkok. The Isthmus of Kra, the southernmost portion of Thailand bordering Malaya, was recognised by the Japanese and the British as strategically important in the event of war. The Imperial Japanese Army needed to land there so that it could capture airfields close to the Malayan border and prepare for a thrust down the west coast towards Penang: this Straits Settlement was earmarked as a base for the Imperial Japanese Navy, whose submarines would soon range across the Indian Ocean as far as Madagascar. There they torpedoed *HMS Ramillies* during the allied takeover of the Vichy island colony. With a hole below her waterline three metres in diameter temporarily repaired, the old battleship struggled to South Africa, where several months work made *Ramillies* seaworthy again in the autumn of 1942. Less fortunate was the tanker *British Loyalty*, which took a torpedo probably intended for the battleship.

Such was the shortage of British warships and even patrol aircraft off the coast of east Africa that Japanese submarines were able to operate securely on the surface against merchant shipping. An eventual reduction in losses to submarine attack owed little to improved British anti-submarine measures and more to Imperial Japanese Navy views about sinking merchant shipping. With a submarine force as large as that of the United States, Japan could have caused havoc along busy sea lanes. It was fortunate for the Allies that a belief in decisive fleet action made attacks on unarmed merchantmen appear singularly unheroic to Japanese submariners. The Americans did not share these qualms and, in an unadvertised campaign as unrestricted as that waged by German U-boats in the Atlantic, their submarines sank hundreds of Japanese merchant vessels. Travel by sea became so risky that these ships sailed with rafts lashed to their rails in expectation of the worst. On the surrender of Japan, all that was left of a merchant fleet totalling 6.4 million tonnes before the Pacific War was 1.5 million tonnes.[14]

Before this savage American submarine offensive took place, the Imperial Japanese Army had overrun all of Southeast Asia.

A British plan to pre-empt its occupation of the Kra isthmus was never put into action, and Japanese troops landed in southern Thailand at Singora. Yamashita Tomoyuki, the general in command of the Malayan campaign, was disappointed that there were no good airfields around Singora that appeared operational after a short period of repair. His immediate reaction was to drive south and occupy better ones in northern Malaya, thereby catching British forces in still incomplete defensive positions. The speed of Yamashita Tomoyuki's advance was to be the decisive factor during the whole campaign, which lasted only 70 days, a month less than Sugiyama Hajime predicted as necessary for the capture of Singapore.

Few shots were fired at the Japanese in Singora, although Tsuji Masanobu, staff officer responsible for operations under Yamashita Tomoyuki, was wounded in the arm. The Thai army contented itself with shelling the beach where the Japanese came ashore on 8 December. Tokyo had presented an ultimatum to the Thai government that morning: either stay neutral or side with Japan. Quickly Phibun reached an agreement with the Japanese that seemed to protect Thailand's independence. He told his cabinet colleagues to "befriend the Japanese" for the sake of the nation.[15] What the Thai strongman feared most was that the Japanese Imperial Army would make use of an excuse to disarm Thai forces and turn Thailand into another Manzhouguo. At first, the people of Thailand were enthusiastic about the Pacific War, and proud to be the only fully independent Asian state in alliance with imperial Japan. But the export of Thai rice, rubber and tin to Japan brought nothing in return because the Japanese economy was entirely geared to war production. The Imperial Japanese Army's overprinting of the Thai currency as a way out of this dilemma merely added runaway inflation to Thailand's woes. Before hostilities went badly against Japan in 1944, conditions in the country had already degenerated to the level of a black-market economy, with recurrent shortages of basic commodities.

The fall of the Japanese premier Tojo Hideki, shortly after the American recapture of the Philippines, seems to have encouraged the National Assembly to vote Phibun out of power. Close contacts soon developed with the US-sponsored Free Thai movement, whose origins went back to the refusal of Seni Pramoj, the Thai ambassador in Washington, to deliver Phibun's declaration of war. The ambassador even broadcast an appeal to Thai living abroad to enlist with the Allies. "We cannot regain our freedom unless we fight for it," Seni said.[16] Unlike Britain, the United States never offered a reciprocal declaration of hostilities, considering that Phibun's action to have been taken under Japanese duress.

In his own account of the Malayan campaign, Tsuji Masanobu contrasts the landings at Singora and Kota Bharu, the capital of Kelantan. At Kota Bharu, the British pillboxes along the beach "were well prepared, and reacted violently with such heavy fire that our men lying on the beach, half in and half out of the water, could not raise their heads". Japanese transports were also attacked from a nearby RAF base and two of the three were sunk. It cost the Imperial Japanese Army 320 men killed and another 538 wounded to penetrate the beach defences and then capture the trouble-some airfield.[17] That some airfields were in Japanese hands by 19 December made these losses worthwhile, for it permitted Yamashita Tomoyuki to call in his own planes and gain air superiority over northern Malaya. Japan's advantage in this aspect of war had already been demonstrated at sea. Ignoring naval advice, Churchill sent two capital ships, the newly commissioned *Prince of Wales* and the *Repulse*, to Singapore as a deterrent. He said of the *Prince of Wales*, in a telegram to Roosevelt, "there is nothing like having something that can catch and kill anything".[18]

The original plan called for the dispatch of the battleship and the battlecruiser along with the aircraft carrier *Indomitable*. Unfortunately, the *Indomitable* ran aground during a fog off Jamaica. No other carrier was available: the *Ark Royal* had just been lost in the Mediterranean, while *Illustrious* and *Formidable* were undergoing repairs in the United States. All that could be spared were ships either too old or too slow to sail eastwards. In addition, their complement of aircraft was quite unequal to the task ahead. So it was that Force Z, the name of Churchill's naval deterrent, arrived at Singapore with only anti-aircraft guns to protect it from aerial assault. Locally, the condition of the Royal Air Force was pitiful. Its 246 aircraft consisted of superannuated fighters and bombers, the most modern of which was the American-built Brewster Buffalo, no match for the Japanese Zero fighter. General Arthur Percival, the British commander in Malaya, commented:

> I was far from happy when I was told that our fighters were a type which I had not heard of as being in action elsewhere . . . However, a fighter is a fighter and we were in no position to pick and choose at the time.[19]

Three days after Pearl Harbor, off the east coast of Malaya, Force Z was intercepted by Japanese aircraft flying from airfields in French Indochina and within hours the battleship and the battle-cruiser were sent to the bottom. Only the presence of three escorting destroyers enabled as many as 2,000 sailors to be saved.

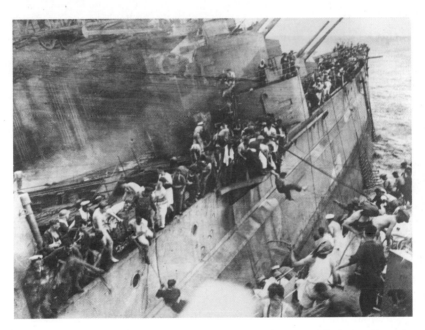

HMS Prince of Wales sinking off the coast of Malaya

As Terence O'Brien, an RAF pilot who was later transferred to Singapore, wrote of sending out the *Prince of Wales* and the *Repulse* without air cover:

> To us who had worked out of St. Eval in Cornwall attacking enemy shipping, and trying to protect our own, it was an

incredible action. Around England even single merchantmen had an air escort, convoys not only had continuous patrol overhead but were also covered by fighter contacts. If the two battleships could not be provided with strong fighter cover they should have been pulled out of the area altogether; they would have been a most valuable adjunct to the Australian navy in the Solomons presently. In the Singapore area, without air cover, they were nothing more than sacrificial targets.[20]

Churchill's gunboat bluff had ended in disaster. After the fall of Singapore, Churchill said that Britain had given to the Soviet Union what was really needed for the defence of Malaya. This was a lame excuse. Just as the sinking of the *Prince of Wales* and the *Repulse* reflected an outdated approach to naval warfare, so on land the complacency of the British garrison almost ensured a Japanese triumph. The diversion of American, British and Canadian resources to aid the Russians was a contentious issue at the time, and became a highly political one afterwards. What the British premier tried to do was pre-empt criticism of the unprepared state of colonial defence by drawing attention to Barbarossa, Hitler's attempt to subdue the Soviet Union.

Political considerations lay behind Churchill's decision to despatch Force Z. The Australian premier, Robert Menzies, was desperately worried about a Japanese attack on his country. He told the First Sea Lord during a visit to London in 1941 that in the absence of a British fleet, there was a pressing need for the "strong reinforcement of our air forces at Singapore" which should "certainly include sufficient quantities of Hurricane fighters".[21] In his diary, Menzies wrote incorrectly that "we are all beginning to see . . . that *air* reinforcement to Singapore and the Far East is the great deterrent". He added, innocently, how "the Jap is reported a poor airman".[22] Neither American servicemen at Pearl Harbor nor British anti-aircraft gunners on board the *Prince of Wales* would have endorsed this verdict. That the battleship could throw up 60,000 bullets and shells a minute made little difference.

In a rapid advance, the Imperial Japanese Army overran British positions in northern Malaya, easily breaking through at Jitra, a strongly fortified line of wire entanglements and deep trenches astride the road to Alor Star. It was expected to be held for three months. An impromptu night attack by barely 500 Japanese soldiers drove off the defenders in a matter of hours. Along with 3,000 prisoners came large stores of ammunition, petrol and food. For the rest of the campaign, these frequent bags of supplies were laughingly called "Churchill's allowance". To turn British positions, baffling tactics were employed, such as night attacks, encirclement, sudden charges and small boat operations. To maintain the momentum of the advance, Yamashita Tomoyuki's men rode bicycles. Tsuji Masanobu recalls how

> the greatest difficulty . . . was the excessive heat, owing to which the tyres punctured easily. A bicycle repair squad of at least two men was attached to each company, and each squad repaired an average of twenty machines a day. But such repairs were only makeshift. When the enemy was being hotly pursued, and time was pressing, punctured tyres were taken off and bicycles ridden on the rims. Surprisingly enough they ran smoothly on the paved roads, which were in perfect condition. Numbers of bicycles some with tyres and some without, when passing along a road, made a noise resembling a tank. At night when such bicycle units advanced the enemy frequently retreated hurriedly, saying, "Here come the tanks!" . . . Thanks to Britain's dear money spent on excellent roads, and to the cheap Japanese bicycles, the assault on Malaya was easy. [23]

And when necessary, the Japanese abandoned pedals and advanced through the jungle, carrying their bicycles on their shoulders. This the British found as disconcerting as attacks from the rear.

It was in fact the jungle that Yamashita Tomoyuki so brilliantly exploited. He realised the potential for outflanking movements when he saw it for the first time near Saigon. His previous posting had been Manzhouguo. Unlike him however, nearly all British senior officers regarded jungle and swampy ground as impenetrable natural obstacles. The shining exception was Ian Stewart, the commanding officer of the 2nd Battalion Argyll and Sutherland Highlanders. Having investigated the problems of fighting under tropical conditions, he took his men on training exercises designed to accustom them to both the advantages and disadvantages of military action in primary as well as secondary jungle. In the process, the Argylls banished any fears they had about plants or animals. "Cross-country movement through the jungle," Stewart wrote, "and living in it for days at a time, not only by large parties but by small groups of three or four officers or NCOs, was practised until the jungle became a friend and not an enemy."[24]

This familiarity saved the Argylls from destruction on several occasions: it also helped inflict an early reverse on the apparently unbeatable Imperial Japanese Army at Grik Road, inland from Penang. There the Japanese were shocked by a counterattack delivered from the jungle on each side of this thoroughfare. As Steward commented:

> One of the arts of rearguard tactics in the jungle is time and space calculation . . . Quite genuinely it is a fascinating game, embodying as it does appreciations of ground, enemy dispositions, and above all the mind and speed of action of the opposing commander. But it is a nervy business, for a commander works with the jungle as a bandage over his eyes; there is no warning of an approaching crisis, and the situation will turn from blue sky to black storm in a minute or two. There are two rules that must never be broken: to hang on desperately to the initiative and to have plans ready and understood by all in anticipation of every eventuality.[25]

Because the British had neither tanks nor an adequate antitank defence, Stewart's use of the jungle alongside roads was critical in the battles which were fought to slow down the Japanese advance.

At the engagement for the bridge at the River Slim in early January 1942, a disastrous British defeat that sealed the fate of Kuala Lumpur, the Argylls improvised road blocks and threw Molotov cocktails at Japanese medium tanks. While the bottle-bombs proved less effective than those used by the Imperial Japanese Army at Nomonhan, there was no shortage of volunteers for the Molotov cocktail party. Through this encounter the Japanese came to respect the courage of Stewart's men, who alone on the surrender of Singapore rode to the Changi prisoner-of-war camp. Impressed by their refusal to hand over their transport, Japanese sentries saluted the column as it went into captivity to the sound of bagpipes. Those Argylls who were sent to work in other parts of the Greater East Asia Co-Prosperity Sphere often found their distinctive bonnets attracted the attention of Japanese officers. In Thailand a sergeant-major was informed that "Argyll Scotsmen number one fighters".

Not that the Argylls' well-deserved reputation for jungle warfare did much to save Malaya or Singapore. Their capture was a foregone conclusion when British military doctrine firmly held that the jungle was impassable for large numbers of troops and that the situation was therefore overwhelmingly in favour of the defenders. It was on this assumption that the so-called fortress at Singapore had been built. Only a threat from the sea was ever seriously considered before the outbreak of the Pacific War. By the time Arthur Percival appreciated what was happening in Malaya, it was too late to adjust to Japanese methods of attack. Percival ordered the adoption of guerrilla tactics. Formations should reduce their transport as far as possible by sending all vehicles that were not immediately wanted well to the rear.[26]

But as Stewart later commented: "New tactics cannot be learnt in the middle of a battle."[27] Another reason for Yamashita Tomoyuki's victory was far better intelligence: he even knew the names of all the Argyll officers. The sheer speed of the Japanese advance gave the British commander-in-chief no chance of regrouping his forces for a last stand in southern Malaya, so that in February 1942 Percival was called upon to conduct his last campaign, the defence of Singapore.

The island's northern defences were almost nonexistent, as the supreme Allied commander, Sir Archibald Wavell, was surprised to discover on his first visit to Singapore. A tough soldier who had fallen foul of Churchill and been transferred from Egypt to India, Wavell was once again expected to accomplish the impossible: operational command over the Dutch East Indies, Burma, the Philippines, Thailand, Malaya, Singapore, and the northern and western coasts of Australia. His headquarters was at Lembang, to the east of Batavia. Thanks to Wavell's prodding and the approach of Yamashita Tomoyuki's army, a limited amount of work was carried out on the northern coast of Singapore. But labour, both civil and military, was in short supply because of the need for repairs to bomb-damaged airfields and docks. According to Tsuji Masanobu, Percival was strongly of the opinion that it was necessary to strengthen the northern defences, but against the opposition of the colonial government he could not carry out the necessary construction work in time. The reason given was that fortification would undermine civilian morale.[28]

Controversy still surrounds the issue, with some blaming the governor, Shenton Thomas, others the general, Arthur Percival. The shortcoming was compounded by the faulty dispositions of Gordon Bennett, as the battle for Singapore was lost in the northwestern part of the island, where Bennett's 8th Australian Division was supposed to hold the coastline. Not only did he fail to incorporate a rear defence line into his overall plan, to deal with any Japanese infiltration, but worse Bennett refused to listen to advice from his trusted chief of staff over troop movements. After the war, this experienced soldier said that the Australian general "would never admit he was wrong".[29] Other extraordinary decisions taken by Bennett towards the end of the siege were to order his men to surrender, without telling Percival; then to leave them behind as prisoners of war while he escaped from Singapore on a native sailing boat. On his arrival back in Australia, he was dismayed to receive a cold welcome from senior army officers, who regarded his escape as a serious error of judgement.[30] Although he sought to place the blame for the fall of Malaya and Singapore squarely on Percival's shoulders, Bennett was never appointed to another command. He even had the temerity to claim later that he, and not Stewart, was the person who first got to grips with the jungle.

"Mr. Quickly-Quickly", as Yamashita Tomoyuki was known to his troops, had pulled off the most gigantic confidence trick. Without in any way disparaging the bravery of the men he led, the fact of the matter was that the Japanese were at the end of their resources when they invaded Singapore. To disguise the lack of shells, Yamashita ordered a colossal bombardment before the leading troops landed, which impressed the defenders, who were still unaware that they actually faced fewer Japanese troops. As Yamashita Tomoyuki himself volunteered,

> my attack on Singapore was a bluff – a bluff that worked. I had 30,000 men and was outnumbered by more than three to one. I knew that if I had to fight long for Singapore I would be beaten. That was why the surrender had to be made at once. I was very frightened that the British would discover our numerical weakness and lack of supplies, and force me into disastrous street fighting.[31]

For the people caught up in the surrender, civilian and military alike, conditions under the victorious Japanese were appalling. The name that Japanese gave to Singapore could not have been more inaccurate: it was never Syonan, "the City of Light and Peace in the South".

A Japanese victory parade at Singapore in early 1942

As in China, the Japanese soldiers went on the rampage, looting, killing and raping at will. They were, according to one eye-witness account, "the Knights of Japan, without fear and without reproach".[32] The scale of the atrocity was not in the same league as Nanjing, but again it fell largely on the Chinese population, for whom Yamashita Tomoyuki harboured great contempt. He ordered a cull of hostile Chinese, later claiming that the mass killings exceeded his orders. Thousands of men between the ages of 15 and 50 were either thrown overboard to drown at sea or executed in improvised prison camps. Despite his protestations of alarm at the abominable behaviour of Japanese soldiers, Tsuji Masanobu did nothing to protect Singapore's residents. In 1941, only two soldiers in the entire Imperial Japanese Army were convicted of rape.[33]

Most feared was arrest by the *Kempeitai*, the Japanese military police. An unsettling aspect of Japanese rule was the arbitrariness of its repression. Failure to bow properly to a soldier was often enough to merit detention or death. When Sinozaki Mamoru went to the *Kempeitai* headquarters in the YMCA building on behalf of the vice-president of the Overseas Chinese Association, an approved society in Singapore, a warrant officer in charge of the case wanted to arrest him as a Japanese traitor. He was uninterested to learn that Sinozaki Mamoru's official role was the protection of civilians. Had a passing *Kempeitai* officer not recognised him, Shinozaki Mamoru would have been immediately locked in a cell. He reflected uneasily how "many Japanese soldiers thought like this warrant officer . . . I felt sad, lonely and dispirited until I remembered myself that the lot of the Singapore people was far worse than mine".[34] At least his severed head would not appear on a pole, a gruesome practice the *Kempeitai* first introduced at Kuala Lumpur. In Singapore, the heads on display were invariably Chinese.

Wavell's troubles really began with the capitulation at Singapore. Because Hong Kong had already fallen, there was nothing to stop the Japanese from spreading throughout Southeast Asia. After long-range bombing by shore-based aircraft, landings took place in Dutch and British Borneo, Sumatra, Sulawesi, Amboina and Timor, a part-Dutch, part-Portuguese island opposite Darwin. Just how stretched the Allied forces were is apparent in the transfer of a Territorial Army anti-aircraft battery to Sparrow Force, an

Australian detachment sent to deny the Japanese use of airfields in Dutch Timor. Originally trained to defend reservoirs near Walton-on-Thames, where public houses enjoyed their custom most evenings, these gunners from Surrey ended up under Wavell's command as the Japanese onslaught engulfed the Indonesian archipelago. At Koepang they gave the impression to the Australians that they had seen action throughout the Battle of Britain. One or two of the gunners felt a little embarrassed by the obvious Australian delight at the arrival of a veteran unit, but it did lift morale.[35] Though Wavell disliked reinforcing small garrisons, the airfields in Timor were essential because short-range planes could not reach Java from Australia without going there to refuel. When news arrived on 19 February of a devastating carrier raid on Darwin, Sparrow Force realised that it was cut off. The same Fuchida Mitsuo who commanded the high-level bombers at Pearl Harbor led the 188 aircraft launched from the carriers *Akagi*, *Kaga*, *Hiryu* and *Soryu*. He thought the raid unworthy of the Imperial Japanese Navy.

Despite having several planes shot down, it was not long before Japanese paratroopers were dropped around Sparrow Force. Regrouping at Babau, to the east of Koepang, the Australians found grim evidence of the treatment that the Japanese gave out to their captives. Several Australians, including one medical orderly, had been tied to trees and had their throats cut. One man had been forced to carry a radio, and when he had collapsed from exhaustion had been brutally bayoneted. He was able to relate his story before dying of his wounds.[36]

Survivors from Sparrow Force were pushed into Portuguese Timor, where they resorted to guerrilla tactics. The Portuguese governor had been instructed not to cooperate with the Allies as it would prejudice Lisbon's neutrality, but he had no choice once fighting spread across the border from Dutch Timor. So effective were the Australian guerrillas that the Imperial Japanese Army had to send extra troops to the island when they could have been better deployed in New Guinea, a desperate campaign in which Japanese soldiers resorted to cannibalism. The year-long guerrilla action coincided with a period of great unrest amongst the native Timorese. In western Timor they were already in revolt against the Dutch before the Japanese arrived and recruited them as anti-European allies: in eastern Timor, however, the Australians were neither attacked nor betrayed as long as their raids harried Japanese garrisons. Some of the eastern Timorese who helped the Australians undoubtedly did so in the mistaken belief that the Australians would eventually help them expel the Portuguese. But when the military initiative passed to the Imperial Japanese Army, the Australians found themselves cornered between the Japanese and warring Timorese factions. Pro-Japanese natives from western Timor exploited local animosities and the Australians were drawn into inter-tribal conflicts that left them in an untenable position. It spelt the end of Allied resistance on the island.

As the invasion of the Dutch East Indies progressed, battles were fought between Allied and Japanese naval forces in the surrounding seas. An American strike at the end of January against a landing at Balikpapan sank four large transports and a patrol boat, but the Japanese took the eastern Borneo town just the same. A Dutch-led naval sortie had no such success. In the Java Sea, 13 warships were lost, including the heavy cruiser *HMS Exeter* of River Plate fame. Despite its efficiency, the *Exeter* was no match for the Japanese cruisers *Haguro* and *Nachi*, each with larger guns and superior armour. They also had 12 fixed torpedo mounts inside their hulls, above their engine rooms. And with a speed almost equal to that of a destroyer, the *Haguro* and the *Nachi* could enter or avoid an engagement as circumstances dictated. Lieutenant Norman Power, the *Exeter*'s cipher officer, summed up the hopelessness of the situation:

> Intelligence told us that the Java and adjoining seas were alive with effective warships and that for ourselves we could only muster a somewhat elderly and decrepit force of mixed nationality Cruisers and Destroyers . . . When it was announced over the tannoy system that an ever increasing number of masts belonging to what turned out to be enemy ships were appearing on the horizon, my heart was as near my boots as it is possible for a heart to be without becoming detached.[37]

His pessimism was justified. When the *Haguro* sank the *Exeter*, survivors were unable to get the boats away and had only floating debris to hold on to in the water. After a couple of hours, Japanese destroyers saved 714 officers and men. They were well treated by the Imperial Japanese Navy, perhaps because of the old relationship with the Royal Navy, but this was not the case when they were handed over as prisoners of war. On land they suffered the same indifferent treatment as surrendered Allied soldiers.

In the Philippines, determined resistance was offered to the Japanese, the rocky island of Corregidor at the entrance to Manila Bay holding out until early May. Fog in Taiwan delayed the Japanese air offensive against the Philippines for six hours after the seaborne strike at Pearl Harbor. Japanese aircrew were therefore surprised that the Americans failed to respond more vigorously to the delayed attack. Only seven Zero fighters and a single bomber did not return to their bases in Taiwan. One reason for this poor start by the Americans was the attitude of Douglas MacArthur, whose lack of respect for Japan verged on outright contempt. Overlooking the fact that the Imperial Japanese Army had taken control of large areas of China, he said in 1939 that:

> It will cost the enemy, in my opinion, half a million men as casualties and upwards of five billion of dollars in money to pursue such an adventure (invading the Philippines) with any hope of success. It has been assumed, in my opinion erroneously, that Japan covets these islands. Just why has never been satisfactorily explained. Proponents of such a theory fail to credit the logic of the Japanese mind.[38]

Incredibly cavalier though MacArthur's outlook was, his subordinates had the good sense to recognise that the forces available to defend the Philippines were hopelessly inadequate. Nor were they in agreement with MacArthur's assertion that if the Japanese came, it would not be until April 1942 at the earliest. Beneath this disdain for Japan's fighting capacity was the same prejudice that informed British thinking: the squinting Japanese could never make good pilots, as Robert Menzies was led to believe in London. The racial stereotype of the Japanese male as a slow-witted and shortsighted dwarf soon gave place to an exaggerated fear of his superhuman stamina and courage, at least until the bloody struggle at Guadalcanal revealed the shortcomings of Japanese tactics. The warnings of Claire Chennault, American liaison officer to the Guomindang, that Japanese pilots in their Zero fighters were of the highest quality fell on deaf ears. As one of those who flew from Taiwan commented, in the invasion of the Philippines, the Zero was "our sword, shield, and buckler".[39]

Bad weather and attacks by surviving American planes hampered the Japanese landings, but with such an extensive coastline to defend it was impossible to resist in strength everywhere. The initial landing was made at Aparri, in the far north of Luzon island, at daybreak on 10 December 1941 by a force of destroyers and transports. Because there was only one company of American soldiers to oppose the landing, within two days Japanese planes were operating from the Aparri airfield. Despite sightings by American submarines of Japanese invasion forces, MacArthur had no clear idea of his opponent's intentions. Knocking out most of his air force at the outset meant that the Japanese could operate without being spotted from the air. They used this advantage to the full. On 2 January 1942, Manila fell, American and Filipino forces having retreated to the nearby Bataan peninsula and the island of Corregidor.

The Japanese attack on Bataan began a week later and was marked by heavy casualties as they ran into prepared American positions. General Homma Masaharu came to the view that it would be wiser to starve its defenders into submission, for which suggestion he was severely reprimanded. In overconfident Tokyo, such a cautious approach was tantamount to defeatism. That he possessed insufficient men to overcome a planned system of defence never occurred to his distant critics. Arguably, this intelligence failure cost Japan dear, if only because dogged resistance in the Philippines tied down troops who could have gone to either Guadalcanal or New Guinea. So annoyed was the Imperial Japanese Army that, after the surrender, American and Filipino prisoners of war were subjected to one of its notorious death marches: 2,250 US and Filipino servicemen died. Japanese soldiers were particularly cruel to the Filipinos, whom they regarded as colonial lackeys. Hardly 40 per cent of the Americans who surrendered in the Philippines were to return home. This indifference to suffering on the part of their captors became patently obvious during the final stages of the Pacific War. At Sandakan in north Borneo 2,428 Australian and British prisoners of war were marched to death in 1945. Just six men managed to escape and survive a deliberate attempt to prevent them from seeing Japan's defeat.[40]

The only action comparable with the American defence of the Philippines was the fighting retreat of the British in Burma. There the last-minute appointment of William Slim turned a potential rout into a taxing withdrawal. On his arrival in March 1942, it was self-evident that the colony would not be able to offer sustained resistance to the 15th Japanese Army, whose tactics paralleled those used by Yamashita Tomoyuki in Malaya. Disaster first struck the British defenders near the Thai-Burma border. Having been forced back into Burma and evacuated the southern port of Moulmein, a stand was attempted at the River Sittang whose long bridge allowed access to Rangoon. The defeat of the 17th Indian Division on the Sittang was a terrible one, but Wavell's strategy of holding up the Japanese as far away from Rangoon for as long as possible, so that reinforcements could be brought in to defeat them via this port, was militarily sound. It permitted the disembarkation of the 7th Armoured Brigade, originally destined for Malaya.

This strategy was unfortunately compromised by the commander of the 17th Indian Division, the highly decorated Jackie Smyth, who overlooked the possibility of Japanese flanking movements as he withdrew his forces to the Sittang bridge. To send the whole division and its transport along a broken-down road was bound to be slow, even if the enemy did not interfere. To have left an inadequate guard on the bridge itself was foolhardy. On 21 February, news reached Smyth that large Japanese forces were already ahead of him en route for the Sittang river. Even though he ordered extra troops to hold the vulnerable eastern side of the bridge, as they took up defensive positions there, they could hear the ominous sound of enemy machine-gun fire. A heavy Japanese attack took place the next day. Smyth got within sight of the bridge, but the failure to establish an effective defence well before the arrival of the Japanese, and the consequent inability to use the approach road, created a serious handicap. The loss of many radios complicated an already confused situation. Some of his troops managed to cross the river by boat, and Smyth set up his headquarters on the other side. Many others were still on the east bank when the order was given to demolish the bridge's central spans on 23 February. Up to the explosion, the Japanese actually thought that they were getting the worst of the fighting. Now they knew that although they could no longer capture the bridge intact, they had won the battle. Appreciating that the defeat meant the loss of Rangoon as well as southern Burma, Wavell sent Smyth home on retirement leave. In a matter of days, William Slim was called in and ordered to salvage what he could.

As the Japanese advanced northwards, Slim fought a series of well-conducted delaying actions. One of them, at Kokkogwa, north of Prome, ended in an unusual humiliation for the Japanese, who were so shaken by the experience that they failed to recover their dead, always a shameful omission. Already the new commander was sowing the seeds of a British recovery in the interest he showed in jungle warfare. He allowed Michael Calvert to raid Japanese lines with his locally trained guerrillas and was pleased to learn that the daring major, after an initial disagreement, got on well with Orde Wingate, Wavell's favourite. The meeting of these two enthusiasts for irregular tactics was to lead to the formation of the famous Chindits. Racing the Japanese and the monsoon, Slim led his battered troops into India with mixed feelings. He had shared their hardships, even sporting a beard like that of so many of his men until he noticed the hairs were coming out white. Thirteen thousand had been killed or wounded against a Japanese total of 4,000. He recalls how on the last day of the thousand-kilometre retreat:

> I stood on a bank beside the road and watched the rearguard march into India. All of them, British, Indian, and Gurkha, were gaunt and ragged as scarecrows. Yet, as they trudged behind their surviving officers in groups pitifully small, they still carried their arms and kept their ranks, they were still recognizable as fighting units. They might look like scarecrows, but they looked like soldiers too.[41]

Japan's New Order in Asia

With the British retreat into India, Japan became the sole colonial power of any importance in Southeast Asia. Pointing up the extent of the collapse of Western influence, the Imperial Japanese Navy's foray across the Indian Ocean during April 1942 terrified Churchill, who thought it presaged an invasion of the subcontinent. He did not know that India, like Australia, was considered by Tokyo as a country too far. Admiral Nagumo's raid nonetheless inflicted damage on the Royal Navy. Had a shortage of water not sent some vessels back to Addu Atoll, a secret base 800 kilometres south of Colombo, losses would have been much greater. As it was, Japanese planes sank the heavy cruisers *Dorsetshire* and *Cornwall*, and then the old aircraft carrier *Hermes* on its way from Trincomalee to Colombo.

The change in colonial fortunes was emphasised on land by the Imperial Japanese Army's policy of humiliating Europeans before local populations. In Malaya, British and Australian captives, stripped to the waist, were made to tackle manual work as a reminder that before the Japanese came, Europeans never undertook such tasks. The *Syonan Times*, the renamed *Straits Times*, announced that the sultans who controlled the various Malay states had paid their respects to Yamashita Tomoyuki, and were looking forward to rebuilding Malaya with Japanese support.

Early restoration of peaceful conditions in occupied territories was of course a primary objective for the Imperial Japanese Army, which needed to free combat units for operations elsewhere in Southeast Asia. Troops were sent on to the Dutch East Indies, where they had not only to take over from the colonial administration but also put down rebellious movements among the native population. In Sumatra and Java, attacks on Europeans and the looting of their houses indicated the start of a revolutionary nationalism that was to embarrass Japan. In Aceh, the anti-Dutch agitation had strong religious overtones. Acehnese religious leaders had taken the initiative in 1939 and set up the All-Aceh Union of Ulamas to modernise Islamic schools. It rapidly became the focus of opposition to Dutch colonial rule and, in the weeks before the Japanese landed in Sumatra, union members began a campaign of sabotage that quickly developed into an all-out assault on European property. The Imperial Japanese Army was forced to intervene to redirect the Indonesian economy to support Japan's war effort. But its efforts tended only to add to the confusion once Indonesia was flooded with occupation currency. Because this currency was worthless, food requisitioning actually led to famine in both Sumatra and Java.

From the outset of the occupation, the Japanese tried to placate Indonesian religious leaders, who they feared could be as difficult to themselves as they had been to the Dutch, while keeping nationalist aspirations firmly under control. Only later, when defeat became inevitable, were Indonesian nationalists given free rein in the hopes of frustrating an Allied reconquest.

The experience of Surabaya, a coastal city in northeastern Java, can be seen as a barometer of the political change inaugurated by the arrival of the Imperial Japanese Army. With the defeat of the hotchpotch Allied naval force in the Java Sea to the north of Surabaya, the city's Dutch residents seriously spoke of killing all European hospital patients if they could not be moved before the Japanese landed. The colonial authorities burned its records and ordered the destruction of all facilities of any conceivable value to the enemy. Concluding that the Dutch were finished, most of the locally recruited police force deserted, an action that gave looters the run of Surabaya city. The lawlessness shocked the Japanese as much as the Dutch when they occupied Surabaya on 8 March. It was fortunate for the survivors from *HMS Exeter* and other Allied warships sunk during the battle of the Java Sea that they were sent to prisoner-of-war camps in parts of Indonesia where the population was less virulently anti-European.

Japanese ignorance of Javanese ways thwarted an eager wish to establish an anti-Western regime, because Dutch knowledge of local conditions was found to be essential for maintaining control. The Japanese were obliged to intern the Dutch colonists so slowly that they were lulled into a false sense of security. While they did not greet the Japanese with any enthusiasm, the Javanese took undisguised delight in the downfall of the Dutch. One Dutch officer based in Surabaya wrote later how

> we had a general notion about the Javanese people. I quite understood that they didn't exactly worship us, but that they harboured such a hatred for us as then appeared came as a surprise to me. I never thought it was so bad. [42]

A visit by Sukarno, the future Indonesian president, three months after the city's capture led to a crackdown on local nationalists. Although the rostrum provided for Sukarno was decked with Japanese flags, and his speech concentrated on blaming the Dutch for Indonesia's ills, the size and excitement of the crowd alarmed the Imperial Japanese Army enough for a prohibition to be placed on all future meetings.

To some educated Indonesians, the Meiji programme of modernisation seemed to point the way for fruitful cooperation with Japan. What they slowly came to appreciate, however, was that the Japanese, as did their Dutch predecessors, intended to control Indonesia for their own imperial interests. Agricultural production was adjusted for the benefit of Japan, with crops such as sugar being artificially depressed to the advantage of farmers at home and in Taiwan. Because sugar estates provided work for the landless Javanese, this policy caused real hardship. The Japanese military leadership was sensitive to the conflicts inherent in the occupation and its policies, but took the view that little could be done until hostilities ended. In Surabaya, uneasy coexistence typified relations between the conquerors and the conquered, even after a civilian administration replaced direct military rule, and its head, Yasuoka Masaomi, learned the Javanese language well enough to use it in public. A retired army officer, Yasuoka Masaomi enjoyed paying visits to government offices and schools throughout the city. Despite a lingering distrust, he tried to employ as many Indonesians as possible, both because this was practical and because of a genuine feeling that Asia belonged to Asians. Yasuoka Masaomi even temporarily released Dutch officials from internment to train Indonesians to take their places in the local administration.

If there was one welcome thing the Japanese New Order did bring to the Dutch East Indies, it was an end to the racial discrimination that had bedevilled colonial relations for centuries. With the single exception of the Simpang Club, which was the preserve of Japanese military officers, there was in Surabaya no bar any longer to membership of clubs or societies on the basis of ethnicity. For the Indonesians, whom the Dutch preferred to go barefoot, this was a significant social improvement. Yet the contradictions in the New Order were soon apparent in the field of education. Popular discontent resulted from censorship of the curriculum, an emphasis on physical training and compulsory lessons in the Japanese language. Another sign of New Order propaganda was the appearance in public places of radios-on-poles. By Sukarno's second visit to Surabaya in 1943, the Japanese were less worried about mass meetings, but they had cause to reflect on the import of his message, for Sukarno said: "The fate of our people is in our own hands and not in those of others."[43]

That year, the growing weakness of Japan in the face of the Allied counterattack brought about a loosening of control, even an attempt to enlist active support in the war effort. But the Movement for the Total Mobilisation of the Javanese People had to be shut down after six months, when the Japanese authorities saw it was being used as a vehicle for nationalist interests. In Surabaya, the movement was never fully disbanded, its members forming the core of the resistance to the return of Dutch rule at the end of the Pacific War. A strong tide was running towards independence, and especially among the young, Mohammad Hatta was equally convinced. Along with Sukarno and other prominent Indonesians, he was chosen by the Japanese to help with the mobilisation movement. In 1927, Hatta had been arrested on the charge of encouraging armed resistance to Dutch rule but, after five months in prison, he was acquitted in the Hague, much to the dismay of the colonial authorities. Meanwhile, Sukarno, an engineer by training, had achieved a united front of the main Indonesian nationalist organisations: his political philosophy denied the need for Islamic reform or its dominance in an independent Indonesia, a stance that was attractive to non-Moslems and non-Malays alike. Two years after Hatta's arrest, Batavia finally moved against Sukarno, who was convicted at Bandung of being a threat to public order and sentenced to four years in the local prison. The anti-Dutch credentials of Sukarno, the future Indonesian president, and Mohammad Hatta, the future prime minister, were therefore impeccable.

Once the Japanese recognised that they were unable to hold the Allies at bay any longer, they asked the two men to devise a formula for cooperation and draft a constitution for an independent republic. The new state was to incorporate under a strong presidency not only the territories of the Dutch East Indies but those belonging to Britain in Malaya and Borneo as well. Because the Indonesian leaders did not want independence as a gift from the Japanese, on 17 August 1945, two days after the surrender of Japan, Sukarno proclaimed the Republic of Indonesia.

The inhabitants of Surabaya had already taken over the running of the city. Because the Netherlands had no troops available, and British forces were already spread thin in Southeast Asia, this unreal arrangement lasted several weeks. Released Dutch internees were just as bewildered on their return to the city, especially when the first British officers to arrive by parachute gratefully accepted the protection of surrendered Japanese soldiers. Collaboration between the Dutch and the British lit the fuse in Surabaya, whose explosive response to the reimposition of colonial rule had by November sent a shockwave round the world. As in Saigon, the colonists started the trouble by direct action. Their attempt to raise the Dutch flag over the British headquarters provoked a popular reaction that could not be contained by the Japanese garrison, the sight of whose bayonets was too much for the Surabayans to stomach. First the Japanese were overwhelmed and killed; then the Dutch found themselves reinterned or slaughtered in their houses; and last of all, a newly arrived British unit was cornered and its commander killed. The subsequent ten-day Allied assault from sea, land and air all but destroyed the city: the sacrifice of the Indonesians in its hopeless defence staggered the British, who were quite unaware of the strength of Indonesian nationalism. Only the Dutch refused to appreciate how changed the situation was in Asia, and shortly afterwards tried without success to reimpose their authority.

In Indochina, the Japanese retained French officials until March 1945. The sudden change of policy left the colonial government gasping but, with the end of the Pacific War in sight, it was still believed that collaboration with Japan had saved French Indochina. Yet the willingness of the Japanese to aid nationalists in Vietnam, as in Java and Sumatra, gave impetus to an independence movement that France was incapable of stopping. Immediately after the Japanese coup in March, the provisional government of Charles de Gaulle in Paris informed the world it would regain Indochina for France, quite overlooking the changes that the Japanese occupation had wrought in Vietnam. Well might the assistance given to nationalist movements have reflected Japan's needs rather than any sympathy with their aspirations, but the Imperial Japanese Army now accepted that it risked damaging its own position by unnecessary repression of the peoples in occupied territories. The primary objective of the conquest of Southeast Asia had been economic, but the systematic exploitation of its assets was frustrated by the wartime disruption of communications, in particular the losses sustained by Japan's merchant fleet. Few ships were left afloat to transport oil, the very product for which Japan began hostilities. In spite of so much violence and hardship, the drive for self-sufficiency within the Greater East Asia Co-prosperity Sphere had come to nothing.

Another reason for a less repressive regime towards the end of the Pacific War was a widespread shortage of food. A terrible famine swept through north Vietnam in early 1945, caused first by drought and then, incredibly, by typhoons. Rice production had fallen steadily during the Japanese occupation, but the unseasonable weather converted a crisis into a disaster. Thousands of destitute people begged in the streets of Hanoi. One resident recorded in his diary: "Sounds of crying as at a funeral. Elderly twisted women, naked children huddled against the wall or lying inside a mat, fathers and children prostrate along the road, corpses hunched up like foetuses, an arm thrust out as if to threaten. Wanted to photograph."[44] As many as half a million Vietnamese may have perished in the famine.

Elsewhere, the Japanese occupation brought semi-starvation and deficiency diseases to local populations. In Malaya, children were especially hard hit, as their rates of growth failed to keep up with their ages. Children of 14 years were no taller than those aged seven or eight. So desperate did the food supply become in Singapore that plans were made for the relocation of 300,000 residents, about 40 per cent of the island's population. Shinozaki Mamoru was uncertain about the attitude of the residents towards the new settlement of New Syonan at Endau, in northeastern Johore. He need not have worried, because "thousands of Singaporeans heard what was happening at New Syonan and applied to settle there, away from the constant pressure of the dreaded *Kempeitai*. To show their appreciation, the settlers presented the settlement's first crop of rice to the mayor of Syonan."[45] Because Shinozaki Mamoru had persuaded the Japanese authorities to let the Chinese settlers at Endau make their own arrangements for law and order, without any assistance from the *Kempeitai*, it is not surprising that the Overseas Chinese Association found "the finest jungle workers in Malaya" to clear the site.

Because the United States had promised independence to the Philippines, the Japanese were more cautious in their occupation, except when it came to surrendered Filipino soldiers. Shortly after Manila fell, talks were held with leading nationalists including Benigno Aquino and José Laurel. These Filipinos eventually called upon their compatriots to accept the American defeat for what it was, a comprehensive Japanese triumph that left no scope for continued resistance. One Japanese officer did not mince his words when he said: "Like it or not, you are Filipinos and belong to the Oriental race. No matter how hard you try, you cannot become white people."[46] Ignoring the American reaction to the Bataan death march, Filipino leaders collaborated throughout the period of the Japanese occupation, José Laurel being appointed in October 1943 as the head of a separate government. As happened in supposedly independent Burma, the Philippines discovered its freedom of action was strictly limited. But Tojo Hideki's delegation of power had its desired effect, since troops released from garrison duties could be redeployed to meet the coming American invasion.

Despite the deteriorating economic situation in the Greater East Asia Co-prosperity Sphere, Tokyo gambled on the possibility that the forces of Asian nationalism might be enlisted against the resurgent Allies. In September 1944, it seemed that the gamble had paid off when Laurel went so far as a declaration of war between the United States and the Philippines. The dividend was small, however, for Filipino guerrilla bands still fought on against the Japanese. They also liaised with the Allied Intelligence Bureau, the Pacific theatre's equivalent of the OSS: its operatives worked with the guerrillas in their jungle hideouts, sending back an invaluable stream of information to MacArthur about Japanese troop strengths and shipping movements.[47] In the shambles of the American reconquest of the Philippines, the testimony of these operatives was to be critical in apportioning praise and blame.

The Fall of the Japanese Empire

Burma and the Philippines were the two colonies most thoroughly fought over during the Pacific War. For Britain, the recapture of Burma was of the utmost political importance, because it had to be demonstrated that British power in Asia was not yet finished. For the United States, on the other hand, the expulsion of the Japanese from the Philippines was a matter of national honour. That was why the Japanese knew that they would have to exert themselves in these colonies.

One liberation movement sponsored by Tokyo had an unexpected impact on Burma. Its aim was the freeing of India from British control and its instrument was Subhas Chandra Bose, who rejected Gandhi's attachment to nonviolence and was impatient to have an Indian army fighting alongside the Japanese. Whether in Germany, where he broadcast and met Indian prisoners of war, or in Japan, to which he travelled in German and Japanese submarines that made a rendezvous off Madagascar, his considerable energy was poured into the task of raising the Indian National Army. A prime target for recruitment was the large number of Indian soldiers who surrendered on the fall of Singapore. With the permission of the Japanese authorities, Bose extracted funds from the Indian business community in Malaya to finance both his government-in-exile and its armed forces. Malaya's own 800,000 Indian residents also offered possibilities for recruitment.

Bose's call for Indians outside India to take up arms attracted 18,000 Tamil workers from the rubber estates, in part because the British never considered that the Tamils, unlike other Indian peoples such as the Marathas, the Rajputs and the Sikhs, possessed the military qualities necessary to join their armed forces. Even Tamil women enlisted in the Indian National Army. By June 1944, some 230,000 Indians in Malaya alone had pledged their support to Bose's provisional government. To give his claim political substance, Tokyo announced that Bose could administer the Andaman and Nicobar Islands, off the coast of Burma. In reality, the British authorities in India were unnecessarily anxious about this administration, for the Imperial Japanese Navy had no intention of handing over the islands to any of Bose's followers. He was flown in for a flag-raising ceremony at Port Blair, a renowned penal colony, and after photographs were taken, flown out again. Yet the declaration of intent did not go unnoticed in India. Hearing of Bose's death in an air crash in late August 1945, Viceroy Wavell breathed a sigh of relief. In his journal he wrote: "His disposal would have presented a most difficult problem."[48]

Among those recruited by the Indian National Army in Malaya were soldiers who were captured at Singapore. Many of these men felt abandoned by the British, who seemed to have lost the will to resist the Japanese. Yamashita Tomoyuki's lightning campaign had been a revelation. When Bose said that the Imperial Japanese

Army would soon do the same in India, there were Indian prisoners of war who believed him. Few Indian officers responded to his call, although they had had to tolerate discrimination before the Japanese victory. The two main clubs in Singapore, the Tanglin and the Swimming Club, were exclusively European in membership. The racism underlying this arrangement became very apparent in the weeks before the Japanese siege of the island, as Indian officers were denied entry, unlike fellow British officers from their regiments. Club members were naturally shocked to discover later that the strictness of committee rules provided no protection at all from Yamashita Tomoyuki and his men.

The attempt made by Bose to suborn Indian troops in the British Fourteenth Army met with little success. One problem was the low morale of the Indian National Army itself, which the Japanese allowed to join their March 1944 attack across the Indian border. Once its soldiers were found incapable of taking part in the bitter hand-to-hand fighting, their role had to be restricted to spreading confusion among the Indian soldiers resisting the Japanese advance. After the Imperial Japanese Army fell back from disastrous reverses at Imphal and Kohima, and retreated into Burma, Bose's soldiers were largely left to their fate. General Slim, the commander of the Fourteenth Army, remembered how they just wandered

> about the country without object and cohesion. They had suffered a good many casualties at the hands of our patrols and during May were surrendering in large numbers, but our Indian and Gurkha soldiers were at times not too ready to let them surrender, and orders had to be issued to give them a kinder welcome. The Gandhi Brigade (of the Indian National Army) took no further appreciable part in operations and what was left of it the Japanese in disgust used mainly as porters.[49]

The costly attempt to invade India had been doomed from the start by the Imperial Japanese Army's usual inability to consider logistics. Without adequate support from the air, Japanese soldiers ran short of supplies and had to eat pack animals as well as grass for food. Their situation was made intolerable by Slim's new tactics, which were to stand firm and fight on whenever positions were

253

surrounded. No supplies were captured as they had been in the Malayan campaign.

The improved strength of the Royal Air Force was another factor, since it was able to sustain hard-pressed garrisons by parachute drops, an innovation that resulted from British activities behind Japanese lines. The Chindits, a long-range penetration force, had pioneered the use of air supply and the radio. They had also led the way in jungle warfare by showing how a small force could wreak havoc out of all proportion to its numbers. If it should be surprised, then the column would disintegrate into small groups, and meet again at a prearranged rendezvous a safe distance away. Food and ammunition were dropped from the skies, and the wounded evacuated by light aircraft, while at the height of the struggle in Kohima, when the Japanese gained possession of the defenders' water supply, planes flew at treetop level to deliver motor-car inner tubes filled with water. By 5 April, the garrison at Kohima was encircled by more than 6,000 Japanese troops, in a triangular area measuring 900 by 1,100 by 1,400 metres. Its survival depended on the daring of RAF pilots, who usually managed to drop supplies within the restricted defensive perimeter. Rarely did the parachutes drift into enemy lines to become "Churchill's allowance".

The rout of the Imperial Japanese Army as it was pressed back in Burma had cost it 100,000 men by the fall of Rangoon in May 1945. One of the heaviest defeats ever suffered, its retreat was characterised by inexplicable acts of valour and violence. To the amazement of their British pursuers, a cut-off group of Japanese soldiers, in full equipment and with closed ranks, marched into the Irrawaddy River until its dark waters closed above their heads. As self-destructive, though more effective, were the human mines used to deal with advancing British tanks. A Japanese soldier would crouch with an aircraft bomb between his knees in a foxhole, and strike the fuse with a stone as the tank passed nearby. Elsewhere, unprovoked attacks on hospitals and the civilian population were signs of Japanese rage.

The invasion of the Indian borderlands was almost the last major operation launched by Japan. During 1943, the outer defences of the Greater East Asia Co-prosperity Sphere began to crumble dramatically. The Solomon and Gilbert Islands were lost, New Guinea

At Cairo in 1943, Franklin D. Roosevelt, Winston Churchill and Chiang Kai-shek

retaken by the Australians and the Americans, the Marshall Islands fell in February 1944, and the Japanese garrison on Truk, in the Caroline Islands, was the same month condemned to a fierce US air and naval bombardment. Whereas the Imperial Japanese Navy was unable to replace the four aircraft carriers sunk at Midway in June 1942, American shipyards were turning out dozens of carriers, which became the core of task forces assaulting Japanese bastions in the Pacific.

While the battle of the Coral Sea a month earlier, the first naval engagement to be decided by carrier-based aircraft, had stopped the Japanese capture of Port Moresby in New Guinea, the American victory was far from decisive. There the *Lexington*, the biggest ship in the American fleet, exploded and went to the bottom. Only at Midway could the United States seize the naval initiative by sinking the pride of the Imperial Japanese Navy, the aircraft carriers *Akagi*, *Kaga*, *Soryu* and *Hiryu*. The first three were destroyed in six minutes by American dive bombers, the fourth was caught later on its own. Admiral Yamamoto Isoroku, who commanded from a battleship, still hoped to salvage something from the ruinous encounter right up to the destruction of the *Hiryu*. Afterwards, he might have turned the American triumph into a Japanese victory had the US Pacific Fleet set off in pursuit, for Yamamoto possessed another carrier, the *Jintsu*, plus nine battleships and numerous heavy cruisers. With only two remaining aircraft carriers to guard Midway Island, and the central Pacific, the Americans moved their ships out of harm's way. Admiral Raymond Spruance's decision was the correct one: in spite of horrendous losses of aircraft and pilots, he had broken Japanese naval-air supremacy without sacrificing more than the *Yorktown*. This carrier succumbed to a Japanese submarine shortly after the battle was over.

After the Midway defeat, Japan was on the defensive in the Pacific, although a few diehards would remain an annoyance to the Allies on recaptured island jungles. From mid-1944 onwards, the Americans began an island-hopping campaign towards Japan, and in October MacArthur was recorded by film cameramen wading in near-deep water as US troops returned to the Philippines. The campaign to liberate the colony did not go according to plan, however. Because of the intensity of the Japanese resistance, an American attempt to keep destruction to a minimum came to nothing and Manila suffered damage on a par with Warsaw and Budapest. More than 200,000 of its residents needlessly died in the month-long assault. The Americans understood early on that the battle for the Philippines would be no ordinary conflict when a new Japanese weapon appeared in the form of the kamikazes.

Admiral Thomas Sprague's task force in the Philippine Sea was the first to come under attack on 25 October, when Zeros suddenly began crash diving on his ships. It took a single kamikaze to destroy the *St. Lo*, while three more carriers were disabled by direct hits. The divine wind, the *kamikaze*, that had thwarted the Mongol invasion of Japan in the thirteenth century, was reincarnated in the bombplanes that had taken off from Mabalacat airfield, north of Manila. Admiral Onishi Takijiro told the suicide-pilots there that

> Japan is in grave danger. The salvation of our country is now beyond the powers of ministers of state, or the General Staff, and lowly commanders like myself. Therefore, on behalf of your hundred million countrymen, I ask of you this sacrifice and pray for your success. Regrettably, we will not be able to

tell you the results. But I shall watch your efforts to the end and report your deeds to the Throne. You may rest assured on this point. You are already gods, without earthly desires. You are going to enter on a long sleep.[50]

With tears in his eyes, the admiral then shook hands with these first suicide-pilots. When Emperor Hirohito was informed of the results of the mission, he said: "Was it necessary to go to this extreme? But they have certainly done a good job."[51] The ferocity of the kamikazes struck terror in Allied seamen's hearts, but they had no real chance of halting the American juggernaut. Japanese planes could not match improved US fighters in the last 18 months of the Pacific War, and whole squadrons of kamikazes were consequently wiped out before they could reach their targets.

General Terauchi Hisaichi, son of the prime minister and governor-general of Korea Terauchi Masatake, had a determination equal to the kamikazes. Since 1943, he had been in command of all Japan's southern armies, with his headquarters first at Singapore, then Manila. He had no intention of giving up the Philippines without a fight. Ordered to move in November to Saigon, Terauchi Hisaichi later suffered the indignity there of handing over his two swords to Lord Mountbatten after the Japanese surrender. One of them currently resides at Windsor Castle. As US troops stormed the beaches of Leyte, an island situated in the middle of the Philippine archipelago, Terauchi Hisaichi never contemplated handing over his ceremonial weapons to the supreme commander of the Southeast Asia Allied Command, since he ordered Japanese soldiers to fight as fearlessly as the suicide-pilots.

Japanese opposition on Leyte threw MacArthur's planning into utter disarray, because he had expected a quick conquest and then an early invasion of Luzon, the main island where Manila is located. Not least because it was already the rainy season on Leyte, the Americans discovered that their jeeps and lorries bogged down in mud. The iron will of Yamashita Tomoyuki added to these problems once he was assigned the defence of the Philippines. As it would take several months to overcome the determined garrison on Leyte, MacArthur had to rethink his whole approach to the Philippine campaign. When he ordered landings on the islands of Mindoro and Luzon, both invasion forces ran into a hornet's nest of kamikazes. The landing on Mindoro surprised Yamashita Tomoyuki, who halted the reinforcement of Leyte better to prepare the defence of Luzon, which he knew was the chief American target. His tactics had to take account of the inability of Japanese pilots to challenge their American opponents. Without command of the skies, Yamashita Tomoyuki could not afford to fight in open terrain where his units would be exposed to aerial attack. So he rejected a repeat of the American withdrawal into the Bataan peninsula and instead decided that his army should

> secure the vital north Luzon area with its main strength, and the mountainous regions east of Manila and west of Clark Field with elements of its forces. The forces in each of these areas will coordinate their operations with the objective of containing American forces on Luzon and destroying [their] fighting strength, and at the same time prepare for protracted resistance on independent, self-sufficient basis.[52]

It was also intended that the Americans would have to accept heavy casualties in the recapture of Manila. And of course all remaining kamikazes would be thrown into Luzon's defence. Twenty-four US vessels were sunk, 30 disabled and 37 damaged. General Herbert Lumsden, Churchill's representative at MacArthur's headquarters, was killed when a kamikaze hit the bridge of the battleship *New Mexico*. Its captain died as well.

In Manila, the fighting was particularly fierce. The Japanese deliberately set on fire large areas of the city to delay the American troops, who were at first greeted by the Filipinos with relief. Their joy soon evaporated as the advancing Americans demolished hundreds of buildings themselves. The last stand of the Japanese was in the Intramuros, Manila's original Spanish settlement, whose moat and stone walls enclosed an area 500 metres square. Once it was realised that the defenders had no intention of giving in, a massive bombardment was quickly followed by an infantry assault that carried the Intramuros' walls. Still unwilling to surrender, the surviving Japanese holed up in Fort Santiago, where they fell eventually victim to flamethrowers, hand grenades and shell fire.

The horror of Manila's liberation remains a permanent blot on MacArthur's campaign. A Filipino woman expressed the general mood when she recalled how

> I spat on the very first American soldier I saw . . . a few seconds before, he had shouted at me from behind a tree in the Malate Street: "Hey you! Wanna get yourself killed?" . . . Our home had been ransacked, put to the torch, its ruins shelled again and again . . . I had seen all the unforgettable, indescribable carnage . . . the carpet-shelling by the Americans which went relentlessly on, long after the last Japanese sniper was a carcass on the rubble . . . and this precious American, awaited desperately for the last three years, pink-cheeked and overfed, tall and mighty, wanted to know, his dear American idioms rising over the crashing of the bullets and the shells, whether I wanted to die. . . So this was Liberation. I was no longer sure what was worse: the inhumanity of the Japanese or the helpfulness of the Americans.[53]

Before Manila was "safely" in American hands on 3 March, the Australians had started a campaign of their own to the south in Borneo. Its objective was to gain control of the oilfields there, since it was a closer source of supply for an invasion of Japan than oil brought all the way from the United States.

The Borneo operation on land was under the command of Leslie Morshead, the outstanding Australian general of the Second World War. His 9th Australian Division had bloodied Rommel's nose at Tobruk, where German casualties were so great in March 1941 that the "Desert Fox" himself received a reprimand. After a stint in New Guinea, these veterans gained control of eastern and western Borneo without tremendous difficulty, adding in the process a seventh Victoria Cross to the impressive divisional tally. They received stalwart support from the Dyaks, native headhunters who hated the Japanese. The Australians duly accepted the surrender of the 37th Japanese Army on the island of Labuan, close to the main oilfields, on 10 September. Morshead's typically understated response to public congratulation about the 9th Division's distinguished war record was "the boys were interested."[54]

The Surrender of Japan

Before the final capitulation, bloody engagements were fought by the United States for the capture of Iwo Jima and Okinawa, two strongly fortified islands on the doorstep of Japan. American losses of almost 27,000 killed on Iwo Jima were greater than the annihilated Japanese garrison. On Okinawa, the Americans lost 12,000 men to kill 80,000 Japanese entrenched in caves and bunkers. Another 37,000 GIs were wounded. This meant that American forces suffered greater casualties in the first six months of 1945 than they did during the previous three years of fighting in the Pacific. Faced with losses on this scale, Washington calculated that between a quarter of a million and half a million more men would have to die to successfully invade Japan itself. Hence the audible sigh of relief when Russia promised to join the Pacific War, although Stalin's motive in becoming a belligerent was the recovery of territories lost to Japan since 1906. Harry S. Truman, the vice-president who succeeded to

After a *kamikaze* attack, *USS Bunker Hill* retires from Okinawa

the presidency on Roosevelt's death, was less convinced than his predecessor about the need for Stalin's help against a Japan determined to fight on. In the ruins of the former German imperial palace at Potsdam at the beginning of August, the United States, Britain and Russia issued a declaration calling upon Japan to cease hostilities or face "prompt and utter destruction". At this conference, Truman told Stalin of a powerful new weapon that had been exploded at a test site in New Mexico. The explosion was the climax of a research project that involved American, Canadian and British scientists, but during the final stages of development, the United States chose to keep secret the method of the atom bomb's actual construction. It was to be this weapon, and not conventional force, that would in Asia restore Western prestige, if not Western colonial power. Even though Stalin's spies had already told him about the Manhattan Project, the Russian leader was shocked by the devastating effect atomic bombs had when detonated over two Japanese cities.

The most controversial act of Truman's presidency, beyond all doubt, was the use of nuclear weapons. On 6 August, shortly before 8.15 A.M., the B-29 bomber *Enola Gay* released its bomb high above Hiroshima. A mushroom cloud spread over the city with a force "brighter than a thousand suns". A hundred and thirty thousand of its inhabitants died instantly, some literally vapourised. An equivalent number suffered terrible burns and the effects of radiation. One survivor trying to help a woman took her "by the hands but her skin slipped off in huge, glove-like pieces". On 9 August, a second atomic bomb was dropped over the city of Nagasaki, killing another 60,000 people. With American public opinion demanding nothing less than unconditional surrender, Truman could well have ordered the dropping of additional bombs had not Japan bowed to the inevitable and surrendered on 15 August. The issue, as Dwight D. Eisenhower said when he first heard of the bombings, is whether it was necessary to "hit them with that awful thing".[55]

By then, American aircraft were having a difficult time finding undamaged targets in Japan. A fire raid by 500 bombers on Tokyo in May had killed 80,000 residents, this time by asphyxiation amid a blazing inferno that caused rivers to boil. Only Hiroshima and Nagasaki were sufficiently without bomb damage to permit an assessment of the destructive capacity of the new weapon.

The second atomic bomb exploding above Nagasaki, 9 August 1945

Besides such a military consideration, another reason for its use was undoubtedly political, since a quick end to the Pacific War would conveniently avoid the need for Russian intervention. Frostiness between Washington and Moscow had already begun to affect the international climate in what was later to be recognised as the Cold War. If Truman had hoped that the Hiroshima bomb might keep Stalin from declaring war on Japan, he was sorely disappointed.

Within hours of the US bombing of Hiroshima, Soviet forces invaded Manzhouguo. Attacking along the whole length of the border, Soviet tanks raced ahead, their progress slowed by shortage of fuel, rather than Japanese resistance. The first serious battle took place at Mudanjiang, southeast of Harbin. Though the Russians largely bypassed the city, bloody house-to-house combat tied up large numbers of infantrymen for several days. Heavy bombing of Mudanjiang was necessary before the Japanese defenders gave any ground.

The timing of the Russian attack was prefect, allowing Stalin to enter the Pacific War before Tokyo could leave it. Between 9 August and 2 September, the day on which the Japanese signed the instrument of surrender, Russian and Mongolian forces completely overran Manzhouguo and captured industries there and in the northern half of the Korean peninsula. After this comprehensive reverse, there was no possibility of Japan remaining on a war footing for long. Had the United States not possessed the atomic bomb, it could well be that the Soviet Union would have invaded Japan first.[56] From northern Sakhalin its troops could have island-hopped to Hokkaido without the need of a vast amphibious assault. Inured as they were to appalling casualties through their hard-won victory over the Germans, Russian soldiers would have had no hesitation in taking on the fanatical adherents of the Japanese emperor. Unlike the American president, Stalin did not have to justify such a bloody campaign to a war-weary electorate. Though denied a role in the Allied occupation of Japan, the Soviet leader still got what had been agreed at Yalta: the return of southern Sakhalin and the acquisition of the Kuriles, an island chain adjacent to Hokkaido.

Only Truman's firmness halted Stalin in his tracks.[57] Reports of the headlong Russian advance convinced Tokyo that there was no alternative but to accept the Potsdam declaration. Since the fall of Tojo Hideki, after the loss of the Philippines, cabinet shuffles had done little to improve the Japanese war effort. The defeat on Okinawa and the German surrender brought about a realisation, however tardily, that Japan would have to find a diplomatic way out of the Pacific War.

News that Nagasaki had suffered the same fate as Hiroshima finally brought the Japanese leadership to its senses. This second explosion obliged them at an imperial conference, hastily called on the evening of the Nagasaki explosion, to contemplate the unimaginable: unconditional surrender. Even then some of the Japanese leaders could not accept the Potsdam terms for peace because so many brave men had fallen in the service of the emperor. The army minister said that it would be totally wrong to surrender then.[58] There was additionally the question of what the Allies meant by "war criminals".[59] After considerable discussion, Emperor Hirohito intervened and said:

> I have given serious thought to the situation prevailing at home and abroad and have concluded that continuing the war can only mean destruction for the nation and a prolongation of

> bloodshed and cruelty in the world. I cannot see my innocent people suffer any longer. Ending the war is the only way to restore world peace and to relieve the nation from the terrible distress with which it is burdened . . . I swallow my tears and give my sanction to the proposal to accept the Allied declaration on the basis outlined by the Foreign Minister.[60]

While this imperial expression of opinion totally altered the atmosphere of the conference, it had no legal authority over state decisions, which remained the preserve of the Japanese cabinet. Early next morning, a dispirited cabinet concurred with the emperor's view and Japan offered to surrender if the Allies accepted the continuation of the imperial house. Neither an abortive military coup nor the ritual suicide of senior army officers could dent Emperor Hirohito's resolve, with the result that a startled nation heard the voice of their ruler for the first time on 15 August broadcast the war's end. No one dared to look at a radio during the brief statement, and afterwards the emperor's message had to be translated from the arcane language of the imperial court into intelligible everyday Japanese.

Between them, President Truman and Emperor Hirohito had ended the Pacific War. It was not a moment too soon. One GI in Luzon, where Yamashita Tomoyuki's men struggled on against the odds, wrote in his diary: "Now that the end is so near, we are all aroused to a new pitch of hate and want to see the Japs utterly smashed if they do not end it soon."[61] Only the terrible shock of the atom bomb jarred Tokyo out of its complacency. Whether it was necessary to drop two bombs is still a matter of debate. Without Emperor Hirohito's personal acceptance of being subject to the decisions of the Allies during the inevitable occupation of Japan, the deadlock over the surrender terms would never have been broken. For a group of British soldiers, this compromise was a lifesaver. Had the Japanese not surrendered, many of them would have been killed during Operation Zipper, the projected reconquest of Malaya, because 3 Commando Brigade was tasked with the capture there of the training school for NCOs in the southern contingents of the Imperial Japanese Army. After the surrender, it was thought a useful exercise to carry on with the coastal landing. In the event, the Royal Marines first got stuck on sandbars some distance from the beach, and then required Japanese guides to find their way inland to the target. This fiasco over, the brigade was rushed to Hong Kong in case the Americans decided to hand over the colony to the Guomindang.[62] It arrived by sea a few days after released British internees had re-established colonial rule. One of them, George Wright-Nooth, found the end of imprisonment at Stanley camp something of a disappointment. The ailing deputy police commissioner had expected to see its commandant commit suicide after the surrender. Contrary to samurai practice, this Japanese officer was observed making a hasty escape with two of his senior staff. [63]

Part 3

Western Decolonisation

Chapter 6

The Beginnings of Withdrawal 1945–50

It was said in the days of the great administrator, Lord Chatham, that you had to get up early in the morning not to miss some great acquisition of territory . . . the no less memorable administration of Mr. Attlee is distinguished for the opposite . . . the British Empire seems to be running off almost as fast as the American loan . . . "Scuttle" is the only word that can be applied.

Winston Churchill in the House of Commons, late 1946

The Post-War Settlement

From a prisoner-of-war camp in Java, Laurens van der Post welcomed news of Hiroshima for a special reason. "This cataclysm," he later wrote, "I was certain would make the Japanese feel that they could now withdraw from the war without dishonour, because it would strike them, as it had us in the silence of our prison night, as something supernatural."[1] His own study of Japan convinced him that the fireball would be associated with divine will, and allow the Imperial Japanese Army to accept defeat by such an overwhelming force. From the Meiji restoration onwards, great play had been made of the imperial family's direct descent from the sun goddess Amaterasu. Its own "divine" authority was the axis around which the newly introduced constitution and a modernised Japanese people had united.[2] Even the imperial regalia was believed to have been passed in remote times by the sun goddess to Emperor Hirohito's ancestors. Whether or not many Japanese reflected on the awful power of Amaterasu that fateful August, they were brought swiftly down to earth on 2 September when *USS Missouri* sailed into Tokyo Bay. General MacArthur, yet another implacable Perry, was on board to oversee the signing of the surrender documents. That the ceremony took place before a corps of press photographers ensured that the whole world was immediately aware of the extent of the Allied victory. A conspicuous witness of the event was Arthur Percival, whom MacArthur insisted

The Japanese arrive for the surrender ceremony aboard *USS Missouri*,
2 September 1945

should be present along with his American counterpart from Bataan, Jonathan Wainwright. Both men had been Japanese prisoners of war, Percival at Changi jail in Singapore. General Yamashita Tomoyuki had visited Changi and later sent the British general a substantial food parcel. Because of the factional fighting among senior officers in the Imperial Japanese Army, Yamashita Tomoyuki never received the public welcome in Tokyo that he believed he deserved. Nor did he have an audience with Emperor Hirohito, the due of all successful commanders. Instead, he was ordered by a jealous Tojo Hideki back to the relative obscurity of Manzhouguo, where he remained until the American invasion of the Philippines in 1944 necessitated his transfer to an active command there. At MacArthur's headquarters in Manila, Percival met Yamashita Tomoyuki once again after the Japanese surrender. As his former opponent entered the room, Percival recalls, "I saw one eyebrow lifted and a look of surprise cross his face—but only for a moment. His face quickly resumed that sphinx-like mask common to all Japanese, and he showed no further interest."[3]

The post-war settlement in Asia that stemmed from the ceremony on *USS Missouri* did not accord with the principles of the Atlantic Charter. President Truman had to look the other way as the British, French and Dutch moved back into their colonies. Yet there was a significant difference in attitude between these three colonial powers. Having elected by a landslide a Labour government, Britain alone would be spared disastrous colonial wars. With a keen awareness of the economic and political changes wrought by Japan's temporary triumph in Asia, the British prime minister, Clement Attlee, took on the thorny issue of decolonisation himself. "The Commonwealth," he said in 1946, "is a free association of free peoples." It would have been quite dishonest to keep peoples within its borders against their will. This new British outlook would have delighted Roosevelt, whose dislike of colonialism had so upset Churchill. It certainly reassured Truman when Attlee replaced Churchill midway through the conference at Potsdam.

Dean Acheson, Truman's secretary of state, reckoned that the strength of Attlee's influence in Washington derived from the mutual regard of prime minister and president. Even though the US-Russian

British internees leaving Stanley Camp on Hong Kong Island

relationship was now more critical than the Anglo-American one, Truman trusted Attlee and valued his opinion. As Acheson noted:

> Churchill never asked, or got so much, as Attlee did. He was a very remarkable man. Attlee was adroit, extremely adroit, his grasp of the situation was masterly. His method was seduction: he led the President on, step by step, to where he wanted to get him. He would make a statement of what the British wanted as though it was a statement of what the Americans wanted, and pause and say, very quickly, "I take it we are already agreed about that," and Truman, who was no slouch himself as a negotiator, would answer "Yes, we are." I was horrified. That's why I began stepping on the President's foot.[4]

In 1950, when things were going badly at the start of the Korean War, Attlee almost persuaded Truman to agree that the atomic bomb would never be used again without British consent. Yet he did persuade the president to stand up to MacArthur, who seemed to believe that he could campaign in China, if he thought it was necessary. Attlee said Truman's difficulties sprang from "the way they did things there": when the president wanted to talk face to face with his commander-in-chief in Korea, instead of recalling him to Washington, he obligingly flew to a meeting on Wake Island. In March 1951, Truman took steps to open peace talks with North Korea, but MacArthur undercut the president by declaring that North Korean and Chinese troops should first surrender. A furious Truman replaced MacArthur with Matthew Ridgway, while Acheson made sure that the American public became aware of how costly all-out war would be with China, along the lines MacArthur advocated.

The biggest problem facing Britain was India, for which Attlee cleverly chose Mountbatten as the viceroy responsible for the handover of power. Lord Louis Mountbatten had been supreme commander of the Southeast Asia Allied Command when the Labour government was formed in July 1945. Earlier that year, when it was still far from certain that the Japanese would be thrown out of Burma, Mountbatten had absorbed the troops of the Burmese Independence Army into his own forces and admitted Aung San, its commander and former supporter of Japan, to a role in shaping affairs after the Imperial Japanese Army was beaten. At a meeting held at Kandy, Mountbatten's headquarters in Sri Lanka, a delegation of Burmese leaders noticed a marked difference in approach to that of the old Burma hands. The governor, Sir Reginald Dorman-Smith, went so far as to decline an invitation to attend on the grounds that he would prefer not to meet a select group of political leaders before his own return to Burma. Then he intended to deal with a wider political range of opinion. Mountbatten, on the contrary, appreciated how the impact of Japanese "Asianism" on emergent nations such as Burma allowed no scope for such a leisurely colonial review. The Kandy conference was very successful, for the good reason that Mountbatten intervened to ensure that the minutes accurately recorded what had been agreed. There was a behind-the-scenes attempt to rewrite them to the Burmese Independence Army's disadvantage, which at the request of Aung San was scotched. This fully restored confidence in Mountbatten's Burmese policy.[5]

The Japanese capitulation did not leave the same power vacuum in Burma that occurred elsewhere in French and Dutch Southeast Asia, because Allied troops were already in occupation. But self-government, Mountbatten tried to tell London, would have to come sooner than planned, and would be dominated by nationalists led by Aung San. His advice was ignored by the Colonial Office, which seemed almost loath to return to the limited degree of home rule granted to Burma after its separation from India in 1935. Dorman-Smith was even encouraged not to recognise the Burmese Independence Army, the dubious creation of "our impetuous friend Dickie".[6] In London, voices were raised questioning the wisdom of the governor's treatment of discontented nationalists. As it was pointed out, Mountbatten had been able to arrive at successful and amicable arrangements with Aung San, so why could Dorman-Smith not do the same? Once Attlee realised what was wrong, he consulted Mountbatten, who recommended that he take the advice of Hubert Rance, his chief civil affairs officer. After half an hour's talk in Downing Street, Rance left Number 10—to his great surprise—as the new governor of Burma.

The speed at which the colony then moved to independence was breathtaking. Not even the assassination of Aung San, by a political rival, caused Attlee to slow down the independence process: in October 1947, Burma became free, and left the Commonwealth. Its withdrawal was not unexpected, Attlee noted, because murder had removed the one man who could have maintained Burmese membership. Misjudging the post-war situation in spectacular fashion, Churchill savaged Attlee's Burma policy. He condemned the agreement in these terms:

> I did not expect to see U Aung San, whose hands were dyed with British blood and loyal Burmese blood, marching up the steps of Buckingham Palace as the plenipotentiary of the Burmese Government.[7]

Yet blood was the very stuff of Burmese politics: assassins machine-gunned Aung San and his entire cabinet three months before the date of Burma's independence. The perpetrators of the massacre were quickly brought to justice, and a period of national mourning lasted for several months. The martyrdom of Aung San had one beneficial effect, albeit only a temporary one, since it left no room for the bickering that typified Burmese political debate. In its grief, the country was not prepared to tolerate unnecessary argument on the eve of independence.

Premier Attlee with Aung San in London, early 1947

Attlee had sorted out Burma himself. So competent was Ernest Bevin as foreign secretary that it is easy to forget that the prime minister was actually Labour's expert on foreign affairs. Though he delegated decision making to Bevin to a large extent, Attlee took the lead whenever he felt urgent action was required, and especially in the field of decolonisation. For Britain's colonial empire was one of the chief casualties of the Second World War. The economic damage caused by fighting the Germans and Italians in Europe and Africa, then the Japanese in Asia, made it impossible for Britain to consider paying any longer for the armed forces that would be needed to protect its array of colonies and dependent territories, although the change of attitude was never just a question of finance. Ballot boxes sent back from soldiers, sailors and airmen serving overseas, whose votes when opened overturned Conservative majorities one after another, indicated a desire for peace and domestic reconstruction, not any protracted colonial struggle.

The temporary triumph of Japan in Asia had totally altered the world's political landscape. There was no easy way back to pre-Pacific War days, in either the European colonies or independent Asian states. China and Japan were as much altered by the experience of war as were French Indochina, British Malaya and the Dutch East Indies. It is to Attlee's enduring credit that he understood the need for the British to accommodate this far-reaching transformation, and put in train an orderly withdrawal from their far-flung empire. His most intractable problem was India, which he also personally handled. The decision he took in granting independence to Britain's largest and most populous possession marked the beginning of the end for Western colonial rule in Asia.

Both the French and the Dutch refused to acknowledge the stark realities of post-war politics. Restoring some kind of imperial presence was for them a psychological as much as an economic necessity. During the Second World War, only a few French colonies opted for de Gaulle; most colonial administrations preferred to cast their lot with the Vichy government, which at least gave the impression of legitimacy. This rejection of the Free French movement stung de Gaulle enough to make him assume the role of defender of the French overseas empire without even having either the means or the authority to do so. He could do nothing to hinder collaboration with the Japanese in French Indochina, so the takeover by Japan in March 1945 came as a welcome relief. For de Gaulle could insist now that France had a duty to recover its Southeast Asian possessions, something neither Roosevelt nor Stalin had wanted to see happen. To complicate matters further, Japan claimed to have liberated Indochina from France and recognised the independent regime of Bao Dai, the former Vietnamese puppet emperor, as well as the royal governments of Cambodia and Laos. Flatly refusing an American proposal for a trusteeship in Indochina, de Gaulle said that France would never forgive the loss of its most developed and prosperous colonial possession, and it would hold the United States solely responsible for the chain reaction of unrest that must follow throughout the remainder of the French empire. The Netherlands was keen to resume control, too, in what was about to become independent Indonesia.

Neither the French nor the Dutch possessed the military strength to reimpose their colonial administrations once Japan surrendered. The first troops to arrive belonged to Mountbatten, who had been ordered to secure southern Indochina, Java and Sumatra, besides Thailand, Malaya and Singapore. French Indochina was a priority because the headquarters of the Imperial Japanese Army in Southeast Asia was once again at Saigon. The sudden end of hostilities, however, caught the British unprepared to assume such a complicated occupation role. As William Slim, the commander of Allied Land Forces Southeast Asia, observed:

> In two of them, Indochina and the Dutch East Indies, nationalist movements, armed from Japanese sources, had already seized power in the vacuum left by the surrender, and were resisting the restoration of French and Dutch sovereignty— fighting had already begun or seemed inevitable. In all areas were intact Japanese forces amounting to about half a million men, whose acceptance of the surrender was not certain, and many thousands of British, Australians, Indians, Americans, Dutch and French, starving and dying of diseases in the brutal and barbaric Japanese prison camps. It was obviously vital that we should occupy all Japanese-held territory at the earliest possible moment, not only to enforce the surrender, but to succour these unfortunates.[8]

There were just too many demands for Slim's troops to tackle, not to say his depleted air force. Long-held hopes of an increase in Royal Air Force strength had been dashed by shortages of material and manpower in Europe, while the invaluable assistance provided by US aircraft was soon lost because of requirements in China, Korea and Japan.[9] Transport planes were in very short supply, with the result that British troops arrived at their destinations by a mixture of flight and voyage. The inevitable delays influenced the unfolding of events in the French and the Dutch colonies, although Slim was most concerned that the vehemently anti-Vietnamese attitude of French settlers could inflame an already uncertain situation.

Above the sixteenth parallel, virtually the border until 1975 between the two independent Vietnams, the Japanese were ordered to hand over their arms to Guomindang troops. Because the Chinese

Manila after the American liberation

soldiers were short of money for supplies, they sold or bartered many of the weapons to the Viet Minh, "the Vietnamese League", set up in 1941 to advance the cause of freedom. Thus the revolutionary supporters of Ho Chi Minh acquired an arsenal of rifles, light machine-guns and ammunition. The Viet Minh refused to acknowledge the restored Vietnamese emperor and, when Japanese units surrendered, its members occupied Hanoi and declared a republic. Upon the withdrawal of Guomindang forces a year later, the returning French recognised with some reluctance Ho Chi Minh's communist regime as a state within the federation of Indochina and the French Union.

Though the constitution of the Fourth Republic, adopted in October 1946, claimed that France intended to lead the peoples for which it had colonial responsibility to the freedom to administer themselves, nothing short of outright independence would ever satisfy Vietnamese nationalists. As soon as it became clear that the French government would stop this from happening, a conflict was unavoidable. On his way to negotiations in Paris, Ho Chi Minh learned that northern Vietnam was to remain separate from the rest of the country: the south had been granted an autonomous government under the titular authority of Bao Dai. In Paris, he found that there was no sign of compromise, possibly because the French believed that they could retake the north by force: the First and Second Vietnam Wars ensued as a consequence of this political intransigence. They are only now seen for what they really were: not a communist triumph but a national struggle for a free and united Vietnam.

The French return was not helped by the British, whose inadequate forces could not guarantee a peaceful reoccupation. Nor was it assisted by the lax attitude of the Chinese, whose sympathies were not pro-French. Such was the shortage of British soldiers in Saigon that the local commander, Douglas Gracey, was allowed to enlist the aid of the surrendered Imperial Japanese Army. On arriving in the city, an RAF pilot said how "everyone is a little dazed with having Japanese chauffeurs and guards, the Japanese being fully armed". The British commander in the Dutch East Indies made a similar use of Japanese manpower. The decision was as bad a mistake in Southeast Asia as it was in China, where Truman chose not to disallow cooperation between Guomindang and Japanese forces against the Chinese Communist Party.

Immediately after the Japanese surrender, the United States threw its weight behind the Guomindang by supplying transport planes to move Chiang Kai-shek's troops to key places in northern and eastern China. When this proved insufficient, US marines landed in large numbers to secure ports and airfields at Qingdao, Tianjin, Qinhuangdao and Beijing. At the end of October, two months after the end of the Pacific War, the American consul in Tianjin reported that the Japanese troops left in control of the vital rail link from Beijing to Qinhuangdao, a port opposite the Liaodong peninsula, were under constant communist attack. He told Washington that the marines in the area "depend almost entirely on former puppet and Japanese troops for the maintenance of order in towns along the line", adding that their position would become untenable unless Guomindang soldiers quickly arrived.[10] A month later, it was publicly admitted that there would be no question of disarming units of the Imperial Japanese Army, because Mao Zedong's guerrillas would not only occupy the areas vacated by the Japanese but acquire their arms and equipment as well.

But the events of 1945 in Asia were probably moving too fast anyway for more than a piecemeal policy. With the desperate need to rebuild a devastated Europe at the start of the Cold War, the United States could not be expected to regard Asian developments as high on the international agenda. Yet the civil war in China, the partition of Korea and the military occupation of Japan deserved more serious attention in Washington. Neglect of Southeast Asia was to prove in the long run an even more costly oversight, once the Americans were drawn into the Vietnam conflict themselves. Apart from Thailand and the Philippines, which returned quietly to their previous existences, the misguided attempts of the French and the Dutch to thwart nationalist aspirations merely served to accelerate political change in Indochina as well as the East Indies. Comparative calm marked the remaining British colonial possessions, but even they experienced discontent at the arrangements being made for their attainment of self-government within the Commonwealth.

The End of the Indian Empire

By the end of the Pacific War, India had some two and a half million men under arms, all volunteers. They fought bravely alongside British and Commonwealth troops, gaining by their exertions 27 Victoria Crosses. It was true that some taken prisoner in Malaya and Singapore enlisted in the Indian National Army, but they were the exception to the rule that Indian soldiers remained loyal to the Allied cause. As in the Mutiny of 1857, many of the deserters felt betrayed by the British, who sent them to war with inadequate weapons under the leadership of poor commanders. Others were opportunists who changed sides for personal advantage, not wishing to endure the privations of a Japanese prisoner-of-war camp. Among the unfinished business in 1945 was the question of the men who had joined the Indian National Army.

Viceroy Wavell had always held a low opinion of this formation, telling Gandhi his opinion when Congress was demanding the removal of the salt tax. What annoyed Wavell above all was Congress' stirring up popular feeling over the trials of the deserters at the Red Fort in Delhi. The first three charged with joining the enemy— a Sikh, a Moslem and a Hindu—allowed nationalist sentiment to unite in defence of those who claimed to have been fighting for independence. Riots in Calcutta left 30 dead and hundreds injured.

Nehru's skilful defence obliged the court martial to pass a sentence of life imprisonment, which was afterwards commuted to cashiering and loss of pay arrears. During the trial, the defendants were concerned that Congress might be embarrassed by giving its support to those who had been involved in the killing. Nehru said its non-violence policy was unaffected by his own undertaking of their defence, which he considered to be an entitlement for anyone who strove for India's freedom. He also indicated that he was not so committed to peaceful opposition to Britain as was Gandhi. Deserters charged with specific acts of violence, such as one man who had a fellow officer beaten to death, collected prison sentences. The general amnesty of August 1947, on the granting of independence, allowed them to be released unnoticed. Later, they were offered reinstatement but with loss of seniority for the period of their Indian National Army service.

For the Labour government in London, the question was no longer whether, but how soon, and to whom, power in India was to be passed. Within Attlee's cabinet, ministers such as Bevin were still imperialists at heart, but even they recognised that the majority were right in relinquishing control as soon as an agreed constitutional settlement was reached. By the late 1930s, the Labour Party had in fact shifted its anti-colonial stance. Instead of being an utter opponent of imperialism, it had committed itself to preserving what was best for Britain and its colonial peoples.[11] In 1945, therefore, preservation was understood to entail independence.

What was critical in a smooth process of decolonisation was for the British to seem to be still in charge. They had to dictate events, and not be driven by them: it was a policy that depended upon gaining the agreement of moderate nationalists by yielding control fast enough to prevent it being seized by extremists. In the 1940s and 1950s, Britain largely achieved this aim by reshaping the old empire into a new framework of more or less equal partners. The exception in Asia was India, where communal differences led to its split into two separate and antagonistic states. Wavell foresaw the coming trouble in early 1947, when he wrote to King George VI in these terms:

> The really fatal thing for us would be to hang on to responsibility (in India) when we have lost the power to exercise it, and possibly involve ourselves in a large-scale Palestine.[12]

American economic aid kept Britain afloat in the immediate post-war years, but there was never sufficient money to underwrite all its foreign and colonial commitments. Well might the Labour government set about restructuring the country's social and economic system, but this was the era of austerity, of queues and ration books.

Wavell's candour did not please Attlee, who regarded his contingency planning as defeatist. As a former professional soldier, it seemed obvious to Wavell that there should be a plan for a staged withdrawal, if necessary, from a hostile subcontinent. Although he appreciated the need to remain on good terms with Congress, none of whose leaders he really trusted, Wavell also attached importance to maintaining good relations with the 90 million Moslem minority in India. Attlee's own view of India, he admitted much later, was formed in discussions with Nehru at Sir Stafford Cripps' house in Gloucestershire during 1938. It was Cripps who had arrived in India, fresh from an embassy to beleaguered Moscow, and promised in March 1942 an elected assembly after hostilities ended in return for Congress' support for the war effort.

Churchill thoroughly disliked the Cripps mission but, fearing a link-up of German and Japanese forces after the fall of India, he accepted the Labour initiative. At the very least, it would keep Roosevelt quiet. The Congress Party ignored Cripps, who returned to London empty handed, mainly because Gandhi had no real understanding of German and Japanese intentions. He had even less knowledge of their brutal methods. The Quit-India campaign was the result. Wavell's appointment had followed shortly afterwards. He was told to vaguely mention constitutional advance, until Churchill became alarmed at his attempt to get both Hindus and Moslems committed to some form of self-government short of dominion status. Churchill spoke bitterly and contemptuously of Wavell as "a self-seeking advertiser" who was "cringing to the Hindus".[13] It has to be said that Wavell's relationship with Churchill's successor was little better, since he regarded Labour policy towards India as being far too trustful of Congress. Wavell blamed this weakness for the breakdown of relations between the Hindus and the Moslems.

Mohammed Ali Jinnah was not unhappy about the situation because it allowed the Moslem League to return to the historic "Pakistan" resolution passed in 1940 at Lahore. The creation of a separate homeland for Indian Moslems was again on the agenda. A part of the problem was Wavell, now completely out of favour in a London impatient for the transfer of power. There was even annoyance at the viceroy's efforts to reconcile Moslem and Hindu leaders, which got nowhere. On 22 March 1947, Wavell was replaced by Mountbatten. Somehow or other Indian independence had to be delivered, and Attlee decided that the time had come for a new man to bring about a decision. Without consulting Wavell, the prime minister lined up Mountbatten for the task, having informed the king of his intention. As King George VI noted:

> Attlee told me that Lord Wavell's plan for our leaving India savours too much of a military retreat and does not realise it is a political problem and not a military one. Wavell has done very good work up to now but Attlee doubts whether he has the finesse to negotiate the next steps when we must keep two Indian parties friendly to us all the time.[14]

On his return home, Wavell was interviewed by the India Committee, which included both Attlee and Cripps. When asked what advice he would like to give them, the penultimate viceroy said they should make a final effort to avoid partition, and if this failed, as it seemed likely to do, start at once on the detailed arrangements for splitting the Indian empire in two. Otherwise, there was a danger of tremendous trouble ahead.

Inspired though Mountbatten's appointment undoubtedly was, it is arguable that Attlee allowed far too short a timetable for India to attain independence, although an early date was fixed as a result of the last viceroy's refusal to travel to Delhi unless the termination of British rule was precisely agreed. In the end, Mountbatten compromised with Attlee by accepting a month, June 1948, instead of an actual day. The worst period for the Labour government occurred between December 1946 and February 1947: a bitterly cold winter that witnessed coal shortages, power cuts and limited supplies of food and milk. Linking a possible colonial collapse with Britain's economic weakness, Bevin had written privately to Attlee in these stark terms:

> You cannot read the telegrams from Egypt and the Middle East without realising that not only is India going, but Malaya, Ceylon and the Middle East is going with it, with a tremendous repercussion on the African territories . . . As Foreign Secretary, I can offer nothing to any foreign country, neither credit, nor coal, nor goods . . . And on top of that, within the British Empire, we knuckle under at the first blow and yet we are expected to preserve the position.[15]

Dismissing Bevin's pessimism, Attlee and Cripps reached an agreement with Mountbatten over the transfer of power in India. Even though Bevin did not approve of Cripps' pro-Congress line, he knew that the prime minister was in agreement with Cripps about a withdrawal from the subcontinent at the earliest possible opportunity. Not that there was anything the British foreign secretary could do to slow down decolonisation, since he belonged to a penurious government frantically searching for a political deal that would permit Britain's disengagement from India at minimum cost. Had Bevin been responsible for Dutch or French foreign affairs, he might not have been so ready to endorse a continued colonial role for any European power: these two countries were already finding the resumption of authority in Southeast Asia well beyond their capabilities.

When Mountbatten reached Delhi on 22 March 1947 to take over from Wavell, India was very unsettled and the situation even more alarming than when he accepted Attlee's offer of the viceroyalty. It was already transparent that partition was going to happen. Despite close relations with the Labour Party, Congress would not concede anything short of its full demands, while the Moslem League was equally determined to obtain an independent Pakistan. Into this entrenched political atmosphere the ambitious 46-year-old Mountbatten was pitched. Notwithstanding his royal connections, he was far removed from the attitudes of previous British rulers of India. He had learned how to manipulate his superiors, allies and subordinates during the Pacific War, becoming a shrewd operator at national and international levels. It is possible that his personal grasp of the political realities of power explains why Attlee chose him at this moment of crisis. For the prime minister was correct in thinking that Indian leaders would welcome someone more experienced in the ways of the world than Wavell.

The two political rivals, Nehru and Jinnah, at a 1946 conference

One of the difficulties facing Mountbatten on his arrival was the vanity of the Indian leadership. Not without conceit himself, Mountbatten was taken aback by the Moslem leader, Jinnah, who positively enjoyed opposing any proposal put to him, and to a lesser extent by Nehru, whose inability to measure his words at press conferences and public meetings was often a source of acute embarrassment afterwards. Both these politicians were satisfied that they knew what was best for their followers. Another difficulty was Gandhi, still a powerful figure in the background. Unlike most Congress leaders, Gandhi could not reconcile himself to partition, and in particular any arrangement devised for it by the British. With justification, Mountbatten feared that the veteran of the struggle for Indian independence might use his enormous influence to wreck any partition plan.

Mountbatten had to deploy all his charm as well as all his guile to meet Attlee's chief instruction, which was for Britain to leave India in a spirit of goodwill. At once he took pains to flatter Gandhi, who responded with pleasure to this last-minute recognition by the highest of all British colonial officials. It had the desired effect. Gandhi was loath to give his consent to partition but, in the end, he advised the Congress Party to accept the plan as the only sure way of securing India's immediate independence. The apparent warmth of the relationship between Mountbatten and Gandhi irked Jinnah, who correctly surmised the viceroy's pro-Congress leanings. He was more angry when Mountbatten's derogatory remarks about his attitude towards negotiations came back to him. Off-the-cuff comments were as dangerous in Government House as anywhere else: at all levels of the civil service, there were people taking sides in anticipation of the reshaping of India at the end of British rule. But it was the viceroy's wife who really soured relations with the Moslems through her passion for Nehru.

To Jinnah it seemed that the Mountbattens had literally got into bed with the Congress Party. This was a foolish lapse, given the uncertainties surrounding the transfer of power. Yet Edwina Mountbatten's infatuation with Nehru at least ensured that her husband, like no previous British ruler of India, was never regarded as an enemy by independence-minded Hindus or Sikhs. Intense dislike was the preserve of the Moslems, who observed the public display of affection with undisguised disdain.

Within a few days of taking up his responsibilities, Mountbatten had informed Attlee that:

> The only conclusion that I have been able to come to is that unless I act quickly I may well find the real beginnings of a civil war on my hands . . . I am convinced that a fairly quick decision would be the only way to convert the Indian minds from their present emotionalism to stark realism and to counter the disastrous spread of strife.[16]

Extensive negotiations with the Congress Party, the Moslem League and the Sikhs quickly revealed the impossibility of keeping India as a single country. On 17 April, Mountbatten reported to Attlee that he saw no alternative to partition, a plan for which he soon submitted. He stressed the need for an early decision, as even in the quieter provinces it feels "that we are sitting on the edge of a volcano and that an eruption might take place through any of the three main craters—Bengal, Punjab and the North-West Frontier Province—at any moment".[17]

Even getting Nehru's agreement to a partition plan was far from easy, because the Congress leader objected to provinces and princely states being allowed to vote for their own independence, either for themselves or in groups. He insisted that they should simply vote to join either India or Pakistan, an amendment that suited Jinnah admirably. On 14 May, Mountbatten flew to London with the amended plan, for which Attlee obtained cabinet approval within weeks. He told his cabinet colleagues that Mountbatten was to return to India, make a final request to preserve a united country, and then announce that power would be transferred to more than one authority on 30 June 1948, the date agreed for the British withdrawal.

To the surprise of many, Churchill stated that the Conservatives would not oppose the necessary legislation. Personally, the ex-prime minister found the post war world hard to accept, but his party was disengaging itself from a long-standing commitment to empire. Alliance with the United States had affected so many aspects of Britain's relations with its dominions as well as its colonies. Australia, and to a lesser extent New Zealand, had been drawn into the American sphere of influence by the Pacific War. The former Australian premier Billy Hughes, the outspoken white supremacist at the Versailles peace conference, cabled Churchill in 1942 about how British influence was in steep decline. The influx of Americans was

> not good. Nearly 90,000 American troops . . . crowd the streets producing great impression on the public mind. MacArthur's confidential report to the Government strongly anti-British. He is highly thought of, is Government adviser, his soldiers are here, the Government leans naturally to America. Strangely forget what they owe to Britain.[18]

To counter this unwelcome political drift, Hughes urged Churchill to send substantial forces to the dominion. There were none to spare, so Australia only received an RAF squadron of Spitfires. A significant part of the problem was the division of the Pacific and Indian oceans into separate operational areas, American and British. It gave MacArthur plenty of scope to vent his frustration at his own defeat in the Philippines on Britain.

In opposition after 1945, a new generation of Conservative leaders concentrated on internal affairs, convincing the British electorate to return them to power in 1951 by jettisoning their traditional image as a party indifferent towards social welfare or full employment. Churchill alone held to a belief in the value of colonial possessions, although he admitted privately that the days of assertive European imperialism were now over. By 1948, the Conservatives had come to speak about "the three unities": unity within the British Commonwealth, unity across the Atlantic and unity with Western Europe. These unities were not seen as incompatible until the Suez crisis of 1956 shattered the Atlantic one.

Anthony Eden's resignation as prime minister at the start of the following year drew a definite line under what was left of Britain's imperial pretensions. Over Suez Eden chose to ignore President Eisenhower's warning about American concern "at the prospect of this drastic action even at the very time the matter is under consideration as it is today at the United Nations Security Council".[19] When the Russians threatened to pepper Western Europe with missiles unless British and French forces quit Egypt, Eisenhower exploded with rage and forced an immediate withdrawal. The anticlimax marked the end of British imperialism and destroyed French chances of holding on in Algeria. Eden's successor, Harold Macmillan, asked for "something like a profit-and-loss account" to be drawn up for each colony, so high was expenditure on the armed forces. Defence spending as a proportion of total government expenditure hardly declined after the defeat of Japan: it was 23 per cent in 1950, 24 per cent in 1960 and still 17 per cent in 1970. Maintaining a world role came expensive and tended to exacerbate Britain's persistent balance of payments problem.

In 1947, however, there seemed no possibility of any rift in Anglo-American relations. Washington could not have asked for more from a Labour administration actively wrestling with its greatest challenge, the start of decolonisation through granting Indian independence. Perhaps its difficulties would have been less severe had Mountbatten refused to be drawn on a date for the transfer of power. At a press conference in Delhi, he said that it could be as early as 15 August, almost one year before the original date announced in London. His suggestion caused consternation among officials in Britain and India, but Attlee insisted that they accept this earlier date. The legislative feat required to put the India Independence Act on the statute book in time for the transfer of power was quite exceptional.

Because the first phases of devising the partition went without real incident, Bengal and the Punjab both endorsing east–west splits, despite a strong feeling among the Sikhs that they merited a province of their own, Mountbatten could overlook an unsatisfactory referendum held in the North-West Frontier Province. A Congress boycott here because of local political reasons led to an overwhelming majority for joining Pakistan. There remained princely India, with a population of more than 100 million and a large number of rulers who had pledged their loyalty to Britain in return for its protection. The princes had no love for the Congress Party, which was republican in spirit and intent on the removal of princely powers. In Kashmir, the Hindu ruler could not decide between Pakistan or India, at least until a force of "volunteers" crossed from Pakistan and attacked Srinagar, his capital. Then he sided with India, starting one of the most protracted post-colonial conflicts of all. In the meantime, communal violence had broken out in the Punjab, the environs of Delhi, Bihar and Tripura, a province close to Burma.

While in most of India, there was rejoicing over the attainment of independence, for two months after 15 August, northern India witnessed slaughter and migration on a massive scale. Mountbatten tried to play down the death toll, but there is no question that some 700,000 people lost their lives in the Punjab and Bengal alone. More than 10 million others migrated: Sikhs and Hindus crossed to safe havens in India, Moslems did the same in Pakistan. This dreadful calamity marred the transfer of power, but Attlee's man of the spot had fulfilled his mission. British public opinion might be unhappy about the necessity of partition, preferring instead that the Indian empire should continue as a single federation of states and provinces, but this was never an option.

The rise of the Moslem League, the demands of the Congress Party and the aimless drift of British policy during the war years were all factors ensuring that Mountbatten had very little room for manoeuvre in 1947. That he achieved what he did in a few months was quite remarkable. His basic problem remained the missed opportunity under the Conservatives to grant India dominion status in the 1930s. Had they been less impressed by the prestige of empire, an earlier devolution of power would have avoided 20 years of frustration and bitterness. Attlee's boldness cut the Gordian knot in India, thereby inaugurating the process of British decolonisation. He did not flinch when Mountbatten pressed for a dramatically accelerated withdrawal, because he knew that unreasonable delay would defeat his cherished aim of remaining on friendly terms with ex-colonies. As a result of Attlee's support for Mountbatten, both Pakistan and India chose to remain in the Commonwealth.

To get Congress to abandon its republicanism to the extent of accepting the British monarch as the head of an international "family" of nations was no mean achievement. To accommodate the Indian republic, a special Commonwealth Conference thrashed out this formula in 1949. Just as India had been the motor of Britain's expanding influence in Asia during the eighteenth century, so in the twentieth its requirement for a different constitutional relationship drove the British Commonwealth to update its arrangements in time for the accession of African, Caribbean, Pacific and Southeast Asian members. It made the Commonwealth—British was dropped from the title—more than a continuation of imperialism by other means. Indian and Pakistani membership of an organisation bound together by choice, mutual interests and support, rather than force, ensured that the Commonwealth had a multicultural and multi-ethnic dimension lacking in many other international associations. By 1997, there were 54 members, including Mozambique, which had had no experience of British rule. With the collapse of *apartheid* in South Africa, the frictions of the 1980s were to disappear and the Commonwealth so dear to Attlee secured for itself an envied niche in the modern world. His vision of an association of free peoples was at long last a reality.

In 1948, Sri Lanka became independent within the Commonwealth, largely because it was next door to India. For some time, the great island had enjoyed a degree of self-government, a circumstance that undoubtedly minimised the impact of the Imperial Japanese Navy's raid in early 1942. Not that Ceylon, as Sri Lanka was then called, lacked troubles of its own. The introduction of electoral politics had sown discord between the Sinhalese and the Tamils, who were largely concentrated in the north of the island. Radical Tamils in Jaffna were dismayed when the Sinhalese used their majority to keep ministerial posts entirely for themselves. A demand for the reservation of posts for Tamil and Moslem minorities was dismissed out of hand by both the Sinhalese and the British colonial government. This failure to recognise their legitimate aspirations would eventually fuel a post-colonial conflict that still rages today. Because the first outbreak of communal violence did not occur until 1956, the Labour government could congratulate itself on avoiding in Sri Lanka a painful Indian-style partition.

Dutch Failure in Indonesia

As in French Indochina, British-led forces arrived in the Dutch East Indies to take over control from the Imperial Japanese Army. The nationalist resistance that these troops encountered at Surabaya, in northeastern Java, was an early indication that the reimposition of

Dutch colonial rule would be difficult and costly. When the Japanese arrived, the nationalist leader Sukarno had no hesitation in supporting them, while making it clear that independence for Indonesia was his ultimate objective. He appreciated the imperialist aims of the Greater East Asia Co-Prosperity Sphere, but the overthrow of three centuries of Dutch rule more than compensated for a Japanese occupation which he thought would be short anyway. Collaboration strained Sukarno's relations with some of his followers, since he acquiesced in the conscription of labourers for Japanese projects throughout Southeast Asia. As many as half a million of them never returned. More than 100,000 labourers from Malaya and Indonesia were estimated to have died in building the infamous Burma railway. Another 12,000 Allied prisoners of war are known to have perished under appalling conditions, at the rate of one death for every 25 metres of track.

General Imamura Hitoshi, the first commander-in-chief in Java, had no doubt about the motive behind Sukarno's helpfulness. "I gained the impression," the general said, "that he was a man of iron resolve. All his thinking was centred on independence, and his passion for it would never desert him."[20] It is possible that the collaboration between Sukarno and Imamura Hitoshi was a blessing in disguise for the Javanese, because the general's comparatively gentle approach to the establishment of Japanese authority greatly displeased his superiors in Tokyo. Impressed by Sukarno's popularity, Imamura Hitoshi decided to make use of him in Java, where the island's large population, if restive, could tie down Japanese troops needed elsewhere.

In talks with the nationalists, Imamura Hitoshi could not commit Japan to granting independence after the Pacific War, but he was able to agree to rallies being held in which the Dutch were blamed for Indonesia's woes. Though the excitement stirred up by these events led to their suspension in cities such as Surabaya, Sukarno's cleverly crafted speeches encouraged his listeners to look upon the Japanese as the guardians of their future freedom. It was an excellent strategy because the argument drew upon two distinct sources of strength: the genuine desire of the Indonesians to be rid of the Dutch and the rash claim of Japan to be freeing Asia for the Asians. Neatly trapping the Japanese in their own propaganda as destroyers of Western colonialism, Sukarno seized the chance to unite nationalist factions publicly and raise demand for independence to fever pitch. Once it became clear that Japan would be defeated, Tokyo's obvious step to frustrate the returning Allies was to let the nationalists declare the establishment of the Republic of Indonesia, which they soon did.

The day after the declaration of independence on 17 August 1945, Sukarno was installed as the Republic of Indonesia's first president with unlimited powers for six months. The first conflict was with British and Indian troops, who began landing in Java in September. At Surabaya, it took them three weeks of hard fighting to gain control of the city, an unexpected contest, which convinced the British that the Indonesians were a people to be reckoned with. An American diplomat reported to Washington that the situation in Java was chaotic, with "lawless armed looters and fanatics out of control". Nobody seemed able to restrain the "armed mobs of hotheaded Indonesian freedom fighters", who were commanded by small-time "gang leaders", each with their own vision of what independence meant.[21] Even Sukarno admitted the gravity of the crisis and agreed to talks with Philip Christison, whom Mountbatten had sent to take control of the Dutch East Indies. What the British general failed to understand was that Sukarno could not control every group of nationalist fighters. Although he personally intervened at the start of the fighting, Sukarno was unable to keep the peace in Surabaya and a full-scale battle took place. Much of Christison's problem derived from London's ignorance about Indonesian determination to resist the return of the Dutch. No one appreciated how strong it was. Mountbatten suspected that taking over from the Japanese would be no easy task and, before assuming responsibility, he asked for sufficient forces and logistical backup. Because he received neither, Christison was obliged to make use of the surrendered Japanese Imperial Army.

The Dutch were so anxious to return to Java that they accepted whatever arrangements might be required. They even tried to enlist Australian military support without success. The United States was equally reluctant to become involved in a potentially bitter colonial conflict. The only troops immediately available belonged to the Royal Netherlands Indies Army, who were largely from Amboina. Because these native soldiers had remained loyal to the

Dutch, the Japanese made about 18,000 of them prisoners of war. In the absence of significant numbers of Dutch forces, the British found themselves in the invidious position of being the advance guard of restored colonial rule.

Parachute regiment soldiers on patrol in Batavia

How bad the situation had already become in Java was revealed to Mountbatten by Laurens van der Post, a recently released British prisoner of war. He told Mountbatten's representative in Batavia that the island was largely in the hands of Indonesian nationalists. All that the surrendered Japanese soldiers could do was haul down Indonesian flags, while at the same time discouraging the display of the Dutch flag, which only served to rouse nationalist fervour to fever pitch. Because the surrender terms obliged it to maintain order until the arrival of the Allies, the Imperial Japanese Army in some places deployed against the local population. In others, it actively fought alongside British-led forces, whose officers were often mistaken for Dutchmen. At Semarang, a port due north of Yogyakarta, John Hudson found himself collaborating with his erstwhile enemy.

> We were so hopelessly outnumbered that it was ridiculous to have fighting men guarding Japanese prisoners . . . The Brigadier put it to Major Kido, as the senior and most effective Japanese officer, that either we fought together or died together. He was delighted. He would love to have his sword back, he would love to fight and kill a few more Javanese in the interests of all . . . Our former detested foe was now our staunchest ally! It was a brave decision by the Brigadier and it undoubtedly saved us all. Numerical superiority could only be countered by highly trained troops and our Ghurkhas backed by the sons of Nippon were a force to respect.
>
> We could imagine questions being tabled in the House back home: "Is the hon. member aware that British forces in Java have enlisted the aid of our former enemies to reinstate Dutch Imperial Rule?"
>
> It was the very stuff of which newspapers are made and politicians destroyed. Some very fine careers were in jeopardy of ruin and undoubtedly heads would roll. What we did not anticipate was that, after the Brigadier had been dealt with, they would hide the facts and that, even to this day, the event would be cloaked in silence.

The combined force took Semarang with "guns blazing". One thing about the Japanese surprised Husdon though, their inability to offer any tactical advice. When asked for his opinion, all that Kido would say was "You give the orders please."[22]

Such a combat role for Japanese soldiers was an embarrassment for Britain, although it was expected that in the absence of a sizable Allied deployment in the liberated Dutch East Indies some reliance on the Japanese would be necessary. Mountbatten had outlined the basic difficulty when he said that, unless there was an accommodation between Holland and the newly declared Republic of Indonesia, troop levels were inadequate to secure more than the key areas of Batavia and Surabaya, which meant using the Imperial

Japanese Army to maintain control elsewhere. A successful reoccupation therefore depended on the harmony that could be established between the Dutch and the Indonesians. Long afterwards, Mountbatten blamed others for the quagmire that Indonesia proved to be for the British as well as the Dutch.

A factor in the deteriorating situation was certainly Hubertus van Mook, the governor of the Dutch East Indies. He resented the apparent lightness of the British touch, because of his own belief that the nationalists could be suppressed with little force. Faced with orders from London to avoid too deep an involvement, Mountbatten encouraged Christison to tread carefully while attempting himself to soften van Mook's approach to the Indonesians. He got nowhere because everything said only confirmed to van Mook what the Dutch feared: that despite assurances that Britain upheld its original policy of returning the Dutch East Indies to Holland, the newly elected Labour government was in fact looking for a way out. As van Mook had no intention of letting Mountbatten repeat his Burma policy in Java, there were to be no conciliatory talks with the nationalists, who were merely anti-Dutch agitators in a "terrorist so-called government". But the Dutch governor conveniently overlooked one significant fact: British and Indian troops were bearing the brunt of Indonesian opposition to the restoration of the Dutch East Indies. With Indian politicians demanding independence for their own country, the role of Indian soldiers in Southeast Asia became a contentious issue, particularly when the Indian National Army trials opened in Delhi. Public opinion in India resented the use of Indian troops in operations designed to reinstate European colonial rule elsewhere in Asia.

Although good Anglo-Dutch relations were valued in London, Britain's foreign minister faced acrimonious inquiries from Labour colleagues and supporters about what was happening in Java, the focal point of Indonesian nationalism. Complicating the situation was van Mook's return to the Hague for talks, and his delayed return, since Bevin was convinced that in January 1946 a negotiated settlement could have been reached. The capital of the Republic of Indonesia had shifted from Batavia to Yogyakarta in central Java, a city without either a Dutch or British military presence. Its representatives stayed in Batavia to consider a belated Dutch plan for a Commonwealth of Indonesia, with varying degrees of self-rule for its constituent provinces. Finally, in February, van Mook met with the "looters and bandits", but within days negotiations had broken down. Even though Sukarno was temporarily sidelined by other nationalist leaders, they discovered that their more moderate approach with the Dutch displeased the majority of the Javanese. As displeased were conservative Dutch politicians who ensured that follow-up talks in Holland, two months later, ended without agreement. One Indonesian commentator pointedly asked: "What is the purpose of negotiations? They are nothing but a downpour of cold water on the raging fire of the Revolution."[23] Attlee took a similar view. The Dutch seemed intent on slowing down negotiations because they assumed continued British military support.

Underlying Attlee's growing exasperation at Dutch intransigence was a concern about a marked deterioration in morale among British as well as Indian servicemen. Many had seen action over several years, home leave being virtually unknown. One commando became the envy of his comrades in Burma when he earned a month's leave in Britain for capturing a Japanese soldier alive: that the prisoner, an imperial guardsman, proved to be a giant amused the intelligence officers who in 1944 had offered the reward. Because this was so unusual a happening, it confirmed the men's belief that they were neglected during hostilities and forgotten after Japan surrendered. They were uneasy, too, about continued service in India and Indonesia because operations in both theatres slowed down the rate of demobilisation.

Mutinies occurred in 1945 and 1946 from India to Singapore. In Malaya, a refusal to parade led to a mass court martial in 1946: more than 200 men of the Parachute Regiment were sent to prison. They had just returned from a tour of duty in Java. Though their protest had a definite connection with poor conditions in camp, long-serving soldiers were worried about finding themselves at a disadvantage in the job market or higher education, if they came back to Britain late. For Indian troops, the position was no less uncertain, especially when the prospect of partition emerged. At the start of 1946, a full-scale mutiny broke out in the Royal Indian Navy, involving 10 naval establishments and 56 ships. The mutiny began at a signals establishment in Bombay when its British commanding officer called a group of sailors "black bastards" and triggered a protest that spread the same day to signal stations as far away as Aden and Bahrain. The spontaneous mutiny was based upon accumulated grievances—poor accommodation and food, bad pay and a perception of an uncaring naval leadership—but it quickly assumed a role in the Indian independence movement. Riots inspired by the mutinous sailors convulsed Bombay, as hundreds were killed or wounded in street battles. Even though order was restored to the city and a commission of inquiry set up, which largely vindicated the sailors' complaints about both dismal conditions and racial harassment, the British were left with a big question mark hanging over the Royal Indian Navy's reliability. Indian tolerance of British condescension was over for good, no matter that the court martials concentrated on a small group of sailors.[24]

Ignoring London's desire for a political settlement, the Dutch went over to the offensive near Batavia. When they ran into trouble and asked for British military support, ostensibly to safeguard the rice-growing area around that city, Bevin insisted that the Dutch should be informed that they could expect nothing more. He had the full backing of Attlee, who was unimpressed by a Dutch request to employ some 20,000 surrendered Japanese as labourers instead of recruiting Indonesians. The United States took little interest in Anglo-Dutch relations in Southeast Asia, other than to insist that trucks supplied originally to the British, and now being used by the Dutch, should have the "US" stencilled on their sides painted out. Once the Dutch invaded territory controlled by the nationalists in July 1947, the Truman administration tried to put as much distance as it could between Dutch use of American military equipment and Indonesian protests over its use. By 1948, as the Dutch need for spare parts and ammunition mounted, ingenious methods were tried to bypass an American embargo on further supplies. There can be no doubt that Holland spent on American arms a substantial part of the aid provided by the United States for post-war reconstruction in Europe.

After the British withdrawal, the Dutch made an all-out attempt to subdue the whole of Java and secure economically important areas in Sumatra. A quick military solution was essential because Holland could ill afford an expensive colonial war, but

British and American opposition to this so-called "police action" prevented a complete conquest. It did not help the Hague that both India and Australia were active in supporting the Indonesian cause at the United Nations, where the Soviet Union lent its support as well. Given Russian interest in the Republic of Indonesia, Truman ditched Holland completely during 1949 with the result that an independent Indonesia became inevitable. While it was diplomatically referred to as the Netherlands-Indonesian Union, nobody expected any mutual relationship to last. One omission from the final agreement was Western New Guinea—or West Irian, as Sukarno called it—where a continued Dutch presence was the source of post-colonial conflict. Not that this represented the limits of Indonesian ambitions, because in the 1960s, Sukarno promoted territorial claims against Malaysia and in 1976 Indonesian forces took over the Portuguese colony of East Timor. Its liberation by an Australia-led international peacekeeping force in 1999 marked the last Asian decolonisation.

Traditionally, Australia had taken comfort from the spread of Western colonies across Southeast Asia as a barrier against Asian threats. The ease with which the Japanese swept through the region in late 1941 and early 1942, and especially their capture of Singapore, shattered the illusion of colonial power and irrevocably altered the political situation. A consequence of this sudden change was Canberra's sympathetic attitude towards nationalist movements there. External affairs minister, Dr. Herbert Evatt, stated in 1947 that they "must be regarded realistically and with understanding".[25] Having helped to write its charter, Evatt was extremely active at the United Nations, being elected the General Assembly's president for the 1948–49 session. His eagerness to refer international disputes to the world body particularly upset Britain, which expected a Commonwealth member to support its own position.

New Zealand was equally annoyed because it saw Evatt's diplomacy as a blatant attempt to claim for Australia a dominant role in Southeast Asian affairs. As did India, Australia used the Dutch offensive in Indonesia to woo Asian nationalists. Its condemnation of Holland led to the Republic of Indonesia nominating Australia as its member on the UN's Good Offices Committee, in spite of continued Asian resentment of the "White Australia" policy. In London the view was "that Australia may not always be Dr. Evatt", so patience should determine Anglo-Australian relations.[26] It was still a relief that Evatt saw the anti-British uprising in Malaya as nothing more than the work of a Chinese communist minority. This suited Australia perfectly because its premier, Ben Chifley, did not want to become militarily involved with the Malayan insurgency. It was the return of Robert Menzies to power in 1949 that re-established Australia as a power willing to intervene militarily abroad, even in Vietnam, a conflict Britain studiously avoided. Although Menzies frequently referred to himself as "British to the bootstraps", his foreign policy has arguably led to American domination of Canberra's international outlook. In the late 1990s, the then prime minister, John Howard, was even prepared to justify Australia's increased military expenditure in terms of acting as America's deputy in Southeast Asia: a policy statement that earned him the title of "Bonsai", meaning Little Bush.

The Communist Triumph in China

The aftermath of the Pacific War was as profound for China and Japan as it was for the European colonial holdings in Asia. Neither country could escape the far-reaching transformation that so dramatically altered the political landscape in the 1940s. While the Japanese lost an empire along with a divine ruler, the Chinese ended their revolutionary travail through the triumph of Mao Zedong. Emperor Hirohito had to heed American guidance at the same time that the Guomindang refused to accept any advice at all from Washington. By the early 1950s, their very different relationships with the United States were reflected in the Korean War: the People's Republic sent Chinese "volunteers" to aid North Korea and, as the Japanese premier Yoshida Shigeru put it, US military procurement was "a gift from the gods", since massive expenditure on the conflict laid the foundation of Japan's present-day economic strength.

In the autumn of 1945, the political situation in China was as strange as in Indonesia or Vietnam. The sudden ending of the Pacific War caught the Guomindang short, while providing ample scope for the Chinese Communist Party to extend its influence. President Truman offered Chiang Kai-shek immediate financial and military assistance and he ordered some of the one million Japanese troops in Manchuria

On 1 October 1949 Mao Zedong proclaims the People's Republic in Beijing

and north China to remain under arms until they could be replaced by Chiang Kai-shek's or US forces. In Chongqing Zhou Enlai asked an American representative there, involved in the peace talks

> why we proclaim non-intervention and then intervene without disarming the Japanese . . . He seemed to have very little faith that any settlement would be forthcoming, though he thought there was a chance that popular pressure from beneath might force the Generalissimo to alter his determination to occupy the entire country. I could not see that he was terribly upset by the continuing erosion of negotiations and the ebbing prospects of peace. He is confident who wins in the end.[27]

There was no easy answer to Zhou Enlai's question. Because of his warlord outlook, Chiang Kai-shek was unable to appreciate that building up a modern army was not enough to hold China, even though it might be furnished with the latest American equipment.

It is possible that the decision of Washington to treat China as a great power, one of the Big Five, only made matters worse, for this elevation gave the Guomindang an inflated view of its own political position. In Shanghai, it moved against the French, the weakest of the Big Five. The trial of Roland Sarly, a senior policemen in the French Concession, provided an opportunity to express publicly a rejection of the old colonial order. Accused of collaboration with Wang Jingwei's regime, and indeed with the Imperial Japanese Army, Sarly's trial uncovered the least attractive side of the Treaty Ports in terms of links with criminal gangs and official corruption.

What goaded the Guomindang into action was the expectation of French residents in Shanghai that the Japanese surrender meant a return of the city to its pre-war position. At Sarly's instigation, consular staff sent out armed groups with tricolour badges to patrol the former French Concession.[28] Under pressure from Japan, the Vichy government had been obliged to renounce the rights and privileges granted to France by the nineteenth-century treaties and pass the concession to Wang Jingwei's puppet regime. From a technical point of view, there was some justification for the French reaction to the end of the Pacific War. Ever since Philippe Pétain had announced on the radio in 1940 that "a collaboration" would take place between France and Germany, the word came to mean a shameful accommodation to a conqueror's will. And the Vichy leader's readiness to do the same in Indochina, when the Imperial Japanese Army moved in, shattered French prestige in Asia more than defeat in the Franco-Thai War of 1940–41.

In Europe, the battles fought by the Free French and the resistance, and the part played by the reconstituted French army in the invasion of Germany, conferred a degree of legitimacy upon the role de Gaulle sought to play. In China, however, there was no respect for France and no possibility that the Guomindang would accept that the French Concession was forcibly relinquished by an illegitimate government. But it was still ironic that the Guomindang failed to understand the necessity of French wartime collaboration, when so many of its own generals had defected to the Japanese side and used their troops against Mao Zedong's guerrillas, giving the distinct impression that Chiang Kai-shek was content to sit out the war. According to a popular rumour in 1944, Chongqing and Tokyo had come to an agreement by which Chiang Kai-shek would not be attacked in his Sichuan stronghold, provided Guomindang forces offered no resistance to Japanese advances elsewhere. Belief in such patent double dealing made the Chinese Communist Party victory almost inevitable.

The shaky Guomindang foundations were not apparent outside China. Mao Zedong had waged an unknown guerrilla campaign in the northern provinces, while the Generalissimo had been praised by Allied propaganda as the determined opponent of the Japanese, bravely holding out in beleaguered Chongqing. American diplomats and military advisers could not be unaware of the ramshackle administration and army that Jiang Jieshi led, but the reports they sent back to Washington were not intended for general consumption because their criticisms would not have squared with accepted attitudes towards China in the United States. Ever since Roosevelt had elevated China to Great Power status, American public opinion looked upon the fate of the country as being synonymous with that of the Guomindang government.

In contrast to the largely inactive Guomindang formations, Mao Zedong's irregulars continually harassed the Imperial Japanese Army, surviving on captured weapons and ammunition, so that their iron determination was unlikely to be bent by imported American firepower. The People's Liberation Army, as communist forces were now called, had in addition a very different attitude to civilians. Foreign observers were amazed at the courtesy displayed. At Tianjin,

> the soldiers looked fierce enough with their big fur caps and ear-flaps, their padded cotton uniforms draped around the cartridge bandoliers and hung with dangerous-looking home-made grenades. All were well armed, with Japanese rifles or automatic weapons of American make. In every group of half a dozen or so there would be one with a scrap of paper in his hand. These we discovered were the addresses of the private houses on which the squads were to be billeted. Several times I saw a soldier approaching a knot of bystanders . . . and, proffering his paper with a polite bow and a smile, ask directions to the street and the house number his group were seeking. These

must have been some of the first occasions . . . of uniformed soldiers using all the forms of Chinese courtesy to ordinary civilians. On the civilians, at first astounded, and in the end mightily pleased, the effect was enormous.[29]

It was an incredible contrast with the recently expelled Guomindang forces. Here, as elsewhere in China, the Chinese Communist Party "was far from private graft, officers and men lived very much together, simply and identically . . . There was almost no maltreatment of the populace. They borrowed extensively but generally returned these articles or made restitutions."[30]

Not that the unusual behaviour of a Soviet puppet's army was considered as noteworthy in Washington, where the powerful "China Lobby" ruled the roost. This well-financed pressure group was to dictate post-war American policy towards China, especially after the Guomindang sought refuge on the island of Taiwan. Its impact was increased through the activities of an errant senator by the name of Joseph McCarthy, whom Truman badly underestimated when he first appeared on the scene in February 1950, claiming that he had a list of "Communists" in the State Department. While Dean Acheson saw an external threat to the United States in what was called the Cold War, McCarthy saw the enemy within the government, and in particular Acheson's own department. Although he always believed that handling the Soviet Union was the key foreign policy issue, Acheson never chose to recognise Mao Zedong's regime, an American position that continued till 1972. Then President Nixon's visit to the People's Republic was to cause a total reshaping of US relations in Asia. It had taken major clashes in 1969 between Chinese and Russian troops to revise the American dogma of a unified communist bloc.

In the late 1940s, however, there was no chance of distinguishing between the aspirations of Russia and China. Once Washington had rejected feelers from Mao Zedong for a top-level conference in Washington, civil war in China could not be avoided. Today, it is difficult to recapture the uncertainties of the time, when neither the United States nor the Soviet Union could distinguish genuine anxiety and political opportunism. In Washington, a city unscarred by war, few appreciated the devastation caused by the

Germans in Russia, which made Stalin so preoccupied with defence in Europe that he even discouraged the Chinese Communist Party from going on the offensive. Totally misunderstanding American intentions, the Russian leader adopted a tough line, and helped to justify anti-Soviet fundamentalism in the United States. Everything Churchill said of an "iron curtain" descending across Europe in his celebrated speech at Fulton, Missouri, in March 1946, seemed to be confirmed. Repressive Communist regimes in Eastern Europe only served to reinforce attitudes that were deftly manipulated by the "China Lobby", as soon as it was apparent that a "bamboo curtain" had descended in China as well.

President Truman had sent his favourite general, George Marshall, to work out a military truce and a political settlement in China. Marshall seemed within an ace of securing a peace as Chiang Kai-shek and Mao Zedong both issued orders to their armed forces to stop hostilities and halt all troop movements in 1946. It was the Guomindang's failure to release political prisoners, however, that marked the beginning of a drawing back from any reconciliation. One reason for Chiang Kai-shek's hesitation was Manchuria. This vast area was never properly incorporated into the terms of the ceasefire, as it was then occupied by the Russians. Marshall seems to have been unwilling to annoy Stalin by making future dispositions of territory still under Soviet control. Both the Guomindang and the Chinese Communist Party intended to gain control of Manchuria when the Russians left, which they did in April after dismantling and removing to Siberia the industries built up there by the Japanese. Taken away were heavy machinery, machine tools, railway materials, even office furniture, along with 700,000 Japanese prisoners of war.[31] By handing over the cities to Guomindang forces, flown in by US aircraft, Stalin revealed that he still thought Mao Zedong was unlikely to win. What Moscow missed was the lack of appetite among the Chinese for a conflict on Chiang Kai-shek's behalf. New recruits to the Guomindang armed forces often had to be roped together to prevent them from running away. Moscow also underestimated the financial crisis that was about to engulf the Guomindang. As an observant American noted on moving from Chongqing to Nanjing, the "economic situation could bring it down . . . Just in the last three or four months the currency note has reached astronomical proportions. No semantic juggling in committee meetings can change what this does to people."[32] How serious inflation had become was plain to see when the Americans purchased a house for embassy staff in Nanjing. The Chinese Central Bank did not have enough notes on hand to exchange for the 60,000 US-dollar draft and the vendor had to wait two days for more to be printed, by which time his money had depreciated by 25 per cent.

The rush to Manchuria was undoubtedly Chiang Kai-shek's greatest mistake. With Mao Zedong's guerrillas in effective control of the northern provinces other than Japanese-garrisoned cities, Chiang Kai-shek simply inherited the military difficulties of the Imperial Japanese Army. Had he chosen to secure the populous southern provinces first, and at the same time tried to reassure the peasants by introducing a measure of land reform, then the Guomindang might have been able to push northwards without peril. Guomindang forces were instead seen to ally themselves with the defeated Japanese and with those Chinese units that had actively cooperated with the invaders. Acheson might protest that American policy had nothing to do with intervention, but the assistance rendered to Chiang Kai-shek seemed oddly like taking sides in China's internal affairs. And the misconduct of US servicemen in Beijing, where the rape of a girl student caused nationwide protests, only increased resentment against the imposition of Guomindang rule.

Chiang Kai-shek's troops recovered large areas previously under communist domination, but this territorial expansion came at a price: the defence of recaptured towns and villages, plus communications between them, meant a dilution of military strength. In the meantime, the People's Liberation Army moved freely through the rural areas, setting up bases for future operations in mountainous areas as far south as the Yangzi river valley. While Chiang Kai-shek was obliged to redeploy troops to counter this dangerous infiltration, Mao Zedong launched an all-out offensive in Manchuria in 1947. The campaign began with the investment of Jinzhou, a key railway centre well to the south of Mukden. This bold attack threatened the supply line and retreat route of the 500,000 Guomindang troops in garrisons to its north. Realising the gravity of the situation, Jiang Jieshi flew in to Mukden to direct a counterattack from there, but there was nothing he could do to save Jinzhou, whose 100,000 defenders surrendered after a fierce assault. Mukden itself fell next as Guomindang morale plummeted and half-hearted resistance became commonplace. Other cities quickly submitted: Jiang Jieshi only admitted the loss of 300,000 troops and glibly informed Washington that the loss of Manchuria was due to Soviet aid.

Giving Chiang Kai-shek no respite at all in 1948, Mao Zedong directed a series of attacks south of the Great Wall, where he gained a decisive victory in Jiangsu province at Xuzhou, a major city on the railway line to Nanjing. In the 65-day engagement, the People's Liberation Army outnumbered the Guomindang forces for the first time, although lacking the tanks and heavy artillery ranged against it. Chiang Kai-shek never recovered from the losses sustained at Xuzhou: between 400,000 and 600,000 men. There was little left to defend Nanjing. Had Mao Zedong ordered an immediate advance, Chiang Kai-shek would have been driven from his capital at once. Instead, there was a pause during which the bypassed northern cities were reduced one by one. Beijing surrendered with a garrison of 200,000 troops. It was obvious that the turning point of the civil war had arrived. On 20 April, advance units of the People's Liberation Army reached the Yangzi. That morning, shells from its field artillery had fallen upon *HMS Amethyst,* killing its captain. The frigate returned fire before running aground on a mudbank at Rose Island, almost midway between Nanjing and Wusong at the river mouth.

Then few people could have expected that the incident would mark the end of gunboat diplomacy. No one could have realised that in spite of a dramatic escape downriver, the Royal Navy's discomfiture was already part of a colonial past. For the shelling effectively restored the Yangzi to Chinese ownership: the great river was no longer an international waterway, a designation forced upon China by the Western powers in the nineteenth century. The crippled ship was supposed to stay there until Britain issued a formal apology for "a violation of Chinese waters", since attempts to come to *Amethyst*'s aid by other members of the Yangzi Flotilla were repulsed. From Nanjing, *HMS Consort* had to turn back after suffering ten men killed, 23 wounded and 56 direct hits, while *HMS London* and *Black Swan*, sailing upriver from the sea, were driven off with 52 dead and wounded. Hidden shore batteries denied these vessels clear targets and gave the communist gunners a tremendous advantage in every exchange of fire.

Even before this rescue attempt was foiled, it was decided to send John Kerans, the British naval attaché in Nanjing, to take over command of the *Amethyst*. He was probably the last person that the Admiralty would have chosen for this difficult task. His posting to a desk job in a distant imperial outpost was a last resort for an officer whose naval career had gone nowhere. That in years to come he should be lionised as a national hero, and indeed become the subject of a successful film, it was quite impossible to foresee when he reached his new command. After he buried the dead, evacuated the wounded and surveyed the damage to the ship, Kerans was stupefied to receive an order to prepare to abandon ship and lead surviving crew members overland to Shanghai. Shifting the *Amethyst* to a more secluded position, Kerans waited upon events in the hope that he would not have to scuttle the frigate. Rightly, he guessed that the People's Liberation Army had mistaken the *Amethyst* for a Guomindang warship and, having realised the error of firing without warning, decided to exploit the incident for propaganda purposes.

In London, there was consternation. While Attlee reiterated the Labour government's policy of remaining uninvolved in the Chinese civil war, it was hard to explain the continued presence of naval and diplomatic personnel in Nanjing when the Guomindang was moving its capital farther south. As unsatisfactory was the explanation for *Amethyst*'s lack of air cover, either on its voyage up the Yangzi or during the two rescue attempts, until it transpired that the absence of aircraft carriers was part of a programme to reduce the Royal Navy's presence east of Suez and trim the defence budget in view of the poor state of the British economy.

Though the *Amethyst* incident struck a deeply patriotic chord in the electorate, the new Labour MP Richard Crossman declared in the *Sunday Pictorial* how "British warships are as out of place on the Yangtse as Chinese warships would be on the Thames".[33] Because the crisis made such good copy for British newspapers, the fate of *Amethyst*'s crew remained the focus of attention during the negotiations held on the Yangzi with representatives of the People's Liberation Army. These dragged on interminably until Kerans determined to make a dash for the sea. He knew it was not a decision to be taken lightly: a court martial would not take a kindly view of outwitting the enemy if his escape bid ended in disaster, not least because he had no reliable navigational charts and there were guns all the way to Wusong.

When on 30 July, Kerans informed the Far East Station of his intention of breaking out that night, Sir Patrick Brind approved to the extent that he turned a Nelson's blind eye to a signal just received from the Admiralty forbidding any such attempt without authorisation from London. In sending the signal back to the Admiralty for rechecking, the commander-in-chief gave Kerans his chance. That the latter also possessed a remarkable degree of luck was evident when, as the *Amethyst* was about to slip anchor, a fully lit Chinese merchant ship steamed past. Kerans realised how it could act as pilot if he followed close astern. In the event, the merchant ship soon fell victim to the communist batteries and the *Amethyst* had to proceed alone, negotiating a twisting channel through treacherous sandbanks in the dark.

At daybreak, Kerans brought the scarred and rusty frigate into the river mouth, after more than a hundred days of captivity. He signalled Brind in Hong Kong that he had "rejoined the Fleet . . . No damage or casualties. God save the King." The monarch responded to the news of *Amethyst's* escape by taking the unusual step of awarding Kerans an immediate DSO. Admiral Bird passed on the king's hearty congratulations to all members of the crew, adding that Kerans had faced nothing on the Yangzi in comparison with the publicity he was going to face now. While the British were celebrating, the Chinese Communist Party reacted with undisguised fury and insisted that the *Amethyst* had fired upon the lifeboats of the merchant vessel before stealing away.[34] Notwithstanding London's denial of any guilt in the loss of life being confirmed by the merchant ship's captain, who said his cargo of coal was set ablaze by People's Liberation Army field artillery and that the unilluminated vessel he then saw passing by him on the river fired at neither his ship nor the shore, the international dispute would not go away.

The aftermath of the *Amethyst's* escape was strained relations between Britain and the People's Republic, which Mao Zedong proclaimed at Beijing on 1 October. On the old capital's surrender earlier in 1949, there was a grand victory parade to mark the communist capture of the city. An American academic there at the time has left this account:

> It unfortunately coincided with the first real dust storm of the winter . . . My face was black with grime by the time I returned home . . . Of chief interest was, of course, the Liberation Army itself. I missed the first contingents of infantry and cavalry, as well as parts of the motorized units. But in what I did see, lasting an hour, I counted over 250 heavy motor vehicles of all kinds—tanks, armoured cars, truck loads of soldiers, trucks mounted with machine guns, trucks towing heavy artillery. Behind them followed innumerable ambulances, jeeps, and other smaller vehicles. As probably the greatest demonstration of Chinese military might in history, the spectacle was enormously impressive. But what made it especially memorable to Americans was the fact that it was primarily a display of *American* military equipment, virtually all of it captured or obtained by bribe from Kuomintang [Guomindang] forces in the short space of two and a half years.

He also noted that the onlookers were "in general quite favourably disposed and obviously deeply impressed by the display of power".[35] They knew Chiang Kai-Shek was a lost cause, something Truman now appreciated as well.

When Marshall came home from China in 1947, the general filled the president's ears with tales of Guomindang incompetence. By the close of the Chinese civil war Truman no longer had any illusions left. Of the 2.5 billion dollars that Washington had given to Chiang Kai-Shek's government, he said: "I'll bet you that a billion dollars of it is in New York banks today . . . It's all for those grafters and crooks; rest of the people in China don't matter."[36] The flight of a Guomindang remnant to Taiwan in December 1949 left Truman unmoved, although his political opponents blamed him and Marshall for "losing" China, as if it were theirs to lose. Giving up the Guomindang because it was a spent force did not mean embracing the "Reds" though, for the Chinese Communist Party had no desire to improve relations with the United States. It was more interested in ties with Moscow than Washington, despite Mao Zedong's insistence that the People's Liberation Army had not expelled the Guomindang so that China would become a Soviet satellite. But any possibility of an understanding with the Americans was about to disappear for 20 years through the Korean War.

Before the start of this conflict on 25 June 1950 with a surprise North Korean attack, Washington was lukewarm about both Taiwan and South Korea. Acheson had told the National Press Club in the capital that they lay beyond the US defence perimeter. Later he admitted that South Korea might have to be abandoned, "whether we like it or not".[37] How wrong Acheson proved to be. Not only would South Korea's defence become a burning issue in the United States but, through Beijing's military assistance to the North Koreans, the Guomindang were relieved to find that Taiwan suddenly had strategic significance too. The Soviet Union's explosion of an atomic weapon seemed to underscore a worldwide communist threat, which led to condemnation of Britain's recognition of the People's Republic on Capitol Hill.

Some politicians actually demanded that sanctions be imposed against London. McCarthyite hysteria combined with a genuine fear of Cold War developments to end any rational discussion of China. Border skirmishes at Hong Kong were never serious enough to deter London from offering recognition to Mao Zedong's regime. As the British acknowledged the legitimacy of Taiwan and refused to agree that Hong Kong was part of the People's Republic, a compromise was reached by which Chinese interests in the colony were entrusted to the New China News Agency, which operated from the Bank of China building.

A few Americans left Hong Kong in protest, but most foreign residents accepted the value of this "unofficial" arrangement. Thomas Dewey, Truman's Republican opponent in the 1948 presidential election, was shocked at the lack of censorship that he encountered in the colony. He could not understand how there were no restrictions placed on newspaper correspondents when reporting Chinese affairs.[38] Apparently, Dewey was reassured by the very different situation in French Indochina, where he learned of determined resistance to the Viet Minh. What Dewey did not really understand was how the French were making a last-ditch effort to retain their colonial holdings there.

The Occupation of Japan

President Truman had more success in Japan than China. He kept the British and the Russians out of the occupation, instructing MacArthur to reshape Japan in the interests of the United States. Not until 1946 would the White House permit the arrival of a token Commonwealth occupation force drawn from Britain, India, Australia and New Zealand. As a British official acutely noted in November 1945, "the Americans now regard Japan and the former Japanese bases which they hold as a bulwark in the Pacific . . . Thus, tragic and paradoxical as it may seem, it is likely that the defeated Japanese will profit from American protection, while the supposedly victorious Chinese will be left to the tender mercies of the Communists whether native or Russian."[39] What Truman desperately wanted to ensure was American prosperity: US industrial production was in post-war decline and unemployment had shot upwards. Integrating Japan into the world market and rebuilding its ruined infrastructure created a golden opportunity for American firms to increase their exports.

General MacArthur set up his headquarters on 8 September 1945 in the Dai-Ichi Mutual Life Insurance building, across the moat from the imperial palace. On his arrival at Yokohama airport, nine days earlier, MacArthur was aware that many Japanese cities were still burning. His journey into Tokyo reassured him because the route was lined with thousands of Japanese soldiers, who stood to attention with their backs to his car. Because this was the position they always assumed when their emperor passed, he knew how the sign of respect meant that his difficult mission had chance of success. Yet there remained a lingering sense of racial superiority, of the Japanese having been somehow cheated of victory in the Pacific War by a more industrially advanced foe. In a letter to his son, Emperor Hirohito explained that:

> Our people believed too much in the imperial country and were contemptuous of Britain and the United States. Our military men placed too much weight on spirit and forgot about science.

Taking over this opinion as his own, Crown Prince Akihito wrote in his diary during September how Japan's defeat was the result of "the overwhelming material superiority of Britain and the United States . . . [They] were defeated at the start [of the Pacific War] because they were not then adequately prepared."[40] Both father and son conveniently avoided mentioning the policy conferences that preceded the outbreak of hostilities, in which the emperor was personally involved. Because his role in bringing about the Japanese surrender only partly compensated for this, the emperor would be regarded for the rest of his life as a "war criminal". A reformed monarchy, however, was such an asset to the US occupation force in Japan that there was never any likelihood of Emperor Hirohito being put on trial.

Similarly to the Japanese people, the emperor had little idea at first of what occupation might bring in the wake of such a catastrophic defeat. He may well have feared that US troops would behave as his own troops had in China: plundering and raping without mercy. Already in Japan itself, the morale of the Imperial Japanese Army had collapsed through widespread looting of military stores and bullying of the civilian population. Men in uniform found themselves suddenly the objects of contempt, an amazing turnaround after half a century of blatant militarism. When he realised that MacArthur was not prepared to tolerate an informal visit, Emperor Hirohito donned formal morning dress with a top hat and went to the American Embassy to pay his respects. Ushered into MacArthur's presence, the general noticed how the emperor's hands were shaking with nervousness, so uncertain was Hirohito of the reception he might get. With memories of Pearl Harbor still fresh, the American public wanted nothing less than the emperor's blood, something his apparent willingness to shoulder the guilt for the surprise attack made feasible. But MacArthur bucked public opinion and threw his energies into reforming Japan. He was fortunate to have been given a free hand, although Truman often chafed at the general's lack of concern for Washington's guidelines. The first meeting with the emperor had a great impact on the American general: quite simply MacArthur and Hirohito hit it off.

Appreciating the impossibility of directly administering a country as different from the United States as Japan, Washington decided to rule through a Japanese government. Having publicly demonstrated the defeat of the Imperial Japanese Army by the presence of occupying forces, MacArthur concentrated therefore on setting up a satisfactory civilian administration, by supervising ministries in Tokyo and checking results locally throughout the country. Because Emperor Hirohito went along with this approach, he became in effect a major partner of the Allied occupation. With the sole exception of the throne, the institutions held responsible for Japanese militarism were swiftly removed, including Shinto as the state religion, and in their place democratic institutions were installed. The amended imperial constitution was an entirely new one based on a set of fundamentally different principles. It transferred sovereignty from the throne to the people, established a parliamentary system of government, outlawed war, allowed trade unions and, for the first time in Japan's history, guaranteed civil liberties. At the same time, MacArthur also placed severe limits on the industrial combines that had so patently profited from a war economy. They had ruthlessly cooperated with the Imperial Japanese Army in the exploitation of Korea, Manchuria and China, as well as other parts of the Greater East Asia Co-Prosperity Sphere. The continuation of the practice of forcing employees to swear loyalty oaths to these companies was looked upon as a dangerous feudal relic. But the attempt MacArthur made to break up combines such as Mitsubishi was thwarted by conservative politicians in the United States, who believed that this policy would slow down Japan's economic recovery.

Even though there was genuine relief that the American general and the Japanese emperor seemed to get along well together, the Japanese people harboured a deep-seated fear about the fate of the imperial house. The famous photograph taken at their first encounter hardly helped. It showed the bespectacled emperor, in formal morning coat and striped trousers, standing as though to attention, with his tie straight and his hands by his side, while next to him stood the taller general in open-necked uniform without decorations, his hands resting casually on his hips. No Japanese could possibly have taken such a frank photograph. The obvious unease of Emperor Hirohito was perceived as soon as newspapers carried the photograph, at the insistence of MacArthur's staff. There had been a marked reluctance to print it at all. When the Japanese government moved to suppress the photograph on the grounds that it was sacrilegious to the imperial house, MacArthur then knew that the emperor would have to stop being regarded as a god.

A less than comfortable Japanese emperor with Douglas MacArthur
in Tokyo, late 1945

He tightened control over the press and welcomed Emperor Hirohito's
subsequent New Year message, which stated:

> The ties between us with our people . . . do not depend on
> mere legends and myths. They are not predicated on the false
> conception that the Emperor is divine and that the Japanese
> people are superior to other races and fated to rule the world.[41]

315

This denial of direct descent from the sun goddess Amaterasu was not given a prominent position in the message, but no Japanese could miss its intention: the emperor was jettisoning all of the imperial pretensions that had defined Japan's history since the Meiji restoration. No longer would its prime objective be to outdo the Western colonial powers in Asia.

MacArthur was delighted that Japan was adjusting once again to the modern world. For the emperor's repudiation of his divinity was crucial for the launch of democratic institutions: at a stroke it deflated right-wing opposition to change. It also helped MacArthur that the emperor was identified as the main sponsor of the new constitution from the day it was presented to elected representatives of the people. This pleased Yoshida Shigeru, who commented:

> As for the Imperial House, the idea and reality of the Throne had come into being among the Japanese people as naturally as the idea of the country itself; no question of antagonism between the Throne and the people could possibly arise; and nothing in the new Constitution could change that fact.[42]

Gratefully, this leading politician saw that the emperor's position had been preserved. That Emperor Hirohito seems to have come to the same conclusion probably explains the many tours of the country he made by car and train. Everywhere he went, his actions were headline news.

One problem was the emperor's inability to shake hands with people who offered to do so, and quickly it became normal to stick with the traditional bow. Yet his down-at-heel appearance somehow compensated for this democratic shortcoming. As an American observer noted, these tours revealed to the Japanese that their emperor was

> short, slight, and round-shouldered, that his coordination was so poor he seemed constantly on the verge of toppling over. He was weak-chinned . . . apart from a stubbly moustache his beard was straggly and he often needed a shave. Thick, horned-rimmed glasses shielded his weak eyes. His clothes were unkempt and his shoes scuffed.[43]

Not that it mattered to a Japan desperately seeking self-esteem after so ruinous a defeat, since Emperor Hirohito's vulnerable image served to endear him to his subjects. Demonstrably not a god, the emperor could now be looked upon as a man, almost a penitent on his circuit of visits to shrines where he paid his respects to those who had died in the Pacific War.

It proved to be a shrewd method of reinventing the monarchy in the years after the Tokyo war crimes trials. General Tojo Hideki had tried to commit suicide in 1946 on learning of his imminent arrest. Because this traditional response to adversity failed and he was recovering in hospital, his former colleagues told the ex-premier that he had to live to protect the emperor. Tojo Hideki accepted that it was his duty to accept the blame for hostilities, which led to him receiving the death sentence, along with five other generals. Only one civilian politician, Hirota Koki, was sentenced to execution. His cabinet had endorsed the actions of the Imperial Japanese Army in north China, thereby facilitating the virtual takeover of government by the armed forces in 1940. As did Emperor Hirohito himself, Hirota Koki saw China as neither a nation nor a people's homeland, but merely a territory that Japan could acquire and use for its own benefit. MacArthur dismissed all appeals for a stay of execution, and all seven were executed by hanging. Their bodies were then cremated and their ashes scattered at sea to prevent them at a later date being enshrined as political martyrs. On hearing the news, Emperor Hirohito wept.

During the trial, the Australian government pressed for charges to be brought against more war criminals, but MacArthur was only interested in pinning the blame on Tojo Hideki, whose testimony he correctly guessed would save the politically useful emperor. The energetic Dr. Evatt was then forcibly representing Australia in foreign affairs. He was determined that his country should play a large part in the post-war settlement on the grounds that Australian and US forces had fought shoulder to shoulder against Japan. Entirely ignored by Herbert Evatt was the contribution made by British, Indian, African and Russian troops, not to mention the efforts of the Chinese, who had tied down the bulk of the Imperial Japanese Army. There is no doubt, however, that he expressed a view widely held in Australia that the events of the war had established a new and different relationship with the United States. This country had replaced Britain as Australia's protector. Yet his advocacy of a major role for Australian troops in Japan did not reap the political dividends that he expected they would at home.

Most of the problems Australian soldiers encountered in Japan were the direct result of the widespread destruction wrought by American bombers. As one Australian infantryman remarked, "You could have what you liked for a cake of soap".[44] Once the Australian public realised that their soldiers were deeply involved with the black market and the underworld, there was an outcry against a continued presence. In 1948, a particularly strong attack was delivered by the Federal President of the League of Ex-Servicemen, after a visit to Japan. He did not spare anyone's blushes when he said the Australian troops there "are spiritually leaderless, bewildered and confused".[45] MacArthur put a gloss on the report that was compiled in response to growing criticism in Australia, when he called its soldiers the "tops". Not so easily explained away was the prevalence of venereal disease, which topped 13,000 cases among the British Commonwealth Occupation Force.

In 1947–48, international tension easily sidelined Australian moral concerns. As Cold War antagonism rose, Truman moved to prepare the United States for the possibility of a Third World War. Already US officials had identified the Soviet Union as the likely enemy.[46] The newly established Central Intelligence Agency was given permission to conduct covert political operations as everything pointed to a confrontation with the Russians, who were worried that the US revival of industry in West Germany would soon threaten them all over again. With Mao Zedong's victory in China, the belligerence of the Soviet Union turned Japan into the key to US policy in Asia. From 1949 onwards, there was a purge of left-wing sympathisers among Japanese politicians, trade unionists, teachers and journalists. This tough American line brought a permanent smile to Yoshida Shigeru's face. Had it been possible the Japanese premier would have smiled even more on the outbreak of the Korean War, for the reason that US military procurement in Japan brought a boom to its struggling economy.

No less a triumph for Japan was the signing in 1951 of the US-Japan Security Treaty, a bilateral agreement through which the Japanese regained full independence in return for creating a small "self-defence" force and allowing US bases on Okinawa and the main Japanese islands. Truman found it easier to get his way here than elsewhere in Asia. In 1945, Washington had secretly asked London about the possibility of establishing strategic airbases in India. It was not pleased to be told that Indian independence, then very much on the Labour government's agenda, would not be of a qualified kind. Delhi would have to make up its own mind about the matter, Bevin insisted, for the good reason that India was already "virtually a sovereign state".[47] In decolonisation, you could not have your cake and eat it too. So pleased were the Japanese to see the end of the Allied occupation that they had no hesitation in agreeing to US bombers flying from their soil to attack the Soviet Union with atomic weapons. For Washington, it was a great relief because Cold War rivalry was already putting a strain on its finances. Not even a superpower such as the United States could afford a prolonged stay in Japan.

Chapter 7

Cold War Complications 1950–99

We all seek a better future for our people. But, given the different circumstances of natural and human resources, agricultural or industrial backgrounds, and industrial and technological competence, we have to chart different courses towards that goal.

*Lee Kuan Yew in 1971 at the first Commonwealth
Conference to be held in Asia*

US Intervention

General Douglas MacArthur met Emperor Hirohito of Japan eleven times before he was dismissed by Truman for having criticised, as commander-in-chief of the United Nations forces in the Korean War, the president's notion of a limited conflict. Now it seems quite incredible that so much power was delegated for so long to this difficult soldier. He can be said to have dominated affairs in Pacific Asia after the surrender of Japan, as a tearful Hirohito acknowledged on MacArthur's recall. The emperor knew that he could never expect to encounter another American as helpful as this general.

The climate of extreme uncertainty created by McCarthyism not only stiffened US foreign policy in Asia, but drew Washington into military alliance with several governments unworthy of support. The first was to be that of Syngman Rhee, whose corrupt and tyrannical methods were widely known. What most concerned the Americans, however, was Syngman Rhee's clamour for unification of Korea by force when South Korea's military strength was far inferior to that of North Korea. That the South Korean electorate also lacked confidence in Syngman Rhee was transparent when in May 1950 his party was left with 56 seats in the National Assembly, while 154 seats went to opposition parties and independents. The next month the North Koreans, thinking that this political disarray offered the perfect moment to strike, launched a surprise attack across the thirty-eighth parallel, the border between the two Koreas.

US troops were shocked by the Korean winter in 1950

Before this invasion by North Korean regulars, there had been sporadic fighting in South Korea between government troops and communist insurgents. Casualties were numbered in thousands, but these figures remain tiny in comparison with the huge losses sustained during the Korean War. The South Korean army would lose 350,000 men killed or missing, and 250,000 wounded; another 100,000 civilians would be forcibly moved to North Korea. Thirty-three thousand Americans would lose their lives and 106,000 would be wounded. Against this, North Korea is estimated to have lost more than half a million men, and China a staggering 900,000. By the end of 1953, few in the West would believe any more that it had been a necessary war.

Stung by McCarthy's criticisms, Truman determined to reverse US policy in Korea and declared his intention of crossing the thirty-eighth parallel and driving all the way to the borders of China and the Soviet Union. Containment was replaced by rollback when the president came to see the North Korean attack as Russia-sponsored aggression, despite Stalin carefully distancing himself from the conflict. At the time, Stalin's fears centred upon the United States, upon its apparent desire to control post-colonial Asia and threaten the Soviet Union from there as well as Europe.

Mao Zedong was less worried about Washington's strategic intentions, at least until United Nations troops approached the frontier of the People's Republic. He preferred to fall back on the traditional Chinese border policy of "letting the barbarians fight each other". Rebuilding China would be so much easier if the Russians and the Americans expended their wealth and energy in global competition. But US protection of the Guomindang on Taiwan galvanised the People's Republic into action: for Mao Zedong, it meant that the Americans had openly taken sides in China's civil war. Just before Kim Il Sung sent his forces against Syngman Rhee's army, Mao Zedong was preparing to cross the Taiwan Strait and settle accounts with Chiang Kai-shek. Annoyed though he was about US intervention, what Mao Zedong disliked most of all was that the Korean War increased Beijing's reliance on Moscow. Worse still, in the two months leading up to the war, both the North Koreans and the Soviets took steps to keep the Chinese in the dark about the military buildup.[1]

Because both the Soviet Union and the United States were preoccupied with European affairs, neither country took full account of the burning desire of Kim Il Sung and Syngman Rhee for a reunited Korea. In Washington, the future of Korea was not a priority before North Koreans attacked on 25 June 1950. The invasion achieved complete tactical surprise and Seoul fell within days. Emergency meetings of the UN Security Council, which the Russians boycotted because of the failure to replace the Guomindang with the Chinese Communist Party, only just agreed to support South Korea. Already the United States had sent arms and ammunition from Japan, while the Seventh Fleet sped northwards from the Philippines. In addition, Truman authorised MacArthur to transfer combat units from Japan to the Korean peninsula. Whatever world opinion thought about the Korean conflict, Washington was now utterly behind Syngman Rhee.

Within little more than a month, all resistance to the North Koreans was concentrated around the port of Pusan in the south-east of the peninsula. A mixed UN and South Korean force of 95,000 men was all that was left to defend this last, unconquered portion of South Korea. For six weeks, it was the subject of attack by day and night, until at last the effort to break through the hastily dug defences exhausted North Korean strength. Gradually, the number of assaults diminished and the defenders were able to push back Kim Il Sung's tired soldiers. The battle cost many lives on both sides, but the failure at Pusan was most damaging for North Korea because MacArthur could supplement his forces with fresh troops through this port because they arrived by sea. The UN commander-in-chief was concerned to turn the North Korean flank too. This he achieved by recapturing Seoul on 28 September through a brilliant amphibious landing at Inchon. Two days later, UN troops invaded North Korea. Although the United Nations gave its consent to the American desire for rollback, Britain was nervous over the widening scope of the conflict. Prime Minister Attlee worried that Truman would be unable to prevent MacArthur from dragging the West into a full-scale war with the People's Republic, since on 24 November nearly 250,000 Chinese soldiers had reacted to his northern drive by coming to Kim Il Sung's aid. No one had heeded Zhou Enlai's warning of possible Chinese intervention, which he gave at a meeting with the Indian ambassador. The United States' growing involvement with Asian affairs, especially its increasing attention to events in French Indochina, Taiwan and the Korean peninsula, deepened Beijing's sense of insecurity. It even accused the Americans of a "military encirclement and economic blockade" of the People's Republic. Zhou Enlai himself went so far as to suggest that American policy aimed at hegemony in Asia, which he said was colonialism under another name.[2]

Had the UN commander-in-chief not been so contemptuous of the idea of a buffer zone along the Chinese border, there is no reason to suppose that Beijing would have opted for war. Conventional warfare was not a method that Mao Zedong would have willingly chosen to maintain a divided peninsula, because it could prove exhausting and dangerous with active American support for South Korea. There was also the chance that Washington might be tempted to back Chiang Kai-shek in a bid to recover the Chinese mainland, perhaps through an invasion from the Korean peninsula. Beijing had always made it perfectly clear that a reconquest of South Korea was acceptable, but never the conquest of North Korea. Brushing aside all restraint, MacArthur ordered his forces to continue the advance northwards to the Yalu River, where they clashed with the People's Liberation Army. Reluctant to accept this engagement as a warning, the UN commander-in-chief was shaken when a full-scale assault fell on his troops with such a devastating impact that they took to their heels in headlong flight. Everywhere carefully laid ambushes awaited the retreating columns, because Chinese units had infiltrated the mountainous interior. This supposedly unpassable terrain provided the advance guard of the People's Liberation Army with a means of entering North Korea unnoticed.

General Omar Bradley called it the worst intelligence failure since the battle of the Bulge in 1944, a remarkable understatement considering how the unexpected German offensive represented only a temporary setback for the Allies. In North Korea, the Chinese advance changed the entire course of the war, ensuring that the peninsula would stay divided as it was at the end of the Pacific War. Bradley was then army chief of staff, having succeeded Dwight D. Eisenhower, the next US president. As early as 1943, when Eisenhower had still to be appointed Allied Supreme Commander in Europe, there were Republicans who saw him as the means of turning the Democrats out of the White House. It is not a little ironic that Eisenhower would sweep into office in the 1952 election on a promise to end the Korean War and protect American interests in Asia as well. Even more bizarre was the declared Republican intention that the United States would in future thwart Stalin's activities, which were aimed at undermining the Free World, as though there had been no American involvement in Chinese and Japanese affairs. But the greater degree of intervention signalled by the new administration would be found as frustrating as Truman's was in the late 1940s. Not even the death of Stalin in early 1953 made any difference to the political dynamics of post-colonial Asia.

The extent of anti-Americanism among Asian nations was to come as a rude shock to Washington in the 1950s and 1960s. A harbinger of this dislike was encountered by the Ulster Rifles in Korea. When two of its men were captured by the North Koreans, they expected the worst. But identified as British soldiers, as distinct from Americans, they were released unharmed.[3] The Ulstermen were lucky because the experience of United Nations soldiers as North Korean prisoners of war was much less pleasant than that of those who surrendered to the Chinese. The latter employed a technique developed to turn Guomindang troops during the Chinese civil war. Though it seemed like "brainwashing" to Westerners, the regime of propaganda rested on a traditional Chinese view that no person was intrinsically bad. Re-education could change an anti-communist into someone with a more sympathetic point of view. Pu Yi, the last emperor of China, had been put through a similar regime as a "war criminal": once deemed to have sufficiently acknowledged his guilt in cooperating with the Japanese, Pu Yi was freed to become a gardener.

General Sir Anthony Farrar-Hockley, the author of the official history of British involvement in the Korea War, was considered irredeemable by the Chinese because he refused to answer military questions.[4] Then a captain with the Glosters, Farrar-Hockley had been captured during the battle on the Imjin River in late April 1951. The heroic stand of its first battalion against overwhelming numbers has since passed into British military legend, but the loss of 622 men could have been avoided if the action had been conducted under the Commonwealth headquarters' direction. The isolated battalion was neither reinforced nor withdrawn, despite the American general in command of this sector being told that "things are pretty sticky down there". He took this to mean uncomfortable.

At the time of the Glosters' surrender, MacArthur was no longer commander-in-chief of the United Nations forces. With China fully committed in Korea, he suggested a blockade of its coastline, bombing its factories, a diversionary attack by the Guomindang from Taiwan and, last but not least, an overland advance into north China. When these proposals were turned down flat in Washington, and the Truman administration chose a peaceful resolution of the Korean conflict, MacArthur blew his top. Used to having his way in Pacific Asia, the general dared to criticise the peace move openly. Bradley quickly got word that Truman considered MacArthur's indiscipline a challenge to the authority of the presidency and called the Joint Chiefs together to discuss the situation. All agreed that MacArthur should be relieved of his command, which he was on 11 April 1951.

Given the Republican surge in popularity then because of McCarthyism, Truman took a calculated political risk when he sacked MacArthur, since the general had even been touted as a future presidential candidate. Privately Truman explained, "I was sorry to have to reach a parting of the way with the big man in Asia but he asked for it and I had to give it to him."[5] General Matthew Ridgway, MacArthur's successor, never compromised the president. Not untypical was the reaction of the New Zealand government to the new commander-in-chief, whose temperate behaviour meant that its greatest nightmare vanished, a damaging split between the United States and Britain over MacArthur's bellicose demands.[6]

The change of leadership had also removed the main obstacle to a negotiated settlement and put a much-needed sense of purpose back into an army henceforth committed to defensive operations. When, in July 1953, the armistice was signed, the agreed ceasefire line was the most heavily fortified frontier in the world. The Korean War was over, although in Washington fear of renewed conflict still led to a plan to use atomic bombs against the People's Republic of China. The plan did "not contemplate a massive atomic strike" but rather "conventional as well as atomic weapons, as appropriate, against military targets in Manchuria and China. . . being used by the Communists in direct support of their operations in Korea".[7] Dropping atomic bombs proved unnecessary because a divided Korean peninsula suited the Chinese as much as the Russians.

The origins of the second setback for US intervention in Asia are to be discovered in the collaboration of the Vichy colonial authorities with the Imperial Japanese Army in French Indochina. It led to what is sometimes called the First Vietnam War, which lasted from the surrender of Japan until the collapse of French colonial rule in 1954. Privately, President Eisenhower called the French "a hopeless, helpless mass of protoplasm".[8] Their difficulties in Vietnam, the focus of resistance to the reimposition of colonial rule, really began during the Pacific War, when the subjection of France to Germany entailed an uncomfortable accommodation of Japanese military demands. After the violent repression of Vietnamese opposition to French rule in the early 1930s, this supine stance was bound to enflame nationalist aspirations. Here was a European colonial power clinging onto a large portion of mainland Southeast Asia by cooperating with an Asian competitor, whose support for Thailand in the Franco-Thai War of 1940–41 demonstrated how weak France had become.

If Japan could not hang on to its wartime conquests, Vietnamese nationalists reasoned, then there was little chance of France keeping its colonies either. What they did not appreciate in 1945 was that a French withdrawal would precipitate direct American intervention, for their reasoning failed to anticipate the influence of the Cold War in Southeast Asia. As long as the United States felt that it needed French assistance, it was prepared to tolerate an overseas empire. On the day of the Japanese attack on Pearl Harbor, Roosevelt had written to Pétain that it was essential to US interests that France continue to exercise control over its colonies. But as the war turned in favour of the Allies, within the Pacific theatre especially, the president became more confident in asserting his own ideas for a post-war settlement.

Admiral William Leahy, the ambassador whom Roosevelt sent to Vichy, reported the state of political paralysis there. He described Pétain as "a feeble, frightened old man... . surrounded by conspirators. . . devoted to Axis philosophy". He added:

> While one may be fully justified in looking at the difficulties
> of the Marshal's ending years with understanding sympathy,
> it seems necessary to reluctantly relinquish what was perhaps

a faint hope that it might be possible for me through friendly
personal relations and pertinent advice to give some semblance
of a backbone to a jellyfish.[9]

So convinced did Roosevelt become of France's inherent weakness
that in 1943 he suggested the detachment of Alsace and Lorraine from
metropolitan France to form another Belgium. It was to be called
Wallonia. The British argued strongly against the dismemberment
of either France or its empire, not least because containing Germany
would be London's main concern after the Allied victory. France
needed to be restored as a powerful European state.

Given that Roosevelt made no secret of his wish to prevent the
French returning as the colonial masters of Indochina after Japan's
defeat, Churchill surmised that the United States would follow up
this policy with the liquidation of nearby British possessions, such as
Hong Kong, Malaya, Singapore and North Borneo, not to mention
the protectorates of Sarawak and Brunei. When Roosevelt indicated
a future role in Asia for Chiang Kai-shek, Churchill tried without
effect to get his American ally to recognise the fundamental weakness of the Guomindang. Though Washington's anti-colonialism
was less strident following Roosevelt's death, US foreign policy
continued to pin its hopes on Chiang Kai-shek until nothing could
save him in China's civil war.

President Truman was more than fortunate then in having in
Attlee someone committed to decolonisation. This was not the case
in France, where the frosty relations between the Americans and
the Russians were used as an excuse to preserve French influence
in Indochina. France's colonial aspirations were doomed, however,
by the events that stemmed from the Japanese takeover on 9 March
1945. The situation was already out of control before the arrival of
Mountbatten's troops in Saigon at the end of the Pacific War. Even
with American help there was no way France could turn back the
flood tide of Vietnamese nationalism. Although most accounts of this
irresistible movement concentrate on Hanoi, an upsurge of resistance
took place throughout Indochina. After the Japanese coup, even
King Norodom Sihanouk had declared Cambodia's independence,
assuming the role of premier over a cabinet formed of administrators
who had previously served under the French. Shortly afterwards

the Laotian monarch was induced to follow suit by the Imperial Japanese Army. The returning French were thus obliged to agree compromises with Cambodia and Laos over autonomy, both countries enjoying a large measure of self-government. Yet it was in Vietnam itself that French dreams of a renewed Asian empire were to be rudely shattered.

In the mountains north of Hanoi, Vo Nguyen Giap had organised a military base area for the Viet Minh, the independence movement founded in May 1941. He had selected the place for its proximity to the Chinese frontier, over which arms and other supplies could easily pass. Chiang Kai-shek disliked the presence of a communist stronghold on his southern border, but from 1943 onwards he acquiesced in the flow of American aid to its forces. Opposed to the Japanese as well as the French, these guerrillas stepped up their activities after the latter were disarmed by the Japanese and the last Vietnamese emperor Bao Dai was restored as the legitimate ruler in March 1945. "The Japanese commanders," Giap later said, "lost the will to use their troops in countering insurgency."[10] Some French officers offered to join forces with the Viet Minh against the Imperial Japanese Army, but they were considered too arrogant to work with, and efforts were therefore directed at winning over rank-and-file members of colonial units.[11] This failure of cooperation did much to colour French attitudes after the surrender of Japan. Because the Imperial Japanese Army needed to concentrate its attention on a possible Allied landing, the Viet Minh had plenty of scope for building up support in readiness for the return of the French. Against them, Giap harboured great bitterness, since his wife, also an ardent nationalist, had died in a French prison along with their baby. In contrast to Giap, Ho Chi Minh was moderate and inclined to favour negotiation.

Now it seems unreal that Emperor Bao Dai's government should have started to function without reference to the Pacific War, the Viet Minh or increasing social disorder. The removal of French statues was an early priority, except in Saigon where, for some unknown reason, the Japanese may have chosen to protect these colonial monuments. More purposeful was the attempt to find and confiscate the French firearms that had fallen into civilian arms. Few were recovered as public confidence in the restored imperial regime was fragile: food shortages, hyperinflation and official corruption combined to undermine its authority.

But the beleaguered emperor understood the need to espouse nationalism and, with Japanese assistance, he broadcast a message to France. Poignantly Bao Dai said:

> You have suffered too much during four deadly years not to understand that the Vietnamese people, who have a history of twenty centuries and an often glorious past, no longer desire and can no longer endure any foreign domination or government. . . I beg you to understand that the only means of safeguarding French interests and the spiritual influence of France in Indochina is to recognise unreservedly the independence of Vietnam and to renounce any idea of re-establishing French sovereignty or French administration here in any form.[12]

This appeal was picked up by the French, upon whom it had no impact. General de Gaulle's overriding aim was to reassert France's status as a global power, which in the wartime context meant a French contribution to the Allied victory over Japan in Indochina. Well might the general proclaim that France would take the fight for freedom to the Greater East Asia Co-Prosperity Sphere, but this grand aim ignored the bankruptcy of its position in Asia. There were not enough French soldiers to reoccupy a peaceful Vietnam at the end of the Pacific War, let alone return to its shores in the teeth of Japanese opposition.

Implementing the agreement made at Potsdam between the United States, the Soviet Union and Britain, Guomindang troops occupied the north of Vietnam, while British and Indian troops moved into the south. The greatest difficulty was expected at Saigon, where the Japanese commander-in-chief, Terauchi Hisai-chi, might decide to ignore Emperor Hirohito's order to surrender. This uncertainty was complicated by MacArthur's determination to accept a general Japanese surrender in Tokyo before any other ceremonies could be held. It prevented the arrival of Mountbatten's forces in Saigon until 11 September, a delay that the Viet Minh exploited to stage such huge rallies in Hanoi and other major cities that Bao Dai was forced to abdicate.

Already critically ill, Terauchi Hisaichi quietly surrendered to Mountbatten on 30 November: he died in Malaya eight months later, thereby escaping trial as a war criminal. Even before the surrender ceremony took place, Terauchi Hisaichi wryly observed how Douglas Gracey, the man sent by Mountbatten to oversee the initial surrender, could not do anything without Japanese military assistance. Landing at Saigon, Gracey found the airport guarded by Japanese soldiers and that the only transport available had armed Japanese drivers. At the airport, he pointedly ignored a waiting Viet Minh delegation, making it transparent that his role was the replacement of Japanese rule with a French colonial administration. His authority, he told those who questioned his actions, came from Mountbatten, who had delegated to him the responsibility for restoring peace.

To Mountbatten, a harassed Gracey explained that "I would stress that although it may appear that I have interfered in the politics of the country I have done so only in the interests of the maintenance of law and order and after close collaboration with senior French representatives."[13] Though ordered by Mountbatten to remain strictly neutral, Gracey was pressured by the French to impose martial law and then finding himself without enough troops to enforce it, he had no choice but use French colonial troops and Japanese soldiers stationed in Saigon. Bitterly Giap commented about the British action, which allowed "soldiers and colonialists who had meekly surrendered to the Japanese only a few months earlier [to show] the utmost savagery in massacring and ill-treating unarmed civilians".[14]

The excesses of the French in Saigon ensured that the inevitable Viet Minh reaction would be all the stronger. Far from minimising British involvement, Gracey had now become hopelessly entangled in France's attempt to reassert its sovereignty. In the crackdown, Mountbatten knew that Gracey had exceeded his authority, but his efforts to rein him in so annoyed the local French residents that on 23 September, some 300 of them, wearing the Cross of Lorraine on their shoulders, staged a coup in the city, expelling the Viet Minh from all pubic buildings. Notwithstanding assurances to the contrary beforehand, Gracey was appalled to learn of the undisciplined behaviour of the French after the coup, which he admitted to Mountbatten he had not tried to stop. Two days afterwards, in the northern part of Saigon, a crowd of Vietnamese killed 150 French civilians, many of whom were women and children, with an equal number disappearing until their mutilated remains were discovered. The area was guarded by Japanese troops, who stood by and let the mob do its dreadful work. All chance of a peaceful settlement had gone by early 1946, the moment a reinforced French army could finally assume full responsibility. On the day he left Saigon, Gracey was publicly honoured by the city for being instrumental in preserving French colonial rule.

General Leclerc de Hauteclocque, one of the first regular officers to rally to de Gaulle in the summer of 1940, had arrived in Saigon shortly after Gracey. With a remarkable mixture of political and military skill, he had gradually reasserted French control over Cochinchina. By November, his troops were entering Cambodia and southern Laos. On a flying visit to Phnom Penh, Leclerc arrested Son Ngoc Thanh, a leading anti-French Cambodian politician, who was exiled to France. Although King Norodom Sihanouk always denied having any part in the arrest, other members of the royal family may have been in contact with Leclerc, once it became clear that Son Ngoc Thanh contemplated armed resistance to the return of the French. A Cambodian prince is known to have visited Saigon just before Leclerc flew in.[15] But reasserting sovereignty south of the sixteenth parallel would never be sufficient to guarantee stability throughout the whole of French Indochina. Something had to be done about northern Vietnam, where Ho Chi Minh had set up an independent government at Hanoi. To Leclerc's surprise, Ho Chi Minh agreed to stationing French troops in the north, so long as there were negotiations in France about Vietnam's future. There is no reason to suppose that, at this stage, the Viet Minh would not have accepted a negotiated agreement with France.

As Mao Zedong had for the Chinese, the Vietnamese leader tried to interest Washington in the aspirations for the Vietnamese people; but Ho Chi Minh received no encouragement at all from the Truman administration, in part because its overseas missions were totally unable to distinguish between nationalist and communist agendas. They missed the significance in Hanoi of the criticism directed at Ho Chi Minh, who was accused by zealous Viet Minh colleagues of being more nationalist than communist. Whilst Leclerc had no illusions about the desire of the Viet Minh for a separate regime in north Vietnam, he appreciated how a peaceful settlement of its differences with France might stop it becoming a communist dictatorship under the control of either Beijing or Moscow. Unfortunately, it did not prevent him from snubbing Giap, whom he met in Hanoi. Other Frenchmen less prescient about future developments were equally disdainful of Ho Chi Minh's diminutive military expert. What they were to discover to their tremendous cost, along with the Americans later on, was that in Giap the Viet Minh possessed the greatest twentieth-century strategist. This ex-schoolteacher had studied Napoleon's campaigns in tremendous detail. In later years, his students recalled the clarity of Giap's lessons on France's first emperor, along with the explanations their teacher gave for his victories as well as his defeats.

After Ho Chi Minh formally declared war against France on 19 December 1946, Giap got his opportunity to demonstrate his knowledge on the battlefield itself. It did the Viet Minh no harm that the French still thought they could impose their will by force of arms: attacks on Haiphong and Hanoi brought Ho Chi Minh overwhelming support from the Vietnamese people, who remembered their age-old tradition of resistance to foreign foes, European and Asian alike. Many joined guerrilla bands or infiltrated the French colonial administration as spies.

As the struggle dragged on, the French were forced to admit the strength of the Viet Minh and the desperate military situation. At first, they enjoyed the advantage of sophisticated weaponry, but their opponents knew the terrain so well that they could move stealthily through the jungle undetected from the air. Giap eschewed set battles: he tied down superior French numbers by ambushes, lightning attacks and sabotage. Soon the French found local recruitment almost impossible, with the result that many of its combat units filled up with mercenaries, whose conduct only served to alienate the Vietnamese people even more. By 1954, the writing was on the wall, in spite of the United States bearing nearly 80 per cent of the war's cost.

With the British getting the better of the communist insurgency in Malaya, Washington came to the conclusion that Ho Chi

Minh should, and indeed, could be beaten. It was a misjudgement that would lead to the tragic Second Vietnam War and the United State's first defeat abroad. In a last gamble to bring the Viet Minh to a decisive battle, the French allowed the garrison at Dien Bien Phu, a fortified base northwest of Hanoi, to be cut off. It was calculated that the Viet Minh supply system would not be able to match supplies flown into the landing strip. The French were wrong. First, Viet Minh artillery hidden in the surrounding hills restricted the use of the airstrip. These guns were entirely of American manufacture, having been taken by the People's Liberation Army from the Guomindang in China or from US formations in Korea. The second reason for the French miscalculation was the attention that Giap gave to logistics: during the siege, his troops received nearly 24,000 tonnes of supplies including 1,500 tonnes of ammunition. More than 130,000 shells were fired on the French defenders before they surrendered on 7 May, when the area under their control had shrunk to the size of two football pitches.

French soldiers take cover at Dien Bien Phu

American reporter Howard Simpson, who survived the siege, recalls how "grizzled French veterans were astounded by the youth and nervousness" of their captors.[16] Possibly 10,000 men fell on each side, although Giap only thought he sustained losses of 7,900 killed and slightly more than 10,000 wounded. The last stand of the French in Indochina, Dien Bien Phu left Vietnam divided at the sixteenth parallel. When French troops finally withdrew in 1955, the United States was left as sole protector of South Vietnam.

Independence in British Southeast Asia

Back in power, Churchill refused Eisenhower's appeal to help the French in Indochina. The president's secretary of state, John Foster Dulles, had urged the sending of a large-scale American expedition, which Ridgway also opposed. That the most senior US soldier was against military involvement prompted Eisenhower to sound out the British premier about joint intervention. Believing the French beyond help, Churchill rejected Washington's domino theory of a communist takeover of Southeast Asia. He had already appointed Sir Gerald Templer to govern Malaya and win "the hearts and minds" of its peoples to beat the communists there. Summing up the situation, Templer said "the shooting side of this business is only 25 per cent of the trouble". With a remit to prepare for independence, the unorthodox general not only contained the communist insurgency but in the election of Tunku Abdul Rahman also produced a premier-in-waiting. This ex-playboy was the brother of the Malay sultan of Kedah, a leader the British feared would aim at some kind of old-fashioned dictatorship. Their fears proved groundless because the Tunku, or "Prince", understood the need for communal harmony and in the so-called Alliance Party he incorporated the Malayan Chinese Association and the Malayan Indian Association along with UMNO, the United Malay National Organisation, which was formed in 1948 as a protest against British moves to create a common citizenship for all inhabitants within a unitary state comprising the Malay sultanates and the Straits Settlements, excluding Singapore.

A shrewd consensus politician, the Tunku even met the communist leader Chin Peng in a jungle village, again much to the anxiety of the British. Although the meeting was not a success, the two men were left in no doubt afterwards about where they stood. With Templer's backing, the Tunku said that there could be no concessions until the armed struggle ceased. Washington was deeply impressed by the emergence of a pro-Western political party in Malaya coincidentally with the terminal decline of French Indochina. Not perhaps so well discerned by the Americans at the time was a British design to protect its commercial interests under the protective umbrella of independence. Just as in the late nineteenth century, the creation of the dominions freed Britain from the task of running large swathes of its empire, so after the Pacific War did effective arrangements for independence in Southeast Asia permit business as usual in ex-colonies wherever reliable economic links and national governments existed. The Tunku's Alliance Party proved an excellent partner in stemming the excesses of Malay nationalism.[17]

But it was not all plain sailing, for in 1957 communal disturbances erupted at Penang. Trouble had been brewing since the decision in 1946 to break up the Straits Settlements and add Penang and Malacca to Malaya. The privations of the Japanese occupation had heightened Penang's sense of difference: its Chinese inhabitants were proud that their island was Britain's earliest settlement in Southeast Asia. Malay residents did not share this view and resented moves to link up with Chinese-dominated Singapore. Despite the creation in 1963 of Malaysia, the Penang Chinese were right about being marginalised under a mainland government, since there has been discrimination in favour of the Malays in the administration, access to education and financial support. Worse still, Penang's free port status was abolished by Kuala Lumpur in 1968, removing the commercial advantage that Francis Light had bestowed on the island nearly two centuries earlier. Stranded by the tide of decolonisation, Penang is today but a shadow of its former self.

If Penang was a problem for the British, the kingdom of the Brookes in Sarawak represented an imperial anomaly of antique proportions. There was no sympathy in London for Vyner Brooke's contention that he ruled a sovereign state. A Labour government could never sustain "the White Rajahs", no matter how benign was the nature of their rule. In 1944, Britain had decided that it would have jurisdiction over Sarawak after the expulsion of the Japanese. However, Sarawak's exiled government in London objected strongly, even though a personal feud between Vyner and his designated successor, the Rajah Muda Anthony Brooke, did much to undermine its opposition: the Rajah dissolved the government in exile and dismissed Anthony. As his wife, Ranee Sylvia, later wrote:

> Above all things, Vyner was an impatient man. He gardened ferociously, played golf with headlong speed, and made love as if there was a time bomb under the bed; so it was not to be wondered at that, as soon as the idea of Cession had crystallized within him, he could hardly wait to have it done with.[18]

Having agreed to cede his kingdom to Britain, the rajah restlessly paced the Astana, his tiny palace at Kuching, where on the opposite bank of the river that bisects that city, a meeting was held on 17 May 1946 to determine Sarawak's future.

Significantly for post-colonial differences between the state of Sarawak and the federal government of present-day Malaysia, the proposal then placed before Council Negri was opposed by the majority of the native members. Acceptance of British control therefore depended on European votes. The extent of local aversion to cession, soon evident in widespread demonstrations, was aggravated by the first colonial governor's authoritarian manner and a ban on Anthony Brooke's entry into the colony. Tension finally came into the open with the assassination of the second British governor in 1949, shortly after his arrival. Despite the public celebration of the murder on a column now standing in Kuching's museum gardens, this patriotic act discredited the anti-cession movement at a stroke. Yet even with this change of mood, it was still a major achievement of the next governor, Sir Anthony Abel, that he restored Sarawak to its usual condition of goodwill through his obvious enjoyment of the 55 distinct peoples living there. A latter-day James Brooke, Abel stayed on at popular request when his repeated terms as governor expired. And he constantly pressed London for early action to show that the colony was indeed headed for self-government.[19] Not long after Abel's departure, Sarawak held its first general election, a timely opportunity to transform itself into a self-governing state before the formation of Malaysia.

Having formally transferred power to Tunku Abdul Rahman on 31 August 1957, the British had to decide what to do about the Borneo territories including oil-rich Brunei. There was additionally the need to prevent Singapore ever becoming an independent communist state, given its strategically important location at the junction of key international sea routes. Even in Sarawak, the attraction of the People's Republic to Chinese youths had caused a worrying exodus to both China and Indonesia. One thousand young men and women left Chinese-medium schools for Kalimantan, where they prepared for armed resistance to the Malaysian federation. They were to fight alongside the Indonesian army during Confrontation, which Sukarno declared in opposition to Malaysia on 13 February 1963.

Tunku Abdul Rahman signs the agreement for Malayan independence

Once Indonesia called off this border war in 1966, Britain knew that Malaysia had solved the problems it faced as the last major Western colonial power in Asia. With Harold Macmillan's attention fixed on the European Economic Community and financial retrenchment, a federation linking all remaining possessions, except Hong Kong, with already independent Malaya seemed a perfect post-colonial solution. At the very last minute, Brunei stood aside, but North Borneo, present-day Sabah, Sarawak and Singapore joined. In Sabah, the chief minister, Donald Stephens, had had to resist objections from both the Philippines and local Malays, who yearned for ties with its Moslem-inhabited islands of Palawan and Mindanao immediately to the north. His determination to protect the Kadazan people, the largest group of native people in Sabah, from exploitation also made him plenty of enemies, but Stephens always had the courage to take an unpopular stand.[20]

For Lee Kuan Yew, Singapore's first prime minister, Malaysia meant a welcome end to British rule but not a military presence, because he seems to have been uncertain over the long-term survival of a predominantly Chinese island community situated in the midst of the Malay world. Lee Kuan Yew was acutely aware that the British provided a substantial part of Singapore's foreign earnings, a circumstance that drove him to stimulate the local economy during the 1970s as Britain steadily withdrew its forces from Asia. After Singapore had quit Malaysia in 1965, this was a matter of urgency, although Lee Kuan Yew reminded Singaporeans how "from 1819 right up to the 1930s there was a prosperous Singapore without either a British naval or air base".[21]

Correct though his assault on discriminatory legislation in Kuala Lumpur was, Lee's own political ambition played a large part in the 1965 withdrawal from the federation and the poor relations between Malaysia and Singapore after the split. Today, the continued vulnerability of Singapore is demonstrated by its close alliance with the sultanate of Brunei, another post-colonial mini-state. Brunei has of course the advantage of oil revenues to pay for the permanent deployment of a battalion of Gurkhas, ostensibly to secure its oilfields. Yet its 380,000 inhabitants uncannily resemble those living in certain Arab sheikhdoms. Substitute jungle for desert and Brunei could be a second Kuwait.

The Tragedy of Vietnam

While Britain accomplished an orderly withdrawal from its colonial possessions in Southeast Asia, the United States was drawn into a disastrous, and ultimately humiliating, military involvement in the Second Vietnam War. Once again, the Cold War dictated the American decision to fight, because it was believed in Washington that a Ho Chi Minh victory would turn all of Southeast Asia communist. A vigorous response was therefore required to support Ngo Dinh Diem, the president of South Vietnam, although his American advisers knew that Ngo Dinh Diem had neither the public support nor the ability to preserve his country. His Roman Catholic faith set him apart from the Buddhists, who constituted 90 per cent of Vietnam's population, but it made him acceptable to many Americans, and notably to John F. Kennedy, the first Catholic to be elected to the White House.

When with the approval of Washington, South Vietnam's president refused to hold in 1956 the elections agreed at the Geneva peace conference just after the fall of Diem Bien Phu, Ngo Dinh Diem took this course of action because he feared that Ho Chi Minh would win. Then, after removing ex-Emperor Bao Dai from the political scene by a rigged election in which Ngo Dinh Diem received a resounding 98.2 per cent of the vote, the South Vietnamese president was free to enjoy the fruits of American aid. He distributed lucrative appointments among his family and ruled in an increasingly authoritarian manner.

Opposition soon became organised, even the Buddhists forming a united front. In May 1963, a Catholic archbishop forbad the display of flags in Hue to commemorate the birthday of the Buddha. In protest, a crowd stormed the local radio station and demanded that a programme be broadcast in the Buddha's honour. Soldiers shot nine of the protesters dead, before tear gas dispersed the rest. No one gave credence to the government claim that the deaths were the work of the Viet Cong, the derogatory name by which Ngo Dinh Diem referred to the Viet Minh. A series of self-immolations by Buddhist monks then caught the attention of the world press. It cost Ngo Dinh Diem Washington's support when a reporter overheard the president's sister-in-law draw a parallel between monks, who neither moved a muscle nor uttered a sound when they were burned to death with petroleum, and Western-style barbecues, a word her daughter had picked up from American military advisers. Her husband Ngo Dinh Nhu, the president's pushy younger brother, added to the furore by offering to supply the fuel if the Buddhists wanted to stage more martyrdoms on Saigon's streets.[22] American public opinion reacted so badly to these tasteless comments that Kennedy was forced to press Ngo Dinh Diem to introduce reforms and listen to US advice.

Frustrated South Vietnamese generals interpreted Kennedy's unexpected anger as their moment to seize power, which they did with the blessing of Henry Cabot Lodge Jnr., the American ambassador. On the morning of 28 October at Saigon airport, Lodge gave the go-ahead on the understanding that the plotters would agree to a continuing US presence.[23] Fifteen minutes later, when he arrived to catch a plane with the American ambassador and Mrs. Lodge for a short break at the presidential retreat in Dalat, Ngo Dinh Diem had no inkling that his fate was already sealed. Within four days, the president and his brother were dead: Ngo Dinh Dem shot in the back of the head, Ngo Dinh Nhu stabbed in the chest and shot many times in the back of the head and the back. Photographs of their blood-splattered bodies dismayed Americans, but not so much as that of Kennedy's assassination in Texas, three weeks afterwards.

At this moment, the United States had only a limited role in Vietnam, a mere 11,000 military advisers as compared with the troop deployment of 525,000 men at the height of the Second Vietnam War. It may be that Lyndon B. Johnson, the next president, would have been less willing to take his country to war had the Republican presidential nominee Barry Goldwater, a conservative senator from Arizona, not demanded a tough military response to what he called worldwide communist aggression. Johnson told his jubilant supporters on winning the 1964 election that "I am not going to be the President who saw Southeast Asia go the way China went."[24]

All hopes in Hanoi of South Vietnam self-destructing before the United States could intervene in sufficient strength to postpone its end, disappeared in the Gulf of Tonkin Incident. A naval confrontation there was used by Johnson to persuade Capitol Hill to give him the right "to take all necessary measures to repel any attack against the forces of the United States and to prevent further aggression". It was this blank cheque to use force as he wished that brought about the tragedy of Vietnam. Over the next four years, evidence appeared that the north Vietnamese interception of US ships in the Gulf of Tonkin was not an unprovoked action at all. The Americans were covertly aiding sabotage operations by mercenaries as well as South Vietnamese commandos.

After the incident, North Vietnam decided there was nothing to be lost by increased military action in South Vietnam, where between 1965 and 1967 the military hierarchy played musical chairs for the leadership of the country. Two strong men eventually came to the fore: Nguyen Cao Ky, an admirer of Hitler, as vice-president and Nguyen Van Thieu as president. At last, Washington seemed to have leaders who promised to provide political stability, a prerequisite for the safety of 300,000 US troops then stationed in South Vietnam. General William Westmoreland, the American commander, took the fight to the Viet Minh with great energy. In January 1967, he moved into the so-called Iron Triangle, a heavily fortified Viet Minh base area situated near the Cambodian border. One of the biggest American operations mounted during the Second Vietnam War, 30,000 US troops were

One-man air-raid shelters in Hanoi during the Second Vietnam War

ordered to destroy all the villages in an area 50 kilometres square. One village by the name of Ben Suc took three days to clear with gas and explosives because the Viet Minh had dug three levels of tunnels beneath its houses. All the Vietnamese men rounded up in the operation were treated as enemies, and even the women and children were regarded as hostile. They were forcibly moved to new settlements, leaving behind a veritable wasteland, a terrible warning of what lay in store for Vietnam if the conflict continued for years.

In Hanoi, there was real concern about the extent of the destruction, and the leadership opted for an immediate and total drive for victory. During a secret visit, a military delegation from North Korea, Cuba and China had just warned of the dangers inherent in allowing the war to go on indefinitely. Though Giap was unhappy about the change of approach, he ordered his staff to prepare for the famous Tet offensive of 1968. Not a little ironic then was its tremendous impact on American public opinion. Taking advantage of the New Year, *Tet* in Vietnamese, Giap launched a massive offensive in which hand-to-hand combat even occurred at the US embassy in Saigon. The Viet Minh lost in excess of 30,000 men, but US and South Vietnamese losses were just as great. Americans at home were so stunned by the scale of the offensive, which hit towns and cities right across South Vietnam, that the question began to be asked about the final outcome of the undeclared war. When Johnson and Westmoreland insisted that it could be won, their optimism was shared by few. Most had come to believe the cost of the war, as shown in the increasing number of bodybags being flown back home, was now too high. Shaken by this decline in popular support, Johnson was next embarrassed by Westmoreland's request for additional troops after the general had claimed that the abortive Tet offensive was a decisive setback for the Viet Minh.

In North Vietnam, the offensive was seen as a failure arising from US strength and Viet Minh errors.[25] Giap had come to the conclusion that from a military point of view the conflict was deadlocked, with neither side in a position to deliver a knockout blow. It was something of a relief to hear that Johnson favoured negotiations, although his decision not to run again for the presidency effectively prevented meaningful peace talks. His successor came to power with a pledge to "end the war and win the peace", but Richard

Nixon's method of winning the peace was to continue direct American involvement in South Vietnam until January 1973. During the first two years of his presidency, the US Air Force actually dropped more bombs than the total tonnage expended by the United States in all theatres throughout the Second World War. The escalation of bombing in North Vietnam was of course counterproductive, because it served to strengthen Vietnamese determination not to yield. Yet Ho Chi Minh, just before his death in 1969 at the age of 79, advised the Hanoi administration to let the United States leave without hindrance, once Nixon's "Vietnamisation" programme had run its course. There was little point in carrying on fighting when it was obvious that South Vietnam could never survive standing alone.

Before Nixon withdrew the troops, however, he backed in 1970 a South Vietnamese invasion of Cambodia, a country hitherto spared the horrors of ground fighting, with the aim of cutting the Ho Chi Minh trail. Considering how King Norodom Sihanouk had said nothing when American bombs had already rained down on eastern Cambodia, the welcome given to Lon Nol's ousting of him in Washington seems obtuse. Crippled in a road accident through Sihanouk's reckless driving, Lon Nol had personal as well as political reasons for his military coup. Guessing that his anti-communist credentials would impress Washington, he seized power when Sihanouk was out of the country and then allowed the South Vietnamese to invade Cambodia, an action that later handed power to the Khmer Rouge.

By early 1973, Lon Nol's authority was restricted to refugee-filled towns, fed by airlifted American rice. When the planes came no more, the Khmer Rouge sent the refugees to the countryside. The decision in 1975 to empty the towns seems to have been a long-standing Khmer Rouge intention, possibly because its rank and file, recruited from the poorest sections of the peasantry, saw it as a just end to the parasitic rule of an urban hierarchy. An impoverished peasantry was no longer prepared to sustain by its toil a privileged modern capital like some latter-day Angkor. Pol Pot himself justified the evacuation of Cambodia's towns and cities in terms of the Paris Commune: this had failed, he said, because the proletariat had not exercised dictatorship over the bourgeoisie.[26] Whatever the exact causes of this extraordinary measure, the resettlement programme decimated the Cambodian people, with as many as three million deaths. Though Nixon referred to the Cambodian intervention as a "sideshow" to the action in Vietnam, the public reaction in the United States was unprecedented. When hundreds of colleges and universities went on strike, the president dismissed the students as "bums" until the killing of four protesters by the Ohio National Guard at Kent State frightened him. He was made even more anxious when Wall Street bankers warned him that a wider war was threatening a stockmarket collapse and a possible financial panic.

Already becoming enmeshed in the Watergate scandal, Nixon was now desperate to play the China card by becoming in 1972 the first American president to step on Chinese soil. The Shanghai communiqué, issued by Nixon and Zhou Enlai at the end of the historic visit, announced that the People's Republic and the United States would oppose any country trying "to establish hegemony" in "the Asia-Pacific region". The Soviet Union was being put on notice of a new political alignment, which arose as much from the 1969 Sino-Soviet border clashes as from the inability of the Americans to avoid defeat in Vietnam. The depth of the Sino-Soviet discord finally

Richard Nixon is greeted at Beijing airport by Zhou Enlai in 1972

blew away the American myth of a unified communist bloc intent of world domination. Perhaps less clearly seen was the weakness of the People's Liberation Army on the battlefield, for the clashes revealed an embarrassing lack of firepower.[27]

Yet this dramatic turnaround in American policy in Asia offered no consolation to the casualties of the Second Vietnam War. More than 300,000 US soldiers were listed as killed, wounded or missing. Of the 56,000 who died in action or related accidents, only 13,000 were regulars. In addition, 4,407 South Koreans, 469 Australians and New Zealanders and 350 Thai lost their lives. South Vietnam's army sustained losses of 137,000 killed and about 300,000 wounded. Maybe 400,000 civilians also perished while a larger number suffered injury. Giap admitted 600,000 casualties. In all, some two million of the combined Vietnamese population of 32 million probably died between 1967 and 1973, the year in which the Paris peace agreement officially ended the Second Vietnam War. That all this blood had been shed in vain could no longer be disguised. The following year, in defiance of the Paris accord, Nguyen Van Thieu did away with the American-model constitution, making himself a presidential dictator. As one Saigon resident said, "There is no more democracy."[28]

Because he realised how difficult it would be to win the projected 1975 election, even with American money behind him, the South Vietnamese leader took this risky gamble to stay in power. But the game was up for his military dictatorship once Hanoi, appreciating that no election was ever going to be held, gave Giap his head. In a lightning campaign, lasting a mere four months, he overran South Vietnam and captured Saigon in April 1975. With Nixon disgraced and the Republicans in no position to contemplate further bombing, there was nothing to do but quit. Nguyen Van Thieu had already made his own escape by US transport plane, taking his family with him as well as 16 tonnes of gold and silver from the vaults of the national bank.

Accommodating China and Japan

In Washington, the Vietnam Memorial, a V-shaped monument of black marble, is a potent reminder of the tragic mistakes of the Johnson–Nixon years. There are those today who maintain that the Second Vietnam War would never have involved the United States had Kennedy survived.[29] It is claimed that a plan for troop withdrawal was reversed by his successor within a matter of days after the assassination. Ambassador Lodge's arrival from Saigon was certainly used as an opportunity to discuss the situation in South Vietnam. Having just got rid of Ngo Dinh Diem, the envoy painted a rosy picture of his successor's ability to beat the Viet Minh. John McCone, director of the CIA, noted how "Lodge's statements were optimistic, hopeful, and left the President with the impression that we are on the road to victory."[30] Whatever the influence of this presentation to Johnson on 24 November 1963, there was already a tough outlook evolving in the White House. Before the end of the month, Johnson had decided to intervene in Vietnam.

The new president told his senior advisers that the Chinese will "think with Kennedy dead, we've lost heart. So they'll think we're yellow and we don't mean what we say". As for the "fellas in the Kremlin", he added, they will also "be taking the measure of us".[31] Totally underestimating Hanoi's resolve to unify Vietnam, Lodge suggested that threatening full-scale US intervention would be enough to force a Viet Minh withdrawal from South Vietnam. But neither Lodge nor Goldwater had a really decisive effect on Johnson's thinking, since he always believed that force should be used wherever communism threatened, as indeed did his predecessor. President Kennedy had seriously considered a pre-emptive nuclear strike against the Soviet Union well before the Cuban missile crisis. It is arguable therefore that Kennedy was as likely as Johnson to intervene militarily in Vietnam.

With such a determined foreign policy, and its bloody consequences for large parts of mainland Southeast Asia, coming to terms with a powerful China and a renewed Japan 20 years after the end of the Second Vietnam War was a sobering experience for Washington. The supremacy that had passed to the United States in Asia, after the liquidation of the Dutch, French and British empires there, was demonstrably beyond the strength of the world's supreme superpower. Political adjustment was in progress, however, well before Sino-American relations reached the top of Washington's agenda.

Independence for the Philippines, together with statehood for Alaska, Guam and Hawaii, had redefined the unofficial American empire in the Pacific. It was a sign that international relations were being transformed by economic power: the Western presence in Asia now took the form of commercial activity, rather than colonial rule. For the retreat of the colonial powers did not mean a return to traditional Asian ways in the liberated territories, but led instead to the emergence of nation-states firmly embedded in a global economy and world affairs. Unfavourable trade balances with China as well as Japan, the two stars of post-Pacific War economic progress, were to become a headache for the United States by the twenty-first century. Long before the breakdown of the Soviet bloc, the Americans already had an intolerable burden of defence expenditure: one reason for the meetings of Nixon and Leonid Brezhnev between 1972 and 1974 was the desire to replace an arms race with bilateral trade, the other was a hope that the Russian leader would help Nixon escape from Vietnam with honour. The second one was entirely misplaced. Although the Soviet Union heavily supplied North Vietnam, Moscow had little control over Hanoi's quest for a united Vietnam.

With trade, there was the prospect of better results, although this did not stop either the Russians or the Americans from modernising their arsenals. Yet it was still a shock to discover in the late 1970s that the United States had to pay so much more for imported oil. The old days of unending wealth and prosperity were now at an end, as the United States had ceased to be the great powerhouse of production. In 1950, it had produced an incredible 40 per cent of the world's goods and services.

For the People's Republic of China, the decade after Mao Zedong's death in 1976 was decisive. The Great Proletarian Cultural Revolution, during which people with Western-style clothes or possessions were harassed in a xenophobia reminiscent of the Boxers, fell into discredit along with Jiang Qing, the third wife of Chairman Mao. In November 1980, she was convicted of hounding 34,274 people to their deaths. It had been a misfortune for Mao Zedong and for China that marshalling millions of Red Guards appealed so strongly to Jiang Qing's thwarted theatrical talents. Under her relentless direction the cultural campaign broadened from an attack on "bourgeois" influences in art and literature into an assault on unacceptable thought in general. A survivor of this period of intellectual tyranny was Deng Xiaoping, a "capitalist roader" whom

Zhou Enlai brought back to Beijing after imprisonment with his family in the provinces. Overcoming renewed attacks by Jiang Qing, he ended in 1978 as the effective leader of the Chinese Communist Party. The judgement of Deng Xiaoping was that the period from 1966 to 1976 had been a "Ten-year Catastrophe".

Deng Xiaoping's strength derived from a realisation of how much the People's Republic yearned for stability: the people simply wanted individual and family security plus an improvement in living standards. They were exhausted by the uninterrupted series of mass movements and incessant political struggle that Mao Zedong had chosen to sponsor. In the countryside, where the overwhelming majority of the Chinese lived, Deng Xiaoping's reforms replaced the communes by means of an equal distribution of land to families charged with responsibility for its cultivation, and a loosening of the restrictions on nonagricultural enterprise in villages and small towns. The old Maoist dichotomy between city and countryside was blurred so that differences in income gradually disappeared.[32] Urban reform, on the other hand, concentrated on removing impediments to greater autonomy in state-owned enterprises. It proved a more complicated

Deng Xiaoping and Gerald Ford inspecting troops in 1976

task than the redistribution of land based on the family production system, because there were problems in estimating the value of industrial activities. And of course the changes introduced could be seen as threatening the status and benefits enjoyed by factory workers.

In contrast to the introduction of market forces in Russia though, Deng Xiaoping's reforms were infinitely more successful because gradual price adjustment gave protection to both workers and consumers, especially in urban areas where there was no possibility of growing one's own food. Although the countryside answered the relaxation of regulation with increased output, the economy as a whole became overheated, as complaints about inflation indicated. For a country that was previously isolated from worldwide inflation, the advent of price rises came as an uncomfortable reminder of the monetary horrors of Chiang Kai-shek's last years on the mainland. Particularly hard hit were the students, who could see their contemporaries earning large sums in street markets and through factory bonuses. Books were expensive, and from 1985 onwards, most students had to pay for higher education. Yet competition remained fierce for entrance to colleges and universities, with fewer than 6 per cent of secondary school leavers going on to higher studies.

Pressures in this bottleneck for the ambitious probably account for some of the demands made by students in the steady buildup of protests that reached such a tragic climax in June 1989. That their supreme gesture of defiance then was to place a statue to democracy next to the Monument of the Heroes in Tiananmen Square was perhaps the saddest aspect of the final demonstration. For this improvised goddess, made from chunks of polystyrene, looked so much like the Statue of Liberty that Deng Xiaoping had no hesitation in blaming the United States for encouraging student dissent. Deng Xiaoping had always made it clear that there were limits to private enterprise—not an unusual notion in a country whose long experience under the imperial system of government had been a high degree of state control. Just in case the inhabitants of Hong Kong missed the message, or mistook student calls for popular reform, he reminded them that they would never be able to use the "cloak of democracy" to turn discontent against China's interests.

Good relations with Britain stemmed from Deng Xiaoping's own recognition of how much the People's Republic benefited from the colony of Hong Kong. By the 1980s, it was China's biggest trading partner and provided 70 per cent of its foreign investment. Deng Xiaoping was most anxious to prevent a flight of capital from Hong Kong on its return to China in 1997, something that Margaret Thatcher, the British prime minister, could do nothing to stop. The people of Hong Kong, in whose interest Mrs. Thatcher professed to speak, were never consulted about the Sino-British accord that she signed at Beijing in 1984. Putting a brave face on the inevitable, she declared as nothing less than a stroke of genius the formula "one country, two systems", quite forgetting that this was always Deng Xiaoping's intention for the money-making colony.

In spite of the careful handling of economic development in the People's Republic, there remained deep disquiet among senior communists about the effect that Deng Xiaoping's espousal of modernisation was having on the young, who were criticised for being indifferent to social issues and overly preoccupied with personal interests. Told though he was to keep out of China's internal affairs, President George Bush got along well with Deng Xiaoping when they met in Beijing shortly after the American president attended the funeral of Emperor Hirohito. There, in early 1989, George Bush learned at first hand how much the Chinese leadership distrusted the Russians, when Deng Xiaoping said:

> Mr. President, you are my friend. I hope you will look at a map to see what happened after the Soviet Union severed Outer Mongolia from China. What kind of strategic position did we find ourselves in? Those over fifty in China remember that the shape of China was like a maple leaf. Now, if you look at a map, you see a huge chunk of the north cut away. . . The strategic position I have mentioned is very unfavourable for China. . . This encirclement has continued from the Khrushchev period through Brezhnev to the present.[33]

This reference to the agreement reached at Yalta between Stalin, Roosevelt and Churchill about post-Pacific War spheres of influence in Asia showed that the preservation of the Mongolian People's Republic still rankled in Beijing. Because Stalin had made the Soviet Union's entrance into the war against Japan conditional on greater influence in Asian affairs, there was little Roosevelt or Churchill could do about Soviet-sponsored Mongolia. What Deng Xiaoping might have added to his complaint about Moscow's most recent detachment of Chinese territory were the vast stretches of Manchuria that had been seized in the 1860s by the tsars. Today, they constitute the largest unresolved issue of the period of Western domination in Asia.

The Tiananmen Square demonstration nearly ended Deng Xiaoping's reforms. Calls for democracy, a free press and an investigation of official corruption left him with little room for manoeuvre, once it became clear that neither the Political Bureau nor the students were prepared to compromise. Conscious of the unpredictable forces that the arrival of Mikhail Gorbachev, the originator of glasnost, could well unleash, several senior communists endeavoured to warn the thousands of student demonstrators camped out in the square that they could face stern repression. Banners calling for Deng Xiaoping's retirement finally provoked an armed response. The military backers of Deng Xiaoping, fearing perhaps a return to the chaos of the Cultural Revolution, bloodily put down the student protest shortly after the declaration of martial law.

The brutal crackdown was watched by millions of people outside China because foreign television crews were still in Beijing after the visit of the president of the Soviet Union. As a result, hardly anyone accepted the official statement that only a small number of "counter-revolutionaries" died on 2 and 3 June 1989. Although the government's authority was reasserted in a way that deterred outright challenges in future, the issues behind student discontent remained to be solved, as did the international fallout from the tragedy. George Bush tried to help with the latter when, on 21 July, he wrote to Deng Xiaoping:

> If some way can be found to close the chapter on the students whose actions were those of peaceful demonstrators, that would help enormously. . . If forgiveness could be granted to the students and, yes, to their teachers, this would go a long way to restoring worldwide confidence. . . It would give me the opportunity to make a statement supporting your position.[34]

The American president even went as far as using his veto against legislation designed to provide sanctuary for Chinese students already in the United States. After a fierce contest on Capitol Hill, it was agreed that the issue would be dealt with administratively, rather than by legislation.

The White House victory was an amazing indication of how far the United States was prepared to go to accommodate the People's Republic. Less tractable for Sino-American relations remains Taiwan, a post-colonial product on a par with Singapore and Brunei. The notable success of the Republic on the island of Taiwan and the mainland People's Republic in weathering the 1990s Asian financial crisis, unlike a lethargic Japan, offers the prospect of an eventual solution. Both are financially strong and their economies now closely interrelated. Some 40,000 Taiwanese businesses have shifted production to the People's Republic, where the greater availability of land and labour permitted a massive expansion of output. Certainly, the changes initiated under Deng Xiaoping have done much to transform the Chinese economy, although subsequent development was driven as much by urbanisation, migration and career mobility as government policy. By the first decade of the twenty-first century, the People's Republic looked less like a country in transition from socialism and more like an industrialising country in transition from its agrarian past. Concerned though the Chinese Communist Party remained about political control, there was greater individual freedom and openness than in Mao Zedong's day. At present, Beijing is trying to recover the country's proper place among the world's powers, without forfeiting the traditional Chinese preference for strong central government: therefore the emphasis on the reunification of Taiwan with the mainland.

Yet no international relationship was ever more sensitive than that between Japan and China. The inability of Tokyo to acknowledge the extent of the atrocities committed by the Imperial Japanese Army in China, let alone apologise for them, has been a significant factor in the continued animosity between the Chinese and the Japanese. Apart from China's insistence on an unequivocal apology for the invasion of the 1930s and 1940s, Japan has deeply resented the return of China to the world stage as a great power. According to Yoshida Shigeru, the Japanese premier until 1955, the choice was a simple one: Free World or Communist. He even suggested that the "old China hands", the United States, Britain and Japan, should combine to thwart Beijing's communist ambitions in Asia.[35] Expressed not long after the end of the Allied occupation of Japan, this proposal now seems as outdated as any of the pronouncements of the pre-Pacific War colonial powers. With some justice, Beijing recently claimed the 1951 US-Japan security alliance was a relic of Cold War thinking, since the demise of the Soviet Union and China's modernisation made it quite unnecessary in Pacific Asia.

Not that relations between the Japanese and the Americans were very cordial during the 1980s and 1990s. Support for US bases was already weakening before the rape in 1995 of an Okinawan schoolgirl by American soldiers. Renewed friction between Beijing and Taipei, however, facilitated the renewal of the security treaty in the ensuing year. If anything, Japan was pleased with the swift American response: the despatch of aircraft carriers from the Philippines to the Straits of Taiwan. From Washington, the Japanese alliance could be seen as a convenient method of balancing growing Chinese power, but its maintenance puts an unnecessary strain on relations with Beijing and reveals the inherent difficulty for the United States of accommodating China as well as Japan. Not until the Americans, as have the other Western colonial rulers, have finally withdrawn from Asia will it be possible to foresee Asia's future. There can be no question that the United States will remain a key player in the Pacific, but the future course of Asian history will not be determined in Washington: its eventual outcome depends on the Chinese and, to a lesser extent, the Japanese.

Post-colonial Conflicts

The issue of language has bedevilled an independent India. With a multitude of languages, the attempt to impose Hindi as the official language was doomed to failure and a compromise of sorts emerged with the retention of English alongside this northern tongue. In Malaysia, on the other hand, the adoption of Malay as the official language had the unfortunate effect of largely cutting off its multilingual population from the rest of the world, so that Malaysian students struggled to make progress at foreign universities. With two notable exceptions, the root cause of India's post-colonial conflicts were religious, rather than linguistic, differences. An internal dispute cost Mrs. Indira Gandhi her life, when in 1984 she was gunned down by a Sikh member of her bodyguard. The disgruntled soldier could not forgive her order forcibly to clear the Golden Temple at Amritsar of Sikh separatists, some 600 of whom were slain in the operation. Mrs. Gandhi was succeeded as prime minister by her son, Rajiv Gandhi. Having subsequently lost office, he was assassinated in turn by a suicide bomber while electioneering in 1991. In this instance, his assassin was a member of the Liberation Tigers of Tamil Eelam, popularly known as the Tamil Tigers, who opposed the deployment of Indian troops in Sri Lanka as part of a peace-keeping force. Rajiv Gandhi's death therefore had a religious dimension as well: the antagonism between the Buddhist Sinhalese, the native majority in Sri Lanka, and the Hindu Tamils, who had migrated from southern India in large numbers during British rule of the island.

Before Sri Lanka gained its independence, the Sinhalese resented the placement of Tamils on the electoral rolls, since these voters qualified by proving not that they were permanently settled but that they had been resident for five years. Because many Tamils regularly visited their own Indian villages, the Sinhalese were convinced that their loyalties lay elsewhere. Religion became really a divisive issue when the Sinhalese insisted that an independent Sri Lanka would have Buddhism as the state religion. Communal tensions increased when Sinhalese governments progressively sought to depress the position of the Tamils. Once Sinhalese replaced English as the official language in 1956, outbreaks of violence led to a demand for a partition of the island. The Tamils wanted their own state of "Eelam", an objective the Tamil Tigers are still fighting for now.

India's long-running quarrel with Pakistan, which resulted in wars in 1947, 1965 and 1971, was also informed by a religious conflict. It was the decision of the Hindu ruler of Kashmir to opt for India on partition that poisoned Indo-Pakistan relations and alienated most of the princely state's population, the Kashmiri Moslems. The first war between India and Pakistan was the longest, lasting more than a year. President Jinnah of Pakistan was as determined as Nehru, the Indian prime minister, to have Kashmir.

Post-colonial South Asia

After instituting an economic blockade, Pakistan launched a full-scale invasion, during the early stages of which India's hurriedly flown-in troops barely held their own, as they battled against tribal warriors as well as Pakistani regulars. An improvement in performance followed substantial reinforcement and better supply. For Indian artillery decided several encounters: at Naushera, a town to the south of the capital Srinagar, the attacking Pakistanis took heavy casualties.[36] Afterwards, shelling brought about the recapture of Pakistani-occupied towns, except in the far north, where the Indians suffered serious reverses, losing control over much of Baltistan and Ladakh. They were to prove permanent, as a ceasefire agreed in December 1948 left large areas behind Pakistani lines.

Although Pakistan was better prepared for the second war in 1964, so was India. In the aftermath of the 1962 border dispute with the People's Republic of China, to which we will turn shortly, American and Commonwealth grants permitted India to purchase automatic weapons, larger mortars and tanks, of both British and Soviet manufacture. The immediate cause of renewed conflict was the granting by Delhi of special status to Kashmir, placing it on a par with other states in India. After a series of border skirmishes, the Pakistani army sent armed infiltrators to foment an uprising among Moslem Kashmiris. After this failed, more conventional engagements were fought on both Pakistani and Indian soil until another stalemate ensued.

Despite the Pakistanis once again starting hostilities, the third Indo-Pakistan War was altogether different in its outcome. Fought on two fronts, in the Punjab and Bengal, the Pakistani army soon discovered that the distance between them put an impossible strain on its defensive arrangements, when it was realised that the prime Indian objective was the capture of all East Pakistan. This daring approach could be adopted by Delhi because the signing of a treaty of friendship with Moscow reduced the possibility of Chinese intervention on Pakistan's behalf. When on 15 December 1971, the Pakistani commander Amir Abdullah Khan Niazi surrendered in Dacca, the Indian army had 90,000 prisoners of war in the bag. Bangladeshi freedom fighters, the Mukti Bahini, could never have achieved independence on their own, notwithstanding growing anger in the late 1960s over West Pakistan's exploitation of East Pakistan. India's ability to truncate the Moslem state relied on a successful defensive strategy along the western front. The loss of Chaamb, a city southwest of Srinagar, was a small price to pay for cutting the Pakistanis down to size. While overwhelming superiority in troops and firepower, in ships and planes, gave an easy victory in East Pakistan, the Indian forces elsewhere had to blunt a very determined effort by the Pakistani army to compensate for the unexpected setback. Their effective resistance meant that, having repulsed its South Asian rival, India was thereafter recognised as the leading regional power.

Exceptions to India's post-colonial conflicts over religion were the wars fought against the Portuguese and the Chinese. The first involved the conquest of Goa in 1961: its annexation ended almost 450 years of Portuguese rule. Until the independence of Brazil in 1822, Lisbon functioned as an entrepôt, importing colonial products and British manufactures, and exporting these industrial products and money back to the colonies. With Brazil gone though, Portugal became one of the most impoverished countries in Europe, an unfortunate consequence of which for Angola, and to a lesser extent Mozambique, was that slavery made up the shortfall in international commerce resulting from the loss of the Brazilian sugar trade. Once Brazil banned the import of slaves in the 1850s, even this source of revenue gradually disappeared, although slaves still toiled in Portuguese colonies until the advent of the republic in 1910.

Unlike Portuguese Africa, the colony of Goa contributed little to Portugal's declining wealth. Apart from a marginal involvement in the export of opium to China, Goa's economy relied from the nineteenth century onwards on small-scale commercial enterprise in the colony and elsewhere in India. There was virtually no industrial development, and mining activities were only accelerated when an independent India laid claim to Goa as well as the pocket-sized enclaves of Diu and Daman, to the north in Gujarat. Out of step with the process of Western decolonisation, the dictatorship of Antonio Salazar endeavoured to strengthen Lisbon's hold over what remained of its seaborne empire. Settlers were sent out to Africa and economic development was stimulated in Goa and East Timor, the other sizable Asian possession. The 1974 coup against the dictatorship arose in fact from the weakening of the Portuguese position in the African colonies. So committed then was Lisbon to a continued imperial role that one in four adult Portuguese males was enrolled in the armed forces.[37] The illiterate Portuguese peasants who came in uniform to Goa surprised the local inhabitants. When they used their thumbprints as a method of identification, a Goan bank clerk wondered, "How is it we are ruled by people who cannot write their own names?" When, in 1961, the revolt in Angola began, India decided to eliminate Portuguese rule on the subcontinent. Despite Salazar's hopes of a stubborn resistance, the Indian army and navy took a mere two days to capture Goa.

In the ensuing year, the Indians found the boot well and truly on the other foot. The People's Liberation Army attacked India, crossing the frontier from Tibet. It turned into a major offensive, with the Indian defenders being pushed back all along the front. There was nothing Britain could do but watch. Prime Minister Macmillan may have felt a quiet satisfaction at Delhi's discomfiture. He had begged Nehru to seek a negotiated end to Portuguese rule in India, since the resort to arms would have "an incalculable influence on many other countries".[38] In Macmillan's mind was the encouragement that India's example might well give to the Indonesian president Sukarno, whose determination to acquire the Dutch colony of West Irian, the western half of New Guinea, was widely known. He was also aware of Sukarno's desire to thwart the creation of Malaysia, which military confrontation on the island of Borneo would shortly fail to achieve. The Commonwealth's buildup of land, sea and air forces in defence of the new state deterred Indonesian military leaders from giving Sukarno their total backing in this border war. To the alarm of the United States, the British transferred troops to Borneo from Germany, thereby weakening the defence of Western Europe. So Washington had no choice but to tone down its friendly policy towards Indonesia and recognise Malaysia.[39]

Though he appreciated that the Indians were having a rough time of it in the Sino-Indian War, Macmillan never subscribed to the American view that Beijing had expansionist aims in Asia. And he seems to have had a salutary influence on the Kennedy administration, because the young president resisted pressure from his hawkish advisers to lend Delhi air support. But Macmillan had no success in persuading Kennedy of the folly of military intervention on mainland Southeast Asia. He never believed that the People's Republic was responsible for all the troubles in Laos and Vietnam. In early 1961, during a boating trip with the American president on the Potomac, Macmillan had remarked how a small flotilla from a local high school was the equivalent of the Laotian navy. Kennedy laughed at the joke, but he was not to be deflected from becoming involved in the Second Vietnam War.

As the Sino-Indian War ended as inexplicably as it had begun, London and Delhi could relax once more. A combination of adverse circumstances lay behind Beijing's decision to invade India: rebellion in Tibet, a worsening split with the Soviet Union and the economic upheaval caused by the Great Leap Forward. The moment seemed right to settle a post-colonial dispute over the McMahon line, the colonial boundary between Tibet and British India. In Ladakh, the Chinese already occupied a vast tract of land claimed by India, the Akai Chin plain, and their construction of a highway across its middle brought a forthright condemnation from Delhi. A swift series of advances allowed Beijing to declare a unilateral ceasefire after less than a month's fighting on 21 October 1962. The People's Liberation Army had shown its superiority on this remote battlefield, using the same infiltration tactics that had proved so effective in the Korean War. Chinese troops surrounded and over-whelmed Indian positions one after the other, wiping out whole battalions of the Indian army.

This brief war was a real one unlike the earlier Chinese bom-bardment of Quemoy and Matsu, offshore islands still under Guomindang control. The shelling in 1958 was really Mao Zedong's way of checking to see how firm was Washington's commitment to Taiwan. US Secretary of State Dulles had answered the question by saying that all force would be used if necessary to keep the two islands from falling into the hands of the People's Republic. Noth-ing like this was said about the Chinese victory in Ladakh, despite a realisation that the operational capability displayed by the Indian army during the 1947–48 war in Kashmir was no longer sufficient to guarantee the country's integrity.

Harold Macmillan was correct about Sukarno's predilection for foreign venture, even when Indonesia had to cope with serious internal troubles of its own. The most persistent post-colonial con-flict was the Acchnese revolt of 1953. Living at the western end of Sumatra, the Acehnese were among the last Indonesians to be con-quered by the Dutch in the nineteenth century and, after the Pacific War, the only people who were never subject to returning colonial rule. Acehnese desire for independence derived from a strong com-mitment to Islam, as well as a memory of past glory. The sudden Japanese surrender left a vacuum that was quickly filled by both of these potent legacies, when the struggle against Holland was declared to be a holy war by a leading cleric in Banda Aceh, the pro-vincial capital. The whole period from 1945 to the outbreak of the Acehnese rebellion in 1953 was marked by a growing divergence between the central government's view of Aceh's position within the Republic of Indonesia and Acehnese aspirations for greater control over local affairs.

Fearful of separatist tendencies in the sprawling archipelago, Jakarta set its face against provinces based on ethnic groupings and sought to link Aceh with other parts of Sumatra. Antipathy towards a Javanese-dominated government's attempt to increase its powers at provincial expense was to be a recurring theme in Indonesia's postcolonial history, but only in Aceh did it encompass years of armed struggle tinged with a belief that Islam was being marginalised. In many aspects, the Acehnese revolt can be recognised as a precursor of present-day movements to found Islamic states. With no end in sight to the rebellion, Jakarta had to concede in 1956 provincial status to Aceh and, three years afterwards, full control over religion, culture and education. The surrender of the last Acehnese rebels in 1962 seemed to have brought matters to a peaceful conclusion. The subsequent establishment of an Islamic institute in Banda Aceh revived its claim to be a centre of religious learning and apparently ensured future influence for the concept of Islam in political, economic and social affairs not just in Aceh but throughout Indonesia.

Australia meets Indonesia: Sir Robert Menzies and his wife with Sukarno

This pious hope led nowhere, however. Sukarno's "guided democracy" threatened Islam because it rested on the support of left-wingers and the armed forces, an uneasy alliance compounded by the president's need to declare a state of siege and pass day-to-day authority to local army commanders. One of these was Suharto, who had joined the Royal Netherlands Indies Army a year before the Japanese invasion. It fell to Suharto in 1965 to deal with an alleged communist coup. Acehnese clerics were delighted with Sukarno's eclipse until they realised that the armed forces, rather than Islam, had gained control of Indonesia. Over the next three years, Suharto gradually pushed the still popular Sukarno from power, ended confrontation with Malaysia, and secured his own political position.

The massive 1973 price increase for oil, initiated by OPEC, helped in the recycling of the debts accumulated under Sukarno, but economic recovery eluded Indonesia during the 1970s and the 1980s. While Thailand and Malaysia developed tourist industries and Singapore took full advantage of its excellent location as a hub for trade and industry, Indonesia still grappled with the problem of disunity. Apart from Bali, the Hindu island where tourism took root, the rest of the archipelago, which contains the world's largest concentration of Moslems, continued along its own obscure course. It may be that this self-imposed isolation should have pleased the Acehnese more than it actually did, but their settled disdain for all things Javanese spilled over into open rebellion on three more occasions. The last uprising ended in early 2007 with the installation of Irwandi Yusuf as the governor of Aceh. Released from a prison sentence for his role in the rebellion, the new governor was urged by Jakarta to work closely with central government agencies for the benefit of the tsunami-hit province.[40] Having won 38 per cent of the vote in the province's first direct election, the Free Aceh Movement and the Acehnese people were at that time ready to give Irwandi Yusuf their trust, provided of course that cooperation with Jakarta excluded meddling with Aceh's own affairs.

Before his downfall, Sukarno had succeeded in adding West Irian to Indonesia. Holland's retention of this part of New Guinea, with the connivance of the United States, lasted until 1962, when the issue was resolved through the United Nations. The Indonesian claim to West Irian had strong emotional overtones, in part because located in its swamps was the Tanah Merah detention camp in which

Mohammad Hatta and other leading Indonesian nationalists were incarcerated during the final decades of colonial rule. In 1952, the Dutch had tried to pre-empt Indonesia's claim by incorporating the colony into the realm of the Netherlands. But for the Indonesians the dispute was anything but closed and Sukarno bolstered in his own popularity by keeping up pressure for annexation.

At the Bandung conference of Asian states in 1955, sympathy was expressed for the Indonesian position. Delegates were also reassured by Zhou Enlai's statement about China's lack of territorial ambitions beyond its borders. Not unlike the Ming admiral Zheng He, he indicated that the People's Republic was content to accept token recognition of the rightful place it occupied in Asia. This line fell on deaf ears in Washington, where the "domino theory" maintained that any concession to communism was a dangerous move. Yet Zhou Enlai struck a chord with his fellow delegates when he reminded them of their common experience of colonialism. "If we seek common ground," he told them, "and remove the misfortune and suffering imposed on us by colonialism, then it will be easy for us to understand and respect each other." He even said that the People's Republic was prepared to sit down at the conference table with the United States so that they could avoid war.[41] What Zhou Enlai unravelled, too, was the anomalous position of the overseas Chinese, of whom nearly three million lived in Indonesia. He reversed Guomindang policy by declaring that no longer would all persons of Chinese descent be automatically regarded as citizens of the People's Republic. Henceforth the 20 million overseas Chinese would have to become citizens of the countries in which they were settled.

This change of policy did not ease the lot of Chinese residents in Indonesia. Those whose families had been in the country for centuries opted for Indonesian nationality, others had to choose between the People's Republic and the Republic of China. Because neither Beijing nor Jakarta regarded the latter state as covered by the agreement reached in Bandung, they were harassed and driven abroad. Opportunist attacks on Chinese shops also marred the whole episode and pointed to future violence, such as the extensive looting of commercial premises in Jakarta immediately after Suharto's enforced resignation in 1998. A consequence of this uncertainty was a steady flow of capital to Singapore, whose banks were kept flush by the profits and savings belonging to the Indonesian Chinese.

Suharto's fall was a great disappointment for Washington. Ever since the removal of Sukarno, a grateful United States had overlooked the less pleasant sides of Suharto's so-called "New Order". The need to favour friends and supporters entailed the reservation of jobs for members of the armed forces upon their retirement from active service, thus ensuring their loyalty to the regime. Ex-military men were employed at all levels, from security guards to chief executives. Control of the large public sector of the economy, plus the practice of granting monopolies for other key activities, gave Suharto and his closest associates access to great personal wealth. That there was no way of hiding the fact that a privileged few were making money at public expense accounts for the criticisms levelled at the Indonesian government in 1998: protesters decried corruption, cronyism and nepotism.

Because he was beyond saving, the United States had to accept a loss of influence in Jakarta through Suharto's fall. But support for a military regime in Indonesia was not a new American policy: in 1957, Washington had backed officers seeking to usurp power in both Sumatra and Sulawesi. US submarines ran military supplies to Sumatra and American aircraft assisted in the Sulawesi insurrection. Neither rebel group prospered, in spite of Britain reluctantly agreeing to a US naval task force basing itself on Singapore. This concession permitted Lee Kuan Yew— the same man who within a decade lamented London's decision to close its base there—to label his main political rival "a colonial stooge" and win extra seats for his party in Singapore's city council election. Few Singaporeans had any sympathy for Indonesia's rebellious colonels. So incensed was Sukarno by the attempted intervention, a CIA report tells us, that the Indonesian president then "transferred the full fury of his anti-Dutch complex to the United States and Britain".[42]

A Suharto annexation that came back to haunt Jakarta was that of East Timor. This Portuguese colony's troubles had begun in 1942 with the arrival of the Imperial Japanese Army. Seen by Tokyo as the gateway to Australia, Timor was a prime target during the southern advance of the Japanese, despite the determined efforts of Lisbon to keep out of the Pacific War. This proved impossible once the largely Australian forces facing the Japanese invaders resorted to guerrilla warfare to prolong resistance right across the island.

Members of Sparrow Force, as the Allied contingent was called, fought on for a year because, for all they knew, the Timor campaign was but a prelude to the invasion of northern Australia.[43] Reinforcement of the Imperial Japanese Army on the island so altered the military situation that Australian intervention had to be abandoned. Of the 30,000 Timorese who died during the Pacific War, the greatest number succumbed to diseases caused by malnutrition.

The Timorese sacrifice was never forgotten in Australia, notwithstanding Canberra's abject failure to raise any objection to Indonesia's takeover of East Timor. Portugal had resumed control in 1945, and done much to rebuild the colony before independence movements became active. The end of Portugal's dictatorial Salazar regime set the stage for increased agitation and, then in 1975, a declaration of East Timorese independence. But it also provided the Indonesians with a convenient opportunity to invade. When at last, in September 1999, Australian troops led an international peacekeeping force to a ravaged East Timor, the response of the Australian public suggested that the country was girding itself for a war of colonial liberation, rather than for a humanitarian rescue mission.

The real sufferings of the ex-Portuguese colony started on 7 December 1975, when Indonesian forces overran its capital, Dili. After a heavy naval and aerial bombardment, the attacking soldiers ran amok, killing and raping the civilian population in the mistaken belief that they had been sent to put down a communist threat to Indonesia, not a people seeking freedom in their own land. Ardent Moslems in the Indonesian ranks were even told that the invasion was a holy war against infidels. More than 2,000 civilians were indiscriminately slaughtered: two Timorese men faced a firing squad because their footwear was judged to have a military appearance.

In Washington, there was no comment at all, just in case it embarrassed ever reliable Suharto. For six years, Indonesia had its bloody way in East Timor, until the killing of 250 Dilians at Santa Cruz cemetery eventually aroused world interest. Some 3,000 mourners were present in 1991 at the internment of an 18-year-old Timorese, who had died from injuries sustained in a fight with pro-Indonesian Timorese. As prayers were being said, a detachment of Indonesian soldiers arrived and opened fire. No shots were returned. Many of those who took shelter behind gravestones, and later escaped the cemetery, sought refuge in the garden of Carlos Belo, the Catholic bishop of Dili. In spite of negotiations with the local army commander, the bishop could not stop a large number of the refugees being forcibly removed and then executed. Although he found it morally reprehensible that some could say that these deaths were a necessary sacrifice to draw international attention to a situation that had been previously ignored, Bishop Belo threw himself into the cause of independence,

The saviour of East Timor, Bishop Carlos Ximenes Belo

whatever the consequences he might suffer himself. Brushing aside death threats and the fears of his closest followers, the bishop managed to gather international support for his downtrodden country.

World attention was unwelcome in a Jakarta preoccupied with secession threats on several islands, but there was no real need for concern because American commercial interests with a stake in Indonesia ensured that the Santa Cruz massacre had little immediate impact on Washington's outlook. Not until 1993, when Bill Clinton moved into the White House, would the United States first express its disapproval. Over the next few years, it became obvious that East Timor had no connection at all with Indonesia: the award in 1996 of the Nobel Peace Prize to Carlos Belo was the turning point—the citation did not mince its words:

> In 1975, Indonesia took control of East Timor and began systematically oppressing the people. In the years that followed it has been estimated that one-third of the population of East Timor lost their lives due to starvation, epidemics, war and terror.[44]

The bad publicity obliged Washington to acknowledge the plight of the East Timorese. When, in 1999, a United Nations team confirmed their wish to separate from Indonesia, Jakarta's tyranny was ended by an international force from Australia, Britain, Canada, France, Italy, New Zealand, the Philippines, Thailand, South Korea and the United States. Thus was the delayed decolonisation of the last Western colony in Asia accomplished.

A not dissimilar betrayal of a colonial people, the Karens, occurred in Burma. Their separatist rebellion endured for far longer than East Timor's independence struggle as it stemmed from the refusal of the Attlee government to contemplate the breakup of existing colonial units unless, like India and Pakistan, there was absolutely no alternative. Because of this policy in London there was never any discussion of Karen aspirations for the establishment of "Karenistan". Possibly the assassination of Aung San in 1947 was a decisive factor in the drift towards armed resistance. Of all the Burmese nationalist leaders, he had the trust of Burma's minority peoples, and especially the Karens, Shan and Mon. After Aung San's violent death, nationalist factions contending for power were only concerned with securing Burman support, reviving in the process age-old ethnic rivalries.

A fundamental difficulty for the Karens was that they did not all live in the same area, although most dwelt in the hill country adjacent to the Thai border. As a consequence of this dispersal, they demanded a larger area than the nationalist leaders could reasonably concede. A compromise of sorts was an agreement to a small but semi-autonomous Karen homeland along with its right to secede from Burma after 10 years.[45] In the anarchy that engulfed newly independent Burma, however, the Karens considered this an inadequate arrangement and, in January 1949, they revolted against Rangoon. The mass desertion of Karen soldiers gave the uprising great strength for, with other hillsmen, they had "formed the backbone of the resistance movements that grew in strength as the Japanese occupation continued".[46]

Field Marshal Slim goes on to recall in his account of the Burma campaign how the staunchly loyal Karens had fallen upon the retreating Japanese columns in 1945 with untold ferocity. "It was not at all difficult to get the Karens to rise against the hated Japanese: the problem was to restrain them from rising too soon."[47] It is arguable that a degree of restraint would have helped the Karen cause from the late 1940s until early 1960s, although Cold War intrigue seemed too good an opportunity to miss. In this key border area between India, China, Laos, Thailand and Burma, a complicated guerrilla war was fought out, the main players being the People's Republic and the United States. To survive and further their cause, the Karens formed alliances with one group of dissidents after another: Guomindang refugees, Burmese and Lao communists, Thai minority peoples. The apparently unending conflict took its toll on traditional Karen ways, as indeed did the import of communist ideas, so that the Karens themselves were riven by ideological differences. Even though it may seem today that warlords rule the roost, the Karen people remain no less determined than they were just after the Pacific War to have a separate state of their own.

The Burmese government also faced armed rebellion in the Arakan, which was not overcome until the mid-1950s. But this Moslem opposition was mild in comparison with the sustained resistance of the Moros in the southern Philippines, a legacy of the Sulu sultanate.

369

From the start of Spain's involvement with the Philippines, the Moslem inhabitants of Mindanao and Palawan had launched raids on its coastal settlements in the islands to the north. Similarly to the troublesome Acehnese in Sumatra, the Moros were not finally brought under direct colonial rule until the late nineteenth century. Then the British refused a request for assistance against the Spanish offensive: Lord Granville, the foreign minister at the time, advised the Sulu sultan to pray instead. The advice was not entirely misplaced as a Dominican friar in Manila had already preached a Christian crusade against Islam.

London was quite happy for the Spaniards to tidy up the last corner of independent Southeast Asia, but no other European power had permission to intrude. Lord Granville had already told King Leopold II in no uncertain terms to keep away from the area, when the Belgium king tried to acquire parts of Sarawak as a way of establishing a colony on the island of Borneo. Given the rapacious nature of that monarch's autocratic regime in the Congo, the peoples of Borneo and adjacent islands were lucky that Leopold gave up any such scheme. This was small consolation for the Moslems in the Philippines, who found themselves forcibly annexed to Spain barely a decade before its colonial empire fell to the Americans. The new rulers never understood Moro dislike of the Philippines, either during the period it was an American colony or after independence; therefore, Washington's bafflement that from 1968 onwards 20,000 Moros were to keep the bulk of the Filipino army at bay. Efforts to negotiate a settlement in late 1976 and early 1977 in Tripoli were founded on the Moro demand for a separate state. The rise of Islamic terrorism may persuade Manila and Washington to think again about the fighting in Mindanao, which has so far consumed 100,000 lives and created ten times that number of refugees. After all, it offers a first-rate training facility for anti-Western extremists.

Of the other post-colonial conflicts, the two major ones both involved Vietnam. The first began on 25 December 1978, with a Vietnamese invasion of Cambodia. It was quickly followed by the occupation of southern Laos. The purpose of these two military operations was the overthrow of the Khmer Rouge, whose leadership fled Phnom Penh for the Thai border. On 10 January 1979, the People's Republic of Kampuchea came into existence: for the Vietnamese, its main task was to prevent Pol Pot from regaining power. Until 1989, when Vietnam withdrew all its forces, the new regime was protected by 200,000 Vietnamese troops. Relieved though they certainly were to be rid of the Khmer Rouge, Cambodians feared that their country would become a colony of Vietnam. They recalled how in the 1830s the Vietnamese emperor Minh-Mang had tried to impose a Vietnamisation programme on Cambodia. Then it took a war between the Thais and the Vietnamese to free Cambodia, whose king Ang Duong wrote to Napoleon III in the mistaken hope that French protection would not mean colonial subjection.

It is hardly credible now that in 1979 the Thai, the Chinese and the Americans allowed their hostility towards the Vietnamese to cloud their judgement to such an extent that they sided with Pol Pot, whose supporters were given sanctuary in camps just inside Thailand. For Pol Pot, this unexpected turn of events meant personal security, even plentiful foreign aid for a couple of years. By 1981 the genocidal activities of the Khmer Rouge became too well publicised for the United States to support Pol Pot openly any longer, so other anti-Vietnamese ploys were tried to keep its client government in Cambodia isolated. With the Cold War diminishing in intensity during the rest of the decade, however, there was a significant shift in the power balance around Vietnam. Mikhail Gorbachev's liberal policies in the Soviet Union, Deng Xiaoping's cautious introduction of a market economy in the People's Republic, and a temporary eclipse of the military in Thai politics, all worked against continued confrontation, especially as the Russians lowered the level of their economic and military aid to Vietnam.

When the Vietnamese finally withdrew their troops from Cambodia in 1989, they left behind many settlers. No subject remains more frequently discussed by present-day Cambodians than the extent of Vietnamese immigration into Cambodia. Rumours often claim that it is part of a long-term plan by which Hanoi intends to expand its influence beyond Vietnam's borders. The Chinese seem to have agreed with this analysis in 1979, when they chose to punish the Vietnamese for border violations. By attacking Moscow's Asian ally, the People's Liberation Army sought to teach a lesson to Vietnam, as well as to the Soviet Union. In the event, the war ended in a costly stalemate or, as far as the Vietnamese were concerned, a Chinese reverse. The exact origin of the conflict is hard to fathom,

although the suggestion that Deng Xiaoping felt sufficiently bothered about Russian influence in Vietnam to favour military action
seems way off target. More likely a reason for giving the People's
Liberation Army its head was his continued need of support in the
run-up to the trial of the Gang of Four. Not until after the public
condemnation of Jiang Qing, Mao Zedong's widow, could Deng
Xiaoping be sure about his own political future. As happened again
a decade later in Tiananmen Square, it was timely military assistance
that saved his leadership and his reform programme.

Last Post in Hong Kong 1997

We were overflown by Flanker aircraft in the South China Sea and when we left Hong Kong even *Britannia* was followed by a Chinese patrol craft.

Prince Charles' reflections on the return of the colony to China.

In spite of the sadness Prince Charles felt about the British withdrawal from Hong Kong, the lowering of the Union Jack on 30 June 1997 ended no more than an era of gunboat diplomacy. This was poignantly underlined by his sailing away on a royal yacht already destined for decommissioning. That Prince Charles mentioned in his speech at the handover ceremony the largest deployment of the Royal Navy in Asian waters for many years should have given him a clue about the reason for a demonstration of Chinese power in the air and at sea. China had not forgotten the destruction inflicted by the steamer *Nemesis* during the British assault on nearby Guangzhou in 1841. A British merchant noted then how the warship was as much admired by his fellow countrymen as it was dreaded by the Chinese, who had no defence against *Nemesis'* guns. He was certain that the iron vessel was worth its weight in gold.

Nor had China failed to recall the last engagement fought with the Royal Navy, which in 1949 had insisted that the frigate *Amethyst* was sailing on international waters when driven aground on the Yangzi, some 300 kilometres from its river mouth. The *Amethyst* incident had revealed the very different perceptions of Britain and China. By disabling the frigate, field artillery belonging to the People's Liberation Army announced the passing of China's vulnerability to Western navies. Even for a Labour government in London, the alteration in the balance of power came as a surprise. After a century of struggle, often humiliating and usually unsuccessful, against foreign aggressors starting with the British during the notorious Opium Wars, China had reasserted its proper position in the world. For there can be no question that the People's Republic lifted the siege that the Chinese had endured for so long.

Afterwards, the British colony of Hong Kong survived on sufferance. London might well claim the island of Hong Kong as sovereign territory, but there could be no argument about the end of the lease on nearby Kowloon. In 1982, Deng Xiaoping's negotiators denied sovereign rights altogether, and declared the whole British occupation illegal. For Beijing, the return of Macao from Portugal and Hong Kong from Britain was never more than the recovery of Chinese territory. What the British missed during the negotiations was Deng Xiaoping's fear over a flight of capital from Hong Kong: its economic activities were of immense benefit to the People's Republic. He simply could not afford to weaken the gradual introduction of a market economy, nor jeopardise the inflow of foreign investment, through making Hong Kong into a convenient colonial scapegoat. He even lauded joint ventures between Hong Kong-based companies and mainland enterprises during his 1992 tour of southern China, whose principal purpose was to further economic reform.

Deng Xiaoping had no time at all for London's sudden conversion to democracy in the colony, however. Whether Chris Patten was on an ego trip as some critics of his governorship thought, or trying to compensate for a patent lack of constitutional development, his drive towards a fully democratic system of government deeply offended Beijing. As Michael Heseltine put it:

> How could one expect the Chinese to accept such a unilateral approach so shortly before 1997. We had governed Hong Kong for long enough to introduce a democratic constitution if we had believed it necessary or desirable. Perhaps it was to our discredit that we did not, but deathbed repentance, however genuine, looked very different when viewed from Beijing.[1]

The Chinese leaders were bound to think that a democratic time bomb was being planted with the sole intention of damaging the People's Republic. They were never going to let this happen and Hong Kong immediately lost the tenuous political control bequeathed by Patten but not its economic freedom. For Beijing wanted the ex-colony to maintain its role as one of the world's great trading cities.

It was no matter that the United States boycotted the rainy handover ceremony because of Beijing's decision to scrap Patten's elected legislative council and replace it with an appointed one. Politely ignored, too, were the words of Prince Charles, when he said that Hong Kong had shown how East and West could live and work together. And there was silence when British newspapers later reported his description of the whole event as "the Great Chinese Takeaway".[2] All that concerned Beijing was the disappearance of the last of the "Ocean Devils" into the mists of the South China Sea.

Chronology

1405	Admiral Zheng He commands the first of seven seaborne expeditions, sailing from Nanjing as far as Sri Lanka and India. In 1409, he places the famous trilingual stele at a Buddhist shrine in Galle.
1411	Emperor Yong Le presents the ruler of Malacca with a war junk. By the time of Zheng He's next visit in 1413, the ruler has converted to Islam.
1415	The sultan of Malindi presents the Chinese emperor with a giraffe, a "celestial horse" and a "celestial stag". King João of Portugal seizes the north African port of Ceuta.
1433	The last Chinese seaborne expedition to the southern oceans.
1437	The Portuguese fail to capture Tangier.
1441	The first black slaves are brought back to Portugal from Guinea.
1460	Death of Henry the Navigator.
1488	Bartolomeu Dias returns to Lisbon with the news that he has discovered the Cape of Good Hope, and a sea route to India.
1498	Vasco da Gama commands the first Portuguese expedition to India.
1500–01	A second expedition under the command of Cabral subjects Calicut to a bombardment.

1505   Franciso d'Almeida appointed as the first viceroy of Portuguese Asia. *Cartaz* system is introduced.

1510   The second viceroy Alfonso de Albuquerque captures Goa, henceforth the headquarters of the Estado da India, Portugal's Asian empire.

1511   Alfonso de Albuquerque takes Malacca as well. Two years later, he is repulsed at Aden.

1517   Portuguese ships reach Guangzhou, or Canton.

1518   The Portuguese occupy Colombo and gain control of the cinnamon trade.

1521   Fernão de Magalhaes reaches the Philippines via Cape Horn. His death there deters Spanish exploration for a time.

1526   Zahir-ud-din Muhammad Babur founds the Mughal empire in India.

1542–43   Portuguese traders arrive in Japan.

1547   St. Francis Xavier stays for six months at Malacca.

1552   Ivan the Terrible captures Kazan and opens the way for Russian penetration of Asia overland.

1556   Akbar the Great succeeds to the Mughal throne.

1560   The Inquisition is established at Goa.

1571   The Spaniards capture Manila, and then fortify the settlement.

1574   The Ming dynasty builds a wall to seal off the Portuguese trading post at Macao.

1578   King Sebastian dies at Alcazar in Morocco with the result that from 1580 until 1640 Portugal passes under Habsburg control.

1592   The Japanese warlord Toyotomi Hideyoshi invades Korea.

1593   Portuguese mercenaries help the Thai to repulse a Burmese invasion at the battle of Nong Sarai.

1598	King Ton of Cambodia permits Diogo Veloso to build a fortress in his kingdom.
1600	Queen Elizabeth I grants a charter to "the Governor and Company of Merchants in London Trading in the East Indies".
1602	The VOC, the United East India Company, is also given a charter over all trade east of the Cape of Good Hope.
1613	King Anaukpetlun destroys Syriam, the stronghold of Filipe de Brito e Nicote in southern Burma. Its Portuguese survivors were recruited as artillerymen.
1614	Christianity is suppressed in Japan.
1616	The Dutch firmly established at Batavia, present-day Jakarta, after conflict with English traders and local Malay rulers.
1623–25	The Dutch blockade Goa.
1627	Acehnese attack on Malacca foiled and "the Terror of Universe" falls into Portuguese hands. It may have been the largest wooden warship ever built.
1632	Mughal forces destroy the Portuguese factory at Hooghly in Bengal.
1638	The Portuguese are expelled from Japan.
1639	The Dutch capture Trincomalee and then start to reduce Portugal's other forts on Sri Lanka. Fort St. George is built at Madras as an English East India Company stronghold.
1641	Portuguese Malacca falls to the Dutch.
1644	The Manchus establish the Qing dynasty, China's last imperial house.
1647–48	The Treaty of Münster acknowledges the independence of Holland.
1652	The first Anglo-Durch War. Three wars were fought between 1652 and 1674.

1658	Aurangzeb usurps the Mughal throne.
1660	Aurangzeb begins a series of campaigns that bring most of India under Mughal rule.
1661	Catherine of Braganza brings Bombay as part of her dowry. As the wife of Charles II, she makes the drinking of tea fashionable in England.
1662	Zheng Chenggong, the Ming patriot, expels the Dutch from the island of Taiwan.
1689	The Treaty of Nerchinsk settles a border dispute between Russia and China.
1690	The English settlement at Calcutta was established.
1707	Bahadur Shah is acknowledged as Mughal emperor after a bitter succession struggle between Aurangzeb's sons.
1717	The Mughal emperor awards Britain customs exemption in Bengal.
1720	Tibet is brought under Qing control.
1739–40	The Iranians loot Delhi and make off with the Peacock Throne, the pride of the Mughals.
1747	At Adyar river in southern India, the French demonstrate how European-trained local troops can match anyone on the battlefield.
1750–51	Robert Clive's successful defence of Arcot.
1756	The "Black Hole" of Calcutta leads in the ensuing year to Clive's victory at Plassey over Siraj-ud-daula. The English East India Company is now dominant in Bengal.
1783	In southern India, the ruler of Mysore, Tipu Sultan, challenges the English East India Company with French support.
1785	Discrimination against Anglo-Indians starts.

1786	Francis Light establishes a base for the Royal Navy at Penang.
1788	Warren Hastings' trial begins in London.
1793	Emperor Qian Long rebuffs the trade mission of Lord Macartney.
1795	The United East India Company goes bankrupt. Henceforth, Dutch colonies survive on British sufferance alone. The English East India Company conquer Dutch Sri Lanka.
1799	Seringapatam, Tipu Sultan's stronghold, falls.
1802	Peace of Amiens. Britain retains Sri Lanka.
1803	Arthur Wellesley defeats the Marathas at Assaye and Argaum, thereby gaining control of the Deccan.
1805	Richard Wellesley is recalled from India.
1806	Military mutiny at Vellore signals growing unease at British domination in India.
1810	The French island of Mauritius is captured by the British.
1811	Stamford Raffles becomes governor of Java.
1819	Raffles founds Singapore as a free port.
1823	First Anglo-Burmese War.
1824	Holland cedes Malacca to the British.
1825	Pangeran Dipanagara's rebellion occurs in Java.
1830	The Dutch introduce *cultuurstelsel*, "the culture system" in Java.
1833	English East India Company loses its monopoly of the China trade.
1838	First Afghan War begins.

1839   Commissioner Lin Zexu is sent to stamp out the opium trade at Guangzhou.
English East India Company seizes Aden.

1840   The First Opium War begins. As a consequence of the Chinese defeat, Hong Kong is ceded to Britain as a sovereign base in 1842.

1841   James Brooke establishes himself in Sarawak.

1845   First Sikh War occurs.

1846   Brunei cedes the island of Labuan to Britain.

1848   Second Sikh War occurs.

1850   The Taipings rebel in China.

1852   Lord Dalhousie annexes lower Burma.

1853   Matthew Perry orders Japan to open its borders to trade.

1856   The *Arrow* Incident leads to the Second Opium War. Oudh is annexed to the Indian empire.

1857   The Indian Mutiny ends with the deposition of Bahadur Shah Zafar II, the last Mughal emperor. He is exiled to Rangoon.

1858   The French occupy Saigon.

1860   An Anglo-French expedition captures Beijing, where Lord Elgin orders the destruction of the Summer Palace. British acquisition of Kowloon, opposite Hong Kong. Russia seizes large areas of Manchuria.

1861   After the death of Emperor Xian Feng, Ci Xi dominates the Qing court and opposes the modernisation of China.

1863   Cambodia becomes a French protectorate.

1867   The enthronement of Emperor Meiji in Japan.

1871	The Anglo-Dutch Treaty of Sumatra clears the way for a Dutch invasion of Aceh. The Malay states of Perak, Selangor and Sungei Ujong accept British residents.
1876	Queen Victoria becomes Empress of India.
1873	Conscription is introduced in Japan.
1878	Second Afghan War begins.
1881	The British North Borneo Company is granted a Royal Charter.
1883	Vietnam ceases to be a Chinese tributary state.
1885	The Congress Party is formed in India. Third Anglo-Burmese War.
1886	Upper Burma is annexed to the Indian empire.
1887	Laos is added to French Indochina.
1888	Sarawak, North Borneo and Brunei become British protectorates.
1893	The French oblige the Thai to cede territories to Laos and Cambodia.
1893–94	The Tonghak uprising in Korea.
1894–95	The Sino-Japanese War is fought in Korea and north China.
1898	Germany obtains a lease on Qingdao, its "Hong Kong" in northern China. The Hundred Days of Reform. Empress Ci Xi imprisons the would-be reformer, Emperor Guang Xu. The Spanish-American War takes place. The United States annexes Hawaii and, in the ensuing year, the Philippines.
1900	The Boxers attack the Legation Quarter in Beijing.
1901	The end of Filipino resistance to the American annexation.

1902   The Anglo-Japanese Alliance.

1904–05   The Russo-Japanese War ends with an acknowledgement of Japan's protection of Korea.

1905   Ho Chi Minh starts to learn French, better to undestand the colonial enemy.

1906   Britain recognises Chinese suzerainty in Tibet.

1909   Bangkok cedes the Malay states of Perlis, Kedah, Kelantan and Trengganu to Britain. In 1943, Japan allowed Thailand to administer them once again.

1910   Japan annexes Korea.

1912   Pu Yi, the last Qing emperor, abdicates and China becomes a republic.

1914   Imperial Japanese Army occupies the German-leased territory of Qingdao.

1915   Mahatma Gandhi returns to India from South Africa, where he had opposed racial discrimination by non-violent means.
            Japan presents China with the Twenty-One Demands.

1916   General Yuan Shikai fails to restore the Chinese empire.

1917   An attempt to restore Pu Yi to the Dragon Throne also fails. A period of warlordism ensues in China.

1919   The Amritsar massacre splits public opinion. It is condemned by Winston Churchill.
            Third Afghan War occurs.
            At the Versailles peace conference the Australian premier, Billy Hughes, blocks a Japanese proposal to outlaw racial discrimination.
            May Fourth Movement in China protests against imperialism.

1921–22   The Washington Naval Conference ends the Anglo-Japanese Alliance. Along with the London Naval Treaty of 1936, it represented an unsuccessful attempt to stop a naval arms race with Japan.

1922	The Imperial Japanese Army quits Vladivostok and the Far Eastern Republic is absorbed into the Soviet Union.
1924	Planning begins for the Singapore naval base.
1928	The Northern Expedition leaves Chiang Kai-shek as China's principal warlord.
1930	Gandhi leads the so-called Salt March, a major civil disobedience campaign.
1931	After the Mukden Incident the Imperial Japanese Army occupies the whole of Manchuria, which soon becomes the puppet-state of Manzhouguo. London Round Table Conference on India is held.
1934	The Long March begins and Mao Zedong is recognised as leader of the Chinese Communist Party.
1935	India Act provides for regional self-government, and separates Burma from India. The Xi'an Incident leads to an anti-Japanese front between the Guomindang and the Chinese Communist Party.
1937	The outbreak of the Sino-Japanese War, which merged in 1941 with the Pacific War. The Nanjing massacre shocks world opinion. Ba Maw government established in Burma.
1938	Singapore naval base is completed but only on a reduced scale.
1939	The Russians defeat the Japanese at Nomonhan. Burma Road is constructed.
1940	Aung San becomes the secretary of the Burma Freedom Block. Wang Jingwei's puppet government is established by the Japanese in Nanjing.
1940–41	The Franco-Thai War ends with a French defeat in Indochina.

1941–42   Japanese attack Pearl Harbor and conquer Hong Kong, Malaya, Guam, the Philippines, the Dutch East Indies and Burma.
Singapore surrenders along with 85,000 troops.
The Imperial Japanese Navy is crippled at Midway.

1943   Sukarno tells the Indonesians that they must secure freedom for themselves.
Gandhi launches the Quit-India campaign.

1944   Subhas Chandra Bose raises the Indian National Army in Malaya.
The Americans return to the Philippines.

1945   After Japanese defeats at Imphal and Kohima, the British recover Burma.
Iwo Jima and Okinawa campaigns occur.
Atomic bombs are dropped on Hiroshima and Nagasaki, followed by the unconditional surrender of Japan.
Sukarno proclaims the Republic of Indonesia.
Emperor Bo Dai appeals by radio to France for Vietnamese independence.

1946   Emperor Hirohito denies his divinity. Tojo Hideki and other war criminals are hanged.
Ho Chi Minh announces hostilities against France.
The First Vietnam War begins.
Vyner Brooke cedes Sarawak to Britain.
The Philippines becomes an independent state.

1947   India, Pakistan and Burma are all granted independence. Only the latter opts to leave the Commonwealth.
The First Indo-Pakistan War occurs.

1948   The People's Liberation Army secures complete control of Manchuria.
Sri Lanka gains its independence.
A state of emergency is declared in Malaya.
Gandhi is assassinated by a Hindu fanatic.

1949	*HMS Amethyst* stranded on the Yangzi River. Mao Zedong proclaims the People's Republic of China, while Chiang Kai-shek flees to Taiwan. The Karens rebel against independence arrangements in Burma. Indonesia gains its independence from Holland.
1950	The Korean War breaks out.
1951	Douglas MacArthur is dismissed by Truman.
1953	The Acehnese rebel against Javanese interference in Sumatra.
1954	The French surrender at Dien Bien Phu.
1955	Bandung Conference of "non-aligned" nations occurs. Malayan Chief Minister Tunku Abdul Rahman speaks to Chin Peng, leader of the Malayan Communist Party. Pakistan becomes an Islamic republic.
1957	Malaya is granted independence. US task force at Singapore backs rebellious Indonesian officers in Sumatra and Selawesi.
1959	Singapore achieves internal self-government.
1960	Malayan Emergency ends.
1961	The Indian Army expels the Portuguese from Goa.
1962	The Sino-Indian War leads to an Indian defeat. Sukarno adds West Irian to Indonesia.
1963	US intervenes in South Vietnam. The Second Vietnam War begins. Malaya, Singapore, Sarawak and North Borneo combine to form Malaysia, which Sukarno then "confronts" on the island of Borneo.
1965	The Second Indo-Pakistan War occurs. Singapore withdraws from Malaysia.
1968	The Moros of the southern Philippines rise in revolt. Tet offensive in South Vietnam shakes the United States.

1970   Washington backs a South Vietnamese invasion of Cambodia.

1971   The Third Indo-Pakistan War ends with the creation of Bangladesh, after the surrender of the Pakistani garrison at Dacca.

1972   President Nixon visits Beijing.

1973   Australia finally abandons ethnic discrimination in its immigration rules.

1975   Indonesia invades East Timor.
            Saigon falls to North Vietnamese troops.

1978   The Vietnamese occupy Cambodia, overthrowing the Khmer Rouge.

1979   The Sino-Vietnamese War ends in a stalemate.

1984   British and Chinese agree on the restoration of Hong Kong to the People's Republic of China.
            Indira Gandhi is assassinated by a Sikh bodyguard.

1989   Vietnamese forces leave Cambodia.

1991   Rajiv Gandhi is assassinated by a Tamil Tiger.

1997   British rule in Hong Kong ends.

1999   The last Western colony, East Timor, secures its independence through international intervention.

Endnotes

Introduction

1. Slim, *Defeat into Victory*, p. 539. Orde Wingate had insisted that the Third West African Brigade should join the Chindits, his behind-enemy-lines force in Burma. Before the fall of France, a major African contribution to the war effort was not envisaged but, as the scale of the Second World War unfolded, Britain was obliged to recruit soldiers whenever it could do so. Bandale's treatment of a Chindit expedition is based on his father's reminiscences. A full account of the contribution made by colonial troops can be found in Jackson, *The British Empire and The Second World War*. According to George MacDonald Fraser, whose *Quartered Safe Out There* is one of the finest memoirs of the Second World War, "probably not even the legions of Rome embraced as many nationalities as the Fourteenth Army", p. 94.
2. Tsuji Masanobu, *Singapore 1941–1942*, p. 281.

Chapter 1

1. Needham, *Science and Civilisation in China*, vol. IV, part III, p. 488.
2. Marco Polo's *Travels*, p. 437.
3. A survey of these distant diplomatic contacts can be found in Filesi, *China and Africa in the Middle Ages*.
4. Chaudhuri, *Trade and Civilisation in the Indian Ocean*, offers a Braudel-like view of the Portuguese seaborne empire, while Whiteway, *The Rise of Portuguese Power in India*, lists some of the atrocities committed in its acquisition.
5. Needham, op. cit., p. 522.
6. Ma Huan, *Overall Survey of the Ocean's Shores*, p. 108.
7. Barros, *Décades de Asia*, décade I, book I, chapter 6.
8. Housley, *The Later Crusades*, p. 287.
9. Needham, op. cit, p. 525.
10. Azurara, *Chronicles*, p. 31.
11. Vogt, "Crusading and Commercial Elements in the Portuguese Capture of Ceuta (1415)", p. 290.

12. Azurara, op. cit., p. 85.
13. Ibid., p. 105.
14. Allmand, *The Hundred Years War*, p. 29. Henry V's policy in France was one of deliberate conquest and settlement, a departure from the previous tactic of extended raids. Those who refused him recognition were deprived of their lands, which the king gave to his English and French supporters. Glorious and profitable though the battle of Agincourt was in terms of ransoms and captured arms, the real enticement for those who followed Henry to France was the chance of acquiring landed property, especially in Normandy. At Ceuta in the same year, however, it was movable goods that most attracted members of the Portuguese expeditionary force. But the principle was the same. After reserving a share for the monarch, the rest of the spoils were shared among all combatants.
15. Phillips, "The growth and composition of trade in the Iberian empires, 1470–1750", p. 50. The Casa da India was then the largest warehouse in the world, access to which in Lisbon was a guarantee of wealth. It contained spices, sugar, molasses and silks.
16. Velho, "The Route to India, 1497–8", p. 13.
17. Ibid., p. 14.
18 Meilink-Roelofz, *Asian Trade and European Influence*, p. 130.
19. Velho, op. cit., p. 30.
20. The Order of Christ's authority overseas, Subrahmanyam, *The Career and Legend of Vasco da Gama*, p. 37.
21. Ibid., p. 163.
22. Greenlee, *The Voyage of Redro Alvares Cabral to Brazil and India*, p. 189.
23. Barros, op. cit., décade I, book VI, chapter I.
24. Albuquerque, *The Commentaries*, IV, p. 24.
25. Piero Strozzi's letter of 20 December 1510, quoted in Subrahmanyam, *Improvising Empire*, p. 5.
26. Celestial portents, Albuquerque, op. cit., Volume IV, p. 44.
27. Thomaz, "Factions, Interests and Messianism", p. 99.
28. Albuquerque, op. cit., vol. III, p. 133.
29. Marshall, "Western Arms in Maritime Asia in the Early Phases of Expansion", p. 17.
30. Manucci, *Storia do Mogor*, vol. II, p. 137.
31. Subrahmanyam, "The Kagemusha effect. . .", p. 106. In sixteenth-century India there were two sources of firearms: the Ottoman Turks and the Portuguese. As Subrahmanyam demonstrates, "the Portuguese who spread the use of these arms were often not emissaries of the Estado da India, but were instead private citizens, traders, mercenaries and even renegades". The latter went over to Asian rulers specifically to offer their military services. So concerned did the Portuguese

authorities become about the activities of European cannon founders and artillerymen in Indian employ that assassins were rewarded for their elimination. One successful assassin sent out from Goa in the 1620s received as a reward the post of clerical assistant to the magistrate at Diu. The problem of renegade gunners, however, was not new. As early as 1506, there were Portuguese deserters making artillery pieces for the ruler of Calicut; Khan, *Gunpowder and Firearms*, p. 61.

32. Reid, "Sixteenth Century Turkish Influence in Western Indonesia", p. 396.
33. Reid, *Southeast Asia in the Age of Commerce*, vol. 2, p. 233.
34. Pinto, *The Travels*, p. 400.
35. Lieberman, "Europeans, Trade and the Unification of Burma, c.1540–1620", p. 211.
36. Pinto, op. cit., p. 401.
37. Ibid., p. 300.
38. The full text of Diogo Veloso's 1598 grant of Cambodian land is quoted in Subrahamanyan, *Improvising Empire*, p. 148.
39. Ibid., p. 153.
40. Winius, *The Fatal History of Portuguese Ceylon*, p. 6.
41. Schurhammer, *Francis Xavier*, vol. III, "Indonesia and India, 1545–1549", p. 242.
42. Boxer, *Race Relations in the Portuguese Colonial Empire*, p. 61.
43. Ibid., p. 70
44. Samuel Purchas' *Pilgrimages*, quoted in Hannaford, *Race*, p. 171.
45. Schurhammer, op. cit., "India, 1541–1545", p. 228.
46. Boxer, op. cit., p. 63.
47. Lach, *Asia in the Making of Europe*, vol. I, book 2, p. 623. This provides an account of Magellan's ill-fated attempt to organise the Philippines as an ally of Spain.
48. Lopez, *The Christianization of the Philippines*, p. 263
49. Chang, *Sino-Portuguese Trade*, p. 53.
50. Boyajian, *Portuguese Trade under the Habsburgs*, p. 236.
51. Pinto, op. cit., p. 278.
52. Schurhammer, op. cit., vol. IV, "Japan and China 1549–1552", p. 77.
53. A report of Luis Frois quoted in McMullin, *Buddhism and the State in Sixteenth-Century Japan*, p. 88.
54. Luis Frois' approval of the Enrayakuji assault, quoted in Lamers, *Japonius Tyrannus*, p. 75.
55. Moran, *The Japanese and the Jesuits*, p. 59.
56. Ibid., p. 53.
57. Sampson, *A History of Japan 1334–1615*, p. 404.
58. Boxer, *Fidalgos in the East*, p. 85.
59. Nelson, *Fort Jesus of Mombasa*, p. 21
60. Parker, "The Making of Strategy in Habsburg Spain", p. 125.

Chapter 2

1. Flores and Vassallo e Silva, *Goa and the Great Mughal*, p. 147.
2. *Empressas militares de Lusitanos* by Lourenco Coelho de Barbuda, Lisbon, 1624, quoted in Boxer, *Portuguese and Dutch Colonial Rivalry, 1641–1661*, p. 9.
3. A comment by the Arab historian al-Djarmuzi, quoted in Padfield, *The Tide of Empires*, vol. 1, p. 159.
4. Goonewardena, *The Foundation of Dutch Power in Ceylon*, p. 146.
5. Boxer, *The Dutch Seaborne Empire*, p. 248.
6. Arasaratnam, *Dutch Power in Ceylon*, p. 231.
7. Leupe, "The Siege and Capture of Malacca from the Portuguese in 1640–1641", p. 47.
8. Prakash, *European Commercial Enterprise in Pre-Colonial India*, p. 181.
9. Rodger, *The Command of the Ocean*, p. 12.
10. Pepys, *The Diary*, vol. VIII, p. 359.
11. Thomas Mun, quoted in Israel, *Dutch Primacy in World Trade 1585–1740*, p. 12.
12. Ibid., p. 415.
13. Charles Boone and Robert Clive, quoted in Watson, "Fortifications and the 'idea' of force in East India Company relations in India", p. 76. The construction of a fort was of course an exercise in sovereignty, because its inhabitants claimed the right to live according to their own laws and beliefs.
14. Prakask, op. cit., p. 240.
15. Subhas Chandra Bose's speech at the tomb of the last Mughal emperor, September 1943. Quoted in Bose, *A Hundred Horizons*, p. 183.
16. Bruijin, *The Dutch Navy*, p. 150.
17. Pillai, *The Private Diary*, vol. III, p. 94. This remarkable document provides an insight into affairs at Pondicherry. Dupleix went on to say that the French victory at the Adyar river was "a sufficient one. What has never befallen the Muhammadans, has now overtaken them. No greater evil could have occurred to them."
18. Parker, *The Military Revolution*, p. 134.
19. Tracy, *Manila Ransomed*, p. 17.
20. Thomas Saunders' letter quoted in Furber, *Rival Empires of Trade in the Orient*, p. 156.
21. One of 23 survivors, John Holwell did not hold Siraj-ud-daula in any way responsible for the atrocity, because early in the morning when the Indian ruler learnt what had happened he at once ordered the prisoners' release. There can be no question, however, that a large number of people suffocated in the "Black Hole" during the night.
22. Clive's view of Siraj-ud-daula, quoted in Moon, *The British Conquest and Dominion of India*, p. 51.
23. Moon, *Warren Hastings*, p. 49.

24. Tracy, op. cit., p. 112.
25. Quoted in Dirks, *The Scandal of Empire*, p. 56.
26. Spear, *Master of Bengal*, p. 146.
27. Quoted in Moon, op. cit., p. 153.
28. Cavaliero, *Admiral Satan*, p. 127.
29. Black, *George III*, p. 334.
30. Quoted in Losty, *Calcutta*, p. 75.
31. Arthur Wellesley's dispatch to his brother in Calcutta dated 24 September 1803 quoted in Cooper, *The Anglo-Maratha Campaigns and the Contest for India*, p. 102.
32. Ibid., p. 106.
33. Moon, op. cit., p. 339.
34. Heathcote, *The Military in British India*, p. 63.
35. The kowtow, actually *koutou*, was a part of everyday court ritual in Beijing. Emperor Qian Long's advisers seem to have appreciated the problems involved for Lord Macartney in following this practice. For a start, there was the difficulty of kneeling in the tight trousers that the ambassador wore. That Macartney's exemption from the kowtow was never forgotten, however, is evident in the unkind response of Chinese journalists in 1982, when Mrs. Thatcher tripped on the steps as she left the Great Hall of the People and fell on her hands and knees. They credited the British premier with knowing how to show proper respect at last. Another British ambassador who refused to kowtow was Lord Amherst, who was in 1816 denied an imperial audience in Beijing. Emperor Ren Zong wondered why the envoy had been permitted to reach the capital if he was known to be unwilling to comply with established court ceremonial.
36. This was the French Revolution, which had started in 1789. See Cranmer-Byng, *An Embassy to China*, p. 32.
37. Lord Macartney's embassy had six specific aims. The first was a treaty of commerce and friendship which provided for a resident ambassador to the Qing court. The second aim was an extension of British trade in China by opening new ports, especially in the northern provinces where British woollens could be sold. Third, Macartney aimed to obtain an island near Guangzhou, where British merchants could reside for the whole year, and where British jurisdiction could be exercised. The fourth aim was a reform of the trading arrangements at Guangzhou. A fifth aim concerned the creation of new markets for British products previously unknown to the Chinese, of which samples were brought by Macartney. The final aim, which indicates London's total misunderstanding of the tributary system, was to open Vietnam and Japan to British commerce with the approval of Beijing.
38. Cranmer-Byng, op. cit., p. 170.
39. Ibid., p. 212.

Chapter 3

1. Letter to William Beresford in Gurwood, *Dispatches of Field Marshall the Duke of Wellington*, vol. XII, p. 529. The word "strategy" did not appear in the English language until 1810, when it was distinguished from tactics. Eight years earlier, William Windam had already complained about its absence from the British war effort, without having available the word to assist him. He said that "we were indeed at war, because we could not be at peace; we were at sea, because we could not be on shore. Yet though reminded of this, the character of the war itself, the grand monitor was wanting. The manner in which it was carried on did not sufficiently mark its nature. The force was centrifugal. It was never converged enough towards the focus from which the danger proceeded", *Parliamentary History*, vol. 36, col. 749, 13 May 1802. Only the ability of the British to subsidise their continental allies permitted the quest for an effective strategy to defeat Napoleon. In 1813, Britain gave more than £7 million to them: Portugal and Spain together received nearly half of this enormous subsidy. £1 million went to Russia. The financial resources of Britain's overseas empire, plus the Royal Navy, more than compensated for the relatively small size of its army. Early in his career, Napoleon had recognised that war between France and Britain would be a war of survival: only one of these two countries could exercise world power. In 1811, the French emperor remarked "in five years, I shall be master of the world: there only remains Russia, but I will crush her."
2. Quoted in Holt, *The Opium Wars in China*, p. 99.
3. Hendrick, *The Tools of Empire*, p. 50.
4. James Matheson, quoted in Fairbank, *The Cambridge History of China*, vol. 10, part I, p. 223.
5. Quoted in Banno, *China and the West*, p. 10.
6. David, *Victoria's Wars*, p. 360.
7. Ibid., p. 401.
8. Sir Seyd Ahmed Khan, quoted in Moon, *The British Conquest and Dominion of India*, p. 751.
9. Ibid., p. 707.
10. Ibid., p. 709.
11. Varma, *Ghalib. The Man, The Times*, p. 130
12. Stark, *Hostages to India*, p. 65.
13. Metcalf, *Ideologies of the Raj*, p. 104. As the author points out, the demonisation of Indian womanhood was but a single part of a more general downgrading of India in the eyes of its British rulers. Oddly, Victorian feminists reinforced the notion through philanthropic works aimed at helping their "degraded" colonial sisters. They could not understand how the secluded lives of Indian women could be anything other than domestic prostitution.

14. James Brooke, quoted in Reece, *The White Rajahs of Sarawak*, p. 23. That good community relations were normal in Sarawak came as a welcome surprise to Australian commandos during the Pacific War. There "they stood a substantial chance of finding friendly natives. Often they were greeted with downright enthusiasm. Where the Dutch had been masters, however, they would encounter only hostility and betrayal", Feuer, *Australian Commandos*, p. xi.

15. Rigault de Genouilly's announcement, quoted in Aldrich, *Greater France*, p. 77. The creation of France's second Asian empire was less the work of its government than of soldiers and sailors whose unilateral actions drew Paris willy-nilly into a colonial role in Indochina.

16. Chandler, *A History of Cambodia*, p. 143. The lost provinces of Battambang and Siem Reap were not evacuated by the Thai until 1907, when France took them over on Cambodia's behalf. A delighted King Sisowath was not permitted to visit them for two more years, however. Briefly they went back to Thailand after the Franco-Thai War of 1940–41.

17. Lee, *France and the Exploitation of China 1885–1901*, p. 13.

18. The Lao people were the earliest known inhabitants of what is now Laos. They seem to have been driven into its mountainous terrain by a gradual migration of Thai-speaking people moving southwards from China. If we take Samsenthai's name literally, in the late fourteenth century he could muster for compulsory labour and military service some 300,000 men. Another 400,000 non-Thais were available too.

19. Reynolds, *Thailand's Secret War*, p. 15.

20. LaFeber, *The American Age*, p. 213.

21. Smith, *The Spanish-American War*, p. 23.

22. Quoted in LaFeber, op. cit., p. 214.

23. Brands, *Bound to Empire*, p. 57.

24. Keene, *Emperor of Japan*, p. 596.

25. Admiral Togo Heihachiro's offensive doctrine, which insisted that the Imperial Japanese Navy should "fight the enemy on sight", is well explained in Marder, *Old Friends, New Enemies: The Royal Navy and the Imperial Japanese Navy. Strategic Illusions, 1936–1941*, p. 318

26. Quoted in Warner and Warner, *The Tide at Sunrise*, p. 204

27. Henry Adam's letter to Elizabeth Cameron written on 10 January 1904. *The Letters of Henry Adams*, p. 419.

28. Because Nebogatov was discharged by an angry tsar for the fleet's surrender, the Japanese government decided to release him from captivity as a noncombatant. Imprisoned on his return to Russia, Nebogatov was later set free and died at home in 1934.

29. The manifesto of the Black Dragon Society, quoted in Beasley, *Japanese Imperialism 1894–1945*, p. 78.

Chapter 4

1. Schroeder, *Matthew Calbraith Perry*, p. 204
2. Keene, op. cit., p. 315
3. Ibid., p. 315
4. Quoted in Jansen, *The Cambridge History of Japan*, vol. 5, p. 710.
5. Saburo, *The Pacific War, 1931–1945*, p. 27
6. Ibid., p. 23.
7. Lone, *Japan's First Modern War*, p. 18.
8. Ibid., p. 45.
9. Owen, *Lord Cromer*, p. 382.
10. Winston Churchill's anti-Bolshevism is put in perspective by Kinvig's *Churchill's Crusade*. On 26 November 1918, Churchill told his constituents at Dundee that the "Bolsheviks hop and caper like troops of ferocious baboons amid the ruins of cities and the corpses of their victims."
11. Grigg, *Lloyd George*, p. 564.
12. Stephan, *The Russian Far East*, p. 149.
13. Quoted in Eddy and Schreuder, *The Rise of Colonial Nationalism*, p. 240.
14. Strahan, *Australia's China*, p. 253.
15. Hyon Chunho's business plea, quoted in Eckert, *Offspring of Empire*, p. 233. Though Korean businessmen did not get all they requested from the Japanese, they were never ignored: Hyon Chunho's complaint was that of an insider, someone who wanted a greater share in the colony's Japanese-driven development.
16. Young, *Japan's Total Empire*, p. 371.
17. Besides showing the cheque, Chinese newspapers published a list of those politicians who had accepted the bribe. Nathan, *Peking Politics 1918–1923*, p. 219.
18. Snow, *Red Star Over China*, p. 155.
19. When the Manchus took control of China in the seventeenth century, they insisted that their Chinese subjects should be visually identified by the queue, as a sign of accepting the rule of the Qing imperial house. Every Chinese man had to shave his forehead and braid his hair into what Europeans called a pigtail. Failure to do so was punishable by death. That Zang Shun retained his queue after the establishment of the Republic is an indication of his imperial outlook. Young revolutionaries such as Mao Zedong had cut off their queues in 1911.
20. Pu Yi, *The Last Manchu*, p. 90.
21. Quoted in Boyle, *China and Japan at War, 1937–1945*, p. 43.
22. Gilmor, *Curzon*, p. 168.
23. Buber, *Pointing the Way*, p. 139.
24. Moon, op. cit., p. 994.
25. Ibid., p. 1113

26. Buber, op. cit. p. 134.
27. Quoted in Watson and Tennyson, *Talking of Gandhi*, p. 151.
28. Maung Maung, *Burmese Nationalist Movements*, p. 16.
29. Slim, op. cit., p. 516.
30. Kratoska, *The Japanese Occupation of Malaya*, p. 32. The adverse comment expressed by *Majilis* was reported in *The Straits Times*, 10 August 1939.
31. Swettenham's view of the Malays comes from the *Annual Report of Perak*, dated 1890. Quoted in Butcher, *The British in Malaya 1880–1941*, p. 9. According to the Colonial Office in 1934, Hong Kong was "the most self-satisfied of all colonies, except Malaya". See Miners, *Hong Kong under Imperial Rule*, p. 89. Opposition to the British in Hong Kong was always more organised than in either Malaya or the Straits Settlements for the good reason that Chinese nationalism was centred on nearby Guangzhou. Well might the Chinese, irrespective of their personal wealth, be denied residence on the Peak, but the British who lived there could do little to control the overwhelming majority of the population who lived on Hong Kong island's lower slopes and shoreline. It was relatively easy for Sun Yatsen's followers to ferment industrial unrest. In response to the shooting of Chinese in Guangzhou and Shanghai, when British police opened fire on anti-colonial demonstrators, 100,000 Chinese workers, a fifth of the population, left Hong Kong in 1925. Many expatriates returned to Britain, and the remainder were forced to do the menial tasks these absent workers had undertaken. A reluctance to handle buckets of night soil, however, led to the governor, Sir Reginald Stubbs, being referred to as "Shit-tubs". Chiang Kai-shek, who had just succeeded Sun Yatsen as leader of Guomindang, commented how "British power in the Orient has passed its peak." Quoted in Gillingham, *At the Peak*, p. 33. Most active in industrial relations was of course the Chinese Communist Party, then the Guomindang's junior partner. After the unrest subsided, a special anti-communist branch was set up by the Hong Kong police department: it was to receive great assistance from the Guomindang until the Xi'an Incident in 1936 temporarily ended the struggle between Mao Zedong and Chiang Kai-shek.
32. Letter to the *Malay Mail* from "Substratum", 30 November 1904.
33. A suggestion made in a Dutch article published in 1890, quoted in Kuitenbrouwer, *The Netherlands and the Rise of Modern Imperialism*, p. 170.
34. Marr, *Vietnamese Anticolonialism*, p. 161.
35. Porch, *The French Foreign Legion*, p. 209.
36. Lindsay, *The Unknown War*, p. 7. Apparently, this senior Japanese officer was unable to do anything about military indiscipline in China before his own retirement in 1942.
37. Morley, *Japan's Road to the Pacific War. Japan Erupts*, p. 139.

38. Honjo Shigeru, *Emperor Hirohito and his Chief Aide-de-Camp*, p. 76. According to Honjo Shigeru, the emperor was in 1933 equally displeased with the Imperial Japanese Navy because several of its senior officers were reluctant to operate within approved policies. What they opposed were the restrictions placed on warship construction by the London naval agreement. See Gow, *Military Intervention in Pre-war Japanese Politics*, p. 243.
39. Coox, *Nomonhan*, p. 742.
40. Chang, *The Rape of Nanking*, p. 99.
41. Quoted in Wickert, *The Good German of Nanking*, p. 101.
42. *The Times*, 28 June 2007. As the article pointed out, Japan's nationalist premier Shinzo Abe had already provoked an international outcry when he said there was no actual proof that the Imperial Japanese Army had ever forced women into prostitution.
43. Telegraph from *HMS Bee* to the senior naval officer in Shanghai, no. 408 in *Documents of British Foreign Policy 1919–1939*. Second Series, vol. XXI. *Far Eastern Affairs*.
44. Ibid, no. 411.
45. Cited in LaFeber, *The Clash*, p. 187.

Chapter 5

1. Wetzler, *Hirohito and War*, p. 195.
2. Boyle, op. cit., p. 294
3. Tarling, *Britain, Southeast Asia and the Onset of the Pacific War*, p. 99.
4. Bangkok communique issued on 14 December 1940, quoted in Morley, *Japan's Road to the Pacific War. The Fateful Choice*, p. 222.
5. Kobkua, *Thailand's Durable Premier*, p. 262.
6. Morley, op. cit., p. 230.
7. Minutes of a meeting held in Tokyo on 3 May 1941, reproduced in Nobutaka, *Japan's Decision for War*, p. 26.
8. Kershaw, *Hitler*, p. 364.
9. The extent of Yamamoto Isoroku's pessimism over conflict with the United States is quoted in Morley, op. cit., p. 274.
10. Quoted in Nobutaka, op. cit., p. 263. Considered too moderate by the Imperial Japanese Army and the Imperial Japanese Navy, Prince Konoe Fumimaro left the cabinet in the hands of Tojo Hideki, the first serving officer ever to be prime minister of Japan. *The Times* had been quick to comment that the new prime minister was "an out-and-out militarist and a staunch friend of the Axis, who has never shown much friendliness towards Great Britain and America. Our presence in the Pacific and in China he resents as an intrusion in the area which Japan covets", 18 October 1941. Hideki Tojo retained the war portfolio and also took over home affairs, a concentration of power which underlined the aggressive nationalism of the new administration. His

foreign minister, Togo Shigenori, was even more anti-American than Matsuoka Yosuke: formerly the Japanese ambassador in Berlin, he had a German wife and strong pro-German sympathies.

11. Ibid., p292.
12. Barnhart, *Japan Prepares for Total War*, p. 169.
13. Quoted in Evans, *The Japanese Navy in World War II*, p. 39.
14. Parillo, *The Japanese Merchant Marine in World War II*, p. 204.
15. Kobkua, op. cit., p. 252.
16. Reynolds, *Thailand's Secret War*, p. 14
17. Tsuji Masanobu, *Singapore 1941–1942*, p. 93.
18. Churchill's cable to President Roosevelt, 1 November 1941, is cited in Marder, op. cit., p. 232.
19. Cull, *Buffaloes over Singapore*, p. 13. This account of the American-built fighter's unequal battle against Japanese aircraft makes sad reading. The root of the problem was the Buffalo's lack of power, which ensured that it was vulnerable when taking off or trying to climb above enemy fighters, and especially the agile Zero.
20. O'Brien, *Chasing After Danger*, p. 165.
21. A note of a meeting held at the Admiralty on 8 March 1941, quoted in Day, *Menzies and Churchill at War*, p. 85.
22. Menzies' own impression of the same meeting, as reported in Martin and Hardy, *Dark and Hurrying Days*, p. 84.
23. Tsuji Masanobu, op. cit., p. 185.
24. Stewart, *History of the Argyll and Sutherland Highlanders*, p. 4. In July 1941, Stuart marched the Argylls from Mersing in Johore to Singapore, a 135-kilometre trek in eight days. They went through the jungle with one platoon in front cutting its way for an hour at a time. Then another platoon would take over. Interviewed by a Straits Times reporter afterwards, Stuart said that the march was "nothing heroic but just part of the training scheme which has put my men among the fittest fighters in this part of the world". What the Argylls had incidentally demonstrated was that there was no impenetrable barrier protecting the northern approaches of Singapore. If the Scottish colonel's men could undertake such a march, so could Japanese soldiers. It was unfortunate that Stuart was regarded as a "crank" by senior British officers in Malaya because he did appreciate how the jungle could be exploited militarily. His tactics were similar to those being developed by the Imperial Japanese Army in French Indochina. So effective was his training that an Argyll prisoner of war was disbelieved when asked by a Japanese officer how many men were in the rearguard on the Kroh to Grik road. When the Argyll scratched on the ground with a stick "35", the Japanese officer added two noughts. He was annoyed when they were both scratched out because the troops he had led down that road were held up for four whole days by the tiny rearguard. Hardly

surprising then was the choice of the surviving 250 Argylls to act as the final rearguard on the British evacuation of Malaya. They were piped across to Singapore just before the causeway was blown up. But their bravery counted for little when the triumphant Imperial Japanese Army captured the island. Near Bukit Timah, a village they had stoutly defended, 12 Argyll prisoners were tied up with barbed wire, bayonetted and shot. Another Argyll was a casualty of the massacre at Alexandra Hospital, where, in their frantic search for valuables such as rings and watches, Japanese soldiers threw the wounded on the floor before bayonetting them. More than 300 patients and orderlies died on 14 February 1942. In all, 53 Argylls escaped to Australia, Sri Lanka and India. Along with two officers and an NCO, Stuart was ordered to Java, then Sri Lanka, so that specialist knowledge of jungle fighting against the Japanese would not be lost. Not until he was certain that the lives of his remaining soldiers were not going to be thrown away in pointless street fighting would Stuart accept this order direct from Wavell. It was his approach to jungle warfare, not that of the errant Gordon Bennett, which formed the basis of successful Australian training manuals. In India, where he stayed with Wavell, Stuart lectured and made a BBC radio broadcast about the Argylls in the Malayan campaign.

25. Ibid., p. 35.
26. HQ Malaya Command Operation Instruction no. 2, 26 December 1941, quoted in Moreman, *The Jungle, the Japanese and British Commonwealth Armies at War 1941–1945*, p. 31.
27. Stewart, "The Loss of Singapore—A Criticism", p. 199.
28. Tsuji Masanobu, op. cit., p. 186. A fundamental difficulty in the defence of Malaya and Singapore was the unhelpful attitude of the colonial administration, which pursued its own course of action and entirely ignored military advice. The governor, Sir Miles Shenton Thomas, believed that it was better not to worry the population unduly. On a practical level, he knew little about military matters.
29. Elphick, *Singapore: The Pregnable Fortress*, p. 284.
30. General Sturdee, then chief of the Australian general staff, told Bennett his escape was ill advised, as reported in Wigmore, *The Japanese Thrust*, p. 384. Bennett's own apologia was published in 1944.
31. Montgomery, *Shenton of Singapore*, p. 194.
32. Low and Cheng, *This Singapore: Our City of Dreadful Night*, p. 5.
33. These convictions occurred in the Philippines. There is little evidence that Japanese commanders regarded the savage behaviour of their troops as wrong. On the contrary, they seem to have looked upon rape and murder as a useful method of cowing occupied territories. A notable exception was the summary punishment of five Japanese infantrymen at St. Steven's Hospital in Hong Kong. They had killed patients

in their beds. When this atrocity was pointed out to a Japanese lieutenant, who spoke perfect English, he ordered their immediate identification and execution. But chillingly he said: "Make it be understood that we deal out punishment to anyone who disobeys the Nippon army. I do it to my men. I do it to you with more pleasure. Just give me an excuse." Quoted in Greenhous, *"C" Force to Hong Kong*, p. 116. Here the victims were of course Westerners, not Hong Kong Chinese. "Since the Japanese believed there was no prospect of collaboration from the Chinese community as a whole, they felt free to victimise them," Hicks, *The Comfort Women*, p. 92.

34. Shinozaki Mamoru, *Syonan—My Story*, p. 60.
35. Paley, *The Sparrows*, p. 138.
36. Ibid., p. 153.
37. Marder, *Old Friends, New Enemies. The Royal Navy and the Imperial Japanese Navy. Volume II: The Pacific War, 1942–1945*, p. 59.
38. Connaughton, *McArthur and Defeat in the Philippines*, p. 87.
39. Evans, op. cit., p. 104.
40. The circumstances of the Sandakan death march are well described in Silver, *Sandakan*. Unanswered questions still surround the baffling Australian failure to mount a rescue operation.
41. Slim, op. cit., p. 109.
42. Frederick, *Visions and Heat*, p. 92.
43. Ibid., p. 138.
44. Marr, *Vietnam 1945*, p. 101.
45. Shinozaki Mamoru, op. cit., p. 83.
46. Brands, op. cit., p. 199.
47. Stahl, *You're No Good to Me Dead*, provides details of these clandestine operations.
48. On Subhas Chandra Bose's death, p. 164 of *The Viceroy's Journal*, Wavell's account of his time in India. Even though the Indian National Army proved to be militarily useless to the Japanese, for propaganda purposes, its value was enormous. During the brief defence of Hong Kong in December 1941, it became obvious that Japan's anti-Western appeal to colonial peoples was already having an impact on Indian policemen and soldiers. Sikh members of the constabulary deserted just before the Imperial Japanese Army landed on the island. Orders were given to Japanese troops to spare Indians who had been obliged to fight on the British side. Once they met determined resistance, however, the treatment of prisoners reverted to its usual barbarity. A contingent of Indian soldiers were machine-gunned in the back of a lorry. See Snow, *The Fall of Hong Kong*, p. 80. Subsequent Japanese efforts to woo the Indians had an effect, because 400 Indian POWs captured on the fall of Hong Kong threw off their allegiance to Britain: some joined the Indian National Army in Malaya, others stayed

on to supplement the Japanese garrison, which lost troops to operations in Southeast Asia. One of the duties undertaken by the latter was guarding British civilian internees at Stanley.

49. Slim, op. cit., p. 327.
50. Axell and Kase, *Kamikaze*, p. 49.
51. Ibid., p. 53.
52. Yamashita Tomoyuki's tactics on Luzon, as they appear in *Reports of MacArthur, I–II*, p. 451.
53. Brands, op. cit., p. 209.
54. Johnston, *That Magnificent 9th*, p. 243.
55. Quoted in Ferrell, *Harry S. Truman*, p. 210.
56. Bellamy, *Absolute War*, p. 681.
57. At first Stalin would not accept Truman's exclusion of the Russians from Hokkaido. His climbdown was the first concession that he made to the United States, as cited in Hasegawa, *Racing the Enemy*, p. 271.
58. Butow, *Japan's Decision to Surrender*, p. 170.
59. Among the war criminals hanged at the end of the Pacific War were Tojo Hideki and Yamashita Tomoyuki. The former was executed in Japan, the latter in the Philippines because his crimes against Filipino civilians were considered a sufficient justification for a local trial. Yamashita Tomoyuki's conduct in Singapore was largely ignored.
60. Butow, op. cit., p. 175.
61. Schrijvers, *The GI War against Japan*, p. 261.
62. Louis, *The Ends of British Imperialism*, p. 350. Hong Kong's future was a bone of contention between Roosevelt and Churchill because the American president saw the British colony as a relic of European imperialism. He wanted Hong Kong returned to China as a gesture of goodwill. Since Churchill had come to see Chiang Kai-shek as nothing more than a US puppet, he strongly resisted this idea. The Guomindang had asked for the return of Hong Kong to China on 29 August 1942, the centenary of the Treaty of Nanjing. After Roosevelt's death, President Truman was willing to let the Imperial Japanese Army in Hong Kong surrender the colony to Britain.
63. Wright-Nooth, *Prisoner of the Turnip Heads*, p. 245. After his release from Stanley camp, Wright-Nooth disarmed a Japanese guard outside his old police station and then waited inside for the welcome return of British forces.

Chapter 6

1. Laurens van der Post, *Night of the Full Moon*, p. 271. He goes on to explain how relieved he was that the dropping of the atomic bombs was a terrible enough warning for the Japanese to contemplate surrender seriously. Otherwise, "the continuation of the war would have left them locked in the old situation of a battle of opposites in which their whole

history, culture and psychology would have demanded death in fighting or by their own hand". That Japan surrendered five days after the bombing of Nagasaki convinced Truman he was right to use the new weapon. In his memoirs, he records how "a number of major Japanese military men and diplomats later confirmed that there would have been no quick surrender without it", Truman, *Where the Buck Stops*, p. 206.

2. Gluck; *Japan's Modern Myths*, p. 78.
3. Percival, *The War in Malaya*, p. 326.
4. Harris, *Attlee*, p. 463.
5. Maung Maung, op. cit., p. 157. Mountbatten was aware of Attlee's support for his Burma policy. As a member of the wartime coalition government, the Labour leader did his best to prepare for the post-war situation. Within days of taking office as the British premier, Attlee gave Mountbatten an unusual freedom of action on military grounds, which the supreme commander employed to bring about fundamental political changes in the colony.
6. Ibid., p. 361.
7. Harris, op. cit., p. 361.
8. Slim, op. cit., p. 520.
9. Probert, *The Forgotten Air Force*, p. 276.
10. The Tianjin consul's cable appears in *Foreign Relations of the United States: Diplomatic Papers*, vol. 7, p. 599.
11. Howe, *Anticolonialism in British Politics*, p. 46.
12. Mansergh, *The Transfer of Power*, vol. 9, p. 807.
13. Churchill's outburst about Wavell, 16 March 1945, quoted in Barnes and Davis, *The Empire at Bay*, p. 1032. As Secretary of State for India, Leopold Amery had the difficult task of putting Wavell's suggestions to Churchill. On this occasion, he was relieved that the prime minister had not asked to see the cables exchanged between Wavell and himself because Churchill "would have gone through the roof".
14. Wheeler-Bennett, *King George VI*, p. 170.
15. Ernest Bevin's private letter to Attlee, 1 January 1947, quoted in *The Oxford History of the British Empire*, vol. IV, p. 334.
16. Harris, op. cit., p. 383.
17. Moon, op. cit., p. 1174.
18. Day, *Reluctant Nation*, p. 13.
19. President Eisenhower's letter to Anthony Eden, 30 October 1956, quoted in Boyle, *The Eden–Eisenhower Correspondence*, p. 181. An antiappeaser in the late 1930s, Eden seems to have believed that only firmness with Gamal Abdel Nasser would keep the Soviet Union out of the Arab world. When on 26 July 1956, Nasser announced the nationalisation of the Suez Canal, the British premier thought the moment for action had come. It is possible that this misjudgement had a connection with his frustration at Britain's political weakness because he told his private

secretary that "all the Americans want to do is replace the French in Indochina themselves. They want to replace us in Egypt too. They want to run the world". See Shuckburgh, *Descent to Suez*, p. 187.

20. Dahm, *Sukarno*, p. 234.
21. Cable sent by the American consul general in Batavia to Washington, 31 October 1945, quoted in Gouda and Zaalberg, *American Visions of the Netherlands East Indies/Indonesia*, p. 165.
22. Hudson, *Sunset in the East*, p. 153.
23. *Lukisan Revolsi Rakjat Indonesia*, section for 1946.
24. Bell and Elleman, *Naval Mutinies of the Twentieth Century*, p. 212. Today the memorial to the naval mutiny proudly declares that "the first war of independence in 1857 started the national uprising for freedom. Netaji Subas Chandra Bose's INA revived it in 1941 and the naval uprising of 1946 accelerated India's independence."
25. Edwards, *Crises and Commitments*, p. 34.
26. The British approach to Evatt's diplomacy, cited in Remme, *Britain and Regional Cooperation in South-East Asia*, p. 104.
27. Melby, *The Mandate of Heaven*, p. 32.
28. Bergère, "The Purge of Shanghai", p. 166.
29. Sprenkel, *New China*, p. 4.
30. Stuart, *Fifty Years in China*, p. 242.
31. Chassin, *The Communist Conquest of China*, p. 66.
32. Melby, op. cit., p. 117.
33. Richard Crossman's newspaper article cited in Kynaston, *Austerity Britain*, p. 342.
34. Murfett, *Hostage on the Yangtze*, p. 214.
35. Bodde, *Peking Diary*, p. 103.
36. Quoted in Ferrell, *Harry S. Truman*, p. 316.
37. Ibid., p. 319.
38. Welsh, *A History of Hong Kong*, p. 447.
39. The comment of J. C. Donnelly, FO 371 AN 3447/4/45, Public Record Office, Kew.
40. Bix, *Hirohito and the Making of Modern Japan*, p. 533.
41. Large, *Emperor Hirohito and Showa Japan*, p. 147.
42. Yoshida Shigeru, *The Yoshida Memoirs*, p. 139.
43. Brines, *MacArthur's Japan*, p. 83.
44. Bates, *Japan*, p. 102.
45. Ibid., p. 176.
46. Leffler, *A Preponderance of Power*, p. 100.
47. Aldrich, *Intelligence and the War against Japan*, p. 318.

Chapter 7

1. Goncharov et al., *Uncertain Partners*, p. 153.
2. Zhou Enlai on US aggression, quoted in Jian, *China's Road to the Korean War*, p. 120.

3. The Ulster Rifles incident is reported in Farrar-Hockley, *The British Part in the Korean War*, vol. II, p. 48.

4. Farrar-Hockley, *The Edge of the Sword*, p. 156.

5. LaFeber, *The American Age*, p. 528.

6. McGibbon, *New Zealand and the Korean War*, p. 237.

7. A Pentagon memorandum cited in *The Times*, 14 December 1994.

8. LaFeber, op. cit., p. 549.

9. Williams, *Pétain*, p. 3398.

10. Quoted in Macdonald, *Giap*, p. 62.

11. Marr, *Vietnam 1945*, p.204.

12. Bao Dai's radio appeal to de Gaulle in France, August 1945, ibid., p. 361.

13. Gracey's cable of 21 September 1945 to Mountbatten, cited in Dennis, *Troubled Days of Peace*, p. 39.

14. Macdonald, op. cit., p. 64.

15. Osbourne, *Sihanouk*, ch.4.

16. Simpson, *Dien Bien Phu*, p. 166.

17. White, *Business, Government and the End of Empire*, p. 168.

18. Vyner Brooke's impatience to cede Sarawak to Britain is explained in Brooke, *Queen of the Headhunters*, p. 168.

19. Porritt, *British Colonial Rule in Sarawak 1946–1963*, p. 21.

20. Granville-Edge, *The Sabahan*, p. 159. The use of customary native land was to become a burning issue in Sarawak as well. Its first chief minister, Kalong Ningkan, fell from power in 1966 when he tried to introduce a land bill. His opponents were led by a Kenyah chieftain from the remote interior. See Ritchie, *Temenggong Oyong Lawai Jau*, p. 79.

21. Josey, *Lee Kuan Yew*, p. 384. He went on to say that the island's survival depended upon three things: a stable society which would encourage investment; the capacity of the population to adapt; and the level of promised British aid. "It would be foolish to believe," Lee Kuan Yew warned, "that others can do for us what we as a people and organised as a representative government must do for ourselves."

22. The incredible remark made by Ngo Dinh Diem's sister-in-law is quoted in Buttinger, *Vietnam*, p. 466.

23. Blair, *Lodge in Vietnam*, p. 66.

24. Lafeber, op. cit., p. 606.

25. Ang Cheng Guan, *The Vietnam War from the Other Side*, p. 136.

26. Short, *Pol Pot*, p. 287.

27. Segal, *Defending China*, p. 192.

28. Dommen, *The Indochinese Experience of the French and the Americans*, p. 891.

29. Jones, *Death of a Generation*, p. 443.

30. Blair, op. cit., p. 97.

31. Jones, op. cit., p. 445.

32. Wang, *China's New Order*, p. 48.

33. Bush and Scowcroft, *A World Transformed*, p. 95.

34. George Bush, *All the Best*, p. 436.
35. Yoshida Shigeru, op. cit., p. 286.
36. Barua, *The State at War in South Asia*, p. 163. Described as a gunners' battle, the Pakistani repulse at Naushera was followed by an Indian counter-attack, which depended on close cooperation between infantry and artillery. At Pir Thal Hill, for instance, 24 field guns pinned down the dug-in Pakistani soldiers while Indian infantrymen assaulted the position from two flanks. Only a hasty retreat saved the Pakistanis from being completely overrun.
37. Holland, *European Decolonization 1918–1981*, p. 293.
38. Horne, *Macmillan 1957–1986*, p. 416.
39. Kahin and Kahin, *Subversion as Foreign Policy*, p. 22.
40. *The Jakarta Post*, 9 February 2007. The front-page article underlined Jakarta's earnest hope for future cooperation, rather than the usual state of conflict. Its spokesman at the ceremony in Banda Aceh said that partnership between the state and the central government should typify the new governor's term of office.
41. Fang and Fang, *Zhou Enlai*, p. 109.
42. Kahin and Kahin, op. cit., p. 226.
43. Wray, *Timor 1942*, p. 77.
44. Nobel Peace Prize citation, quoted in Kohen, *From the Place of the Dead*, p. 176.
45. Tinker, *Burma*, vol. II, p. 759.
46. Slim, op. cit., p. 113.
47. Ibid., p. 499.

Postscript

1. Heseltine, *Life in the Jungle*, p.459.
2. "The Great Chinese Takeaway", *The Times*, 13 February 2006. Prince Charles found Chris Patten's speech so "moving" that he ended up with a "lump" in his throat. What he disliked most about the handover ceremony was "at the end of this awful Soviet-style display we had to watch the Chinese soldiers goose-step on to the stage and haul down the Union Jack and raise the ultimate flag". The prince especially hated "the artificial way in which the flags were made to flutter enticingly". But he admitted that the Chinese foreign minister, next to whom he sat at a banquet, "must have had considerable difficulty in knowing what to make of me".

Bibliography

Abernethy, D. B., *The Dynamics of Global Dominance. European Overseas Empires 1415–1980*, New Haven, 2000.

Adams, Henry, *Letters of Henry Adams (1892–1918)* (ed.), W.C. Ford, Boston, 1938.

Agawa, Hiroyuki, *The Reluctant Admiral: Yamamoto and the Imperial Navy*, translated by J. Bester, Tokyo, 1979.

Ageron, C., *L'Anticolonialisme en France de 1871 à 1914*, Paris, 1973.

Albuquerque, Alfonso de, *The Commentaries of the Great Alfonso Dalboquerque, Second Viceroy of India*, translated by W. de Gray Birch, London, 1874.

Aldous, R., *Macmillan, Eisenhower and the Cold War*, Dublin, 2005.

Aldrich, R., *Greater France. A History of French Overseas Expansion*, Basingstoke, 1996.

Alfian, Teuku Ibrahim, "Aceh Sultanate under Sultan Mohammed Daud–syah and the Dutch War", in Sartono Kartodirdjo (ed.), *Profiles of Malay Culture, Historiography, Religion and Politics*, Jakarta, 1976.

Allen, L., *Japan, the Years of Triumph*, London, 1970.

——, *Singapore 1941–1942*, London, 1977.

——, *Burma. The Longest War 1941–45*, London, 1984.

Allmand, C., *The Hundred Years War, c. 1300–c. 1400*, Cambridge, 1988.

Ames, G. J., *Colbert, Mercantilism and the French Quest for Asian Trade*, Dekalb, Illinois, 1996.

Ambrose, S. E., *Rise to Globalism. American Foreign Policy Since 1938*, New York, 1971.

Andaya, L. Y., *The Kingdom of Johor, 1641–1728, Economic and Political Developments*, Kuala Lumpur, 1975.

——, *The Heritage of Arung Palakka: A History of South Sulawesi (Celebes) in the Seventeenth Century*, The Hague, 1981.

Anderson, B. R. O'G., *Java in a Time of Revolution and Resistance, 1944–1946*, Ithaca, 1972.

Anderson, J., *Mission to the East Coast of Sumatra in 1823*, London, 1826, reissued Kuala Lumpur, 1971.

Andrew, C. M., and Kanya–Forstner, A. S., *France Overseas: the First World War and the Climax of French Imperial Expansion*, London, 1981.

Andrews, K. R., *Trade, Plunder and Settlement. Maritime Enterprise and the Genesis of the British Empire*, Cambridge, 1984.

Ang Cheng Guan, *The Vietnam War from the Other Side. The Vietnamese Communists' Perspective*, London, 2002.

Arasaratnam, S., *Dutch Power in Ceylon 1658–1687*, Amsterdam, 1958.

——, *Merchants, Companies and Commerce on the Coromandel Coast, 1650–1740*, Delhi, 1986.

Atwell, P., *British Mandarins and Chinese Reformers: The British Administration of Weihaiwei (1898–1930) and the Territory's Return to Chinese Rule*, Oxford, 1985.

Aubin, J., "L'Apprentissage de l'Inde. Cochin, 1503–1504", *Moyen Orient et Ocean Indien*, 4, 1987.

——, "D. João II Devant Sa Succession", *Arquivos do Centro Cultural Portugues*, 27, 1991.

——, "Ormuz au Jour le Jour à Travers un Registre de Luis Figueira, 1516–1518", *Arquivos do Centro Cultural Portugues*, 32, 1993.

Aung–Thwin, M., *Pagan: The Origins of Modern Burma*, Honolulu, 1985.

Axell, A., and Kase, H., *Kamikaze. Japan's Suicide Gods*, London, 2002.

Aymonier, E., *Notes sur le Laos*, Saigon, 1885.

Aziz, M. A., *Japan's Colonialism and Indonesia*, The Hague, 1955.

Azurara, Gomes Eannes de, *Cronica de Ceuta*. It is translated as *Conquests and Discoveries of Henry the Navigator, being the chronicles of Azurara*, by Virginia de Castro e Almeida, London,1936,

Baer, G. W., *One Hundred Years of Sea Power. The US Navy, 1890–1990*, Stanford, 1993.

Baiao, Antonio, Magalhaes Basto, A. de. and Peres, Damiao (eds.), *Diario da Viagem de Vasco da Gama*, Lisbon, 1945.

Bandele, Biyi, *Burma Boy*, London, 2007.

Banno, Masataka, *China and the West 1833–1860*, Cambridge, Massachusetts, 1964.

Barnes, J., and Nicholson, D. (eds.), *The Empire at Bay: The Leo Amery Diaries*, London, 1988.

Barnett, R., *North India Between Empires: Avadh, the Mughals and the British, 1720–1801*, Berkeley, 1980.

Barnhart, M. A., *Japan Prepares for Total War. The Search for Economic Security, 1919–1941*, Ithaca, 1987.

Barros, João de, *Décadas da Ásia*, originally published 1552–1615. A facsimile edition of the 1777–1778 Regia Oficina Tipografia edition was published by Livaria Sam Carlos, Lisbon, during the 1970s.

Barua, D. P., *The State at War in South Asia*, Lincoln, Nebraska, 2005.

Bastin, J., *The native policies of Sir Stamford Raffles in Java and Sumatra: An economic interpretation*, Oxford, 1957.

Bates, P., *Japan and the British Commonwealth Occupation Force 1947–52*, London, 1993.

Battesti, M., *Trafalgar: les aleas de la strategie navale de Napoleon*, Paris, 2004.

Bayly, C. R., *Imperial Meridian: The British Empire and the World 1780–1830*, London, 1989.

Bayly, C. R., *The New Cambridge History of India*, vol. II. 1, *Indian Society and the Making of the British Empire*, Cambridge, 1988.

——, *The Raj: India and the British 1600–1947*, London, 1990.

——, *The Birth of the Modern World 1780–1914*, Oxford, 2004.

—— and Harper, T., *Forgotten Armies. The Fall of British Asia 1941–1945*, London, 2004.

—— and Harper, T., *Forgotten Wars. The End of Britain's Asian Empire*, London, 2007.

Bearce, G. D., *British Attitudes Towards India, 1784–1858*, Oxford, 1961.

Beasley, W. G., *Japanese Imperialism 1894–1945*, Oxford, 1987.

——, *Japan Encounters the Barbarian. Japanese Travellers in America and Europe*, New Haven, 1995.

Beightler, R. S., *Report on the Activities of the 37th Infantry Division 1940–1945*, Washington, 1945.

Bell, C. M., and Elleman, B. A., *Naval Mutinies in the Twentieth Century. An International Perspective*, London, 2003.

Bellamy, C., *Absolute War, Soviet Russia in the Second World War*, Basingstoke, 2007.

Beranger, J., and Meyer, J., *La France dans le Monde au XVIIIe Siècle*, Paris, 1993.

Bergère, Marie-Claire, *Su Yat–sen*, translated by J. Lloyd, Stanford, 1998.

——, "The Purge in Shanghai, 1945–46: the Sarly Affair and the End of the French Concession", in *Wartime Shanghai*, edited by Wen-hsin Yeh, London, 1998.

Best, A., Britain, *Japan and Pearl Harbor. Avoiding a War in East Asia*, London, 1995.

Betts, R., *Assimilation and Association in French Colonial Theory, 1890–1914*, New York, 1961.

Bickers, R. A., "Shanghailanders: The Formation and Identity of the British Settler Community in Shanghai, 1843–1937", *Past and Present*, CLIX, May, 1998.

Bizot, F., *The Gate*, translated by E. Cameron, London, 2003.

Black, I., *A Gambling Style of Government: The Establishment of Chartered Company Rule in Sabah, 1878–1915*, Kuala Lumpur, 1971.

Black, J., *War and the World. Military Power and the Fate of Continents 1450–2000*, New Haven, 1998.

Blair, A. E., *Lodge in Vietnam. A Patriot Abroad*, New Haven, 1995.

Blussé, L., "Brief Encounters at Macao", *Modern Asian Studies*, xxi, 3, 1988.

——, *Strange Company: Chinese Settlers, Mestizo Women and the Dutch in VOC Batavia*, Dordrecht, 1986.

Bodde, D., *Peking Diary. A Year of Revolution*, London, 1951.

Bond, B., and Kyoichi Tachikawa, *British and Japanese Military Leadership in the Far Eastern War, 1941–1945*, London, 2004.

Bonner, R., *Waltzing with a Dictator. The Marcoses and the Making of American Policy*, London, 1987.

Boomgaard, P., *Children of the Colonial State: Population Growth and Economic Development in Java, 1795–1880*, Amsterdam, 1989.

Borg, D., *The United States and the Far Eastern Crisis of 1933–1938*, Cambridge, Massachusetts, 1964.

Bose, R., *A Will for Freedom: Netaji and the Indian Independence Army in Singapore and Southeast Asia, 1943–1945*, Singapore, 1993.

Bose, S., *A Hundred Horizons. The Indian Ocean in the Age of Global Empire*, Cambridge, Massachusetts, 2006.

Bouchon, G., *Albuquerque, le lion des mers d'Asie*, Paris, 1992.

—— and Thomaz, L. F., *Voyage dans les Deltas du Gange et de l'Irraouaddy. Relation Portuguese Anonyme (1521)*, Centre Culturel Portugais, Paris, 1988.

Bowen, H. V., Lincoln M. and Rigby, N. (eds), *The Worlds of the East India Company*, Woodbridge, 2002.

Boxer, C. R., "The Siege of Fort Zeelandia and the Capture of Formosa from the Dutch, 1661–6", *Transactions and Proceedings of the Japan Society of London*, xxiv, 1926–1927.

——, *The Christian Century in Japan*, Berkeley, 1951.

——, *A Portuguese Embassy to Japan (1644–1647)*, London, 1953.

——, *South China in the Sixteenth Century. Being the Narratives of Galeote Pereira et al*, London, 1953.

——, *The Great Ship from Amaco. Annals of Macao and the Old Japan Trade*, Lisbon, 1959.

——, "Portuguese and Dutch Colonial Rivalry, 1641–1661", *Centro dos Estudaos Historicos Ultramarinos*, Lisbon, 1958.

——, *Race Relations in the Portuguese Colonial Empire, 1415–1825*, Oxford, 1963.

——, "Asian Potentates and European Artillery in the 16th–18th Centuries", *Journal of the Malay Branch, Royal Asiatic Society*, xxvii, 2, 1965.

——, *The Dutch Seaborne Empire, 1600–1800*, London, 1965.

——, *Fidalgos in the Far East, 1550–1770*, Oxford, 1968.

——, *The Portuguese Seaborne Empire*, New York, 1969.

——, "A Note on Portuguese Reactions to the Revival of the Red Sea Trade and the rise of Atzeh, 1540–1600", *Journal of Southeast Asian Studies*, x, 3, 1969.

——, "Portuguese and Spanish Projects for the Conquest of Southeast Asia, 1580–1600", *Journal of Southeast Asian Studies*, x, 3, 1969.

——, *Jan Companie in War and Peace, 1602–1799. A Short History of the Dutch East India Company*, Hong Kong, 1979.

——, *João de Barros. Portuguese Humanist and Historian of Asia*, New Delhi, 1981.

——, *Portuguese Conquest and Commerce in Southeast Asia, 1500–1700*, London, 1985.

——, *Portuguese Merchants and Missionaries in Feudal Japan*, London, 1986.

Boyajian, J. C., *Portuguese Trade in Asia under the Habsburgs, 1580–1640*, Baltimore, 1993.

Boyle, J. H., *China and Japan at War 1937–1945. The Politics of Collaboration*, Stanford, 1972.

Boyle, P. G. (ed.), *The Eden–Eisenhower Correspondence, 1955–1957*, Chapel Hill, 2005.

Brand, M., *Fighter Squadron at Guadalcanal*, Annapolis, 1996.

Brands, H. W., *Bound to Empire. The United States and the Philippines*, Oxford, 1991.

Brendon, P., *The Decline and Fall of the British Empire 1781–1997*, London, 2007.

Brewer, J., *The Sinews of Power: War, Money and the English State 1688–1783*, London, 1989.

Brines, M., *MacArthur's Japan*, New York, 1948.

Brocheux, P., *Ho Chi Minh. A Biography*, translated by C. Duiker, Cambridge, 2007.

Broeze, F. (ed.), *Bridges of the Sea. Port Cities of Asia from the 16th to 20th Centuries*, Honolulu, 1989.

Brook, T., *Collaboration. Japanese Agents and Local Elites in Wartime China*, Cambridge, Maassachusetts, 2005.

Brooke, James, *Narrative of Events in Borneo and Celebes Down to the Occupation of Labuan: From the Journals of J. Brooke*, London, 1848.

Brooke, S. L., *Queen of the Headhunters. The Autobiography of H. H. the Hon. Sylvia Lady Brooke*, London, 1970.

Brown, J. M. (ed.), *The Oxford History of the British Empire*, vol. 4: "The Twentieth Century", Oxford, 1999.

Brown, M., *War in Shangri–la. A Memoir of Civil War in Laos*, London, 2001.

Bruijin, J. R., *The Dutch Navy of the Seventeenth and Eighteenth Centuries*, Columbia, South Carolina, 1993.

——, Gaastra, F. S., and Schoffer, I. (eds.), *Ships, Sailors and Spices. East India Companies and their Shipping in the 16th, 17th and 18th Centuries*, Amsterdam, 1993.

Brune, P., *Those Ragged Bloody Heroes. From the Kokoda Trail to Gona Beach 1942*, Sydney, 1991.

——, *A Bastard of a Place. The Australians in Papua. Kokoda. Milne Bay. Gona. Buna, Sanananda*, Crows Nest, New South Wales, 2003.

Brunschwig, H., *French Colonialism 1871–1914. Myths and Realities*, London, 1966.

Buber, M., *Pointing the Way*, translated by M. Friedman, London, 1953.

Buckley, R., *Occupation Diplomacy: Britain, the United States and Japan 1945–1952*, Cambridge, 1982.

——, *The United States in the Asia–Pacific Since 1945*, Cambridge, 2002.

Bullock, A., *Ernest Bevin: Foreign Secretary, 1945–1951*, London, 1983.

Burton, R., *Railway of Hell. War, Captivity and Forced Labour at the Hands of the Japanese*, Barnsley, 2002.

Bush, G., *All the Best: My Life in Letters and Other Writings*, New York, 1999.

Butcher, J. G., *The British in Malaya 1880–1941. The Social History of a European Community in Colonial South-East Asia*, Oxford, 1979.

Butow, R. T. C., *Japan's Decision to Surrender*, Stanford, 1954.

——, *Tojo and the Coming of War*, Stanford, 1981.

Buttinger, J., *Vietnam: A Political History*, New York, 1968.

Cady, J. F., *The Roots of French Imperialism in East Asia*, Ithaca, 1954.

——, *A History of Burma*, Ithaca, 1958.

Cain, P. J. and Hopkins, A. G., *British Imperialism: Innovation and Expansion 1688–1914*, London, 1993.

——, *British Imperialism: Crisis and Deconstruction, 1914–2000*, London, 1993.

Callahan, R., *The East India Company and Army Reform, 1783–1798*, Cambridge, Massachusetts, 1972.

Cannadine, D., *Ornamentalism: How the British Saw Their Empire*, London, 2001.

Carruthers, S. L., *Winning Hearts and Minds: British Governments, the Media and Colonial Counter-Insurgency, 1944–1960*, London, 1995.

Castesão, A. (ed.), *A Suma Oriental de Tomé Pires e o Livro de Francisco Rodrigues*, Coimbra, 1978.

Castle, T. N., *At War in the Shadow of Vietnam. US Military Aid to the Royal Lao Government, 1955–1975*, New York, 1993.

Cavaliero, R., *Admiral Satan. The Life and Campaigns of Suffren*, London, 1994.

Chan Lau Kit–ching, *China, Britain and Hong Kong, 1895–1945*, London, 1990.

Chandler, D. P., *A History of Cambodia*, Boulder, Colorado, 1983.

Chang, I., *The Rape of Nanking. The Forgotten Holocaust of World War II*, New York, 1997.

Chang, T'ien–tse, *Sino–Portuguese Trade from 1514 to 1644. A Synthesis of Portuguese and Chinese Sources*, Leyden, 1934.

Chappell, J. D., *Before the Bomb. How America Approached the End of the Pacific War*, Lexington, Kentucky, 1997.

Charlesworth, N., *British Rule and the Indian Economy, 1800–1914*, London, 1982.

Chassin, L. M., *The Communist Conquest of China. A History of Civil War, 1945–1949*, translated by T. Osato and L. Gelas, London, 1965.

Chaudhuri, K. N., *The Trading World of Asia and the English East India Company 1660–1760*, Cambridge, 1978.

——, *Trade and Civilisation in the Indian Ocean. An Economic History from the Rise of Islam to 1750*, Cambridge, 1985.

Chaunu, P., *L'expansion europeene du XIIIe au XVe siècle*, Paris, 1983.

Ch'en, J., *Mao and the Chinese Revolution*, Oxford, 1965.

Chin Kee Onn, *Malaya Upside Down*, Singapore, 1946.

Chinnery, P. D., *March or Die. The Story of Wingate's Chindits*, Shrewsbury, 1997.

Chippington, G., *Singapore. The Inexcusable Betrayal*, Hanley Swan, 1992.

Chon, Won-loy, *Burma. The Untold Story*, Novato, California, 1986.

Clayton, A., *The British Empire as a Superpower, 1919–1939*, London, 1986.

——, *The Wars of French Decolonization*, London, 1994.

Clements, J., *Pirate King. Coxinga and the Fall of the Ming Dynasty*, Stroud, 2004.

Clemens, M., *Alone on Guadalcanal. A Coastwatcher's Story*, Annapolis, 1998.

Clifford, C., *Retreat from China: British Policy in the Far East, 1937–1941*, London, 1967.

Clodd, H. P., *Malaya's First British Pioneer: The Life of Francis Light*, London, 1948.

Clymer, K., *The United States and Cambodia, 1969–2000. A Troubled Relationship*, London, 2004.

Coates, A., *A Macao Narrative*, Hong Kong 1987.

Coates, J., *Bravery Above Blunder. The 9th Australian Division at Finschhafen, Sattelberg and Sio*, Melbourne, 1999.

Coble, P. M., *Facing Japan: Chinese Politics and Japanese Imperialism*, Cambridge, Massachuetts, 1991.

Coen, T. C., *The Indian Political Service: A Study in Indirect Rule*, London, 1971.

Cohen, P. A., *History in Three Keys: The Boxers as Event, Experience and Myth*, New York, 1997.

Cohen, S. P., *The Pakistan Army*, Berkeley, 1984.

Collis, M., *Raffles*, London, 1966.

Collar, H., *Captive in Shanghai*, Hong Kong, 1990.

Colvin, J., *Not Ordinary Men. The Battle of Kohima Re-assessed*, London, 1994.

Connaughton, R., *MacArthur and Defeat in the Philippines*, New York, 2001.

——, Pimlot, J. and Anderson, D., *The Battle for Manila. The Most Devastating Untold Story of World War II*, London, 1995.

Cookson, J. E., *The British Armed Nation 1793–1815*, Oxford, 1997.

Coombes, D., *Morshead. Hero of Tobruk and El Alamein*, Melbourne, 2007.

Cooper, K. W., *The Little Men. A Platoon's Epic Fight in the Burma Campaign*, London, 1973.

Cooper, M. (ed.), *The Southern Barbarians: the First Europeans in Japan*, Tokyo, 1971.

Cooper, R. G. S., *The Anglo-Maratha Campaigns and the Contest for India. The Struggle for Control of the South Asian Military Economy*, Cambridge, 2003.

Coox, A. D., *The Anatomy of a Small War. The Soviet-Japanese Struggle for Changkufeng/Khasan*, 1938, Westport, 1977.

——, *Nomonhan. Japan against Russia, 1939*, Stanford, 1985.

——, *The Unfought War: Japan 1941–1942*, San Diego, 1992.

Correia–Alfonso, J. (ed.), *Indo–Portuguese History: Sources and Problems*, Bombay, 1981.

—— (ed.), *Intrepid Itinerant. Manuel Godinho and his Journey from India to Portugal in 1663*, Bombay, 1990.

Corrigan, G., *Wellington. A Military Life*, London, 2001.

Cotterell, A., *The Imperial Capitals of China. An Inside View of the Celestial Empire*, London, 2007.

Cowan, C. D., *Nineteenth–Century Malaya: The Origins of British Political Control*, London, 1961.

Cranmer-Byng, J. L., *An Embassy to China. Being the journal kept by Lord Macartney during his embassy to Emperor Ch'ien-long 1793–1794*, London, 1962.

Crosby, Sir J., *Siam: The Crossroads*, London, 1945.

Crossley, P., *A Translucent Mirror: History and Identity in Qing Imperial Ideology*, Berkeley, 1999.

Crouch, H., *The Army and Politics in Indonesia*, Ithaca, 1988.

Crouzet, F., *De la superiorite de l'Angleterre sur la France: l'economique et l'imaginaire, XVIIe–XXe siècles*, Paris, 1999.

Currey, C. B., *Victory at Any Cost. The Genius of Viet Nam's Gen. Vo Nguyen Giap*, London, 1997.

da Costa, A. Fontoura (ed.), *Roteiro da Primeira Viagem de Vasco da Gama (1497–1499)*, Lisbon 1969.

Dahm, B., *Sukarno and the Struggle for Indonesian Independence*, translated by M. F. Somers, Heidhus, 1969.

Dalrymple, W., *The Last Mughal. The Fall of a Dynasty, Delhi, 1857*, London, 2006.

Danvers, F. C., *The Portuguese in India*, London, 1894.

Darby, P., *British Defence Policy East of Suez 1947–1968*, Oxford, 1973.

Darwin, J., *The End of the British Empire: The Historical Debate*, Oxford, 1991.

Das Gupta, A. K., "Aceh in the Seventeenth Century Asian Trade", *Bengal Past and Present*, 81,1, 1962.

David, S., *Victoria's Wars. The Rise of Empire*, London, 2006.

Davison, P. B., *Vietnam at War: The History 1946–1975*, Novato, California, 1988.

Davis, R., *The Industrial Revolution and British Overseas Trade*, Leicester, 1979.

Day, C., *The Policy and Administration of the Dutch in Java*, New York, 1904.

Day, D., *The Great Betrayal. Britain, Australia and the Onset of the Pacific War 1939–42*, Melbourne, 1988.

Day, D., *Menzies and Churchill at War*, Melbourne, 1993.

De Carne, L., *Voyage en Indo-Chine et dans l'Empire Chinois*, Paris, 1872.

De Graaf, H. J., *Islamic States in Java 1500–1700*, The Hague, 1975.

Dc Madariaga, I., *Ivan the Terrible*, New Haven, 2005.

de Silva, C. R., *Sri Lanka: A History*, New Delhi, 1989.

——, *The Portuguese in Ceylon 1617–1638*, Columbo, 1972.

de Silva, K. M., *A History of Sri Lanka*, London, 1981.

Dennett, T., *Roosevelt and the Russo–Japanese War*, New York, 1925.

Dennis, P., *Troubled Days of Peace. Mountbatten and South East Asia Command, 1945–1946*, Manchester, 1987.

Devillers, P., *L'Histoire du Vietnam de 1940 à 1952*, Paris, 1952.

Dewey, C., *Anglo-Indian Attitudes. The Mind of the Indian Civil Service*, London, 1993.

Dewey, G., *Autobiography of George Dewey, Admiral of the Navy*, New York, 1916.

Diffie, B. W., and Winnius, G. D., *Foundations of the Portuguese Empire*, Minneapolis, 1977.

Dirks, N. B., *The Scandal of Empire. India and the Creation of Imperial Britain*, Cambridge, Massachusetts, 2006.

Disney, A. R., *Twilight of the Pepper Empire: Portuguese Trade in Southwest India in the Early Seventeenth Century*, Cambridge, Massachusetts, 1978.

Dobson, J., *Reticent Expansionism: The Foreign Policy of William McKinley*, Pittsburgh, 1988.

Dockrill, S., *Britain's Retreat from the East of Suez. The Choice Between Europe and the World*, Basingstoke, 2002.

Documents on British Foreign Policy 1919–1939. Second Series, vol. XXI. Far Eastern Affairs, November 6, 1936–July 27, 1938, London, 1984.

Dodge, E. S., *Islands and Empires. Western Impact on the Pacific and East Asia*, Oxford, 1976.

Dodwell, H., *Dupleix and Clive: The Beginning of Empire*, London, 1920.

Dommen, A. J., *The Indochinese Experience of the French and the Americans. Nationalism and Communism in Cambodia, Laos and Vietnam*, Bloomington , 2001.

Dower, J. W., *Empire and Aftermath: Yoshida Shigeru and the Japanese Experience 1878–1954*, Cambridge, Massacusetts, 1979.

Drachman, E. R., *United States Policy Toward Vietnam, 1940–1945*, Cranbury, New Jersey, 1970.

Dreyer, E. L., *Zheng He. China and the Oceans in the Early Ming Dynasty, 1405–1433*, New York, 2007.

Duara, P. (ed.), *Decolonization. Prospectives from now and then*, London, 2004.

Duiker, W. J., *The Communist Road to Power in Vietnam*, Boulder, Colorado, 1981.

——, *Sacred War: Nationalism and Revolution in a Divided Vietnam*, New York, 1995.

——, *Ho Chi Minh, A Life*, New York, 2000.

Dunn, P. M., *The First Vietnam War*, London, 1985.

Durand, Sir H. M., *The First Afghan War and its Causes*, London, 1879.

Durrani, M. K., *The Sixth Column*, London, 1955.

Duus, P., *The Abacus and the Sword: The Japanese Penetration of Korea 1895–1910*, Berkeley, 1995.

Earle, T. F. and Villiers, J., *Albuquerque, Caesar of the East: Selected Texts by Alfonso de Albuquerque and His Son*, Warminster, 1990.

Eastman, L. E., *The Abortive Revolution: China Under Nationalist Rule 1927–1937*, Cambridge, Massachusetts, 1974.

Eckert, C. J., *Offspring of Empire. The Koch'ang Kims and the Colonial Origins of Korean Capitalism 1874–1945*, Seattle, 1991.

Eddy, J. and Schreuder, D. (eds.), *The Rise of Colonial Nationalism: Australia, New Zealand, Canada and South Africa First Assert Their Nationalities, 1880–1914*, Sydney, 1988.

Edgerton, D., *England and the Aeroplane. An Essay on a Militant and Technological Nation*, Basingstoke, 1991.

——, *Warfare State. Britain, 1920–1970*, Cambridge, 2006.

Edwards, A., *Saigon. Mistress of the Mekong*, Oxford, 2003.

Edwards, E. W., *British Diplomacy and Finance in China , 1895–1914*, Oxford, 1987.

Edwards, P., *A Nation at War: Australian Politics, Society and Diplomacy During the Vietnam War, 1965–1975*, London, 1977.

——, *Crises and Commitments. The Politics and Diplomacy of Australia's Involvement in Southeast Asian Conflicts*, Sydney, 1992.

Eichelberger, R. L., *Our Jungle Road to Tokyo*, Nashville, 1989.

Elphick, R., *Singapore: the Pregnable Fortress. A Study in Deception, Discord and Desertion*, London, 1995.

——, *Far Eastern File. The Intelligence War in the Far East 1930–1945*, London, 1997.

Endicott, S. L., *Diplomacy and Enterprise. British China Policy, 1933–1937*, Manchester, 1975.

Evans, D. C. (ed.), *The Japanese Navy in World War II. In the Words of Former Japanese Naval Officers*, Annapolis, 1986.

Evans, D. C. and Peattie, M. R., *Kaigun. Strategy, Tactics and Technology in the Imperial Japanese Navy 1887–1941*, Annapolis, 1997.

Fairbank, J. K. (ed.), *The Cambridge History of China*, vol. 10, part I: *Late Ch'ing*, Cambridge, 1978.

Fang, P. J. and Fang, L. G. J., *Zhou Enlai—A Profile*, Beijing, 1986.

Farrar-Hockley, A., *The Edge of the Sword*, London, 1954.

——, *The British Part in the Korean War*, London, 1995.

Fay, P. W., *The Forgotten Army. India's Armed Struggle for Independence 1942–1945*, Ann Arbor, 1993.

Fergusson, B., *Beyond the Chindwin. Being an Account of the Adventures of Number Five Column of the Wingate Expedition into Burma, 1943*, London, 1945.

Ferrell, R. H., *Harry S. Truman. A Life*, Columbia, Missouri, 1994.

Feuer, A. B., *Australian Commandos. Their Secret War Against the Japanese in WW II*, Mechanicsburg, Pennysylvania, 1996.

Filesi, T., *China and Africa in the Middle Ages*, translated by D. L. Morison, London, 1972.

Fitzgerald, C. P., *China and Southeast Asia since 1945*, London, 1973.

Flores, J. M., "The Straits of Ceylon and the Maritime Trade in Early Sixteenth-Century India: Commodities, Merchants and Trading Networks", *Moyen Orient et Ocean Indien*, 7, 1990.

Flores, J. and Vassallo e Silva, N. (eds.), *Goa and the Great Mughal*, Lisbon, 2004.

Flynn, G. Q., *The Draft, 1940–1973*, Lawrence, Kansas, 1993.

Fok, K. C., "Early Ming Images of the Portuguese", in R. Ptak (ed.), *Portuguese Asia. Aspects of History and Economic History*, Stuttgart, 1987.

Ford, R. E., *Tet 1968. Understanding the Surprise*, London, 1995.

Foreign Relations of the United States: Diplomatic Papers, 1945, vol. 7, Washington, 1949–1969.

Forrest, Sir G. W., *The Life of Lord Clive*, London, 1918.

Frederick, W. H., *Visions and Heat. The Making of the Indonesian Revolution*, Athens, Ohio, 1989.

Freeman, D. B., *The Straits of Malacca. Gateway or Gauntlet?*, Montreal, 2003.

Friedberg, A. L., *The Weary Titan: Britain and the Experience of Relative Decline, 1895–1905*, Princeton, 1988.

Furber, H., *Rival Empires of Trade in the Orient 1600–1800*, Minneapolis, 1976.

——, *John Company at Work: a Study of European Expansion in India in the Late Eighteenth Century*, Cambridge, Massachusetts, 1948.

Gallagher, J., *The Decline, Revival and Fall of the British Empire*, Cambridge, 1982.

Gallagher, O. D., *Retreat in the East*, London, 1942.

Garnier, D., *Ayutthaya. Venice of the East*, Bangkok, 2004.

Garnier, F. et al., *Voyage d'exploration en Indo-chine effectué pendant les années 1886, 1867 et 1868*, Paris, 1873.

Gasster, M., *Chinese Intellectuals and the Revolution of 1911*, Seattle, 1968.

Ghosh, K. K., *The Indian National Army*, Meerut, 1969.

Ghosh, L., *Burma: Myth of French Intrigue*, Calcutta, 1994.

Gilchrist, Sir. A., *Malaya 1941. The Fall of a Fighting Empire*, London, 1992.

Gillin, D. G., *Warlord Yen Hsi-shan in Shansi Province 1911–1949*, Princeton, 1967.

Gilmour, D., *Curzon*, London, 1994.

Glamann, K., *Dutch-Asiatic Trade, 1620–1740*, Copenhagen, 1958.

Glantz, D. M., *Soviet Operational and Tactical Combat in Manchuria, 1945. "August Storm"*, London, 2003.

Gluck, C., *Japan's Modern Myths. Ideology in the Late Meiji Period*, Princeton, 1985.

——, and Graubard, S. R. (eds.), *Showa. The Japan of Hirohito*, New York, 1992.

Gois, Damiao de, *Cronica do Felicissmo Rei Dom Manuel*, Coimbra, 1949–1955.

Goldsworthy, D., *Colonial Issues in British Politics, 1945–1961*, Oxford, 1971.

Goncharov, S. N., Lewis J. W. and Xue Litai, *Uncertain Partners. Stalin, Mao and the Korean War*, Stanford, 1993.

Goodman, G. K., *The Dutch Impact on Japan (1640–1853)*, Leiden, 1967.

Goonewardena, K. W., *The Foundation of Dutch Power in Ceylon, 1638–1658*, Amsterdam, 1958.

Gopal, S., *British Policy in India, 1858–1905*, Cambridge, 1965.

Gottesman, E., *Cambodia after the Khmer Rouge. Inside the Politics of Nation Building*, New Haven, 2003.

Gould, L. L., *The Presidency of William McKinley*, Lawrence, Kansas, 1980.

Gow, I., *Military Intervention in Pre-war Japanese Politics. Admiral Kato Kanji and the "Washington System"*, London, 2004.

Grant, I. L., *Burma: The Turning Point. The Seven Battles on the Tiddim Road Which Turned the Tide of the Burma War*, Chichester, 1993.

Grant, I. L. and Kazuo Tamayama, *Burma 1942: The Japanese Invasion. Both Sides Tell the Story of a Savage Jungle War*, Chichester, 1999.

Granville–Edge, P. J., *The Sabahan. The Life and Death of Tun Fuad Stephens*, Dataran Palma, Selangor, 1999.

Green, D., *Captured at the Imjin River. The Korean War Memoirs of a Gloster, 1950–1953*, Barnsley, 2003.

Greenhous, B., *"C" Force to Hong Kong. A Canadian Catastrophe, 1941–1945*, Toronto, 1997.

Grewal, J. S., *The Sikhs of the Punjab*, Cambridge, 1994.

Grigg, J., *Lloyd George. War Leader 1916–1918*, London, 2002.

Gullick, J. M., *Rulers and Residents: Influence and Power in the Malay States, 1870–1920*, Singapore, 1992.

Gupta, P. S., *Imperialism and the British Labour Movement*, London, 1975.

Hack, K., and Blackburn, K., *Did Singapore Have to Fall? Churchill and the Impregnable Fortress*, London, 2004.

Haggie, P., *Britannia at Bay: The Defence of the British Empire Against Japan 1931–1941*, Oxford, 1981.

Hall, C., *Britain, America and Arms Control 1921–1937*, London, 1987.

Hall, D. H., *British Strategy in the Napoleonic War, 1803–1815*, Manchester, 1992.

Hall, K. R., *Maritime Trade and State Development in Early Southeast Asia*, Honolulu, 1985.

Halpern, P. G., *A Naval History of World War I*, London, 1994.

Harding, R. (ed.), *The Royal Navy, 1930–2000. Innovation and Defence*, London, 2005.

Harper, L. A., *The English Navigation Acts*, New York, 1939.

Harries, M. and S., *Soldiers of the Sun. The Rise and Fall of the Imperial Japanese Army*, New York, 1991.

Harris, K., *Attlee*, London, 1982.

Harrison, B., "Malacca in the 18th century: Two Dutch Governors' Reports", *Journal of the Malay Branch, Royal Asiatic Society*, 27, 1, 1954.

Harvey, G. E., *British Rule in Burma: 1824–1942*, London, 1944.

Hasegawara, Tsuyoshi, *Racing the Enemy. Stalin, Truman and the Surrender of Japan*, Cambridge, Massachusetts, 2005.

Haslem, J., *The Soviet Union and the Threat from the East, 1933–41. Moscow, Tokyo and the Prelude to the Pacific War*, Basingstoke, 1992.

Haudrere, P., *La Compagnie Francaise des Indes au XVIIIe siècle 1719–1795*, Paris, 1989.

Havinden, M. and Meredith D., *Colonialism and Development. Britain and its Tropical Colonies, 1850–1960*, London, 1993.

Hayashi Saburo, with A. D. Coox, *Kogun. The Japanese Army in the Pacific War*, Tokyo, 1980.

Headrick, D. R., *The Tools of Empire: Technology and European Imperialism in the Nineteenth Century*, New York, 1991.

Heathcote, T. A., *The Military in British India. The Development of British Land Forces in South Asia, 1600–1947*, Manchester, 1995.

Heinlein, F., *British Government Policy and Decolonisation 1945–1963. Scrutinising the Official Mind*, London, 2002.

Heseltine, M., *Life in the Jungle*, London, 2000.

Hevia, J. L., *Cherishing Men from Afar: Qing Guest Ritual and the Macartney Embassy of 1793*, New York, 1995.

Hickey, M., *The Unforgettable Army. Slim's XIVth Army in Burma*, Tunbridge Wells, 1992.

Hicks, G., *The Comfort Women. Sex Slaves of the Imperial Japanese Army*, London, 1995.

Hill, J., *China Dragons. A Rifle Company at War, Burma 1944–45*, London, 1991.

Hixon, C. K., *Guadalcanal. An American Story*, Annapolis, 1999.

Hodson, H. V., *The Great Divide: Britain, India, Pakistan*, London, 1969.

Hoe, S. and Roebuk, D., *The Taking of Hong Kong. Charles and Clara Elliot in Chinese Waters*, Richmond, 1999.

Holland, R. F., *European Decolonization 1918–1981. An Introductory Survey*, Basingstoke, 1985.

Holt, E., *The Opium Wars in China*, London, 1964.

Honjo Shigeru, *Emperor Hirohito and His Chief Aide-de-Camp. The Honjo Diary, 1933–1936*, translated by Mikiso Hane, Tokyo, 1982.

Hooper, B., *China Stands Up: Ending the Western Presence, 1948–1950*, Sidney, 1986.

Hopkins, T., "Macmillan's Audit of Empire, 1957", in Clarke, P. and Trebilcock, C. (eds.), *Understandng Decline: Perceptions of Realities in British Economic Performance*, Cambridge, 1997.

Horne, A., *Macmillan 1957–1986*, London, 1989.

Hough, R., *The Fleet That Had to Die*, London, 1958.

Housley, N., *The Later Crusades. From Lyons to Alcazar, 1274–1580*, Oxford, 1992.

Howe, S., *Anticoloniulism in British Politics. The Left and the End of Empire, 1918–1964*, Oxford, 1993.

Howe, S. E., *In Quest of Spices*, London, 1946.

Hudson, J., *Sunset in the East. Fighting against the Japanese through the siege of Imphal and alongside them in Java 1943–1946*, Barnsley, 2002.

Hughes, E. R., *The Invasion of China by the Western World*, London, 1937.

Hyam, R., "Churchill and the British Empire", in Blake, R. and Louis, W. R. (eds.), *Churchill*, Oxford, 1993.

——, *Britain's Imperial Century, 1815–1914: A Study of Empire and Expansion*, London, 1993.

——, *Britain's Declining Empire: The Road to Decolonisation, 1918–1968*, Cambridge, 2006.

Ike, Nobutaka, *Japan's Decision for War. Records of the 1941 Policy Conferences*, Stanford, 1967.

Iriye, A., *After Imperialism: The Search for a New Order in the Far East 1921–1931*, Cambridge, Massachusetts, 1965.

——, *Pacific Estrangement. Japanese and American Expansion, 1897–1911*, Cambridge, Massachusetts, 1972.

——, *The Origins of the Second World War in Asia and the Pacific*, London, 1987.

Irwin, G., *Nineteenth-Century Borneo: A Study in Diplomatic Rivalry*, Singapore, 1967.

Israel, J. I., *The Dutch Republic and the Hispanic World 1606–1661*, Oxford, 1982.

——, *Dutch Primacy in World Trade, 1585–1740*, Oxford, 1989.

——, *The Dutch Republic. Its Rise, Greatness and Fall 1477–1806*, Oxford, 1995.

Issac, A. R., *Without Honor. Defeat in Cambodia and Vietnam*, Baltimore, 1983.

Jackson, A., *The British Empire and the Second World War*, London, 2006.

Jackson, Sir W., *Withdrawal from Empire*, London, 1990.

Jalal, A., *The Sole Spokesman: Jinnah, the Muslim League and the Demand for Pakistan*, Cambridge, 1985.

Jansen, M. B., *The Japanese and Sun Yat-sen*, Cambridge, Massachusetts, 1954.

——, (ed.), *The Cambridge History of Japan*, vol. 5, *The Nineteenth Century*, Cambridge, 1989.

Jayne, K. G., *Vasco da Gama and His Successors*, London, 1910.

Jian Chen, *China's Road to the Korean War. The Making of Sino-American Confrontation*, New York, 1994.

Johnson, M., *Fighting the Enemy. Australian Soldiers and their Adversaries in World War II*, Cambridge, 2000.

——, *That Magnificent 9th. An Illustrated History of the 9th Australian Division 1940–1946*, Crows Nest, New South Wales, 2002.

Johnson, R. H., *Improbable Dangers: US Conceptions of Threat in the Cold War and After*, New York, 1994.

Jones, F. C., *Japan's New Order in East Asia: Its Rise and Fall, 1937–45*, Oxford, 1954.

Jones, H., *Death of a Generation. How the Assassinations of Diem and JFK Prolonged the Vietnam War*, Oxford, 2003.

Jones, J. R., *The Anglo–Dutch Wars of the Seventeenth Century*, London, 1996.

Josey, A., *Lee Kuan Yew. The Crucial Years*, Singapore, 1968.

Kahin, A. R., and Kahin, G. M., *Subversion as Foreign Policy. The Secret Eisenhower and Dulles Debacle in Indonesia*, New York, 1995.

Kahler, M., *Decolonization in Britain and France. The Domestic Consequences of International Relations*, Princeton, 1984.

Karl, R. E. and Zarrow, P, *Rethinking the 1898 Reform Period: Political and Cultural Change in Late Qing China*, Cambridge, Massachusetts, 2002.

Karnov, S., *In Our Image: America's Empire in the Philippines*, New York, 1989.

Keay, J., *Last Post. The End of Empire in the Far East*, London, 1997.

——, *Mad about the Mekong. Exploration and Empire in South- East Asia*, London, 2005.

Keene, D., *Emperor of Japan. Meiji and His World, 1852–1912*, New York, 2002.

Kelly, T., *Hurricane and Spitfire Pilots at War*, London, 1986.

——, *Hurricane in Sumatra*, London, 1991.

Kennedy, P. M., *The Rise and Fall of British Naval Mastery*, London, 1976.

Kershaw, I., *Hitler. 1936–45: Nemesis*, London, 2000.

Khan, I. A., *Gunpowder and Firearms. Warfare in Medieval India*, New Delhi, 2004.

Khodarkovsky, M., *Russia's Steppe Frontier. The Making of a Colonial Empire, 1500–1800*, Bloomington, 2002.

Kiernan, B., *The Pol Pot Regime. Race, Power, and Genocide in Cambodia under the Khmer Rouge, 1975–79*, New Haven, 1996.

Killingray, D. and Omissi, D. (eds.), *Guardians of Empire. The Armed Forces of the Colonial Powers, c. 1700–1964*, Manchester, 1999.

Kinvig, C., *Scapegoat. General Percival of Singapore*, London, 1996.

——, *Churchill's Crusade. The British Invasion of Russia 1918–1920*, London, 2006.

Kirk, T. A., *Genoa and the Sea. Policy and Power in an Early Modern Maritime Republic, 1559–1684*, Baltimore, 2005.

Kling, B. B. and Pearson, M. N. (eds.), *The Age of Partnership. Europeans in Asia before Dominion*, Honolulu, 1979.

Koen, R. Y., *The China Lobby in American Politics*, New York, 1970.

Kohen, A. S., *From the Place of the Dead. Bishop Belo and the Struggle for East Timor*, Oxford, 1999.

Kong Kim Hoong, *Merdeka: British rule and the struggle for independence in Malaya*, Kuala Lumpur, 1984.

Krancher, J. A., *The Defining Years of the Dutch East Indies, 1942–1949: Survivors' accounts of Japanese invasion and enslavement of Europeans and the revolution that created Indonesia*, London, 1996.

Kuitenbrouwer, M., *The Netherlands and the Rise of Modern Imperialism. Colonies and Foreign Policy 1870–1902*, translated by H. Beyer, New York, 1991.

Kynaston, D., *Austerity Britain 1945–51*, London, 2007.

Lach, D. F., *Asia in the Making of Europe*, vol. I, book 2, "The century of discovery", Chicago, 1965.

LaFeber, W., *The American Age. US Foreign Policy at Home and Abroad. 1750 to the Present*, New York, 1989.

——, *The Clash. US-Japanese Relations Throughout History*, New York, 1997.

Lai, Tse-Han, Myers, R. H. and Wei Wou, *A Tragic Beginning. The Taiwan Uprising of February 28, 1947*, Stanford, 1991.

Lamers, J. P., *Japonius Tyrannus. The Japanese warlord Oda Nobunaga reconsidered*, Leiden, 2000.

Lampton, D. M., *Same Bed, Different Dreams. Managing US–China Relations, 1989–2000*, Berkeley, 2001.

Large, S. S., *Emperor Hirohito and Showa Japan. A Political Biography*, London, 1992.

Latimer, J., *Burma. The Forgotten War*, London, 2004.

Laurie, W. F. B., *Our Burmese Wars*, London, 1885.

Lawford, J. P., *Britain's Army in India. From its Origins to the Conquest of Bengal*, London, 1978.

Lawson, P., *The East India Company. A History*, London, 1993.

Le Thanh Khoi, *Le Viet-Nam, histoire et civilisation*, Paris, 1955.

Lee, B. A., *Britain and the Sino-Japanese War, 1937–1939. A Study in the Dilemmas of British Decline*, Stanford, 1973.

Lee, Ki-baik, *A New History of Korea*, translated by E. W. Wagner, Seoul, 1986.

Lee, Leo Du-Fan, *Shanghai Modern. The Flowering of a New Urban Culture in China 1930–1945*, Cambridge, Massachusetts, 1999.

Lee, R., *France and the Exploitation of China 1885–1901. A Study in Economic Imperialism*, Oxford, 1989.

Lee, S. H., *Outposts of Empire. Korea, Vietnam and the Origins of the Cold War*, Liverpool, 1995.

Leech, M., *In the Days of McKinley*, New York, 1959.

Leffler, M. P., *A Preponderance of Power. National Security, the Truman Administration, and the Cold War*, Stanford, 1992.

Legge, J. D., *Sukarno: a Political Biography*, Harmondsworth, 1972.

Lenman, B., *Britain's Colonial Wars 1688–1783*, Harlow, 2002.

Leupe, P. A., "The Siege and Capture of Malacca from the Portuguese in 1640–1641", *Journal of the Malay Branch, Royal Asiatic Society*, 14, 1, London, 1936.

Leur, J. C. van, *Indonesian Trade and Society*, The Hague, 1955.

Lewis, D., *Jan Compagnie in the Straits of Malacca 1641–1795*, Athens, Ohio, 1995.

Lewis, J., *Changing Direction: British Military Planning for Post-War Strategic Defence, 1942–1947*, London, 1988.

Ley, C. D. (ed.), *Portuguese Voyages, 1498–1663*, London, 1947.

Lieberman, V. B., "Europeans, Trade and the Unification of Burma: c. 1540–1620", *Oriens Extremus*, 17, 2, 1980.

Lindsay, M., *The Unknown War. North China 1937–1945*, London, 1975.

Lindsay, O., *The Battle for Hong Kong, 1941–1945. Hostage to Fortune*, Staplehurst, 2005.

Lombard, D., *Le Sultanat d'Atjeh au Temps d'Iskandar Muda (1607–1636)*, Paris, 1967.

Lone, S., *Japan's First Modern War. Army and Society in the Conflict with China, 1894–95*, Basingstoke, 1994.

Losty, J. P., *Calcutta, City of Palaces*, London, 1990.

Lopez, R., *The Christianization of the Philippines*, Manila, 1965.

Louis, W. R., *In the Name of God Go! Leo Amery and the British Empire in the Age of Churchill*, New York, 1992.

——, *Imperialism at Bay, 1941–1945: The United States and the Decolonization of the British Empire*, Oxford, 1977.

——, *British Strategy in the Far East, 1919–1939*, Oxford, 1971.

——, *Ends of British Imperialism. The Scramble for Empire, Suez and Decolonialization, Collected Essays*, London, 2006.

Low, N. I. and Cheng, H. M., *This Singapore: Our City of Dreadful Night*, Singapore, 1946.

Lu, Suping, *They Were In Nanjing. The Nanjing Massacre Witnessed by American and British Nationals*, Hong Kong, 2004.

Ludowyk, E. F. C., *The Modern History of Ceylon*, London, 1966.

Lyman, R., *Slim, Master of War. Burma and the Birth of Modern Warfare*, London, 2004.

Ma Huan, *The Overall Survey of the Ocean's Shores (Yingya Shenglan)*, translated and edited by J. V. G. Mills, Cambridge, 1970.

MacArthur, D., *Reports of General MacArthur*, vol. II, parts I and II: "Japanese Operations in the Southwest Pacific Area", Washington, 1967.

Macdonald, P., *Giap. The Victor in Vietnam*, London, 1993.

Màdaro, A., *The Boxer Rebellion*, translated by E. Tomlin, Treviso, 2001.

Majumdar, R. C., *The Sepoy Mutiny and the Revolt of 1857*, Calcutta, 1957.

Malozemoff, A., *Russian Far Eastern Policy, 1881–1904*, Berkeley, 1958.

Mansergh, N. et al. (eds.), *The Transfer of Power, 1942–1947*, London, 1970–1983.

Manucci, Nicolao, *Storia do Mogor, or Mogul India*, translated by W. Irvine, London, 1906–08.

Marder, A. J., *Old Friends, New Enemies: The Royal Navy and the Imperial Japanese Navy. Strategic Illusions, 1936–1941*, Oxford, 1981.

——, Jacobsen, M. and Horsfield J., *Old Friends, New Enemies. The Royal Navy and the Imperial Japanese Navy*, vol. II: *The Pacific War, 1942–1945*, Oxford, 1990.

Marks, T. A., *Counterrevolution in China. Wang Sheng and the Kuomintang*, London, 1998.

Marr, D. G., *Vietnam 1945. A Quest for Power*, Berkeley, 1995.

——, *Vietnamese Anti-Colonialism, 1885–1925*, Berkeley, 1971.

Marshall, P. J., *Problems of Empire: Britain and India, 1757–1813*, London, 1968.

——, "Western Armies in Maritime Asia in the Early Phases of Expansion", *Modern Asian Studies*, 14, 1, 1980.

——, *The New Cambridge History of India*, vol. II. 2, *Bengal: the British Bridgehead. Eastern India 1740–1828*, Cambridge, 1987.

Marston, D. P., *Phoenix from the Ashes. The Indian Army in the Burma Campaign*, New York, 2003.

Martin, A. W., *Robert Menzies. A Life. Volume One, 1894–1943*, Melbourne, 1993.

—— and Hardy, P. (eds.), *Dark and Hurrying Days. Menzies' 1941 Diary*, Canberra, 1993.

Martin, J., *L'empire renaissant, 1789–1871*, Paris, 1987.

Martins, J. P. O., *The golden age of Prince Henry the Navigator*, translated by J. J. Abraham and W. E. Reynolds, London, 1914.

Mason, P., *A Matter of Honour: an account of the Indian army, its officers and men*, London, 1976.

Mathew, K. S., *Portuguese Trade in India in the Sixteenth Century*, New Delhi, 1983.

——, *The Portuguese and the Sultanate of Gujarat (1500–1573)*, New Delhi, 1985.

Maung Maung, U, *Burmese Nationalist Movements 1940–1948*, Edinburgh, 1989.

May, E. R., *Imperial Democracy: The Emergence of America as a Great Power*, New York, 1961.

Maybon, C. B., *Histoire Moderne du Pays d'Annam*, Paris, 1920.

McCoy, A. W. (ed.), *Southeast Asia Under Japanese Occupation*, New Haven, 1980.

McGiburn, I., *New Zealand and the Korean War. Volume I, Politics and Diplomacy*, Auckland, 1992.

McMullin, N., *Buddhism and the State in Sixteenth-Century Japan*, Princeton, 1984.

McLeod, M. W., *The Vietnamese Response to French Intervention 1862–74*, New York, 1991.

McNeill, I., *To Long Tan. The Australian Army and the Vietnam War 1950–1966*, Canberra, 1993.

Meilink-Roelofz, M. A. P., *Asian trade and European influence in the Indonesian archipelago from 1500 to about 1630*, The Hague, 1962.

Melby, J. F., *The Mandate of Heaven. Record of a Civil War. China 1945–49*, London, 1969.

Metcalf, T. R., *The New Cambridge History of India*, vol. III. 4, *Ideologies of the Raj*, Cambridge, 1995.

——, *The Aftermath of Revolt: India, 1857–1870*, Princeton, 1964.

Meyer, C., *La Vie Quotidienne des Francais en Indochine, 1860–1910*, Paris, 1985.

Milner, A., *The Invention of Politics in Colonial Malaya: Contesting Nationalism and the Expansion of the Public Sphere*, Cambridge, 1994.

Miners, N., *Hong Kong Under Imperial Rule, 1912–1941*, Hong Kong, 1987.

Moffat, J. and McCormick, A. H., *Moon Over Malaya. A Tale of the Argylls and the Marines*, Stroud, 2000.

Moon, Sir P., *Warren Hastings and India*, London, 1947.

——, *Gandhi and Modern India*, London, 1968.

——, *The British Conquest and Dominion of India*, London, 1990.

Moore, R. J., *Escape from Empire. The Attlee Government and the Indian Problem*, Oxford, 1983.

Morgan, H. W., *America's Road to Empire: The War with Spain and Overseas Expansion*, New York, 1965.

Morgan, J. F., *The Japanese and the Jesuits. Allesandro Valignano in the sixteenth-century Japan*, London, 1993.

Morgan, K. O., *Labour in Power 1945–51*, London, 1984.

Moreley, J. W., *The Japanese Thrust into Siberia*, New York, 1957.

——, (ed.), *Japan's Road to the Pacific War. The China Quagmire. Japan's Expansion on the Asian Continent, 1933–1941*, New York, 1983.

Moremann, T. R., *The Jungle, the Japanese and British Commonwealth Armies at War, 1941–45. Fighting Methods, Doctrine and Training for Jungle Warfare*, London, 2005.

Morrison, I., *Malayan Postscript*, London, 1942.

Moscotti, A., *British Policy and the Nationalist Movement in Burma 1917–1937*, Honolulu, 1974.

Mozingo, D., *Chinese Policy Toward Indonesia, 1949–1967*, Ithaca, 1976.

Mukerjee, A., *British Colonial Policy in Burma: An Aspect of Colonialism in South-East Asia 1840–1885*, New Delhi, 1988.

Mukerjee, R. and Subramaniam, L., *Politics and Trade in the Indian Ocean*, New Delhi, 1998.

Murfett, M., *Fool-Proof Relations: The Search for Anglo-American Naval Cooperation during the Chamberlain Years, 1937–1940*, Singapore, 1984

Murfett, M. H., *Hostage on the Yangtze. Britain, China, and the Amethyst Crisis of 1949*, Annapolis, 1991.

Murray, M. J., *The Development of Capitalism in Colonial Indochina (1870–1940)*, Berkeley, 1980.

Nambiar, O. K., *Portuguese Pirates and Indian Seamen*, Bombay, 1955.

Naw, A., *Aung San and the Struggle for Burmese Independence*, Copenhagen, 2001.

Needham, J., *Science and Civilisation in China. 4: Physics and Physical Technology*, III: *Civil Engineering and Nautics*, Cambridge, 1971.

Nelson, W. A., *Fort Jesus of Mombasa*, Edinburgh, 1994.

Newbold, T. J., *British Settlements in the Straits of Malacca*, Kuala Lumpur, 1971.

Newitt, M. (ed.), *The First Portuguese Empire*, Exeter, 1986.

Ngo Vinh Long, *Before the Revolution: The Vietnamese Peasants under the French*, New York, 1991.

Nguyen Phut Tan, *A Modern History of Vietnam*, Saigon, 1964.

Ni Ni Myint, *Burma's Struggle Against British Imperialism: 1885–1889*, Rangoon, 1983.

Nish, I. H., *Alliance in Decline. A Study in Anglo-Japanese Relations, 1908–1923*, London, 1972.

——, *The Origins of the Russo-Japanese War*, London, 1985.

Noer, D., *The Modernist Muslim Movement in Indonesia, 1900–1942*, Singapore, 1973.

Nowell, C. E., *The Great Discoveries of the First Colonial Empires*, Ithaca, 1954.

O'Brien, T., *Chasing After Danger. A Combat Pilot's War Over Europe and the Far East, 1939–42*, London, 1990.

Olson, L., *Japan in Postwar Asia*, New York, 1970.

Omissi, D. E., *The Sepoy and the Raj: The Indian Army, 1860–1940*, Basingstoke, 1994.

Osbeck, P. A., *A Voyage to China and the East Indies in 1747–1748*, London, 1771.

Osborne, M., *The French Presence in CochinChina and Cambodia*, Berkeley, 1971.

——, *Sihanouk. Prince of Light, Prince of Darkness*, London, 1994.

——, *The Mekong: Turbulent Past, Uncertain Future*, St. Leonards, New South Wales, 2000.

——, *Phnom Penh. A Cultural and Literary Guide*, Oxford, 2008.

Owen, R., *Lord Cromer. Victorian Imperialist, Edwardian Proconsul*, Oxford, 2004.

Ozbaran, S., "The Ottoman Turks and the Portuguese in the Persian Gulf, 1534–1581", *Journal of Asian History*, 6, 1, 1972.

Padfield, P., *Tide of Empires: Decisive Naval Campaigns in the Rise of the West*, London, 1979.

Paley, T., *The Sparrows*, Worcester, 1992.

Palmer, D. R., *The Summons of the Trumpet: a History of the Vietnam War from a Military Man's Viewpoint*, New York, 1984.

Pannikkar, K. M., *Asia and Western Dominance*, London, 1959.

Parillo, M. P., *The Japanese Merchant Marine in World War II*, Annapolis, 1993.

Parker, G., *Philip II*, London, 1979.

——, *The Military Revolution: Military Innovation and the Rise of the West*, Cambridge, 1987.

——, "The making of strategy in Habsburg Spain: Philip II's 'bid for mastery', 1556–1598", in *The Making of Strategy. Rulers, States and War* (ed.) Murray, W., Knox, M. and Berstein, A., Cambridge, 1994.

Parry, J. H., *The Discovery of the Sea*, Berkeley, 1981.

Parry, J. H., *The Spanish Seaborne Empire*, Berkeley, 1990.

Payne, R., *Chiang Kai-shek*, New York, 1969.

Pearson, M. N., *Merchants and Rulers in Gujarat. The Response to the Portuguese in the Sixteenth Century*, Berkeley, 1976.

——, *The Cambridge History of India*, vol. I. 1, *The Portuguese in India*, Cambridge, 1987.

Peers, D. M., *Between Mars and Mammon: Colonial Armies and the Garrison State in India*, London, 1995.

Pepys, S., *The Diary of Samuel Pepys*, edited by R. Latham and W. Matthews, London, 1970–1983.

Percival, A. E., *The War in Malaya*, London, 1949.

Perville, G., *De l'Empire Francais à la Decolonisation*, Paris, 1991.

Phillips, C. R., "The Growth and Composition of Trade in the Iberian Empires, 1450–1750", in *The Rise of the Merchant Empires* (ed.), Tracy, J. D., Cambridge, 1990.

Pillai, A. R., *The Private Diary of Ananda Ranga Pillai*, translated by Sir J. F. Rice, Madras, 1914.

Pinto, Fernão Mendes, *The Travels of Mendes Pinto*, translated by R. D. Gatz, Chicago, 1989.

Pires, Tomé, *Suma Oriental*, translated by A. Cortesão, London, 1944.

Platt, D. C. M., *Finance, Trade and Politics in British Foreign Policy, 1815–1914*, Oxford, 1968.

Pleshakov, C., *The Tsar's Last Armada. The Epic Voyage to the Battle of Tsushima*, Oxford, 2002.

Polachek, J. M., *The Inner Opium War*, Cambridge, Massachusetts, 1992.

Pollack, O., *Empires in Collision: Anglo-Burmese Relations in the Mid-Nineteenth Century*, Westport, 1979.

Polo, Marco, *The Travels*, translated by R. Latham, London, 1958.

Porch, D., *The French Foreign Legion. A Complete History*, London, 1991.

Porritt, V. L., *British Colonial Rule in Sarawak 1946–1963*, Kuala Lumpur, 1997.

Powell, A., *War by Stealth. Australians and the Allied Intelligence Bureau 1942–1945*, Melbourne, 1996.

Prakash, O., *The Dutch East India Company and the Economy of Bengal, 1630–1720*, Princeton, 1985.

——, *The New Cambridge History of India*, vol. II. 5, *European Commercial Enterprise in Pre-Colonial India*, Cambridge, 1998.

Praval, K. C., *The Indian Army after Indepedence*, New Delhi, 1987.

Prefer, N. N., *Vinegar Joe's War. Stilwell's Campaigns for Burma*, Navato, California, 2000.

Price, R., *An Imperial War and the British Working Class*, London, 1971.

Pringle, R., *Rajahs and Rebels: The Ibans of Sarawak under Brooke rule, 1841–1941*, Ithaca, 1970.

Pritchard, E. H., *Anglo-Chinese Relations During the Seventeenth and Eighteenth Centuries*, Urbana, 1929.

Probert, H., *The Forgotten Air Force. The Royal Air Force in the War Against Japan 1941–1945*, London, 1995.

Ptak, R. (ed.), *Portuguese Asia: Aspects in History and Economic History (Sixteenth and Seventeenth Centuries)*, Stuttgart, 1987.

Pu Yi, *The Last Manchu. The Autobiography of Henry Pu Yi, Last Emperor of China*, translated by P. Tsai and edited by P. Kramer, London, 1967.

Puri, B., *Kashmir: Towards Insurgency*, New Delhi, 1993.

Quiason, S. D., *English Country Trade with the Philippines, 1644–1765*, Quezon, 1966.

Rabb, T. K., *Enterprise and Empire. Merchant and Gentry Investment in the Expansion of England, 1575–1630*, Cambridge, Massachusetts, 1967.

Radwan, A. B., *The Dutch in Western India 1601–1632. A Study in Mutual Accommodation*, Calcutta, 1978.

Rao, R. P., *Portuguese Rule in Goa, 1510–1961*, Bombay, 1963.

Reece, B., *The White Rajahs of Sarawak. A Borneo Dynasty*, Singapore, 2004.

Ready, J. L., *Forgotten Allies. The Military Contribution of Colonies, Exiled Governments, and Lesser Powers in the Allied Victory in World War II*. Vol. II. *The Asian Theatre*, Jefferson, North Carolina, 1985.

Reginer, P., *Singapore. City-State in South-East Asia*, London, 1987.

Reid, A., *Southeast Asia in the Age of Commerce 1450–1680*, vol. 1, *The Land below the Winds*, New Haven, 1988.

——, *Southeast Asia in the Age of Commerce 1450–1680*, vol. 2, *Expansion and Crisis*, New Haven, 1993.

——, "Sixteenth Century Turkish Influence in Western Indonesia", *The Journal of South-East Asian Studies*, vol. 10, 1969.

Remme, T., *Britain and Regional Cooperation in South-East Asia, 1945–1949*, London, 1995.

Reynolds, E. B., *Thailand's Secret War. The Free Thai, OSS and SOE During World War II*, Cambridge, 2005.

Richards, J. F., *The New Cambridge History of India*, vol. I. 5, *The Mughal Empire*, Cambridge, 1993.

Richie, J., *Temenggong Oyang Lawai Jau. A Paramount Chief in Borneo. The Legacy*, Kuching, Sarawak, 2006.

Ricklefs, M., *A History of Modern Indonesia since 1300*, London, 1993.

Roberts, D. R., *Spotlight on Singapore*, London, 1965.

Robinson, F. C. R., *Islam and Muslim History in South Asia*, New Delhi, 2001.

Rodger, N. A. M., *The Command of the Ocean. A Naval History of Britain 1649–1815*, London, 2004.

Roe, M., *Australia, Britain and Migration,1915–1940*, Cambridge, 1995.

Rosen, S. P., *Societies and Military Power: India and Its Armies*, Ithaca, 1996.

Roux, J.-P., *Histoire des Grands Monghuls: Babur*, Paris, 1986.

Rumold, Sir A., *Watershed in India, 1914–27*, London, 1979.

Runciman, S., *The White Rajahs: A History of Sarawak from 1841 to 1946*, Cambridge, 1980.

Russell-Wood, A. J. R., *A World on the Move: the Portuguese in Africa, Asia and America, 1415–1808*, Manchester, 1992.

Ryan, N. J., *A History of Malaysia and Singapore*, Kuala Lumpur, 1976.

Saburo, Ienaga, *The Pacific War, 1931–1945. A Critical Perspective on Japan's Role in World War II*, New York, 1978.

Sadka, E., *The Protected Malay States, 1874–1895*, Kuala Lumpur, 1968.

Saeed, Ahmad, *The Battle of Chaamb, 1971*, Rawalpindi, 1973.

Saliq, Siddiq, *Witness to Surrender*, Karachi, 1977.

Sampson, Sir G., *A History of Japan 1334–1615*, Stanford, 1961.

Sanger, C., *Malcolm MacDonald: Bringing an End to Empire*, Montreal, 1995.

Sardeshpande, S. C., *Assignment Jaffna*, New Delhi, 1992.

Sarkisyanz, E., *Buddhist Backgrounds to the Burmese Revolution*, The Hague, 1965.

Sarvelpalli, G., *British Policy in India, 1858–1905*, Cambridge, 1965.

Scammell, G. V., *The First Imperial Age. European Overseas Expansion, c. 1400–1715*, London, 1989.

Scholfield, V., *Wavell. Soldier and Statesman*, London, 2006.

Schrijvers, P., *The GI War Against Japan. American Soldiers in Asia and the Pacific During World War II*, Basingstoke, 2002.

Schroeder, J. H., *Matthew Calbraith Perry. Antebellum Sailor and Diplomat*, Annapolis, 2001.

Schurhammer, G., *Francis Xavier: His Life and Times*, Rome, 1975–82.

Scott, I., *Political Change and the Crisis of Legitimacy in Hong Kong*, London, 1989.

Scott, L. V., *Conscription and the Attlee Governments. The Politics and Policy of National Service, 1945–1951*, Oxford, 1993.

Segal, G., *Defending China*, Oxford, 1985.

Semmel, B., *The Rise of Free Trade Imperialism*, Cambridge, 1970.

Sen, S. P., *The French in India, 1763–1816*, New Delhi, 1971.

Shai, A., *Origins of the War in the East. Britain, China and Japan, 1937–1939*, London, 1976.

Shetlat, J. M., *Akbar*, Bombay, 1959.

Shennan, M., *Out in the Midday Sun. The British in Malaya 1880–1960*, London , 2000.

Shinozaki Mamoru, *Syonan—My Story: The Japanese Occupation of Singapore*, Singapore, 1975.

Short, P., *Pol Pot. The History of a Nightmare*, London, 2004.

Shuckburgh, E., *Descent to Suez: Diaries, 1951–56*, London, 1986.

Sideri, S., *Trade and Power. Informal Colonialism in Anglo–Portuguese Relations*, Rotterdam, 1970.

Simson, I., *Singapore: Too Little, Too Late. Some Aspects of the Malayan Disaster in 1942*, London , 1970.

Silver, L. R., *Sandakan. A Conspiracy of Silence*, Bowral, New South Wales, 1994.

Simpson, H. R., *Dien Bien Phu. The Epic Battle America Forgot*, Washington, 1974.

Singh, P., *The Indian Army Under the East India Company*, New Delhi, 1976.

Singhal, D. P., *British Diplomacy and the Annexation of Upper Burma*, New Delhi, 1981.

Slackman, M., *Target: Pearl Harbor*, Honolulu, 1990.

Slim, W., Viscount, *Defeat into Victory*, London, 1956.

Slocomb, M., *The People's Republic of Kampucea 1979–1989. The Revolution after Pol Pot*, Chiang Mai, Thailand, 2003.

Small, J. and D. S., *The Undeclared War. The Story of the Indonesian Confrontation, 1962–1966*, London, 1971.

Smith, C., *Singapore Burning. Heroism and Surrender in World War II*, London, 2005.

Smith, C. F., *Vladivostok under Red and White Rule*, Seattle, 1975.

Smith, J., *The Spanish-American War. Conflict in the Caribbean and the Pacific 1895–1902*, London, 1994.

Smith, M., *British Air Strategy Between the Wars*, Oxford, 1984.

Smith, M. S., *Bloody Ridge. The Battle that Saved Guadalcanal*, Navato, California, 2000.

Smith, R. B., *The First Age of the Portuguese Embassies, Navigations and Peregrinations to the Kingdoms and Islands of South–East Asia, 1509–1521*, Bethesda, 1968.

Snow, E., *Red Star Over China*, New York, 1961.

Snow, P., *The Fall of Hong Kong. Britain, China and the Japanese Occupation*, New Haven, 2003.

Souza, G. B., *The Survival of Empire. Portuguese Trade and Society in China and the South China Sea, 1630–1754*, Cambridge, 1986.

Spear, T. G. P., *The Nabobs: a Study of the Social Life of the English in Eighteenth-Century India*, London, 1932.

Spence, J., *God's Chinese Son. The Taiping Heavenly Kingdom of Hong Qiuquan*, New York, 1996.

Sprenkel, O. B., van der Guillian, R. and Lindsay, M., *New China, Three Views*, London, 1950.

Stahl, B., *You're No Good to Me Dead. Behind Japanese Lines in the Philippines*, Annapolis, 1995.

Stanley, B., *The Bible and the Flag: Protestant Missions and Imperialism in the Nineteenth and Twentieth Centuries*, Leicester, 1990.

Stanley, H. E. J., *The Three Voyages of Vasco da Gama and His Viceroyalty*, London, 1869.

Stark, H. A., *Hostages to India or the Life of the Anglo-Indian Race*, Calcutta, 1936.

Steensgaard, N., *The Asian Trade Revolution of the Seventeenth Century. The East India Companies and the Decline of the Caravan Trade*, Chicago, 1974.

Steinberg, D., *Philippine Collaboration in World War II*, Ann Arbor, 1967.

Stephan, J. J., *The Russian Far East. A History*, Stanford, 1994.

Stevenson, R., "Cinemas and Censorship in Colonial Malaya", *Journal of Southeast Asian Studies*, 5, September, 1974.

Stewart, I. M., *History of the Argyll and Sutherland Highlanders. 2nd Battalion. Malayan Campaign 1941–1942*, London, 1947.

——, "The Loss of Singapore—A Criticism", *Army Quarterly*, 56, 2, 1948.

Stowe, J. A., *Siam Becomes Thailand. A Story of Intrigue*, London, 1991.

Strahan, L., *Australia's China. Changing Perceptions from the 1930s to the 1990s*, Cambridge, 1996.

Stuard, J. L., *Fifty Years in China*, New York, 1954.

Stueck, W., *Rethinking the Korean War. A New Diplomatic and Strategic History*, Princeton, 2002.

Subrahmanyam, S., "The Kagemusha effect. The Portuguese, firearms and the state in early modern south India", *Moyen Orient et Ocean Indien*, vol. 4, 1987.

——, *Improvising Empire: Portuguese Trade and Settlement in the Bay of Bengal, 1500–1700*, New Delhi, 1990.

——, *The Political Economy of Commerce: Southern India, 1500–1650*, Cambridge, 1990.

——, *The Portuguese Empire in Asia, 1500–1700: A Political and Economic History*, London, 1993.

——, *The Career and Legend of Vasco da Gama*, Cambridge, 1997.

Subramanian, L. (ed.), *The French East India Company and the Trade of the Indian Ocean*, Calcultta, 1999.

Sun, S., *The Long March*, London, 2006.

Sutherland, L. S., *The East India Company in Eighteenth-Century Politics*, Oxford, 1952.

Swettenham, F., *British Malaya. An Account of the Origin and Progress of British Influence in Malaya*, London, 1906.

Taboulet, G., *La Geste Francais en Indochine*, Paris, 1956.

Tanaka, Yuki, *Japanese War Crimes in World War II*, Boulder, Colorado, 1996.

T'ang Leang-li, *The Puppet State of "Manchukuo"*, Shanghai, 1935.

Tanizaki, Junichiro, *Childhood Years. A Memoir*, translated by P. McCarthy, London, 1990.

Tarling, N., *The Fall of British Imperialism in South–East Asia*, Singapore, 1993.

—— (ed.), *The Cambridge History of Southeast Asia. Vol. 1. From Early Times to c.1800*, Cambridge, 1992.

—— (ed.), *The Cambridge History of Southeast Asia. Vol. 2. The Nineteenth and Twentieth Centuries*, Cambridge, 1992.

——, *Britain, Southeast Asia and the Onset of the Pacific War*, Cambridge, 1996.

——, *Imperialism in Southeast Asia*, London, 2001.

Taylor, A. M., *Indonesian independence and the United Nations*, Ithaca, 1960.

Teitler, G., *The Dutch Colonial Army in Transition: the Militia Debate, 1900–1921*, Rotterdam, 1980.

Thobie, J., Meynier, G. and Coquery–Vidrovitch, C., and Ageron, C., *Histoire de la France coloniale, 1914–1990*, Paris, 1990.

Thomaz, L. F., "Factions, Interests and Messianism: The Politics of Portuguese Expansion in the East, 1500–1521", *The Indian Economic and Social Review*, 28,1,1991.

——, *De Ceuta a Timor*, Lisbon, 1994.

Tomich, V. M., *Warships of the Imperial Russian Navy*, San Francisco, 1968.

Thorne, C., *Allies of a Kind. The United States, Britain and the War against Japan, 1941–1945*, London, 1978.

Tidrick, K., *Empire and the English Character*, London, 1990.

Timperley, H. J., *Japanese Terror in China*, New York, 1938.

Tinker, H., *A New System of Slavery. The Export of Indian Labour Overseas 1830–1920*, London, 1920.

——, *The Union of Burma: A Study of the First Years of Independence*, Oxford, 1961.

Tracy, J. D. (ed.), *The Rise of the Merchant Empires. Long-Distance Trade in the Early Modern World 1350–1750*, Cambridge, 1990.

—— (ed.), *The Political Economy of Merchant Empires. State Power and World Trade 1350–1750*, Cambridge, 1991.

Tracy, N., *Manila Ransomed. The British Assault on Manila in the Seven Years War*, Exeter, 1995.

Trask, D. F., *The War with Spain in 1898*, New York, 1981.

Trotter, A., *Britain and East Asia, 1933–1937*, Cambridge, 1975.

Truman, Harry S., *Where the Buck Stops. The Personal and Private Papers*, edited by M. Truman, New York, 1989.

Tsuji Mansobu, *Singapore 1941–1942. The Japanese Version of the Malayan Campaign of World War II*, translated by M. E. Lake, Singapore, 1988.

U Nu, *Burma under the Japanese*, London, 1954.

Uzielli, G., "Piero di Andrea Strozzi: Viaggiatore Fiorentino del Secolo delle Scoperte", *Memorie della Societa Geografica Italiana*, vol. V, Rome, 1895.

Valone, S. J., *A Policy Calculated to Benefit China. The United States and the China Arms Embargo, 1919–1929*, New York, 1991.

Van der Post, L., *The Night of the Full Moon*, London, 1970.

Van Mook, Dr. H. J., *The Netherlands and Japan. Their Relations 1940–41*, London, 1944.

Van Niel, R., *The Emergence of the Modern Indonesian Elite*, The Hague, 1960.

Vandenbosh, A., *Dutch Foreign Policy Since 1815. A Study in Small Power Politics*, s'–Gravenhage, 1959.

Vansittart, H., *A Narrative of Transactions in Bengal*, London, 1766.

Varma, P. K., *Ghalib: The Man, the Times*, New Delhi, 1989.

Velho, Alvaro, *Roteiro da Primeira Viagem de Vasco da Gama*, (ed.) Neves Aguas, Lisbon, 1987.

——, "The Route to India, 1497–8", in *Portuguese Voyages, 1497–1663*, (ed.) C. D. Ley, London , 1943.

Vincent, R. (ed.), *Pondichery, 1674–1761: l'echec d'un reve d'empire*, Paris, 1993.

Viraphol, S., *Tribute and Profit: Sino-Siamese Trade, 1652–1853*, Cambridge, Massachusetts, 1977.

Vogt, J. L., "Crusading and Commercial Elements in the Portuguese Capture of Ceuta (1415)", *Muslim World*, 59, 1969.

Voigt, J. H., *India in the Second World War*, New Delhi, 1987.

Waley, A., *The Opium War Through Chinese Eyes*, London, 1958.

Wang Gungwu, *Community and Nation: Essays on Southeast Asia and the Chinese*, Singapore, 1981.

Wang Hui, *China's New Order*, Cambridge, Massachusetts, 2003.

Warner, D. and Warner, R., *The Tide at Sunrise. A History of the Russo-Japanese War, 1904–1905*, London, 2002.

Warren, A., *Singapore 1942. Britain's Greatest Defeat*, London, 2002.

Wasserstein, B., *Secret War in Shanghai. Treachery, Subversion and Collaboration in the Second World War*, London, 1998.

Watson, F. and Tennyson, H., *Talking of Gandhi*, London, 1969.

Watson, L. B., "Fortifications and the 'Idea' of Force in Early East India Company Relations in India", *Past and Present*, 88, 1980.

——, *Foundation for Empire: English Private Trade in India, 1659–1760*, Delhi, 1980.

Watt, A., *The Evolution of Australian Foreign Policy 1938–1965*, Cambridge, 1967.

Wavell, *The Viceroy's Journal*, edited by Sir Penderel Moon, Karachi, 1997.

Weigley, R. F., *The Age of Battles. The Quest for Decisive Warfare from Breitenfeld to Waterloo*, Bloomington, 1991.

Weinberg, G. L., *Hitler, Germany and World War II. Essays in Modern German and World History*, Cambridge, 1995.

Weinstein, F. B., *Indonesia Abandons Confrontation: An inquiry into the functions of Indonesian foreign policy*, Ithaca, 1969.

Welsh, F., *A History of Hong Kong*, London, 1997.

Wesseling, H. L., *Imperialism and Colonialism*, Westport, 1997.

Wetzler, P., *Hirohito and War. Imperial Tradition and Military Decision Making in Prewar Japan*, Honolulu, 1998.

Wheeler-Bennett, J., *King George VI*, London, 1958.

White, N. J., *Business, Government, and the End of Empire. Malaya, 1942–1957*, Kuala Lumpur, 1996.

Whiteway, R. S., *The Rise of Portuguese Power in India, 1497–1550*, London, 1898.

Wigmore, L., *Australia in the War 1939–1945. The Thrust South*, Canberra, 1957.

Wills, J. E., *Pepper, Guns and Parleys. The Dutch East India Company and China 1622–1681*, Cambridge, Massachusetts, 1974.

——, *Embassies and Illusions. Dutch and Portuguese Envoys to K'ang–hsi, 1666–1687*, Cambridge, Massachusetts, 1984.

Winborn, B. R., *Wen Bon. A Naval Air Intelligence Officer Behind Japanese Lines in China in WWII*, North West Texas, 1994.

Winnius, G. D., *The Fatal History of Portuguese Ceylon. Transition to Dutch Rule*, Cambridge, Massachusetts, 1971.

Winstead, R. O., *A History of Malaya*, Singapore, 1935.

Wong, J. W., *Deadly Dreams. Opium, Imperialism and the Arrow War (1856–1860) in China*, Cambridge, 1998.

Woodside, A. B., *Vietnam and the Chinese Model: A Comparative Study of Vietnamese and Chinese Government in the First Half of the Nineteenth Century*, Cambridge, Massachusetts, 1971.

Wright, H. R. C., *East-Indian Economic Problems in the Age of Cornwallis and Raffles*, London, 1961.

Wray, C. C. H., *Timor 1942. Australian Commandos at War with the Japanese*, Melbourne, 1990.

Wyatt, D. K., *The Politics of Reform in Thailand: Education in the Reign of King Chulalongkom*, New Haven, 1969.

——, *Thailand. A Short History*, New Haven, 1982.

Wright-Nooth, G., *Prisoner of the Turnip Heads. The Fall of Hong Kong and Imprisonment by the Japanese*, London, 1994.

Xue Zhigeng, *Lest We Forget: Nanjing Massacre, 1937*, translated by Zhang Tingquan and Lin Wusun, Beijing, 1995.

Yapp, M. E., *Strategies of British India. India and Afghanistan 1798–1850*, Oxford, 1980.

Yeager, M., *The Muslims of Burma: A Study of a Minority Group*, Wiesbaden, 1972.

Yeh, Wen-hsin (ed.), *Wartime Shanghai*, London, 1998.

Yen Chin Hwang, *The Overseas Chinese and the 1911 Revolution*, Kuala Lumpur, 1976.

Yoshida, Shigeru, *The Yoshida Memoirs. The Story of Japan in Crisis*, translated by Kenichi Yoshida, London, 1961.

Young, A. N., *China and the Helping Hand, 1937–1945*, Cambridge, Massachusetts, 1963.

Young, D. M., *The Colonial Office in the Early Nineteenth Century*, London, 1961.

Young, L., *Japan's Total Empire. Manchuria and the Culture of Wartime Imperialism*, Berkeley, 1998.

Young, L. K., *British Policy in China, 1895–1902*, Oxford, 1970.

Yu, M., *OSS in China. Prelude to the Cold War*, New Haven, 1996.

Zaheer, H., *The Separation of East Pakistan: the Rise and Realization of Bengali Muslim Nationalism*, New York, 1994.

Ziegler, P., *Mountbatten: the Official Biography*, London, 1985.

—— (ed.), *Personal Diary of Admiral the Lord Mountbatten: Supreme Allied Commander, South-East Asia, 1943–1946*, London, 1988.

Index